Wermouth

"WILL BECOME AS INDISPENSABLE TO BABY BOOMERS AS DR. SPOCK WAS TO THEIR PARENTS." —*New York Daily News*

From countdown to parenthood to fifth birthday, Dr. Mom tells it all with astonishing thoroughness, in the relaxed, easy manner of a seasoned veteran who's seen it all, at home and in the office. She takes the panic out of emergencies by giving clear, concise descriptions and wise, often unconventional solutions to problems as wide-ranging as childbirth methods, sibling preparation, colic, techniques of discipline and punishment, breast feeding, sleep patterns, tantrums, and much, much more.

As up-to-the-minute and original as it is remarkably wise and easy to use, *Dr. Mom* is the one must-have child care guide for the new parents of the '90s.

DR. MOM

MARIANNE NEIFERT, M.D., is a pediatrician, associate clinical professor of pediatrics at the University of Colorado School of Medicine, and the medical director of the lactation program at Presbyterian/Saint Luke's Medical Center in Denver. The mother of five children, she was chosen as one of *Glamour* magazine's ⬛⬛⬛⬛⬛⬛⬛⬛⬛⬛⬛⬛⬛ omen. She is also ⬛⬛⬛⬛⬛⬛⬛⬛⬛⬛ s with her husban⬛⬛⬛⬛⬛⬛⬛⬛⬛⬛ enver, Colorado.

ANNE PRI⬛⬛⬛⬛⬛⬛⬛⬛⬛⬛⬛⬛⬛thored *The Breastfe⬛⬛⬛⬛ ⬛⬛⬛⬛ ⬛⬛⬛⬛ ⬛⬛⬛⬛man* and *Successful Breastfeeding*. Ms. Price is the mother of a daughter and two sons and Ms. Dana is a mother of two sons.

DR. MOM

A Guide to
Baby and Child Care

by Marianne Egeland Neifert, M.D.

with Anne Price
and Nancy Dana

A SIGNET BOOK

SIGNET
Published by New American Library, a division of
Penguin Putnam Inc., 375 Hudson Street,
New York, New York 10014, U.S.A.
Penguin Books Ltd, 27 Wrights Lane,
London W8 5TZ, England
Penguin Books Australia Ltd, Ringwood,
Victoria, Australia
Penguin Books Canada Ltd, 10 Alcorn Avenue,
Toronto, Ontario, Canada M4V 3B2
Penguin Books (N.Z.) Ltd, 182–190 Wairau Road,
Auckland 10, New Zealand

Penguin Books Ltd, Registered Offices:
Harmondsworth, Middlesex, England

Published by Signet, an imprint of New American Library,
a division of Penguin Putnam Inc.

This is an authorized reprint of a hardcover edition published by
G. P. Putnam's Sons. A hardcover edition was published simultaneously
in Canada by General Publishing Co. Limited.

First Signet Printing, May 1987
25 24 23 22 21 20 19

Illustrations by Richard L. Penney on pages 32, 38, 90, 103, 111, 132, 190, 220,
221, 223, 225, 227, 229, 231, 233, 235, 237, 239, 259, 266, 276, 298, 312, 323, 334,
344, 356, 389, 399, 401, 402, 404, 444, 466, 478, 482.

Illustrations by Sheldon Ciner, D.D.S., on pages 30, 31, 59, 115, 142, 295, 296,
310, 422.

Illustrations by Kenneth Reseigh Waters on pages 180 and 185.

The graph on page 78 is reproduced by permission of C. B. Mosby Co. from an
article by F. Battaglia and L. Lubchenco, "A practical classification of newborn
infants by birth weight and gestational age," published in *Journal of Pediatrics*,
71: 159–163, 1967. Copyright © 1967 by C. V. Mosby Co.

 REGISTERED TRADEMARK—MARCA REGISTRADA

Printed in the United States of America

NOTE TO THE READER
The ideas, procedures, and suggestions contained in this book are not intended
as a substitute for consulting with your physician. All matters regarding your
health require medical supervision.

CONTENTS

ACKNOWLEDGMENTS

I gratefully acknowledge the following individuals who contributed directly to this manuscript or who indirectly influenced the work by their impact on my professional growth and development:

My husband, Larry, for sustaining me and giving me wings;

My children, Peter, Paige, Patrice, Heather, and Mark, for perpetually uplifting and replenishing me;

My parents, Andrew and Annabelle Egeland for their unconditional love, high expectation, and personal example;

My brothers and sisters, Andy Egeland, Marcy Poncelow, Aleta Egeland and Tommy Egeland, for both nurturing and needing me;

Joy M. Seacat, C.H.A., M.S., for her steadfast loyalty and professional partnership;

Nancy Gary, C.H.A., M.S., for her long-time friendship and support;

Velois Whiteside, for her confidence and frequent encouragement;

Debbie Akana Holcomb for her years of sensible parenting advice;

Watson A. Bowes, Jr., M.D., for his model of competence and caring;

John L. Lightburn, M.D., for his insight and guidance;

The late C. Henry Kempe, M.D., for his enduring example and mentorship;

Susan L. Merrill, M.D., and Roger Barkin, M.D., for graciously reviewing the medical portions of the manuscript;

Sally Berga, M.D., Ph.D., and Marion Galant, for their helpful review of the entire manuscript;

Richard Penney, for his talented illustrations comprising the lion's share of the artwork;

Sherry Robb, my literary agent, for launching the project;

Judith Mintz, assistant editor at Putnam, for her dedicated handling of the manuscript;

Patricia Romanowski, for her superb copyediting;

Chris Schillig, Associate Publisher and Senior Editor at Putnam, for her initial foresight, ongoing encouragement, professional guidance, and remarkable efficiency in bringing it all about;

Gypsy da Silva at Putnam for final copy editing heroics;

NAL and Carole Hall, editor, for giving the book another life in paperback;

My students everywhere, from whom I've drawn my energy;

The children and parents who have touched my life and for whom the book was written.

MARIANNE EGELAND NEIFERT, M.D.

Introducing . . .
Dr. Mom

THIS IS THE BOOK that I wish I had when my first baby was born in 1968. I was then barely twenty years old and had no experience with babies. My mother was 5,000 miles away, and my sailor husband, who had been overseas for the last six months of my pregnancy, returned home just a week before our baby's birth.

I was so naive that when someone mentioned adding rice cereal to a bottle of formula, I wondered to myself how the little grains of rice fit through the nipple openings, and breathed a sigh of relief that I was breast-feeding. The day I took my son home from the hospital I worried at length about how to remove his pullover T-shirt without injuring his head. His routine bath was a daily ordeal that I postponed for the slightest excuse.

Having read that a newborn slept up to eighteen hours a day, I planned to resume my heavy course load at the university a week after delivery, fully expecting to have ample time to maintain my schedule. Instead, I seemed to spend eighteen hours each day just looking after one small baby, every aspect of whose care was foreign to me. My only reassurance was voiced by a matronly neighbor who promised, "The first one lives through anything." Miraculously, he did.

Over the next seven years, I finished college, graduated from medical school, completed a pediatric residency, and gave birth to four more children. Most pediatricians have their own first child well into their medical training, and thus can't really identify with the concerns of typical new parents. Throughout my medical education, however, I recalled my own fledgling parenting experiences and found myself repeatedly empathizing with new parents. By tuning in to their needs and listening to their feelings, I gradually arrived at a child-rearing perspective somewhat different from that of traditional health professionals.

With slight embarrassment I recall my early attempts at parenting, when I accepted outdated standards of success. I started solids at three weeks and toilet trained at a year, convinced by my contemporaries that these "milestones" were accurate indicators of my baby's developmental skills and my parenting abilities. We measured the baby's intelligence by his clothing size and the number of teeth present at a given age.

And yet, early in my parenting career, I began in little ways to challenge standard recommendations and tailor them to my own situation and needs. Although I had read that an infant should sleep in his own room, our tiny baby looked too isolated in the expanse of his new crib in the next room. But swaddled in the small bassinet at my bedside, where I could reach over to nurse him as soon as he stirred, he seemed cozy and secure. Despite all the admonitions, I failed to perceive the much-discussed ill effects of a contented baby asleep at my side. After experiencing a few more years of parenting and developing a lot more confidence, I began to examine traditional recommendations more critically. Shortly after starting my internship, I brought my eight-month-old third child to a pediatrician at the medical center for treatment of an ear infection. During the visit, I mentioned that she had been more wakeful at night and that I had been going to her room to comfort her. The pediatrician replied that I was "spoiling her" and that I should let her "cry it out" instead.

The next day, still feeling uncomfortable about the physician's advice, I stealthily pulled my baby's chart from medical records and reviewed the physician's notes. "Doubt if mother will comply" read the assessment. I tried to picture myself as a "noncompliant mother," refusing to cooperate with the latest medical opinion, potentially damaging my own baby with my obstinacy. Finally, it occurred to me that this pediatrician had no children of his own. He was a trained doctor, not a trained parent, and therefore couldn't appreciate the value of mothering instincts. While his "cry it out" advice might have been helpful to another parent who indeed wanted to "break the habit," it simply didn't fit with my own instincts to comfort my infant.

Just a few years ago, an encounter with a perseverant, intuitive mother finally crystallized for me the optimal role of the health professional. I had counseled this woman at length about how to teach her premature infant, who had been tube-fed and then bottle-fed in the nursery, to nurse at the breast. I gave her a dozen suggestions and tried to radiate confidence, as I assured her that she could successfully breast feed, though I had my own doubts.

A short time later, beaming with pride and joy, she thanked me for all my advice and support. Pleasantly surprised, I asked which of my suggestions worked best for her. "Oh, actually I did the opposite of what you told me, Dr. Neifert," she replied, oblivious of my startled look, and her esteem for me clearly undiminished. As I turned to nurse my wounded ego (how could a patient be so successful doing the *opposite* of what I had recommended?), I realized the hidden compliment in what had transpired. I had managed to offer a variety of suggestions, but more importantly, I had instilled confidence in the mother. Then *she* had creatively discovered a method of teaching her little boy how to nurse based on their relationship and her ability to read his cues. I had simply facilitated the process by providing support and encouragement and some practical suggestions, which she had effectively modified to best serve her own baby's needs. In essence, I had done for this woman what I wished pediatricians had done for me fifteen years earlier.

Few of you will be as naive as I once was, and fewer yet will acquire an M.D. degree and pediatric certification during your early years of parenting. But most of you will have many of the same questions and concerns that I did. Each of you will begin with good intentions, careful observations, and basically sound intuition. All you will need is a solid base of information and the permission to make healthy decisions and choices that fit comfortably into your parenting style.

By now you can probably tell that I love babies, children, and parents. I have experienced parental growing pains myself and have listened long and hard to the parents I have encountered. I have tempered my sometimes rigid, traditional medical training with personal experience and my patients' feedback. I have learned from all of you and now want to give back to parents everywhere, and thereby to their precious little ones, a gift of gratitude.

MY PHILOSOPHY OF PARENTING

As a pediatrician, medical educator, wife, and mother of five delightful preteens and adolescents, I write about child rearing from a special perspective. Because my own children were born while I was in college, medical school, internship, and residency training, motherhood influenced every aspect of my medical education, as well as my professional relationships with parents and my philosophy of child rearing. All the time I spend doctoring, I'm still a mom. All the time I spend mothering, I'm still a doctor. The paths of pediatrician and parent cross and recross and run together, enhancing both roles.

I had decided to become a physician at an early age and never wavered from this aspiration. So engrossed was I in achieving my goal that I gave little thought to marriage or children. Frankly, I had no model for meshing the two roles, so I ignored potential boyfriends and concentrated on the academic requirements for becoming a surgeon. Despite carefully laid plans, however, something unexpected happened to me in the summer after graduation from high school in Hawaii. I fell hopelessly in love—you know, "twitterpated," as in *Bambi*. Within five months, Larry and I were engaged, and a year later we were married. We set up housekeeping in a little apartment, where I smuggled in the embalmed cat I was dissecting for embryology lab, still resolute in my premed commitment. Children, it seemed, might fit into my agenda some ten years later.

I distinctly remember when something changed in my mind. Barely a month after our marriage, Larry showed me a school snapshot of himself, a little 1" × 2" portrait with the year printed at the bottom. Suddenly that youngster seemed the dearest thing to me and the thought of creating someone new out of our love became the first priority in our brand-new marriage, illogical as the timing appeared.

A year later, Peter was born amid physics, advanced quantitative analysis, physical chemistry, and forgotten humanities. He was the child of our inexperience, and his birth was the greatest adjustment we ever had to make, both individually and as a couple. Peter was six months old when I entered medical school at the tender age of twenty, the world at my fingertips.

I initially thought subsequent children would wait until I'd completed all my education. Perhaps it was the painful daily separation from my infant that made me long to have another baby right away instead. A year later Paige was born after class on a Friday afternoon. She was the child of our emerging confidence, and with a little creativity, I arranged a babysitter across the street from the hospital, so that I could nurse her between classes.

My dreams of being a surgeon soon vanished as I acknowledged that I lacked the technical skills (I actually cut off the tip of my glove during an operation!) and realized I wasn't the surgical personality type. Increasingly, I was drawn to pediatrics, largely because of the influence of my own growing family.

The medical school in Hawaii had not yet added its third and fourth clinical years of training, so transfer to the mainland was mandatory at the end of the second year. Larry and I arrived in Colorado with our one-year-old and two-year-old. We were reluctant, homesick, isolated, financially depleted, and somewhat scared. Following a six-month adjustment period, we had formally established our new home and felt ready to bring another baby into our family.

Tricie arrived early in the fourth year of medical school. The child of our transition, she brought new joys and new adjustments. I had arranged a luxurious ten-week break between clinical rotations and basked in the leisure of caring for her full time. Once back in school, however, I faced the periodic trauma of staying at the hospital all night and not seeing any of my kids for thirty-six hours at a time. Larry took on new responsibilities at home as my duties at school expanded. The stark reality of putting the needs of others ahead of my own family began to set in. I still thought I could give enough to everyone.

After graduation, I was accepted into the pediatric internship of my choice and embarked on the final grueling "initiation rites" of medicine. I can't explain why I decided to get pregnant shortly after internship commenced. Much of that year is now a blur of sheer physical and emotional exhaustion. My being on call every other or every third night rendered "quality time" an empty phrase. Everyone else's sick child came ahead of my own healthy children. "It's only a year," I told myself repeatedly, but its becoming a life-style was what I feared.

Heather was born late in the internship year, the child of our hopes in the midst of discouragement. I did a radical thing and announced to the appropriate powers that the standard two-week vacation would not give me enough time with my baby. I requested one month and lied "I'll make the time up next year." For thirty glorious days, I cherished every nursing, marked the days on the calendar as the month sped by, and cried all the way to the hospital on my first day back to work, knowing I was on call that night. Motherhood on these terms was a bittersweet experience. I simply took things one day at a time, and somehow we all survived. Meanwhile, the parent-doctor conflict mounted.

Two years later, on the final day of my residency training, Mark's arrival signaled the end of my formal medical education. He was the child of our vast experience, bringing me a new focus and joy. For the first time in my life, I had no future commitments. No educational program awaited me in the next phase of the making of a physician. My medical training was complete, but I was without immediate career plans. I just wanted to go home to my family for a while.

Thus in the summer of 1975, I found myself with five kids—seven years and under—a fully trained pediatrician seeking the best way to blend my formal education and personal experiences. Frankly, I was still mentally and physically exhausted, but applying my knowledge and experience in a professional setting remained important to me. Although I initially felt guilty for spending that summer at home instead of practicing medicine, I actually learned more in those two months about pediatrics, priorities, and parenting than I had learned from any two-month block of formal training. At last I was the kind of mother I had longed to be and I relished the realization that our family had emerged intact from the previous seven years. (Thank you, Larry.) Having always returned to school a few days to a few weeks after delivery, I delighted in parenting full time for a while.

Both physically and emotionally refueled, I began work as an instructor in the department of pediatrics at the prestigious medical school where I had trained. There I endeavored to educate students and house staff by personal example and formal lecture in the sensitive care of families, as well as the medical management of disease. Wherever possible, I tried to change hospital routines to accommodate parental requests, to treat patients the way I would want to be treated, and to listen to families' complaints and concerns.

As a teacher, I attempted to nurture my students with compliment and encouragement instead of the criticism and scorn frequently encountered in traditional medical education. It was my belief that positive support would help to preserve the warmth and enthusiasm students brought to medical school that was often snuffed out in an atmosphere of discouragement. I resolved to teach the art of caring for others by first demonstrating that I cared for them.

As I watched my techniques work with students, who in turn treated patients with greater sensitivity and compassion, it occurred to me that the professor-student relationship in many ways paralleled the pediatrician-parent relationship. Like a first-year medical student, every new parent looks forward to caring for others, filled with optimism and anticipation, as well as apprehension about the magnitude of responsibility. I believed that nurturing new parents by acknowledging their good intentions and sound intuition, while supplying them with factual information, better equips them to meet their children's needs than filling them with insecurities, fostering dependency, and criticizing their sincere efforts. It was also evident that this educational model provided a successful formula for parent-child relationships. As parents, we are, in fact, the most influential teachers, mentors, and role models our children will ever have. Similarly, our children are the most attentive students we will ever encounter. By fostering their self-esteem, complimenting their positive behavior rather than hounding them with criticism, letting them know we trust them instead of continually prophesying misbehavior, and loving them always apart from their performance, we bring out the best in our children.

Over the years, I became an authority on breast feeding, a role that has taken me all over the country and to distant parts of the world. This particular expertise has brought me into contact with thousands of new parents. In interacting with them and listening at length, I began to recognize the impact of early parenting experiences, such as breast feeding, on long-term parental competency.

Choosing to breast-feed is simply one of many conscious choices new parents make about their baby, and it doesn't always proceed smoothly. I noticed that parents judged their breast-feeding experience according to their own definition of "success." For example, if a mother had been forced to relinquish breast feeding before she had desired, due to lack of support or practical knowledge to solve a particular problem, she was often left with lingering disappointment and guilt. Occasionally, these inadequate feelings spilled over into other aspects of her parenting, causing her to lose confidence in her mothering abilities. But a woman who received necessary support and information, which enabled her to breast-feed as long as she had planned, tended to look back on her experience with pride and satisfaction. Her confidence radiated to other areas of mothering, and she viewed herself as a competent and successful parent. The issue wasn't really how long a woman nursed; rather it was whether she had been supported in reaching her own breast-feeding goal.

Similarly, a couple who chose to formula-feed for their own convincing reasons felt proud and confident. A mother who decided to formula-feed because she feared she would fail at breast feeding often felt guilty and dissatisfied. The parenting recipe seemed to be:

Awareness of Options + Conscious Decision +
Support and Encouragement = Achievement of Goal
and *Competency Grooming*.

Conversely,

Unrecognized Options or Imposed Decision or Lack of
Support and Encouragement = Unattained Goal and
Inadequacy Priming.

Using the breast-feeding model I had observed and reflecting on my own parenting "successes" and "failures"
in a variety of areas, I adopted a philosophy of facilitating
parents' informed decisions and doing all in my power to
see that they are able to reach their specific parenting goals.
Whether it's infant feeding or one of the many other
parenting responsibilities we face, I believe that feelings of
adequacy or inadequacy largely depend upon whether we
make informed choices and receive support in fulfilling
our options, rather than relinquishing choices and abandoning goals.

In 1984 *Glamour* magazine recognized me as one of their
Top Ten Outstanding Young Working Women. The honor
came at a time in my career when I really needed and
appreciated such validation of my work. But what made
the award especially meaningful was the fact that I had
been nominated by the mother of a child previously under
my care.

Cindy, a well-intentioned and hardworking woman, had
always been a high-achiever as a student, employee, and
housewife. She remains one of the most organized and
conscientious young mothers I know. The inadequate weight
gain demonstrated by Jenessa, her new breast-fed infant,
had resulted in medical alarm by her referring pediatrician,
judgmental remarks from her own mother, and mild scorn
by her sister-in-law, whose bottle-fed infant had boasted
phenomenal growth.

For months I consulted on Jenessa's case and supported
her parents in their efforts to induce weight gain in her.
Cindy discontinued breast feeding, only to find the baby
grew no better on formula or solids. Endeavoring to mask

my own distress as Jenessa's weight curve steadily drifted further below the lowest percentile, I discreetly ordered necessary tests to rule out medical causes of failure to thrive, while overtly radiating optimism about her overall health and well-being. I commiserated with Cindy and Frank over their fruitless efforts to produce a robust baby, but objectively acknowledged that the developmental milestones of their bright-eyed and responsive infant were quite appropriate. I made a home visit and there endorsed Cindy's feeding practices. I defended her against the onslaught of negative comments from relatives and tried to assure her that she was indeed an exemplary mother but one who happened to have a slow-gaining baby.

Initially Cindy felt inadequate and insecure about her mothering abilities. For a time, her self-confidence hinged on ounces Jenessa gained each week. Gradually Cindy began to realize that she had tried as hard as any mother could have (in fact, harder than most!) in feeding a difficult baby, and that the body habitus of her petite little girl was somewhat predetermined. (In fact, Cindy weighs barely one hundred pounds soaking wet!)

Several years later, Cindy gave birth to a chunky boy who nursed vigorously, ate voraciously, and gained weight rapidly. Michael soon outweighed his delicate older sister, and we all laughed at the difference between the two siblings. If Michael had been born first, how confident Cindy would have been in her parenting of such an obviously thriving infant. With such a background of success, she probably would not have blamed herself for Jenessa's painfully slow weight gain. It was not really until Michael's birth that she finally acknowledged that the rate of Jenessa's growth did not reflect on her competence as a mother.

Why am I telling you all this? And what compelled Cindy to nominate me for the *Glamour* award? I didn't make an exotic diagnosis or rescue Jenessa from the ravages of a life-threatening disease. Yet Cindy will always remember me for being supportive and helpful, as someone who nurtured her during those painful, early months of motherhood when she was unfairly under attack by relatives and professionals. All I did was recognize her diligent and conscientious efforts to be a good mother. I was determined to build her up and enhance her confidence, rather than feed into any developing insecurities.

Nothing I learned in medical school told me to do that, but everything I remember from my own first experiences as a parent urged me to "mother" this industrious new mother until her confidence was restored. That's why the name "Dr. Mom" is so special to me. Not just because I am mom to five children of my own, but also because I believe so strongly in the importance of nurturing new parents, in order to bring to blossom their long-term competency. That's what I hope this book will do for you!

1 ON BECOMING A PARENT

SINCE PARENTING really is the oldest profession in the world, you'd think there would be some pretty clear-cut guidelines about how to parent. The truth is that a wide range of parenting styles seems to produce well-adjusted, productive, and happy adults. Even within the same family, parenting styles may change from the first to last child, as our philosophy of child rearing evolves with experience and wisdom. This book will provide you with the fundamentals of child care, while allowing you to fine-tune your own parenting techniques to fit your individual life-style.

Each of us views having children a little differently. We each have our own reasons for becoming a parent. Why did you have children? What are your parenting goals? There is no single right answer to these questions, but an honest self-analysis of your underlying reasons for becoming a parent can add valuable insight to your parenting priorities and clarify your expectations. How do you feel about your own parents? What would you like to do similarly and what things do you plan to do differently? For better or worse, most of us are creatures of habit and products of our past. We are likely to parent very much as we were parented, unless we make a conscious effort to change in a specific way.

By and large, I liked the way my parents raised me. Without consciously planning it, I had five children after being raised as one of five. I work full time just as my mother did. We emphasize academic performance with our children, perhaps because my mother was a schoolteacher.

I find myself perpetuating in our home many holiday traditions, favorite meals, and games from my own childhood. Having been raised in a large family, I always wished I had had more opportunities to do things one-on-one with my parents. Recalling that desire, I now make a conscious effort to arrange individual experiences with my own children, such as taking one child with me on each out-of-town trip.

RESPONSIBILITIES OF PARENTHOOD

Many, if not most, new parents initially feel overwhelmed by the total responsibility for the care and survival of a human being they love so profoundly. When faced with the magnitude of this responsibility, parents may be temporarily oppressed by the long-term commitment to protect and nurture their baby. Even immediate small acts of care, such as changing another diaper in the middle of the night, may seem for a moment to require too much from you. When my first baby was about three weeks old, I was absolutely exhausted one night and remember thinking irrationally, "I'll never survive eighteen years of waking up every three hours." My husband detected my distress and cared for Peter while I slept several hours and awoke more optimistic.

"This too shall pass" is sage advice my parents shared with me. In fact, even the magical moments and happiest times will indeed pass all too quickly. With experience on our part, and gradual maturation on the baby's part, those early conscious and time-consuming acts of parenting eventually come naturally and will scarcely seem disruptive. Then, by the time your child starts kindergarten, you'll worry how you'll get through the morning without having him around!

Loving your baby probably sounds like the easy part, especially if he fulfills all your expectations. (But that hasn't happened since the Gerber Baby agreed to perpetually smile from the label of a baby food jar!) Too often, we expect our baby to be perfectly formed, even gorgeous, as well as delightful and precocious. We look forward to the enhancement of our own self-esteem through this thoroughly marvelous extension of ourselves—our cute, bright, and healthy baby. By trying to fulfill ourselves through our children's accomplishments, we place a burden on them. Many children ultimately feel loved only because of their athletic prowess, academic ability, good looks or other attribute meriting reward. True parental love, however, is unconditional love. It's loving our baby with a birth defect, our youngster with a behavior problem, our child with a learning disability—loving him just because he was given into our care.

I recently read a newspaper story about a young father who had been a star gymnast in high school and had learned to strive for perfection in everything. His first son was born with a cleft lip, an unexpected imperfection in his otherwise perfect world. In the touching story, this sensitive father candidly described his initial disappointment with his son and his reluctance to attach to the "flawed" child. As he began to hold and respond to his son, however, he was suddenly struck by the child's innocence and the realization that he "was mine." This maturation process was accompanied by an outpouring of love toward the little boy. A few days later, the initially disappointed father was unwilling to trade his precious child for any other infant. That was unconditional love, not present at birth, but blossoming in full within a few short days.

Unconditional love, parental love, is unearned and unending. It has no strings attached, no conditions that must be met. Many of our other relationships in life depend on reciprocal benefits, but parental love is given freely to both gifted and retarded child, beautiful and blemished child, precocious and handicapped child, planned and unplanned child, boy and girl child. When delightful or obnoxious, we continue to love our child. It's the most selfless thing we ever do, sometimes the bravest thing we ever do, and surely the most important thing we ever do. We love simply because it comes so naturally and because someone once did it for us.

Unconditional love fosters in our child self-esteem, or one's own sense of self-worth—that key ingredient for mental health, the successful accomplishment of goals, and satisfaction in all of life's relationships. Our own healthy model of self-esteem plays a significant role in developing our child's sense of self-esteem. But the most vital ingredient is our unconditional love, for it convinces our child that he is worthy of love.

In addition to loving, several concrete responsibilities accompany parenthood. Among these is the obvious necessity to protect your baby from physical and emotional trauma. A baby is helpless to defend himself against the outside world. We must be vigilant about assuring his automobile safety, screening his caretakers, safety-proofing his environment, and supervising his play. Of course we will make mistakes, and fortunately we often will be lucky. The constant diligence necessary to see him safely into adult life is one of the most tedious jobs of parenthood.

Certainly we need to provide nourishment for our child, and with this particular responsibility we encounter a wide range of options, with some basic ground rules. We can breast-feed, formula-feed, or even do both. But we can't decide to raise our newborn on skim milk, rice water, or carrot juice. We can introduce commercial solids or make our own, provided we offer all essential food groups. We can bake bread from scratch or dine at fast-food restaurants. We can keep kosher, become vegetarians, or banish junk foods. We can use paper plates, watch TV during dinner, or eat by candlelight. But we must guarantee that our child will receive enough of the right foods for adequate growth and development. Furthermore, we need to introduce him to early eating habits that will foster lifelong sound nutrition.

Meeting a child's emotional needs is equally important. Whether you work full time or stay at home, are a single parent or a married partner, live in a high-rise or out on a farm, your children need to feel loved and to be raised in an emotionally secure environment that allows them to trust their caretaker adults. The creation of this emotional security begins with your regular response to your newborn's physical needs and develops fully in a loving home environment where children are complimented, encouraged, and valued. Emotional security is always jeopardized if children are abused, victimized, or regularly criticized.

Comprehensive health care should be the birthright of every child, and that includes good prenatal care, safe delivery practices, routine childhood health maintenance visits, and prompt emergency care when necessary. You are encouraged to be an active participant in your child's health care, not just a passive recipient, and to make educated decisions about many matters that our parents never even considered. But you don't have the right to jeopardize your child's health because of your own personal beliefs or withhold necessary medical treatment just because you don't agree with it.

We are also responsible for providing our child with quality educational opportunities, whether in a public school, private institution, religion-sponsored program, or by home tutoring. If your child has special educational needs, such as a learning disability or speech impediment, you are obligated to seek intervention for such problems. We never have the right to deny our children formal education, to ignore learning problems, or fail to foster prodigious talents.

When we fulfill these parental responsibilities to the best of our ability, we maximize the chance that our child will develop in every way to his fullest genetic potential. Whether or not he becomes the Einstein we had predicted, our child will be the very best that he was destined to be.

RIGHTS OF PARENTHOOD

Parenting brings many rewards and joys. Your child's babyhood is the courtship phase of the long love relationship you are building. As in any courtship, it feels terrific to love with complete abandon. You have every right to soak it up and enjoy the growing love that is blossoming between you and your baby. You are entitled to thoughtfully sift through all the advice you receive and ultimately to raise your child in the way that you feel is most conducive to his development and your own parenting style, as long as his safety and well-being are protected. Similarly, you have the right to receive full explanations about his health care, and the right to participate in decisions when a choice among types of care is available. When making a nontraditional choice, like deciding never to spank, or not to have a circumcision performed, or to share custody jointly with your ex-partner, you should feel good about the appropriate decision you make, despite being bombarded with outside criticism and caution.

In most jobs, making mistakes and learning from them is met with understanding. As parents, however, we often feel we must be perfect, and that every mistake will have lifelong consequences. Not only does this impossible expectation create undue pressure for the parent, it also provides a highly unrealistic model for our children. As with any job (and parenting may be the toughest one you'll ever have!), you do have the luxury of making some mistakes without suffering or inflicting permanent damage. As your children grow, they will appreciate your honest confession of occasional errors and your sincere apologies. In fact, they will respect you more for it. As it turns out, simply being a "good enough" parent, instead of a perfect parent, is pretty commendable. So go easy on yourself.

Once we have a baby, we often feel pressured, both by ourselves and others, to become "all parent." Sure, there are sacrifices to be made, but one of them is not abandoning everything that we were before we became parents. You can continue to be the husband or wife, the hobbyist or sports enthusiast, the employee or employer, the bowler or bridge player that you were before you became a parent. And preserving those other dimensions of your life will actually enhance your parenting. After the birth of my first child, I considered giving up my plans for medical school to be a full-time mother. After struggling with this decision, I realized that sacrificing a long-planned medical career might leave me personally unfulfilled, thus making me a less effective mother in the long run. I decided instead to try to combine medicine and motherhood, as long as my child did not seem adversely affected. In the end, I am confident I made the right decision for myself and my family. Martyrs make poor parents!

HOW PARENTING HAS EVOLVED

Although the basic responsibilities and rights of parenting have not really changed much over time, many aspects of parenting have changed radically, even in the last generation. Being a parent today is hard, perhaps even harder than ever. Certainly it is far different than it was in our parents' time. Consider the impact on families brought about by the following societal changes.

IN OUR PARENTS' GENERATION	IN OUR GENERATION
The average family consisted of Dad, who supported the family, Mom, who cared for the family, and numerous children. Divorce was rare.	Today both Mom and Dad can either stay home or work outside the home. Fifty percent of all marriages end in divorce, and single-parent families are headed by either Mom or Dad. Stepparents and step-siblings are common. We see many more single-child families and fewer large families. In fact, the "average" family no longer exists.
Traditional parenting (translated as "mothering") values were based on doing things for your children. A good parent cooked and sewed and cleaned for her children, and kept them clean as well.	Today's society values "doing with" more than "doing for." Parents today know about "quality versus quantity time" and the importance of family relationships.
The extended family often lived in the same town, perhaps in the same neighborhood, if not in the same home.	In our mobile society, a young family may move often and far from their extended family and the models and support it provides.
Parents of large families struggled just to get by and were content if they could simply feed and clothe their children.	Parents of smaller families often place a higher premium on each child. By trying to do more for each child, they experience increased "pressure to perform."

IN OUR PARENTS' GENERATION	IN OUR GENERATION
Most couples first became parents while still in their early twenties.	Many couples today postpone childbearing until their thirties and are often better educated and more financially stable than their own parents were when they first had children.
Poverty was usually due to men being out of work.	Now the majority of poor families are headed by women.
Parents were encouraged to be stern and strict, so that a child would learn self-control.	Parents are encouaged to provide loving guidance, so that children learn to make reasoned decisions on their own.
Gender-role identification predominated as the model for all types of behavior.	Gender-role identification still prevails to a great degree, but as a society, we are beginning to see that it is not always the healthiest model for our children.
The idea of a child having a gay or lesbian parent was inconceivable.	Gays and lesbians are less closeted, and their special challenges and rights as parents are being recognized.
Parents and children bowed to authority. ("I don't like it, but my doctor says my husband can't be in the delivery room.")	Challenging authority and actively participating with authority figures is considered admirable. ("My doctor agreed to let my older child attend the delivery.")

IN OUR PARENTS' GENERATION	IN OUR GENERATION
Teachers freely imposed their values and disciplinary standards on their students.	Teachers have limited influence on students' values and less authority to discipline, thus placing greater responsibility on parents.
Divorce impacted primarily on adolescents.	Today divorce widely impacts even infants and preschoolers. Families seldom "stay together" for the sake of the children.
In a divorce, mothers were almost always awarded custody of children, and fathers were granted visitation rights.	There is a growing trend toward more fathers being awarded custody, and more shared custody arrangements are being negotiated.
Mothers mothered, fathers fathered, so that each child had one complete "parenting unit." Girls modeled their mothers and boys modeled their fathers.	Each parent can and should function as a separate (but joined, if a couple) total parenting unit, offering children of either one- or two-parent families better parenting potential and better models. Girls and boys can emulate the qualities of sensitivity, strength, independence, and warmth exhibited by both parents.

Rapid technological advances in recent years also have had direct impact on families and children, as well as society as a whole.

IN OUR PARENTS' GENERATION	IN OUR GENERATION
The threat of war meant the frightening possibility of losing a son, a brother, or a father.	Now the threat of war means the terrifying possibility of the total annihilation of the human race. We are seeing the effects of this ever-present fear on the emotional health (depression, anxiety, and apathy) of children raised in the nuclear generation.
Regardless of the ethical issue, abortion was not a legal choice.	Abortion is a legal choice (although not always financially feasible) that impacts on ethical concerns, family planning, and genetic counseling.
There was little way to know if a woman was carrying a healthy baby, much less a boy or a girl.	Current procedures, such as ultrasound screening and amniocentesis, can forewarn a family of possible health problems in the baby, as well as tell the number and sex of the baby/babies present in utero. With the availability of abortion, many difficult societal and parental questions are now posed.
Most very sick and/or small babies did not survive.	Many premature or sick babies are being kept alive by modern technology and equipment. One consequence is an increased number of babies who survive with severe handicaps, raising more hard questions.

IN OUR PARENTS' GENERATION	IN OUR GENERATION
Little data was available about parenting concerns such as parent-infant "bonding" or breast feeding. Parents did whatever their parents had done, or what seemed right for them at the time.	The vast research in these areas has been publicized to the lay community, so that educated parents today can make informed choices about their parenting.
The family and community had great influence on children, and controlled most of their experiences. A farm child and a city child had little in common.	The family's influence on children is diminished by two leaps in technology that expose children to more of the world—travel and TV. Children today see more of the world firsthand, and also experience that great cultural equalizer—TV. From farm or city, what child doesn't know who Michael Jackson is?

Yes, in many ways parenting today is more challenging than ever before. The decisions are surely tougher, and the rewards may be greater. No simple recipes are possible because our individual backgrounds, life-styles, and priorities vary so widely. Whether you are having your first child or your fifth, whether you are single or married, whether you work outside the home or parent full time, whether you began your family at nineteen or waited until thirty-nine, whether your child is healthy or has a medical problem, it is my hope that this book will speak personally to you. I have tried to provide understandable explanations of necessary medical information and present a range of safe options within which you can select the approach to parenting that best fits your own philosophy and life-style. By giving you the information you need and permission to thoughtfully apply it in your own situation, I hope to instill confidence in your innate parenting abilities and foster a lifetime of competent child rearing.

No matter what choices you make, parenting is a hard, twenty-four-hour-a-day job. According to an old Russian proverb, "You can't pay anyone to do what a parent will do for free." We not only do it; we enjoy it. Few of us could be persuaded to provide round-the-clock care for a senile, bald, edentulous, and incontinent adult, yet we *choose* to lovingly care for a toothless, hairless, speechless, helpless, diapered newborn. We make meals, make beds, make mistakes, make exceptions, and mostly make do. It's parenting—loving, living, laughing, learning, and more loving.

2 COUNTDOWN TO PARENTHOOD

PREPARING FOR your new baby is probably the most pleasant part of your pregnancy. In anticipation of your baby's arrival, you will be evaluating childbirth options, choosing a name, decorating the nursery, buying baby equipment, selecting health-care providers, rehearsing your trip to the hospital, and making numerous other plans.

The magnitude of impending parental responsibilities is often overwhelming and frightening. The more deliberate preparations involve making physical and emotional adjustments, and evaluating professional and common-sense advice. You will find that advance preparation can add to your confidence and make the big adjustment easier.

CHILDBIRTH OPTIONS

In the past, women routinely gave birth at home. More recently a highly structured hospital birth has been the norm. Today we encounter a variety of both birthing places and "methods."

Childbirth Classes

When I had my first baby, no childbirth classes were available to me, so I was ignorant and unprepared for labor and delivery. By the time classes were popular and easily accessible, we already had several children and felt we were supposed to already "know it all." In retrospect, I wish we had taken a formal class and a refresher course with each pregnancy.

Childbirth classes offer you an understanding of what happens to your body during labor, and they help you assume as much control over the birthing process as possible. Your labor will be a more positive experience if you are prepared. In addition, going through classes with your partner often brings you closer together and makes the birth a more shared experience. You cannot expect the same sort of loving attentiveness from a labor nurse as you can from your partner. Without childbirth classes, however, your partner may be at a loss as to how to help you through your labor and delivery.

You might find a variety of childbirth classes to choose from if you live in a big city, or only one or two if your community is smaller. Those you might expect to find include:

Lamaze: Lamaze is the largest and most popular system of childbirth education. Couples who take Lamaze classes are almost always happy with their results. Lamaze is not strictly a "natural childbirth" approach, but a "prepared childbirth" course, as medication options are presented in class and are acceptable within the Lamaze philosophy. You can read more about Lamaze childbirth in the book *Preparation for Childbirth: A Lamaze Guide* by Donna and Roger Ewy.

Hospital- or OB-office-sponsored classes: Some hospitals or OB offices sponsor their own classes, which are often a combination of techniques from other childbirth methods. In general, these classes will teach you the stages of labor and some management techniques and will display a very accepting attitude toward medication, probably thoroughly outlining the options.

The Bradley Method: The Bradley method is a "natural" approach to birth in which the use of medication is discouraged. A "consumerist" attitude is taught, and a great deal of information is transmitted. Bradley students are very aware of their birth options and they rarely use any medication during delivery. There are a few basic differences from Lamaze in breathing and focusing techniques. The book *Husband Coached Childbirth* by Robert Bradley, M.D., explains the Bradley philosophy in greater detail.

Grantly Dick-Read: The Dick-Read method is not as specific in its contents as most other methods. It preceded the Lamaze method, but has never been as popular. The basic idea behind the Dick-Read method is breaking the cycle of fear-tension-pain. The method emphasizes education as a way of minimizing fear. The laboring woman is taught to use voluntary muscle relaxation and a relaxed inward focus. A source of emotional support is important, but not as specifically defined as "the labor coach." Dr. Grantly Dick-Read's book *Childbirth Without Fear* offers a thorough explanation of his philosophy.

Erna Wright: Erna Wright studied both the Dick-Read and Lamaze approaches before defining her own method. It is based on psychoprophylaxis (prevention of pain). She teaches four levels of breathing, described as less active than the breathing techniques of Lamaze, with no panting until the urge to push. Erna Wright believed that her method improved on the others by being more specific.

Vaginal Birth after a Caesarean: This is not a system of childbirth education, but bears mentioning here. The old saying "Once a section always a section" is simply no longer true, provided the uterine scar is transverse (horizontal rather than vertical). Each woman needs to be evaluated individually, but in general, half of women with a previous C-section can successfully deliver subsequent babies vaginally, under close medical supervision. Although a vaginal birth is usually optimal, do not allow yourself to become so caught up in the idea of a "perfect birth" that the baby's safety becomes secondary. If you do require a Caesarean, you may feel disappointed, but focus instead on your beautiful, healthy baby.

Place of Birth

Where will you give birth? You are lucky to be giving birth in a consumerist era; your choices are broader, safer, and more humanistic than ever before.

A Hospital: A hospital is still by far the most common place to give birth. In a traditional hospital birth, the mother may labor in one room, deliver in another, and recover in still a third room before being transferred to the ward. The advantage of hospital birth is that in case of emergency, the appropriate personnel and equipment are readily available. Possible disadvantages include the inconvenience of being moved, some unnecessary interventions, a less personal atmosphere, and periodic mother-baby separation. Most hospitals, however, are revising their policies to give parents flexible options and more control of their birthing experience.

The Hospital Birthing Room: This approach has done a great deal to make hospitals more appealing to parents today. In a birthing room, a mother can labor and give birth in the same bed. Generally a smaller professional staff is present, probably your doctor and one nurse. In many hospitals you have the option of inviting family and friends into the birthing room to share the birth of your baby with you. Located in a hospital, a birthing room offers all the medical services that might be needed in an emergency. Unfortunately, few hospitals have enough birthing rooms to assure one is always available.

A Birthing Center: Another option that is growing in popularity and availability is the birthing center. This facility is usually staffed by certified nurse midwives, is less structured and more homelike than a hospital, but is attached to or very close to a hospital in case of emergency. Your prenatal care is given at the birthing center by the midwives. The care you receive is often more personal and generally your nurse midwife remains with you throughout labor and delivery. The people of your choice, including your other children, can be present at any time.

Like birthing rooms, birthing centers are available only to women without pregnancy complications.

Homebirth: In the United States, interest in homebirth is increasing. It is understandable that a woman would feel more comfortable and in control in her own home. However, a medical emergency cannot be handled effectively in one's home, and could jeopardize mother's or baby's life. Because complications at birth can be so devastating and are often unpredictable, the majority professional opinion strongly disapproves of homebirth. I personally would never accept the medical risks involved.

Regardless of where you choose to give birth, read, inform yourself, and by all means take childbirth classes of some type. Look at your options critically, with your baby's safety as your highest priority.

IT'S TIME!

Once you've made your decisions about childbirth education and the place you will give birth, make a plan for getting from your home to the hospital or birthing center. Here are some proven strategies to help you through those intense moments.

√ Pack your suitcase for the hospital two or three weeks in advance. Include a nightgown that will be convenient for nursing, a receiving blanket, an outfit to dress the baby in for her homecoming, toiletries, a nursing bra, and a good reference book on breast feeding if you plan to nurse. Remember that your going-home clothes will come from your maternity wardrobe—you won't be back into your favorite nonmaternity clothes immediately.

√ Bring along snacks. During your labor you may be reluctant to let your partner leave even long enough to grab a sandwich. Take simple, high-protein snacks like nuts and cheese, so he won't become weak and even more tired. Fruit is also a good idea.

√ Install an infant car seat in your car a couple of weeks before your baby is due. Be sure to follow the manufacturer's installation instructions.

√ If you have any other children, plan in detail who will care for them. You may need both a day plan and a night plan as well as a back-up system. Some familes even rent a pager several weeks before the due date for the person who will care for your children. That way, no matter where they are when you go into labor, you can reach them immediately. It is also a good idea to have your partner carry a pager near the end of your pregnancy, so he can be reached anytime, anyplace.

√ If you have a pet, make arrangements ahead of time with a friend or neighbor to come over and care for it.

√ Have a list of everyone who will need to be called

immediately. For example, you'll probably want to call your bosses to inform them that neither of you will be coming to work today or notify clients or others with whom either of you have meetings. If someone will be photographing the birth or caring for your children or pets, have their numbers handy.

√ Don't make your trip to the hospital to give birth your first drive there. Chances are, you will already have been to the hospital for preregistration and a maternity floor tour. But even if you have no reason for going, drive there once during your pregnancy so you won't need to figure out the best route on the way.

Only you know the essentials in your life. You will probably need to add to or alter these suggestions for your "hospital plan," but the point is, do plan ahead. Everything will go more smoothly if you do.

PREPARATION FOR BREAST FEEDING

In general, you need to do little preparation if you plan to breast-feed. Information and confidence are your best preparation. Although you may have heard that your sister rubbed her nipples with a towel, your neighbor did "nipple pulls," and your friend religiously applied lanolin to her nipples daily, there is no proof any of this is necessary or helpful. In fact, rubbing with a towel too vigorously may actually irritate your nipples.

During pregnancy, nature prepares your nipples for breast feeding. You may notice the emergence of little protrusions, known as Montgomery tubercles, on your areola. They secrete an unnoticeable fluid that keeps your nipple and areola clean and increases their pliability. Because this fluid cleanses your nipples, during the last couple of months of your pregnancy, avoid washing your nipples with soap, as it will dry them.

Attend La Leche League meetings. You will learn more from other breast-feeding mothers than you can learn from any book. Try to attend the full series of four monthly meetings before the birth of your baby. Take down the leader's name and phone number so you can call her with any questions or problems you encounter once your baby is born.

Buy at least one reference book on breast feeding. Good choices include *Successful Breastfeeding* by Nancy Dana and Anne Price (Meadowbrook Press), *Breast Is Best* by Drs. Andrew and Penny Stanway (American Baby Books), and The *Womanly Art of Breastfeeding* by La Leche League (NAL).

NURSING BRA

Buy one nursing bra in the size you're wearing at the end of your pregnancy. Look for cotton content and an easy opening and closing device. After you've tried several, you can better decide what type of bra you like.

Examine your nipples to see if they are inverted. Place your thumb on top and your index finger on the bottom of the areola and squeeze gently. Does your nipple protrude or invert? Inverted nipples pull inward and so are difficult for the baby to grasp. Inverted nipples are managed quite successfully by wearing breast shields, also known as milk cups or breast shells, during the latter months of pregnancy. The devices provide gentle suction to draw the nipple out. Breast shields are not noticeable under clothing and can be worn throughout the day but should be removed at night.

**Inverted nipple pulls inward when areola is compressed
between thumb and forefinger.**

If you plan to return to work after your baby is born, it
is still possible to breast-feed. You will want to obtain a
breast pump; compare pumps first and choose one with
your specific needs in mind. You'll find *The Breastfeeding
Guide for the Working Woman* by Anne Price and Nancy
Bamford Dana a helpful resource.

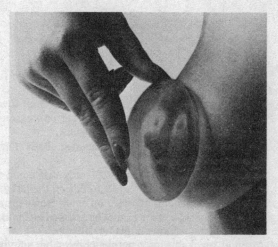

BREAST SHIELD
(Happy Family Products, Inc.)

BABY-PROOFING YOUR HOUSE

As you make your "parent preparations," you should also think about baby-proofing your house for your infant's long-term safety. You won't actually need to implement your plans until your baby is mobile, but since your life-style and habits are so ingrained already, you should start making changes in your household that prepare you for living with an infant. Measures that you will eventually need to take include:

- √ Covering electrical outlets with guards, so little fingers cannot probe.
- √ Placing baby-safe latches on the inside of your lower cabinet doors so your baby cannot get into cleaning products or other dangerous substances.
- √ Protecting stairs with a stair gate (see Baby Equipment, page 59).
- √ Checking for exposed electrical cords that could be pulled, causing a heavy object to fall on the baby.
- √ Keeping the handles of pots on your stove turned toward the back, so they cannot be grabbed and pulled down, causing serious burns.
- √ Moving breakable or tearable objects out of your baby's reach. If you think you will be able to "teach" your baby not to touch, you will only be setting up

yourself and your baby for failure. Instead, you will
want to allow your baby to explore appropriately, and
keep only safe "explorables" within her reach.

Naming Your Baby

Preparation for your baby involves both practical and
mental tasks. Part of your mental preparation is choosing a
name for your baby, enabling you to more easily envision
a real person. Expectant parents are typically depicted
poring over name books, debating the attributes of each
possibility, eventually narrowing the list to a favored few
and finally settling on the two names that are just right.
You, too, are probably putting such time and effort into
the selection of a name. Don't underestimate the importance of the name you choose for your baby. Her name
will be a significant part of her identity throughout her life.
Will you give her a gift or a burden?

Names have connotations for us all. We often get a
mental image of someone from their name before we even
meet them. What kinds of images are conjured up by the
names you are considering? For some reason we get very
different mental pictures when we hear names like Oswald
and Mabel than we do when we hear David and Susan,
and different ones yet for Troy and Vanessa. It has even
been scientifically established that teachers react to their
students partially according to the connotation of their
names. And haven't we all rejected very fine names on the
grounds that we once knew someone we disliked with that
name?

You may prefer common, traditional names like John or
Elizabeth because they have a solid sound and feel to
them. Or you may lean toward uncommon names like
Miranda or Seth because they are more individualistic.
This is really just a matter of taste. An interesting study
has shown that for a disadvantaged person (i.e., poor,
uneducated) an unusual name may be a handicap, but for
someone with more social advantages, an unusual name is
often an asset.

The selection of purposefully odd names like Moon Suit
or Sundown may be a hindrance to a child and should be

avoided. Odd names are not simply uncommon names like Kyle or Jade. They are names (Moonstar or Rainbow) that are not normally personal names, or names that are so old-fashioned that they are out of use (Hazel or Percival), or made up multisyllabic names that are difficult to decipher. Consider carefully before choosing an odd name.

Some individuals have provided such strong and long-lasting name connotations that they have virtually retired a name, like Elvis, Lucretia, or Romeo. An extreme example would be Adolf. A lighter example would be that no boy named Alvin could escape being connected with a cartoon chipmunk.

It's not my intent to recommend what type of name to choose—common names, family names, original names, short or long names are all fine. But I do recommend that you give serious thought to your choice and that you keep several important points in mind as you contemplate your baby's name. Is the name easy to pronounce? If not, your child is in for a lifetime of repeating his name correctly. Does the spelling of the name help or hinder someone who reads it for the first time (i.e., Jorga for Georgia)? Is the spelling standard (and thus more understandable) or a cute variation (Leesa for Lisa or Mikehal for Michael)? To avoid misspelling a name by accident, look it up first. Do the initials of the baby's name spell something embarrassing? One family changed their plan to name their son Paul Ivan Garrity after reflecting on the initials. Brenda Ann Davis would also be a problem. Forego humor. Your child's identity is not a joke. No matter how tempting combinations like Brigham Young or North West are, pass them by. Most important, choose a lifelong name, not a name suitable for a small child only (Muffy or Scooter) or only for an old person (Oscar or Mabel). Some parents choose to put a nickname on the birth certificate as the proper name, like Teddy instead of Theodore, or Cindy instead of Cynthia. Try to imagine your child as an adult and ponder whether the full name might not be a more appropriate choice for the birth certificate.

Consider how the name blends with your last name:

√ For vowel sounds: Steve Wheeler (too many E's)

√ For consonant sounds: Joy Seacat (sounds like Joyce Eacat)

√ For length: Montgomery Jeremiah Livingston (too long)

√ For meaning: Morgan David (sounds like Mogen David)

√ For rhyming: Bryce Price.

√ For pronounceability: Josh Salzman, Brad Dodds, Travis Davis, Seth Schwartz.

√ For rhythm: If you have a one-syllable last name a longer first name sounds better. For example, Daniel Ku instead of Pat Ku. But if the two one-syllable names have long sounds like Mark Strain, it can sound full and strong. Also, if you have a one- or two-syllable last name, it generally sounds better to have more syllables in the first name than in the last, like Amanda Galant. If you have a multi-syllabic last name like Caracciolo, a one- or two-syllable first name sounds best, like Dana or Jenn.

√ For identity: If you have a common last name, to avoid confusion, choose a less common first name, like Evan Smith instead of John Smith

How common is the name you're considering? Find out. First-time parents are often unaware of trends in names. "You mean there are other Jennifers (or Jasons)?" Is the likely nickname undesirable to you? If you hate the name Bobby, maybe you should reconsider the name Robert.

If you are expecting twins, please resist giving them "matching" names like Sharon and Karen. This contributes to each child feeling like half of a set. Distinctly different names will help your twins feel more like individuals.

When choosing a middle name, check again for a nicely flowing sound, no unfortunate initial combinations, and a reasonable combined length. You can also opt for two middle names or none. A guideline for choosing a middle name is that if you are using long first and last names, use a short middle name, and vice versa. If the baby's first and last names have the same number of syllables, be sure the middle name has a different number.

If you are considering naming a son Junior, remember that not all Juniors are happy with their names. While some boys feel it is special to have their father's name, others feel it is a lifelong burden. In a sense being named after Dad deprives your child of having his very own name. In addition, calling the boy "junior" can be like calling him "diminutive." Some juniors are reminded of their smallness by having "little" attached to the front of their name. The worst real-life example I recall is a family with "big Dick" and "little Dick."

Namesakes present other concerns. Are you obligated to use a name you don't like? How about using it as a middle name instead of a first name?

Some parents try to build a choice into their name selection, like the parents who chose the name Amy Elizabeth for their daughter. Their thought was that if she didn't like the name Amy, she could choose from the variety of names stemming from Elizabeth (Beth, Liz, Libby, Betty, Liza, Betsy, Elli).

If your last name is a hyphenated name, consider its length in relation to your favorite names. Will a middle name make it too unwieldy? What last name will the baby have, just one or the hyphenated version?

Avoid calling your child by a nickname that reflects a physical attribute, such as Shorty or Red. These names often stick, cause embarrassment and resentment in the child, and call attention to something the child may prefer not to highlight.

Are you using a replacement name, perhaps using the same name as a child of yours who was stillborn or a SIDS (Sudden Infant Death Syndrome) victim? If so, are your expectations fair? Will this baby be allowed to just be herself, or will she always be filling someone else's shoes?

Giving siblings similar names like Alicia and Leticia, or even using the same letter for siblings like Jeff and Josh can be more confusing than one would suspect. Also avoid binding yourself to a concept like the geologists who named their children Rocky, Sandy, Pebbles, and Cliff.

It can be confusing to others and frustrating for the child to have a name that is normally used as an opposite-sex name, like Kevin for a girl, or to reverse traditional male/female spellings, like Frances and Francis.

Finally, write out the whole name you're considering. Does it look as good as it sounds? You've got it! The right name.

Some parents have chosen their child's name by the time the pregnancy is confirmed. While it is not essential to have the matter finalized this early, it is wise to have names selected or at least narrowed down by the end of your pregnancy. Parents who have not decided on names before the birth may be feeling some ambivalence about the baby, and they should discuss their feelings before the birth. Perhaps they are unable to choose a name for one sex because of a strong preference for the other. Of course, they might just be having trouble coming up with a name they both can agree on. Or, they need to see the baby before selecting the final name that fits the best.

Discussing names does in fact make the coming baby more real and is a very healthy step toward adjusting to the idea of parenthood. For many, selecting a name is the first of numerous joint decisions about your child. How you decide this matter may reflect your joint approach to many important future issues.

FORETHOUGHT ON THE FORESKIN

You should be aware of the pros and cons of neonatal circumcision, so you can make an informed decision in case you have a baby boy. Circumcision is the removal of some of the foreskin from the tip of the penis, so that the glans, or head of the penis, is exposed. Circumcision is usually performed by your obstetrician or pediatrician during your baby's nursery stay, but it is sometimes delayed until the eighth day and performed as a religious ritual.

Although most of the male members of your family are probably circumcised, you should realize that the majority of the world's men are not circumcised, and they get along just fine. This procedure originated in various parts of the world in ancient times, suggesting that it might indeed be a useful operation. On the other hand, you would think that if circumcision were really necessary, nature would have tended to such an important matter herself.

Circumcision became almost universal in the United States during this century because of medical recommendation and social acceptance. Ten or fifteen years ago, it was performed routinely on newborn males with little

CIRCUMCISED   **UNCIRCUMCISED**

thought given to whether or not it was necessary or the possibility of associated risks. Laboring women were often asked to "sign here in case you have a boy." Seldom was the procedure ever discussed with the doctor, nor did it involve any decision making on the part of the family.

Members of the medical profession have since questioned and reevaluated the risks and benefits of some "routine" medical procedures, such as tonsillectomy, smallpox vaccination, and routine circumcision. After carefully examining the issues on both sides, the American Academy of Pediatrics recently concluded that routine neonatal circumcision is not medically necessary, provided that good hygiene of the penis is maintained and that an uncircumcised child is taught to retract his foreskin and clean beneath it during bathing. (See page 111.) In light of these new recommendations, increasing numbers of parents are choosing to forego circumcision of their baby boys.

The risks of circumcision are few, but some complications can occur, as in any surgical procedure. These include excessive bleeding, infection, or surgical injury to the penis during the operation. Furthermore, circumcision is almost always performed on the newborn without any anesthesia and clearly causes discomfort.

Some of the questions parents need to ask themselves about circumcision are:

√ Do you have religious or cultural reasons for your decision to circumcise?
√ Do you feel strongly about your son "looking like" his circumcised father or brother?

✓ Are you comfortable with the routine cleansing of the uncircumcised penis and later teaching your son how to do this himself?

There is no right or wrong answer to the circumcision question. But parents should play the most important part in making the decision. This responsibility may place a bit more stress on you, but it is undoubtedly better than the old "sign here in case you have a boy" approach. Whatever your decision, it should be based on true informed consent, rather than ignorance or simple tradition.

SELECTING YOUR HEALTH-CARE PROFESSIONALS

One of the basic responsibilities of parenthood is providing your child with quality health care. Selection of the practitioners who will give your baby care should be made before her arrival, so you can evaluate carefully and not feel pressured to select either the pediatrician closest to your house or your best friend's doctor, but rather the person or persons you feel are best qualified and most compatible with your own parenting style.

You will want to examine your own feelings and philosophies about health care before selecting doctors for your baby. Plan ahead. Selecting your baby's doctor is an important decision, so take your time and choose carefully. As you meet prospective doctors, keep in mind that it is important to feel comfortable and compatible with both your doctor's philosophy and personality. It is worth spending the necessary time to find out if this person is someone you can respect and trust, and with whom you can communicate comfortably.

Keep in mind that you'll be changing the focus of your primary medical relationship. During pre- and post-natal care, women often become emotionally attached to their obstetrician or midwife, making it hard to give up the frequent and personal contacts typical of routine prenatal care. After your baby's birth, however, you will see your obstetrician for your six-week checkup and then probably only once a year for a Pap smear.

Now your baby becomes the major focus of medical attention. Your baby's doctor becomes your primary health-care contact, the person to whom you bring your questions and concerns. As expectant parents, you will probably be seeking a pediatrician's care for your baby. Of the many types of health-care providers available, most new parents choose a pediatrician because of the confidence that comes with knowing your doctor is trained specifically in children's health needs and has ongoing experience with children. A personal recommendation from a like-minded friend who uses this doctor is worth a great deal.

Other parents select a family practitioner who can provide all members of the family with most types of care. Many physicians now employ nurse practitioners, child health associates, or physician's assistants to expand the services they can offer. You should be aware that these health practitioners are well trained professionals who can be of great help to you and may be able to spend more time discussing your concerns.

In addition to receiving a personal recommendation and forming your own general impressions, it is very useful to interview a prospective doctor. Most competent professionals welcome a brief consultation visit and are happy to tell you about their practice and philosophy.

Many people, however, are uncomfortable with the prospect of interviewing a doctor. Some parents exercise more discretion in selecting an auto mechanic than in choosing their baby's doctor. They imagine that the doctor will be offended if subjected to screening. On the contrary, most health professionals will not only agree to an interview, but will respect you and appreciate your informed interest in your baby's health care.

Here are some practical guidelines to use in preparing for your interview:

Your attitude should be confident, not meek. It is your right and responsibility to select health care that will meet your personal goals.

Make a list of questions before you go. Include issues of philosophy, medical procedures or practices, and even office policy. Questions are a layperson's best tool for evaluating a health professional. With a thorough list, you will feel more confident and be less likely to forget any important questions.

You may ask a prospective pediatrician, "Are you in favor of breast feeding?" Virtually every pediatrician will respond, "Yes, I encourage breast feeding." To really learn how this doctor manages breast-feeding mothers in the practice, follow up with more specific questions, such as:

√ What percentage of mothers in your practice are still breast-feeding at six months? At one year?
√ What would you advise if I felt my milk supply was low?
√ Under what circumstances might you recommend supplementing with or weaning to formula?

If you ask a question like the last one, beware of a reply like "Only if absolutely necessary." What does that mean? What might be specific examples of what the doctor considers to be "absolutely necessary" reasons for weaning?

After you meet a prospective doctor, ask yourself some questions. Are your feelings, opinions, and information given weight in discussions or decisions? Does this doctor volunteer information and advice, or do you leave with unanswered questions? One who generously shares information and recommendations with you will be more helpful. Look for good communications skills. There are no right or wrong answers to your interview inquiries. What you are looking for is understanding and flexible responses that consider your philosophy and life-style.

During your office visit, look into the following: Are patients kept waiting too long for their scheduled appointments? Are phone calls returned promptly?

Does this doctor have partners? Have you met them? Are you equally comfortable with and confident in their care? What is the atmosphere in the office? You'll deal with office personnel as much as with the pediatrician. Is the staff friendly and considerate, and are you comfortable with the office procedures?

What type of payment policies does this doctor have? Does the practice expect payment at the time of the visit? Will they bill you? Will they bill your insurance company?

Does your doctor's waiting room have separate rooms or sections for sick and well patients, so healthy children in for routine checkups are not exposed to the others' illnesses?

While these office features are important, good communication is still the essential for getting what you want from any health-care relationship. If you can't communicate with the practitioner, don't be satisfied just because that person has a good reputation. You may end up with technically excellent care that is not right for you.

What You Can Give to Your Doctor

Much has been written about choosing doctors according to your expectations of them, but we seldom consider that the patient-professional relationship is a two-way street. Parents can greatly influence a physician's practice by setting examples and giving feedback.

For instance, many doctors have admitted that their traditional medical education did not prepare them for the practical management of breast feeding, and that they ultimately learned this art from their patients. This type of education can be effective only if patients are willing to communicate openly and honestly.

Let's look at a scenario. Until recently, solid foods were regularly introduced to the baby's diet at an inappropriately early age. Some well-informed mothers, realizing their babies did not need the solid foods yet, did not always begin the suggested foods "on time." One such woman explained how she would wait until the day before the baby's next appointment to give a taste of the food prescribed at the previous visit. This way she could tell the physician the next day that the baby was "doing just great on applesauce."

Unfortunately, however, she failed to use the opportunity to teach her doctor that a breast-fed baby can grow beautifully without the addition of solids during the early months of life. Instead, the doctor continued to attribute the baby's excellent progress to the early introduction of solids.

Here's another scene. Let's say that you have several small children and you are employed part time. You are incredibly busy and hassled. One of your children has an ear infection and needs an antibiotic. The pediatrician prescribes one that should be given four times daily for ten days. Your child is impossible to medicate, and every dose sparks a major battle. You manage to give three doses a day for five days, and then the bottle spills during the latest struggle. "Oh well," you might say. "the child seems better anyway."

When you return for the ear recheck, the infection has not cleared. Assuming you gave all the antibiotic, the physician may presume that the infection was resistant to the medication, or that your child will be chronically prone to ear infections.

On the other hand, your admission that you were unable to give all the medication, that giving medicine is quite difficult for you with your hectic schedule, and that your child spits, gags, and sputters on every dose, may be very effective in providing new insight for your physician. With a better understanding of individual home situations, your doctor may begin to do some of the following:

- √ Ask all patients if they really can give all the medication being prescribed at the proper intervals;
- √ Prescribe an antibiotic that can be given every twelve hours instead of every six;
- √ Give a stronger concentration of medication, so that only half the amount needs to be given to resistant children;
- √ Begin to ask all patients if they were indeed able to complete the full course of prescribed medication instead of assuming that they did.

Such feedback can be provided in a variety of areas, such as child-birthing preferences, parenting attitudes, and dietary beliefs. Most physicians bring to their practices a strong personal bias from their own experiences. But through honest communication, you can introduce them to new ideas or other practices that are also effective and help them round out their philosophies and become more broad-minded and insightful.

SIBLING PREPARATION

If this is your second or subsequent pregnancy, you may be appropriately concerned about your "current baby's" adjustment to your new baby. Your child will need help with this adjustment, and the time to begin is well before the birth.

Your child's age will determine how much you can discuss the events and feelings surrounding the birth of the new baby. A child under two will not have the verbal skills, so you'll have to keep your explanations brief and simplistic. Do not imagine, however, that a child under two is unaware of your pregnancy or unable to understand a basic discussion of the changes to come. It is essential that you talk about it.

What to Say

Regardless of your child's age and verbal skills, some basics must be covered. Make sure that the news of your pregnancy comes from you. Don't wait so long that your child overhears this information from someone else. Talk about the baby, explaining in simple terms where the baby is (a special place inside Mommy called the uterus), and how the baby will come out. Don't say that the baby is in your "tummy." It is confusing and could give your child the idea that you "ate" the baby. Talk with your child about having been pregnant with her and tell the story of her birth. Let her feel the baby move.

Give her a realistic idea of what a new baby will be like. Talk about the size and helplessness of a new baby. Many "expectant siblings" imagine a baby who can play. When I was pregnant with my fifth child, I already had a son and three younger daughters. Peter strongly hoped for a younger brother to play "spacemen" with. He was absolutely delighted when Mark was born and showed great interest in his daily routine. As the baby's total dependence and immaturity became evident, Peter expressed his disappointment to me. "I just realized Mark can't play spacemen with me, and by the time he's seven, I'll be fourteen and I might not like to play spacemen anymore!"

SIBLING PREPARATION *(Phil Stietenroth)*

Prepare your child for the fact that you will need to care for, nurse, hold, change, rock, and generally attend to the baby. Go on in great detail about how you lovingly performed these same tasks for her when she was the baby. This would be a good time to pull out her baby book and pore over it with her. Tell her about the things she'll be able to help with the baby's care, like bringing you a diaper or covering the baby with a blanket.

It is crucial that you thoroughly discuss your upcoming absence with your child. Explain who will care for her while you're in the hospital and where she'll stay. Promise that you'll say good-bye before you go to the hospital and DO, even if you need to wake her up in the middle of the night. Describe where you'll be and what a hospital is. Maybe you can drive by or visit the hospital with her in advance so she'll have a mental image of it. Tell her what you'll be doing there; give her a pleasant description of delivering the baby, resting afterward, and perhaps some other interesting details of hospital life, like the bed that goes up and down. Explain when you'll come home. Be realistic, don't make a promise you might not be able to keep.

Go over this information with your child so often that she has it memorized. Be careful, though, not to prepare your child for events that may not come off as described. Don't promise anything that is subject to change. For example, don't lead your child to believe that "When Mommy and Daddy go to the hospital, Grandma will come and pick you up," if you really mean that Grandma will come if it's daytime and the next-door neighbor will come if labor starts during the night.

Most important, tell her how much you love her and that you will always love her the way you do now. The new baby won't change that. (It's true, but she may not buy it.)

What to Expect

Typical reactions of "displaced" children vary considerably, but one fact you can count on is that your child will feel jealous and angry, and rightfully so. It is the intensity of the feelings and the degree of expression that vary. When you love someone, you want to be everything to them and it is hard to accept that they may want someone else in their life, too.

A well-known analogy can help us understand the inevitability of jealousy in the toddler as she anticipates the arrival of a new baby.

HUSBAND TO WIFE
"Sweetheart, I have some wonderful news. I'm going to bring home a second wife! I love you *so* much, I just can't wait to have another wonderful wife like you. I

was thinking how nice it would be for you to have some help and company during the day. And, you know, she'll be *our* wife, and we'll both love her. I will have to pay lots more attention to her in the beginning, like I did to you when we were first married. Now I'll need my reliable old wife more than ever to help me look after the new one. Of course, I won't love you any less. We'll all love each other."

This scenario helps us realize that no amount of explanation can soothe the unbearable jealousy that your older child will initially feel. Please do not believe your child is being "good" if she expresses no jealousy toward the baby, and "naughty" if she shares her inevitable jealous and angry feelings with you. Three-year-old Hedy had a very normal response to her brother's arrival. After he had been home from the hospital a short time, this conversation took place:

Hedy: Mommy, couldn't we take Adam back to the hospital and leave him there?
Mother: No, honey, Adam's part of our family now; he's always going to live with us.
Hedy: Well then, couldn't we just move him into the garage?

If your child displays jealousy, she's being normal. Even if she doesn't express jealousy, you can still assume that she's feeling it. You should help her express her feelings and allow her to see that you still love her even when you know she can't stand the baby. Of course, you do need to make a clear distinction between permission to dislike the baby and permission to hurt the baby. It is not uncommon for a toddler to hit or otherwise hurt a newborn, so you must keep an eye on them and avoid leaving them alone in a room together until the jealous feelings have been somewhat resolved.

In addition to jealousy, you can expect your child to be angry with you for having upset her life. Her behavior may be temperamental and tearful. Put it in perspective, accept it, and take consolation in knowing that your child is secure and trusting enough to express these feelings.

Some regression, or babyish behavior, is also normal in the older child when a new baby arrives. The baby's typical behavior is so clearly appealing to you, that of course she wants to be a baby. Wetting, extra crying, baby talk, and sleep problems are all typical temporary behaviors. Do not punish your child; heap on extra love and reassurance and the behavior will gradually fade away. Instead of encouraging the "big sister syndrome," it is helpful to offer your child opportunities to be babyish. You can say, "Would you like me to rock you now just the way I rocked the baby?" Or, "How about if I cover you with a baby blanket?"

Give your child the impression that nothing you do for the baby is really denied her, but rather that she has outgrown most of these "services." Sometimes, however, it will be important to set age-appropriate limits based upon the fact that she really has outgrown some needs. Then when your child expresses resentment, acknowledge and accept her anger with understanding.

What to Do

To help your child adjust to a new sibling as easily as possible, you can implement some of the following suggestions. They have been helpful to other parents.

If your child is still in a crib during your pregnancy, make a point of putting the crib away and getting a bed for her several months before the new baby arrives. Put the crib (and any other equipment you plan to pass on) away and out of sight. She'll forget about that furniture and become accustomed to her new furnishings. By the time you pull out the "baby furniture" for the new baby, she probably won't think of it as hers and won't feel as slighted at its transfer.

Buy a present (something your child will really like), wrap it, and bring it to the hospital. When your child comes to "meet her baby," the baby can "give" her the present. For nearly a year after my last child was born the older children all referred to the toys "Baby Mark" had given them.

Buy your older child a doll. All children like to mimic

nurturing behavior with a doll. They will nurse, diaper, kiss, and care for their dolls as you do for the baby. Many children also throw, hit, and kick their dolls, and this is a perfectly acceptable outlet for their anger at the baby.

When my second child, Paige, was two, I was about to deliver my third baby. Paige was a bright, articulate, and stubborn young lady. After reading about sibling rivalry, I set out to prepare Paige for the upcoming birth. At this particular time, Paige carried a doll called Baby Tender Love with her everywhere—to the sitter, to the store, and to bed. I was pleased that she was obviously an attentive, loving mother.

One day, I set up the bassinet and purchased an infant seat for the new baby. I brought Paige into the bedroom and showed her the "new baby's things." I was satisfied with my explanation that Mommy would have a new baby and we would put the baby into the bassinet and infant seat. Her eyes brightened and she promptly announced that Baby Tender Love would sit in the seat, thrusting the doll into the chair. At first I thought "How cute; she's getting the idea," but I soon realized that possession is nine tenths of the law. I ended up buying a second infant seat for the real baby and letting Baby Tender Love live out her years in the original infant carrier. It turned out not to be a bad idea, as little Paige mimicked much of my care of her new sister through her doll. We bought her a doll front pack that went with her everywhere (and years later would transport baby bunnies on walks around the block before experiencing a smelly demise). The baby sister was probably better accepted by unknowingly relinquishing her first infant seat to her big sister's "baby."

When you come home from the hospital, the older child may be less upset if the father carries the baby into the house and the mother walks in empty-handed, appearing available. Remember, after being separated, the child wants her mother, not the baby. Let your child briefly greet the baby. Then focus your attention on the older child. She needs to feel reassured that you're still *her* parents and that she is still very special to you. When you arrive home, do as many familiar things as possible with her. Helping her feel confident about your relationship with her will go much further toward her acceptance of her new sibling than showing her all the appealing features of the baby.

Try to balance the attention. Friends and relatives will come in droves to admire the baby. "Isn't he sweet!" "He's so beautiful." "Look at his tiny hands and feet." "Wow, he has so much hair!" The raving is endless. Your older child may feel quite invisible during all this glowing. Do help her out by bragging about her and her wonderful characteristics within her hearing. Sensitive visitors may pick up on your efforts and join in as well.

When visitors bring presents for the baby, your older child may feel left out. Let her open the presents. After all, most of the fun is in the opening. You'll see that she doesn't care at all about the crib sheet in the package, just as long as she had the privilege of opening it. Despite her job as opener, the abundance of presents for the baby may take its toll on your older child. Have some small gifts stashed away for those low moments. These presents do not need to be expensive—crayons or books are fine—as long as they're specifically for her and they're wrapped.

Don't start calling your older child "my *big* girl or boy" and continually emphasize her oldness and bigness. It may be very clear to her that there is nothing better in the universe than to be a tiny baby, so hearing herself constantly called "big" may not make her feel as special as you imagine. The arrival of the baby may cause her to wish for nothing more than to be a baby herself. One two-year-old boy who had recently become a big brother insisted on being referred to as a "baby" and as "small." "Tiny" was even better. His father complimented him on a job well done by saying, "You're really a big help!" The boy responded, highly insulted, "I am not. I'm a *little* help!"

You can, however, build in some advantages to being "the oldest" in more subtle ways. "You're big enough to come to the circus with us, but the baby is so small, we need to leave her home with Grandma." Even running errands with one parent, or receiving some spending money can include a gentle reference to her being "old enough" for it.

Try to give your child the impression that the baby adores her. Make comments like, "Look, the baby just can't take his eyes off you," or "Oh, look at the way the baby kicks and gets excited when he sees you!"

It may help somewhat to point out families with more than one child to her subtly so she realizes that this is a normal pattern, not a personal rejection of her.

Don't criticize your older child's attempts to help. Even if her efforts are less than helpful, she may feel more congenial toward the baby if she thinks she's contributing to her care. Don't allow your overprotective feelings toward your baby to create unnecessary distance between the older child and baby. The baby probably doesn't mind her awkward attempts at care and affection, and this contact will serve to build their relationship.

You may experience difficulty adjusting to some aspects of your new family constellation as well. You may have found the difficult behavior of your toddler understandable and tolerable before the birth of your baby; your toddler then seemed like a baby herself. But now she looks huge and mature to you—like she's just about ready to enter school! This change in your perception may also cause your expectations of your toddler to change. In comparison with your innocent and angelic infant, your toddler's behavior may seem unbearable. Suddenly typical two- or three-year-old behavior will seem too babyish and you may expect more maturity than she can possibly display.

You may also find that the pressures and fatigue accompanying a new baby make your toddler's behavior seem even worse than it is. Or she may be genuinely harder to get along with, picking up on your fatigue and stress and reflecting that in her own crankiness and misbehavior. It is not unusual for parents in this situation to take out some of their frustration on the toddler and/or older children. As a result, these children may be over disciplined and subjected to unrealistic expectations.

During the period of adjustment after the baby's birth, try to loosen up expectations and standards for your toddler and other children. It is crucial for you to acknowledge how genuinely difficult it will be for your child to share you.

Successfully adjusting to a new baby will be easier for your child if she feels secure in your love and if she has a solid sense of self-esteem. Build these feelings for your child as you prepare her for "siblinghood." It will take time, but with your unconditional love and your sensitivity to her mixed emotions, she'll eventually blossom into a happy and proud big sister.

Whether the baby you are expecting is your first, second, or even fourth, the preparations for this baby (physical, emotional and mental) may at times feel monumental. Most days, preparing for your baby is exciting and fun, but on other days it can cause anxiety. Almost all expectant parents, regardless of which baby they're expecting, share this experience.

Do what you can to prepare. Try to temper your expectations with reality. Take time selecting the best health care possible for your infant. Ponder carefully as you choose your baby's name. And if you already have a child, lovingly prepare her for the adjustment she, too, will be making.

Then sit back and realize that you are as prepared as any parent has ever been. The rest will fall into place, as it has for each of us, once your baby finally arrives.

3 Practical Preparation: Buying Baby Equipment

AS YOU IMAGINE caring for your baby at home, you envision your whole life, including your immediate environment, changing. Your home fills with baby equipment and, once baby-proofed, every room becomes the baby's room.

You will want to prepare for your baby's arrival by arranging his nursery and having clothes and baby items waiting for him. You will feel more prepared, and your early days with your baby will be easier if they're not spent in frantic shopping. (Although admittedly we stopped at a department store on the way home from the hospital to pick up the crib we had ordered a week earlier!)

Deciding what baby equipment you want to buy and which type, model, and brand of each item will be best can be exhausting. The selection appears endless. To make this job easier for you, I've categorized different baby equipment under the headings "Essential Items," "Desirable Items," "Luxury Items," and "Unnecessary Items." Although these lists provide you with guidelines, your personal taste and desires may vary somewhat. As you make your selections, remember that your first consideration should always be safety. Everything else is secondary.

When shopping, remember that borrowed or used items are perfectly acceptable to your baby. The new model is for you. If you really want it, fine. But don't feel guilty or think that your baby will be deprived if you've opted for a used stroller rather than the top-of-the-line European model. Your baby will never know! Another money-saving idea is to pick up sale items throughout your pregnancy.

ESSENTIAL ITEMS

Parents differ in what they consider to be essential baby equipment. An item one parent simply couldn't live without may never be found in another family's home. Every parent has his or her own favorite baby items, but among most parents, the following group emerges as truly essential.

Diapers

An early decision you'll make is whether to use your own cloth diapers, a diaper service, disposable diapers, or a combination of these.

Cloth Diapers have some advantages over disposables. They are more comfortable and allow the skin to breathe, if worn without rubber pants. In addition, cloth diapers are reusable, ecological, and less expensive in the long run. If you decide to buy cloth diapers, you will need at least four dozen. Some parents prefer prefolded diapers or those with extra padding in the middle. Cloth diapers are now available with Velcro tabs to eliminate the need for safety pins.

The major disadvantage of cloth diapers is that they need to be washed, although few parents find this difficult. If you are on an outing you must bring wet or soiled diapers home in a plastic bag. And you will use and wash plastic pants in addition to diapers. If you use your own cloth diapers, you will need to buy a large diaper pail with a tight-fitting or locking lid to contain unpleasant odors. Most lids have a place for a deodorizer.

A Diaper Service may be no more expensive than buying and washing your own diapers, and is less expensive than using disposable diapers. You can feel assured that diapers from a diaper service are thoroughly cleaned, rinsed, and treated against bacteria.

Service diapers are almost as convenient as disposable ones—you do not even need to rinse off a new baby's soft stool before putting the diaper in the pail. If you decide to use a diaper service, start with an order of seventy-five or one hundred newborn-size diapers a week. (The service will supply the diaper pail.) As your baby grows older, your order will decrease.

Disposable Diapers are easiest to use. You do not need to add plastic pants, used diapers can be thrown away, and the newborn-size fits a new baby's bottom better than a regular cloth diaper. However, disposable diapers are less ecologically sound and more expensive.

New disposable diapers are now available, made with materials that lock wetness inside the diaper itself and away from the skin. Recent studies suggest that these new disposable diapers are more effective than cloth diapers or conventional disposable diapers in preventing diaper rash.

Disposable diapers now come in many types: with and without printed patterns, with and without elastic in the legs and waist, and with and without reusable tapes. You'll find newborn through toddler sizes and daytime and nighttime absorbencies.

Combining cloth and disposable diapers is a practical alternative. You can balance the pros and cons of each method by using cloth diapers at home and disposable ones when you are away from home.

Clothing

You will want to acquire some clothing before your baby arrives, so you'll have an outfit to dress him in when you bring him home from the hospital and practical baby wear for the early weeks. It really is fun to buy baby clothes! Suggestions for a layette include:

4+ dozen cloth diapers (You'll still need at least a dozen cloth diapers for burping and mop-ups even if you use disposables.)

6 safety diaper pins

8 to 12 pairs of plastic pants
or
several boxes of newborn disposable diapers (Your baby will use approximately 350 disposable diapers during the first month.)

6 to 10 cotton undershirts

6 newborn gowns

3 saque sets

6 newborn stretch suits

12 square cotton receiving blankets

6 lap pads

3 blanket sleepers

6 crib sheets

3 to 6 absorbent bibs

2 mattress pads

1 snowsuit or bunting if winter

8 to 12 crib blankets

4 crib pads

2 sweaters or light jackets

2 to 3 baby bath towels

4 pairs of socks or booties

12 baby washcloths

If you do not own a washing machine and dryer, you may want to buy additional quantities of these items to cut down on trips to the laundry room or laundromat.

There are general guidelines to follow whenever you purchase baby clothes. Your baby will be more comfortable in cotton clothing or clothes with a higher cotton content and in clothes that are easy to put on and take off. You will change your baby often, and in the beginning, this may be an awkward process. Also, most babies dislike being dressed, so the faster and more smoothly you can do it, the better. You'll find yourself leaving those little shirts with the tight collars in the drawer and reaching for the nice stretchy ones instead. Choose pants or outfits with easy access for diaper changes instead of those adorable one-piece outfits that have no snaps and a zipper up the back.

Avoid outfits with little balls (or other objects) on the front. Your baby will nap in his play clothes and probably sleep on his stomach. These little decorations can be quite uncomfortable and are not conducive to sleep.

Buying adorable and appealing baby clothes is one of a parent's greatest pleasures, so don't feel you always need to be practical. It's definitely fun to occasionally buy one of those irresistible outfits.

Although you may want to buy clothes a little larger than your fast-growing baby, clothes that are neither too tight nor excessively large are the most comfortable. Be aware, however, that sizes vary from one brand to another.

Remember to check for "nearly new" shops that carry (or even specialize in) children's clothes. These shops resell used clothes, generally in good condition, and they can really stretch your clothing budget. In the tiny sizes, you may even find things for resale that have never been worn.

Sleepwear

Although children's sleepwear is usually made of synthetic fabrics like polyester, many parents prefer cotton sleepwear for their babies because of its greater comfort, so they use various alternatives to standard sleepwear. Some sew gowns or pajamas themselves or have a seamstress make them. Certain imported European cotton playsuits can be used as sleepwear. In the summer, a diaper and a cotton undershirt serve as great P.J.s. And for an older baby, cotton "long johns" make ideal pajamas.

Crib

A crib is probably the first piece of baby equipment expectant parents think of. In addition to a place to sleep, a crib is also an easy place to change the baby, dress him, or leave him safely watching his mobile while you rinse out a diaper.

Almost any crib is suitable. If you are borrowing one or buying a used crib, make sure it does not predate the 1973 federal safety regulations for cribs. These regulations require that the crib slats be no farther apart than 2⅜", that the mattress not exceed 5" in depth, and that you not be able to fit more than four fingers between the mattress and the side of the crib.

Bumper pads along the sides of your crib give the baby something to look at, protect his head if he rolls against the side, and block drafts. Fabric ones are softer, while plastic ones are easier to clean.

Car Seats

Thousands of children are killed or maimed in auto accidents each year. Most of them could have been spared if they had been using a car restraint.

Owning a car seat is not only essential for any responsible parent, it is required by law in many states. All infant car seats must meet federal safety standards, so you can assume any car seat you buy new is reasonably safe.

Compare the many models on the market for features that are important. Some seats fit infants of a certain age range only, but most can be used for both newborns and toddlers. Some can be adjusted for comfort. You will want to find a buckling system that is easy to use, since buckling up will be repeated thousands of times over the next few years and you would need to release your child quickly in an emergency. If buying or borrowing a used seat, make sure it was manufactured after the 1981 Federal regulations for safety standards and that it has not been involved in a serious accident.

Car Seat Covers and Headrests

Two important supplements to your car seat are a cloth car seat cover and a cloth-covered foam headrest. Both are sold in baby goods stores where car seats are found. The cover is important because vinyl seats can become hot enough in the summer to burn your baby. Also, a car seat cover makes it easier to keep the seat clean.

Prior to the availability of car seat headrests, young babies slept in their seats with their necks flopped over at striking angles. A headrest is a worthwhile investment for a small infant and can be used in strollers, infant seats, and swings as well.

Shoes

Your baby need not wear shoes before he starts walking. Once he is walking, the only reason for shoes is protection. Contrary to popular belief, shoes do not improve the shape of his feet. If he is happier in the house in bare feet or socks, feel free to leave him that way.

When you do buy shoes, be sure your baby's feet are measured accurately and the shoes are fitted correctly. Don't feel you need to buy the top-of-the-line white high-tops. Inexpensive cloth or leather shoes are fine. Baby sneakers work very well and don't slip easily on smooth floors. High-top sneakers stay on especially well. Avoid vinyl shoes; they don't breathe and are less comfortable.

Booties

Avoid booties in the summer (even if his grandmother knit him two dozen pairs), because your baby may be too hot with his feet covered. A baby's feet are normally cool. (If you are checking his body temperature, feel his tummy, not his feet.) In the winter, however, your baby may need booties if his feet aren't covered by a stretch suit. Most booties fall off; sometimes stretchy socks stay on better. Make sure that the booties or socks are not too tight, as they can cut off circulation.

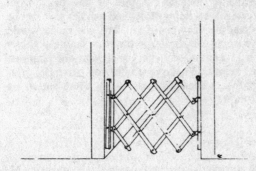

Stair Gate

If you have stairs in your house, you will need a stair gate until your baby learns to safely climb up and down. Do not imagine that you can teach your baby to stay away from the stairs! It's simply impossible given a small baby's abilities and natural desire to explore. Blocking the stairs is essential to protect your baby from serious injury. Stair gates can also be used to keep babies out of rooms with dangerous contents.

Unfortunately, stair safety gates themselves have some problems. You will need to keep a watchful eye on your baby even when the gate is in place. The X-joint gates have the potential to strangulate a baby, and the joints can be used by a toddler as toeholds for climbing. The plastic mesh type gates also offer toeholds for climbing toddlers, and the pressure type gates could possibly be forced loose by a strong toddler. Make sure the gate is always tightly in place.

Stroller

No modern parent could possibly manage without a stroller. Although large baby carriages and the more bulky baby strollers are still in use, the umbrella-style stroller is the most popular for good reason: it is light, portable, easy to lift and push, and comes in many variations. Features worth investigating include canopies or tote bags, front wheels that swivel, reclining seats, and handles that can be changed so that the baby can either face you or the world ahead. Try pushing the stroller in the store before you buy it, since handle lengths vary and you'll want one comfortable for your height. Whatever stroller you purchase, your baby will probably spend endless happy hours surveying his world from it.

Diaper Bag

Although you don't need a "diaper bag" specifically, you do need something sturdy and big enough to carry your baby's diapers, changes of clothing, wipe-ups, toys, baby food, and whatever else may be necessary. It really doesn't matter what type you select; some parents use a backpack, others a general tote bag or carryall.

Bottles

If you plan to bottle-feed your baby, you'll need at least a dozen bottles or four holders for disposable bottle bags. Each type of bottle has its advantages: Glass bottles are easier to clean, plastic ones are unbreakable, and bottle bags are disposable. Some dentists prefer the orthodontic nipple or Playtex Nurser for their shape, although dental concerns are probably exaggerated. Any bottle and nipple combination your baby likes is just fine. Remember that your baby will probably be fed in the hospital with traditional bottle nipples and may be reluctant to switch to another shape once he gets home.

Buy bottles in both four-ounce and eight-ounce sizes for your baby's changing milk requirements. A bottle brush will be necessary to thoroughly clean bottles. Bottle sterilizers are no longer necessary provided you have a sanitized water supply.

High Chair

Once your baby is sitting up and eating solid foods, he will need a high chair. Besides keeping your baby safe while he eats, a high chair also allows him to be conveniently included in your mealtimes. The social aspect of eating may be as important to your baby as the food itself.

Make sure the high chair is stable and has a safety belt. Convertible high chairs that sit within a square table can later be converted into a low play table for the child. Because of their square shape, these tables are especially stable. Many parents appreciate a special feature on some high chairs that allows them to remove the tray easily from the front with one hand. The high chair should not have cross-bars on the legs because babies may be tempted to scale them, and the high chair may then topple over.

A wonderful new innovation, the portable high chair is available under many brand names. It unfolds and fits onto a regular table (but is not for use with glass tables or tables more than three inches thick). The seat hangs from your table, with arms supporting it above and below your table top, permitting the baby to eat directly from the table. Without legs to be bumped into or knocked over, the chair is quite safe. The portable high chair can be used routinely instead of a regular high chair or used simply for eating out in a restaurant or at a friend's house.

Chest of Drawers

You will need something in which to store your baby's clothes. It could range from one of those little cardboard chests to the most expensive wooden chest on the market, as long as it serves the purpose. The chest should be stable and not top-heavy, as toddlers who scaled unsturdy ones have knocked them over onto themselves.

If You're Breast-feeding (See pages 29-31.)

You will want to purchase a nursing bra before your baby is born. After you have decided if you like the opening and closing system, the straps, the fabric, and style, buy several more. Also purchase a few boxes of nursing pads. You'll use these regularly in the early part of your nursing experience. Most women buy the disposable type, but reusable, washable cloth nursing pads are also available. Cloth pads can also be made from cotton diapers or handkerchiefs.

Health-Care Equipment and Supplies

Of course, you'll need to keep a few items on hand for dealing with childhood illnesses. Most parents buy a thermometer before their baby is born and gradually acquire other items as they need them. Please see pages 290 and 397-98 for a complete list of supplies.

DESIRABLE ITEMS

You could raise your child without the items in this category, but many parents rate these items highly for their usefulness and convenience.

Lamp

A small lamp or night-light is suggested for your convenience. With one, you'll be able to find whatever you need, feed your baby, and put him back to bed without stimulating him into full wakefulness. If you can avoid turning on a bright light when your baby awakens for a

BABY CARRIER *(Happy Family Products, Inc.)*

night feeding, you will better encourage the practice of going right back to sleep.

Baby Packs

A front carrier for your baby is a must for many parents, and you'll understand why once you've used one. Babies like to be held most of the time. That's not being spoiled; it's being normal. All of the front packs accomplish the same purpose, holding your baby close to you while allowing your arms to be free. Choose one with features you want in a price range you can afford.

Backpacks are also very popular. They provide an easy way to transport your older baby, especially in a crowd or in an area where strollers are not practical. Older babies are usually quite happy in a backpack, since the motion and the closeness to Mom or Dad are comforting. However, babies cannot be safely carried in backpacks until they can sit well, and parents may find that as the baby grows older, his weight contributes to a weary back.

Bassinet

A bassinet can be any small bed, such as a travel bed, a baby basket, or any other small portable crib. Most new parents like the convenience and reassurance offered by moving the infant from room to room with them throughout the day and the ease of having the baby by their bedside at night. And some authorities believe that a new baby feels safer in the smaller sleeping space than in the relatively huge expanse of a crib.

Infant Seat

Many parents would claim that an infant seat is, in fact, essential. It allows you to seat your baby safely where he will usually be happy for short periods, especially if he can see you. There are two basic types of infant seats.

The first is the cloth bouncing seat that fits on a metal frame. The seat bounces gently with the baby's motion and is quite comfortable. It provides enough support for a new baby and enough stability for an older baby.

The second is the bulky plastic seat. This seat is durable and has a carrying handle. Some have a storage compartment in the back, and many of them rock. Unfortunately, most are not very portable since they are awkward to carry.

Playpen

Some parents couldn't live without a playpen; others never purchase one and don't miss it at all. A playpen can serve many functions, and so is worth considering. A new baby can be kept safe from the advances of a toddler or pet. On the other hand, a toddler can take his special toys with him into the playpen, where he can escape a crawling baby. When you're busy, the baby can be placed in the playpen where he can move around safely. If your house or a place you are visiting is not yet baby-proofed or has any other potentially hazardous feature (like stairs, a fireplace, and so on), your baby will be safer in the playpen than any place else, regardless of how many people might be watching out for him. And when you are traveling, camping, or involved in any other outdoor activities, the playpen can serve as a portable crib. Most pens fold up easily and are quite portable.

Mobiles and Decorations

Babies really do respond to mobiles and other eye-catching displays hung over the crib, changing table, playpen, or bassinet. More than just a baby room decoration, a mobile stimulates the baby and can give you a short break while your baby is being entertained. The mobiles that wind up and have music boxes are especially nice, but your baby will also love a nice, safe, homemade mobile that can be changed and varied much to his delight.

Pacifier

Your baby will decide whether or not you need this item. Some babies have very strong sucking urges and need additional sucking on a pacifier in order to be content. Other babies refuse a pacifier and clearly don't need one.

If your baby seems to need a pacifier, start out with a very small soft one. If your baby doesn't like the first one you offer, try another type. Some babies are pretty particular about what they put in their mouths! Keep in mind, though, that tying a pacifier on a string around a baby's neck is extremely unsafe. If you feel you need to attach it to your baby, it's better to tie a short string to the pacifier and pin it to his outer clothing.

Do not use a bottle nipple stuffed with cotton for a pacifier, although many nurseries fashioned pacifiers this way in the recent past. I know one baby who sucked the cotton through the nipple opening! Use only commercial pacifiers.

Teething toys could also be included in this category. A teether, especially one you can freeze, is usually welcomed by a teething baby. It is probably a good idea to buy one or two.

Cleaning Products and Ointments

Very few of the health and grooming products made for babies are necessary or even desirable. The few items I recommend are: tear-free shampoo, a mild baby soap, and Desitin or A&D Ointment for diaper rash.

Baby wipes are extremely handy when changing a messy diaper, especially when away from home. Most of these towelettes are moisturized with a lanolin-based solution to minimize irritation to a baby's bottom. Tri-fold paper towels kept moist in a clear plastic margarine tub also make effective wipe-ups. Soft cotton washcloths are always excellent for comfortably cleaning a baby's bottom.

LUXURY ITEMS

Some equipment may make your parenting easier or more pleasant, and that is reason enough for you to want it. This category contains luxury items that are not essential to baby care but may be of value to you.

Bathtub

Many parents bathe their babies in the kitchen sink or in the bathtub with them. Others prefer to use a standard small infant bathtub. Inflatable bathtubs, cited as being safer and easier to use, are also quite popular. However, in an inflatable tub the baby is not as deeply immersed in water and may be colder than he would be in a traditional baby tub.

The shampoo hat is a device probably invented by the parent of a shampoo-phobic baby. It is a large, soft vinyl disk with a hole in the middle for your baby's head. It is placed around the hairline like a shield and it allows water and shampoo to drain off without dripping in his face. These hats work well for babies who hate to be shampooed.

Jumping Seat

Some babies enjoy these seats, which hang from a doorway and bounce on springs. A deluxe model is available that includes a headrest.

Crib Cuddle

The crib cuddle is a relatively new product consisting of a cloth hammock suspended from the crib posts over the crib mattress. In addition to providing a more comfortable and secure sleeping surface for a newborn, the hammock contains a battery-operated mechanism that reproduces the sounds and vibrations of a human heartbeat. The vibrations radiating through the entire hammock are thought to enhance peaceful sleep.

Foam Bedroll

When your baby is napping away from home without a crib, he is in danger of rolling off a bed or getting into an unsafe position on the floor. The foam bedroll consists of two foam tubes that open parallel to each other to create a surface protected on both sides. The baby is placed on the cloth between the rolls. Of course, an older baby could crawl away, but a new baby would be quite safe napping this way. This device also offers a clean surface for changing your baby in public and may be a real convenience for parents who are away from home a great deal.

Changing Table

You don't need a changing table. You can and will change your baby in his crib, on the floor, on your bed, on the couch, and in many other places. Many parents, however, find a changing table convenient because of its height and storage compartments. Remember, even if the table has a rim, an unattended baby could easily roll off. Never turn your back for even a second while your baby is on a changing table.

Breast Pump

Breast-feeding mothers who are either going back to work or foresee the possibility of being away from the baby may want to purchase a breast pump. If you will need to express milk only occasionally, several cylinder-type hand pumps are available through large pharmacies, maternity shops, and hospitals. Battery-operated hand pumps are also gaining popularity. If you will be working full time and pumping regularly, you might consider purchasing a small electric breast pump or renting a full-size electric breast pump. One novel idea is for several nursing women at an employment site to jointly split the rental expenses of an electric breast pump. A more thorough description of pumps is available in *The Breastfeeding Guide for the Working Woman*.

Infant Swing

Since babies vary in their reactions to swings, it is a good idea to borrow one and try it before purchasing one. Some babies are happy swinging, while others shriek and hate it. If you do buy a swing, notice the windup mechanism. Swings that stay wound up longest are the most convenient. The easiest and quietest model is an electric swing that is turned on and off with a switch.

MANUALECTRIC BREAST PUMP (*Medela, Inc.*)

ELECTRIC BREAST PUMP (*Medela, Inc.*)

BATTERY-OPERATED BREAST PUMP (*Ameda/Egnell*)

THE FAULTLESS DELUXE BREAST PUMP SYSTEM (*Ross Laboratories*)

UNNECESSARY ITEMS

This category includes all that "baby goop" that is marketed as if it were as vital to your baby's health as food or love. Your baby does not need baby oil, baby lotion, or any of those miscellaneous ointments, creams, or powders created for babies. If you feel compelled to rub your baby with lotion or oil, please avoid his face and hair, because clogging his pores causes cradle cap.

You do not need and should not use baby powder. Powder serves no purpose, and the talc can be harmful to your baby if inhaled. If you insist on using baby powder, pour only a small amount on your hand and rub it on the baby to minimize airborne particles. The only sure way to keep your baby's bottom dry and free from diaper rash is to change him frequently.

A baby scale is not only unnecessary but it can lead to overconcern about your baby's weight. Furthermore, scales sold for home use are highly inaccurate.

AS YOUR CHILD GROWS OLDER

The growing child needs some specific items in addition to those you purchased for your baby. Much of what you buy will depend on your lifestyle and your child's preferences, but a few items are sufficiently universal to warrant mention.

Potty Chair

When your child is between two and three and you begin to teach him toilet skills, you will need a potty chair. Some parents like to have the potty chair in the bathroom a couple of months before the child uses it, so he can become familiar with it and have the opportunity to ask questions about it.

Potty chairs that sit on the ground rather than fit onto the toilet are preferred. They foster independence in toilet use, which you are encouraging. A child still needs adult help to get onto the seats that fit over the toilet, unless it has an attached step stool.

Since toilet learning is a new and sometimes anxiety-provoking experience for the child, it is important that he feel as safe as possible when he uses the toilet. For that reason, be sure the potty chair is stable. The potty chair that resembles an adult toilet is especially stable.

Booster Chair

Once your child is old enough that he can easily climb up and down from a chair, he can "graduate" from his high chair to a booster chair placed on one of your chairs for mealtime. Stability is the feature you want most in a booster chair. The booster chair can be easily taken in the car when you are invited out to eat and makes reaching the table and eating easier for your toddler.

Toy Box

You'll need a toy box as soon as your baby has acquired several toys. When shopping for a toy box, look for one that's large and has a lid that cannot fall onto your child's head as he reaches in for a toy. Many toy boxes have lids that come off rather than lift up. Another option is to simply remove an attached lid.

Bed

When your child is between the ages of two and three, you'll probably want to take down his crib and replace it with a regular twin bed. Most parents worry that their child will fall out of the "big bed." And most children do fall out a few times. You can roll a blanket and place it next to him on the outside as a precaution or buy a portable side rail that attaches to the bed between the mattress and the box spring. The advantages of a water bed are that it is heated, so the child is warmer when blankets are kicked off; it is harder to roll out of a water bed; and water beds are very comfortable. Any type of bed will be fine as long as it doesn't have a sagging mattress.

Bathroom Stool

As your child learns hygiene skills like brushing his teeth and washing his hands, the logistics of reaching the bathroom sink become a problem. A little stool placed in front of the sink allows your child easy and independent access to the sink. Be sure it is skid proof.

The possibilities for furnishing your baby's world are

endless. You'll be looking at your finances, your tastes and desires, and consumer considerations as you make your selections. Keep in mind that only a minimum of equipment is really essential, but your goal will be to acquire those items that will make your parenting easier and more enjoyable.

4 Your Amazing Newborn

FOR THE MAJORITY, having a baby today brings new parents into contact with modern delivery, aftercare, and nursery hospital practices. There have been tremendous improvements since I had my first baby years ago amid strict hospital procedures, routine anesthesia, the exclusion of fathers and other family and friends from the delivery room, restricted family visits, and extended hospital stays. Although well educated, I was still ignorant about normal pregnancy body changes and stages of labor. Furthermore, I was isolated from my extended family, and none of my friends had ever been pregnant. I felt powerless to make choices regarding my own body and I found the miracle of childbirth to be unnecessarily frightening and lonely. It excites me today to witness the replacement of "standard obstetric protocol" with prepared childbirth and a wide range of birthing procedures and settings. Briefer hospital stays now offer rooming-in and liberal visiting policies for the whole family. Campaigning for such maternity options has been tremendously gratifying to me in my professional career, and to this day, providing newborn care remains one of my favorite roles as a pediatrician. Despite an active homebirth movement in various parts of the country, I strongly believe that a homelike hospital birth is the safest method of childbirth and can combine the best in medical expertise with a homelike birthing experience.

This chapter will familiarize you with typical hospital nursery routines, procedures, and terminology. It will fully explain the events of your recent hospital stay if you are already home with your baby.

Whether you experienced prepared, unmedicated childbirth or a Caesarean birth with general anesthesia; whether your partner was present in the delivery room or paced the floor outside; whether your special doctor delivered or a partner was on call; whether you received an intravenous catheter, an enema, a shave, or an episiotomy matters not a bit at this point. Whether you adopted or delivered, in fact, you have your baby and are now a parent. You have entered into that world of love and sacrifice, of responsibility and reward, of fulfillment and commitment. You've had a baby! Congratulations!

DELIVERY ROOM ROUTINES

Your infant begins generating a great deal of interest from the moment you enter the hospital in labor. A pediatrician has been prepared to attend her birth at the slightest indication of fetal distress, prematurity, prolonged labor, or any other complication. If labor progresses uneventfully, the delivery room nurse and your obstetrician are fully prepared to care for your infant at birth.

Immediate Handling

Immediately after birth, the umbilical cord connecting your infant to the placenta is clamped and cut. The infant is placed under a warmer and promptly dried with blankets to prevent chilling. This gentle rubbing also stimulates her to cry and breathe. Babies are NOT slapped or spanked at birth to start them crying. Mucus and amniotic fluid are suctioned from her nose and mouth to clear her air passages for easy breathing. Very soon after birth, she is clearly identified as your infant by an ID bracelet whose number matches your own, and her footprint is recorded on her hospital birth record.

Apgar Score

Within the first few minutes after her birth, your baby is given an Apgar evaluation, which assesses her adjustment to life outside your body. Dr. Virginia Apgar developed this scoring system in the 1950s. The evaluation covers five categories and these can be remembered by the letters of Dr. Apgar's name:

A = Appearance (color blue, partially blue, totally pink)
P = Pulse (absent, slow, normal)
G = Grimace (no facial response to a catheter placed in the nostril, slight response, or vigorous response)
A = Activity (limp, moving slightly, or moving vigorously)
R = Respiration (absent, irregular, regular, and crying)

An infant is given a 0, 1, or 2 for each of the five categories, so that an Apgar score can range from 0 to 10. Apgar scores are assigned at both one minute and five minutes of age. Most commonly, healthy babies obtain an Apgar score at one minute of 7 or higher. A one-minute Apgar score quickly tells the caretakers if immediate attention is necessary for the next several minutes. Usually warmth, drying, and gentle stimulation are all that are needed, but occasionally oxygen and artificial respiration may be indicated if the Apgar score is very low.

Nearly all infants will have a five-minute Apgar score of 7 or higher, indicating that the baby is adapting well to her new surroundings. A low one-minute Apgar score with a high five-minute Apgar score suggests a short period of fetal distress with rapid recovery and is thus little cause for concern. Good prenatal care, careful checking during labor, and the availability of expert medical care at delivery all contribute to a high Apgar score for your infant.

Introduction to Her Family

Following initial stabilization, an infant is no longer routinely whisked away to the nursery as in former days. Rather, she is placed in the arms of one of her parents and properly welcomed into her family. If she appears interested and her mother is able to put her to the breast, she may nurse while still in the delivery room. After a period of time, she is brought to the nursery (often carried in her father's arms), where she undergoes some brief but important medical screening and evaluation.

NURSERY ROUTINES

Measurements

In the nursery your infant is accurately weighed and measured. Although parents usually think in terms of pounds and ounces, hospital personnel frequently work with kilograms and grams. There are 1000 grams in one kilogram and one kilogram equals 2.2 pounds. The conversion table on page 77 should help you estimate your own baby's birth weight in kilograms or grams.

A full-term infant normally weighs between 5½ pounds (2.5 kilograms or 2500 grams) to 9 or more pounds (4.1 kilograms or 4100 grams), with about 7½ pounds (3.4 kilograms or 3400 grams) being average. Subsequent babies often weigh more than first babies. An infant's birth weight is important, not only for her baby book and all her interested family and friends, but because the weight can be a helpful clue to alert nursery personnel to observe your baby more carefully for certain problems.

Your infant's length and head circumference will also be measured, and each of her measurements will be plotted on a newborn growth curve to determine if they fall within the normal range.

Gestational Age

Next, an estimate is made of your infant's gestational age, or how close she is to being full term.

Calculated Dates: When your pregnancy was confirmed, your due date was probably calculated by a simple formula using the first day of your last menstrual period. Your obstetrician took your recollected date, added seven days and then counted back three months to calculate the due date. Thus, if your last period began on June seventh, your baby's due date would be March fourteenth.

CONVERSION TABLE FOR
CHANGING POUNDS AND OUNCES TO GRAMS

POUNDS

	0	1	2	3	4	5	6	7	8	9	10	11	12
0	0	454	907	1361	1814	2268	2722	3175	3629	4082	4536	4990	5443
1	28	482	936	1389	1843	2296	2750	3203	3657	4111	4564	5018	5471
2	57	510	964	1417	1871	2325	2778	3232	3685	4139	4593	5046	5500
3	85	539	992	1446	1899	2353	2807	3260	3714	4167	4621	5075	5528
4	113	567	1021	1474	1928	2381	2835	3289	3742	4196	4649	5103	5557
5	142	595	1049	1503	1956	2410	2863	3317	3770	4224	4678	5131	5585
6	170	624	1077	1531	1984	2438	2892	3345	3799	4252	4706	5160	5613
7	198	652	1106	1559	2013	2466	2920	3374	3827	4281	4734	5188	5642
8	227	680	1134	1588	2041	2495	2948	3402	3856	4309	4763	5216	5670
9	255	709	1162	1616	2070	2523	2977	3430	3884	4337	4791	5245	5698
10	283	737	1191	1644	2098	2551	3005	3459	3912	4366	4819	5273	5727
11	312	765	1219	1673	2126	2580	3033	3487	3941	4394	4848	5301	5755
12	340	794	1247	1701	2155	2608	3062	3515	3969	4423	4876	5330	5783
13	369	822	1276	1729	2183	2637	3090	3544	3998	4451	4904	5358	5812
14	397	850	1304	1758	2211	2665	3118	3572	4026	4479	4933	5386	5840
15	425	879	1332	1786	2240	2693	3147	3600	4054	4508	4961	5415	5868

(OUNCES along the side scale)

One pound equals 454 grams; one ounce equals 28 grams; grams have been rounded off to the nearest whole number.

Example: To convert 7 pounds 12 ounces to grams, read down from "7" on the top scale and across from "12" on the side scale. Answer is 3515 grams, which would be 3.515 kilograms.

The calculated due date may have been modified during your prenatal checkups, depending upon results of ultrasound, the size of your uterus, or when your baby's heartbeat was first heard. Generally, your due date is forty weeks from the first day of your last period. Full term is considered to be two weeks on either side of the due date, or from thirty-eight to forty-two weeks. Premature is defined as being more than two weeks early, or less than thirty-eight weeks. Postterm is defined as being more than two weeks late, or more than forty-two weeks. Your actual delivery date is compared with your due date as one estimate of whether your infant was born prematurely, on time, or past term.

Clinical Examination: In addition to the calculated dates, nursery personnel perform a brief exam of your baby and use certain physical criteria to estimate her gestational age.

The exam includes inspecting the baby's skin and hair, breast tissue, ear cartilage, creases in the sole of the foot, and a variety of other features that develop while the baby is in the uterus.

For example, an infant born ten weeks early has little cartilage in her outer ear. If you bend the ear down, it does not spring back quickly into place. A full-term infant, however, has a generous amount of ear cartilage with lots of "spring back." The lack of cartilage at birth causes no problem, but such features that develop over time can be used to estimate the baby's gestational age.

Gestational Age Categories: Finally, the birth weight and gestational age are linked together in the graph:

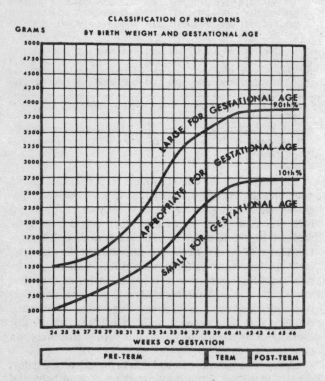

CLASSIFICATION OF NEWBORNS
BY BIRTH WEIGHT AND GESTATIONAL AGE

A hypothetical average infant (3400 grams) is plotted along her gestational age (thirty-nine weeks) and falls at a point between the 10th percentile and the 90th percentile, making her weight appropriate for her gestational age. An infant weighing 4100 grams at the same gestational age would be above the 90th percentile, or Large for Gestational Age. An infant weighing only 2300 grams at thirty-nine weeks would be below the 10th percentile, or Small for Gestational Age. Hospital personnel often refer to babies by the abbreviations AGA, LGA, or SGA.

Now plot your own baby on the graph and determine her birth weight-gestational age category. You can use the conversion table on page 77 if you need to change pounds and ounces to grams.

Risk Factors: Categorizing babies by size and gestation is important, because risk factors vary with weight and gestational age. Preterm infants are at risk for respiratory distress, low blood sugar, jaundice, and other problems. Postterm infants are prone to low Apgar scores. SGA babies may have low blood sugar and LGA infants are at greater risk for birth trauma. Each infant is closely watched by nursery personnel for the kinds of problems known to be more common for her size and gestational age.

Vital Signs

Upon her arrival in the nursery, your baby's pulse and respiratory rate are counted, and her blood pressure is measured in both an arm and a leg to be sure they fall within the normal range. Her temperature is taken to check that she is neither too cold following delivery, nor running a fever, which might indicate an infection.

The baby's temperature, pulse, and respiration checks are repeated each eight-hour shift as a guide to her overall well-being. Sometimes a rapid breathing rate, a low temperature, or a rapid heart rate can be the first sign of serious illness in a baby. In some hospitals, all babies must be brought to the nursery each shift to be checked. Obviously, it is preferable to measure your baby's vital signs right at your bedside in order not to disrupt rooming-in and to keep you better informed.

Blood Glucose Level

Within the early hours of life, your infant will probably be screened for low blood sugar, or hypoglycemia. The few drops of blood needed will be obtained by pricking her heel. Since the newborn brain is dependent upon sugar, or glucose, for its energy, and since the stress of birth can rapidly deplete the body's stores of glucose, it is a good idea to screen infants shortly after birth to be sure they are not hypoglycemic. Hypoglycemia in an infant can cause jitteriness, lethargy, poor color, or poor feeding. Severe and prolonged low blood sugar can cause more serious problems. Low blood sugar is more common among premature infants, small infants, postmature infants, and infants with low Apgar scores, so these babies are screened even more closely. If the initial blood glucose level is normal, and the infant is healthy and feeding well, it is quite rare for hypoglycemia to develop later. On the other hand, if the first glucose level is low, and the infant is in a high-risk group, low blood sugar may persist for hours or days if it is not treated.

Hypoglycemia is treated with glucose, or sugar, either by feeding the baby every few hours or by starting an intravenous line to provide glucose water if the infant is unable to eat due to prematurity or illness. Once a normal feeding pattern is established, the problem almost never recurs.

Hematocrit

Most adults have red blood-cell counts, or hematocrits, between 40 percent and 50 percent, whereas a normal hematocrit in a newborn is usually 50 percent to 60 percent or higher. A low hematocrit, below 45 percent, indicates anemia, perhaps due to blood loss at birth or the rapid destruction of red blood cells. Anemia can cause an infant to appear pale and to tire easily with feedings.

A high hematocrit, above 65 percent, may be due to extra blood flowing to the baby from the placenta at the time of birth. A high red blood-cell count can lead to sluggish flow of blood, known as hyperviscosity. This can cause lethargy, poor muscle tone, and poor feeding.

Your baby's blood count will be obtained within the first few hours of life. If it is abnormally high or low, further tests may be ordered to determine the cause of the high or low count. If the first screen is normal, problems seldom arise later.

Eye Prophylaxis

We have known for hundreds of years that severe eye infections, or conjunctivitis, acquired in the birth canal can erode the cornea and lead to blindness. A century ago, neonatal conjunctivitis was one of the leading causes of blindness. Before the discovery of antibiotics, doctors started instilling the chemical silver nitrate into a baby's eyes after birth to prevent eye infection. Now, all fifty states have laws requiring that the eyes of newborns be treated at birth to prevent neonatal conjunctivitis.

Since silver nitrate irritates the eyes, many hospitals now use less irritating antibiotic eye ointments. Also, instead of being administered in the delivery room, treatment is now commonly delayed for several hours to allow the baby time to look at her parents without the temporary blurring of vision or eye irritation sometimes caused by the ointment.

Gonorrhea is the most common cause of serious eye infection shortly after birth, but fortunately, pregnant women are screened for gonorrhea during their prenatal care, so that detected cases can be treated before delivery. Organisms other than gonorrhea can also cause neonatal conjunctivitis. Although silver nitrate does not prevent other infections, the commonly used antibiotic ointments are effective against them.

Vitamin K

Vitamin K is necessary for normal blood clotting, but newborns temporarily have low levels of Vitamin K after birth. Several decades ago, infants occasionally died of massive hemorrhage due to Vitamin K deficiency. For this reason, all infants are routinely given an injection of Vitamin K after birth.

Blood Typing

If her mother's and father's blood types are not the same, a baby may be born with a blood type different from her mother's. Such differences include the major ABO blood groups and a marker on red cells known as the Rh factor. Sometimes when blood type differences exist, a mother's body produces antibodies against her baby's red blood cells. These antibodies may enter the baby's bloodstream and destroy some of the baby's red blood cells causing anemia and/or jaundice in the infant.

To check for blood type problems between baby and mother, blood is taken from the umbilical cord at birth to determine the baby's blood type and to check for maternal antibodies against the baby's red blood cells. Thus potential problems can be anticipated and the infant observed more carefully if indicated.

Cord

The umbilical cord, which has been your infant's nutritional lifeline in the uterus, is clamped off at birth. Now that your infant is breathing through her lungs and utilizing her own digestive tract, she no longer needs this source of oxygen and nutrients.

The cord contains three large blood vessels that will gradually dry up. But in the first few days these vessels could serve as a port of entry for infecting organisms if the cord stump is not kept clean. Triple Dye, a blue dye that inhibits the growth of organisms, is commonly painted on the cord shortly after birth. Triple Dye also helps the cord dry up so that it heals quickly and falls off. The clamp applied to the cord in the delivery room is usually removed after twenty-four hours.

ROUTINE NEWBORN CARE

Rooming-in

Following the initial assessment and screening, there is no reason why your healthy infant cannot room-in with you throughout the rest of the hospital stay. The purpose of the postpartum stay is to assure your own recovery, to guarantee your infant's healthy adjustment to life in the world, and to build your confidence in your ability to provide all the care necessary for your baby under the watchful eye of the nursery personnel.

This is best accomplished by rooming-in with your baby whenever possible, amid the loving support of close family and friends. Many hospitals have discarded outdated restrictive visiting policies and now allow siblings and other family members to visit with you and the baby. Those that have done so, with appropriate screening of visitors, have not reported an increased rate of infections as was traditionally feared. Instead, they have witnessed an increased level of family satisfaction.

Feeding

Many infants are ready to eat shortly after birth. They have been sucking on their fingers, hands, or tongues in the uterus and have a natural reflex to "root" toward a nipple. Following an uncomplicated delivery, a full-term infant with a good Apgar score will be alert, make mouthing movements, and be ready to feed in the first few minutes after birth. If circumstances permit, your infant can be put to the breast in the delivery room or recovery room. Only a small amount of colostrum, or early milk, is produced on the first day, but a healthy infant needs no more than this. The slow drip of colostrum will be the perfect way to help her learn to eat outside the uterus and to coordinate her suck and swallow reflexes. Within a few days, milk is produced in abundance.

The bottle-fed infant can be offered water or formula by her parents in the recovery room and start experiencing being held and fed, and learning to suck. In general, most hospital schedules allow for breast-fed infants to be nursed every three hours and bottle-fed infants to be fed every four hours. "Demand feeding" means that whenever an infant awakens and indicates hunger by sucking on her hands or making mouthing movements or crying, she is fed until she appears to be satisfied. Unfortunately, most hospital personnel who claim to feed "on demand" actually are bound by tradition to look at the clock and proclaim, "She shouldn't be hungry yet." With true demand feeding, the infant is allowed to feed whenever she is hungry regardless of the time. The interval between feedings will usually range from one to four hours.

You and your partner should try to offer as many of your baby's feedings yourself as possible. If you are breast-feeding, it will be important for your infant to learn to nurse well before you go home. Each time she is given a bottle in the nursery by a well-intentioned nurse, she misses an opportunity to perfect her breast-feeding technique and thus jeopardizes successful nursing. And if you are bottle-feeding, you will want to learn your baby's special feeding habits and preferences.

Since you can't take the nursery personnel home with you, it does no good to have them learn to feed and handle your baby comfortably while you remain inexperienced. You will probably find that in the long run, additional experience and confidence in caring for your baby in the hospital will allow you to get more rest at home, since things will go more smoothly.

If you are breast-feeding, you may find that nursery personnel encourage supplementing the infant's milk intake with water, since the volume of colostrum produced on the first day tends to be low. In fact, very few babies require extra liquid and most babies will nurse less effectively if they routinely receive bottle feedings. Unless your baby's physician prescribes the supplement for a medical reason, it is preferable to nurse exclusively and avoid bottle feedings in the hospital. Within forty-eight to seventy-two hours after delivery, you should have an abundant milk supply that contains adequate quantities of all nutrients.

If you are bottle-feeding, you should be aware that the formula fed to your baby in the hospital will depend largely upon which brand is provided free by the manufacturer that month. If your baby is doing well on the formula, you may want to continue using that brand at home. If you had planned to use another product, however, there is no harm in switching once you get home.

Standard bottle nipples are generally used in the hospital, so if you wanted to use a specially shaped nipple, you might introduce it while still in the hospital, before your baby grows accustomed to the standard type.

Stools

Because the cells that line the gastrointestinal tract multiply and slough off very quickly, and because infants in the uterus swallow amniotic fluid, there is some fecal material formed in an infant's gut even in the uterus. This dark, sticky, tarlike first stool is known as meconium.

Most infants pass their first meconium stool within the first twenty-four hours after birth. By the second day, the stools usually have changed to "transitional," or looser greenish-brown. By the third day, they become more typical milk stools: yellow, seedy, or curdy. Thereafter, breast-fed infants have frequent, loose, soft yellow stools for the first several weeks, whereas formula-fed infants tend to stool once or twice a day and pass a more formed stool.

Although meconium is not normally passed until after birth, under conditions of stress or lack of oxygen, the infant may pass some meconium into the bag of waters before birth. This results in amniotic fluid that is stained dark green or yellow, and it can be one indicator of fetal distress. Rarely, an infant will inhale some of the meconium-stained fluid into her lungs where the meconium can block off her air passages or cause a chemical pneumonia. If meconium-stained fluid is noted when the bag of waters breaks, the baby will be carefully monitored during labor, and any meconium will be suctioned from her airway at birth.

Weight Loss

Don't be surprised if your baby loses weight in the first several days. It is typical for newborns to lose several ounces (or approximately 5 percent of their birth weight) as they begin feedings in limited amounts. By the end of the first week, however, most infants have begun to gain weight. By the end of the second week, almost all babies will have regained their original birth weight, and most will weigh even more.

If a baby is still below birth weight by two weeks of age, there is usually no great cause for alarm. However, a careful feeding history needs to be taken by your baby's physician, appropriate feeding changes should be made, and another weight check should be scheduled in a few days to be sure the feeding problem has been corrected.

Jaundice

Nearly half of all newborns develop a yellowish skin color, known as jaundice, during the first week of life. The yellow color, which usually is worst between the third and fifth days of life, is due to an excess of bilirubin, a yellow pigment formed by the breakdown of red blood cells. Our red blood cells are normally breaking down and new ones are being produced all the time, but we don't become jaundiced because our liver removes the bilirubin formed. Jaundice occurs when either an excess of bilirubin is formed or the removal of bilirubin is impaired.

An infant is born with a high red blood cell count, contributing to the formation of bilirubin. During the first week of life, however, her liver is not yet sufficiently mature to handle all the bilirubin produced, so temporary jaundice often results.

Bilirubin levels are monitored very carefully in a jaundiced infant, since high levels of bilirubin can cause brain damage. In addition, a high bilirubin level may be associated with an underlying problem needing treatment, such as an infection.

Jaundice is seldom severe enough to require intervention, but you may need to bring your baby back to the office or hospital laboratory after you go home in order to recheck her bilirubin level until it begins to decrease. (See pages 99-101 for specific treatment of jaundice and interpretation of bilirubin levels.)

Screening Tests

With recent advances in medical technology, it is now possible to screen infants at birth for a variety of medical conditions, so any necessary treatment can be started before symptoms arise and, therefore, complications can be minimized. Blood is usually taken from the baby's heel prior to leaving the hospital and a week or two may pass before the test results are available. Parents are always notified if any abnormality is found, but normal results are not routinely reported to parents. State laws vary, but all states screen for one or more of the following diseases:

Hypothyroidism: Older children and adults who develop hypothyroidism, or low levels of thyroid hormone, may have constipation, cool skin, a hoarse voice, dry hair, and other symptoms. Treatment with thyroid hormone will correct the problem. If hypothyroidism is present at birth, however, a baby can develop irreversible brain damage within a few months unless thyroid hormone is started in the first few weeks.

Phenylketonuria (PKU): PKU is an inherited disease in which the body cannot metabolize the amino acid phenylalanine. Toxic levels of phenylalanine build up and cause permanent brain damage unless a special diet low in phenylalanine is started in the early weeks of life. In addition to the blood test in the hospital, a second test is usually performed at ten to fourteen days of life to assure that no affected infants have been inadvertently missed.

Sickle-cell disease (SCD): Sickle-cell anemia is an inherited disorder of the red blood cells that occurs commonly among blacks. Children with sickle-cell disease are chronically anemic and are prone to serious infections. Although there is no cure, many complications can be prevented by identifying the disease early in life and providing specialized medical care.

Cystic fibrosis (CF): Cystic fibrosis is an inherited disorder that affects many glands in the body. It results in chronic respiratory problems, intestinal malabsorption, and poor growth. Although no cure is available, complications of cystic fibrosis may be minimized by detecting the disorder early in life and beginning respiratory therapy, diet management, and close medical follow-up.

Screening is also available for several rare, inherited metabolic diseases that require a special diet to be started early in life to prevent death or retardation.

Routine neonatal screening now makes it possible to detect these diseases before symptoms are present or a problem is even suspected, thus making it possible to start treatment before permanent damage has occurred. In addition, nurseries routinely screen newborns for hearing impairment prior to discharge. Feel free to ask about the screening procedures at your hospital.

Length of Hospitalization

Over recent decades, the routine American postpartum hospital stay has steadily decreased from seven to five to three or fewer days. Longer stays were necessitated by the routine use of heavy medications during childbirth, the high rates of postpartum infections, and the overall view of birth as a medical problem. Since routine pediatric visits did not begin until six weeks, longer observation in the hospital seemed warranted. Now, postpartum stays of twenty-four hours or less are not uncommon, and pediatric outpatient care is beginning as early as five days, and almost always by two weeks of age.

While short postpartum hospitalization can be medically safe, socially practical, and economically attractive, a variety of factors should be considered in deciding how long you should stay. The length of hospitalization should depend upon your rate of recovery from labor and delivery, the availability of help at home, the condition of your baby, the accessibility of follow-up pediatric care, and the success of infant feeding.

Interestingly, if a mother requires extended postpartum care, the infant is welcomed in the nursery for as long as her mother is hospitalized. However, if an infant must remain an additional day or two because of jaundice, for example, it is almost unheard of for the mother to be allowed to remain with her infant. My first baby had severe jaundice requiring an exchange transfusion, and I will always appreciate being allowed to remain in the hospital with him the whole time. Although my second child, born at a different hospital, was less jaundiced, she remained for several days, while I was discharged without an infant in my arms. Nothing seemed more unnatural. I now make every effort to avoid parent-infant separation among my patients.

Obviously, rising costs of medical care dictate many such policies. Nevertheless, individualized discharge orders rather than rigid policies should result in safe early discharge for the majority and prolonged joint stays for the few. If you must be discharged without your infant, try to visit and feed her as often as possible. Some hospitals have sleep-over arrangements for parents. Ask what is available at your hospital.

NEWBORN EXAMINATIONS

Regardless of her length of stay, your baby will undergo at least four examinations. The first brief assessment occurs in the delivery room during which Apgar scores are assigned and the baby's transition to life outside the uterus is evaluated. The second occurs during the "transition period" covering the next several hours. This exam includes vital signs, measurements, the estimate of gestational age, and several screening laboratory tests.

The third exam is more formal and includes the physician's thorough medical exam of every organ system and the ultimate pronouncement that your baby is healthy in every respect. Some practitioners will perform this examination at your bedside and offer helpful explanations of their procedures and findings.

The final exam is performed at the time of hospital discharge and includes giving parents instructions about feeding and caring for their infant at home and arrangements for follow-up medical care. Some hospitals even require that you attend a newborn class before discharge in order to assure that you have all the basic knowledge necessary to care for your infant at home.

To make you more comfortable with handling your baby, some typical newborn physical findings are described and explained as follows:

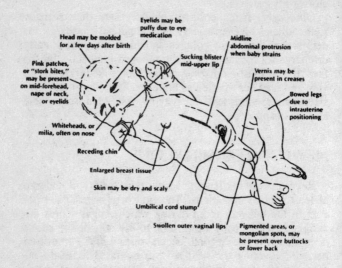

Head may be molded for a few days after birth

Eyelids may be puffy due to eye medication

Pink patches, or "stork bites," may be present on mid-forehead, nape of neck, or eyelids

Sucking blister mid-upper lip

Midline abdominal protrusion when baby strains

Vernix may be present in creases

Bowed legs due to intrauterine positioning

Whiteheads, or milia, often on nose

Receding chin

Enlarged breast tissue

Skin may be dry and scaly

Umbilical cord stump

Swollen outer vaginal lips

Pigmented areas, or mongolian spots, may be present over buttocks or lower back

Head

The bones of the newborn skull are soft and separated by narrow spaces known as sutures. Two sutures join to form a "soft spot," or fontanel, near the front of the skull and a smaller one near the back. During the birth process, the head is molded due to its soft, moveable bones in order to pass more easily through the birth canal. This molding often creates a temporarily elongated head, which assumes a normal shape within one or two days. Molding is more prominent with firstborn infants.

If a fetal scalp monitor was used during labor to check the baby's heartbeat, a small scab may be seen over the back of the head. Occasionally the birth process will be traumatic enough to cause some bleeding into the scalp, leaving a black and blue discoloration. Rarely, a small lump will be noted over the back of the head due to bleeding just above one of the skull bones. These lumps may take a few weeks to reabsorb and the blood may break down to form bilirubin and cause jaundice. Usually, these swellings, known as cephalohematomas, have no great significance.

Eyes

The eye medication used to prevent infection may irritate the eyes and result in some lid swelling or eye discharge. This usually lasts only a day or two. If jaundice is present, the whites of the eyes will appear yellow. Occasionally a small hemorrhage may be seen in the whites of the eyes due to the birth process. The blood may take a week or two to reabsorb.

Your infant can see quite well at eight to twelve inches, about the distance from your arms to your face during feeding. She can even follow your face for short distances after she has focused on it. Occasionally, infants may not focus their eyes together and thus may appear cross-eyed at times. If crossed eyes are persistent or still noticeable by a few months of age, then you should take your baby to an ophthalmologist (see page 166).

Ears

An infant can hear well at birth and responds best to her own mother's voice or a similarly pitched voice. She can turn her head in the direction of a voice or sound to which she has attuned.

Nose

Infants are nose breathers, so it is important to keep the nasal passages clear of mucus. Since the nose and mouth are connected at the back of the throat, it is not uncommon for a newborn to vomit out the nose and mouth together. This should not cause alarm, but the nose should be cleared well afterward.

Mouth

Small white cysts are often present on the roof of a newborn's mouth. These are known as Epstein's pearls and are of no consequence. Neonatal teeth can be present, and if loose, they may need to be pulled to prevent the chance of the baby choking on them.

Chest

Newborns frequently breathe in a seemingly irregular fashion, several seconds of short, shallow breathing, followed by a few seconds without breathing. They breathe at a faster rate than adults, approximately forty to sixty times a minute. Signs of difficulty in breathing include noisy breathing, tugging in between the ribs, flaring of the nostrils, or a bluish color. An infant's heart rate is faster than an adult's and varies from 100 to 160 beats per minute.

Both girl and boy babies will have a little nubbin of breast tissue just under the nipples as a result of the mother's pregnancy hormones. Rarely, these little breasts will release a drop of milk, but usually they just shrink and disappear over the first few weeks of life.

Abdomen

The umbilical cord stump should drop off in one to three weeks. Infants' abdomens are gently rounded and usually move up and down with breathing. Sometimes a piece of normal cartilage may stick up at the bottom of the breastbone, or a soft sausage-shaped protrusion may be intermittently present, extending from the breastbone to the umbilical cord. Both are normal and have no significance.

Extremities

An infant can move her arms and legs symmetrically. Her legs may appear bowed due to her position in the uterus, and this bowing will probably persist several months or more. Her hands and feet will usually feel cooler than the rest of the body. Hip dislocation may be discovered shortly after birth, and if treated promptly, should not have long-term consequences. Because of the importance of discovering a dislocated hip, the hips should be carefully checked at every pediatric visit for many months.

Genitals

A baby girl usually has puffy outer vaginal lips due to the mother's pregnancy hormones. A small amount of clear whitish vaginal discharge is commonly found, and occasionally slight vaginal bleeding may occur several days after birth due to the withdrawal of these same hormones. The sticky, whitish, cheesy material between the inner and outer vaginal lips is vernix, the substance that covers the infant at birth. It may still be present a week or two later.

A baby boy's foreskin is tightly bound to the glans, or head of the penis. The penis will usually become erect just before urination. The urine stream should be thick and strong. His scrotum may appear enlarged due to a small amount of fluid surrounding the testicles. This fluid, known as a hydrocele, gradually will be absorbed over weeks or months.

If a boy was circumcised using a Plastibell, a small plastic bell-shaped device will remain tied in place at the tip of the penis for a few days. There may be some yellowish discharge over the head of the penis and slight swelling of the skin overlying the Plastibell. Redness or swelling that spreads toward the body suggests an infected circumcision site and should be examined by a physician immediately. If a circumcision was performed by another method, no Plastibell will be present, but the same signs of healing will be noted. (See pages 110-11 for further discussion of both the circumcised and uncircumcised newborn penis.)

Reflexes

A newborn demonstrates a variety of reflexes, including the grasp of a finger or similar object placed in her palm; a startle reflex in which she throws out her arms and cries when exposed to a sudden noise or movement; an automatic walking reflex in which she seems to take steps when held up with her feet touching a hard surface; a rooting reflex in which she turns toward a stimulus against one cheek; a crawling reflex in which she appears to crawl when placed on her abdomen and the soles of her feet are pressed; and a dozen or more similar automatic responses. The presence of these reflexes helps determine gestational age and overall wellbeing. Each of these primitve reflexes will gradually be lost and replaced by purposeful movements.

Skin

A newborn's skin is usually a reddish color shortly after birth. If the baby was overdue, some peeling of the skin normally may be noted, especially on the palms, soles, scrotum, and trunk. The hands and feet may appear bluish during the first day. Jaundice may begin to appear after forty-eight hours and usually subsides by the seventh day. Jaundice is first noted on the head and face and the whites of the eyes, and progresses down to the trunk and legs when it reaches higher levels.

Newborns commonly have little whiteheads, known as milia, over their nose, for the first few weeks. They can have a harmless blotchy red rash with small central whitish bumps that comes and goes during the first week. Mongolian spots, or bluish-black patches, are common above the buttocks of dark-skinned babies. These are often mistaken for bruises, but are of a uniform color that gradually fades over years. Infants with long nails may scratch themselves and leave temporary marks.

Birthmarks occur commonly and can be of varying size, location, and consequence. Birthmarks made of blood vessels are known as hemangiomas. They may be flat, raised, or extend beneath the skin. Flat hemangiomas, known as "stork bites," are commonly seen over the eyelids and at the nape of the neck. They gradually fade away in the early months of life. Raised hemangiomas can grow in size over the first few years of life and often cause parents great anxiety. After several years, however, these "strawberry" hemangiomas usually begin to shrink and disappear completely by school age.

Darkly pigmented birthmarks should be examined by a dermatologist. Some of these are at risk of later developing skin cancer, and for this reason, elective removal in the early years of life may be recommended. Café-au-lait spots, which are light brown (like coffee with cream), do not have this risk.

Another common birthmark is a raised, oily, yellowish-orange mark, often on the face or scalp. It should be followed by a dermatologist and removed electively before adolescence, since it can later develop into skin cancer.

ALL THIS may seem like an excessive amount of handling, evaluating, and screening, but I hope you now have an appreciation for the great lengths to which your pediatrician has gone in order to answer that seemingly simple question posed by all parents at delivery: "Is my baby all right?"

NEWBORN COMPLICATIONS

Occasionally a medical problem is evident at birth or becomes manifest during the nursery stay. Your baby may be whisked away to a high-risk nursery, placed in an incubator, and attached to monitors, IVs, and oxygen. Without accurate information, you may be left panicked and ignorant about her condition and your role in her care. A discussion of some newborn medical problems should help familiarize you with terminology and the possible treatments a sick newborn might receive.

Prematurity

Approximately 7 percent of infants are born prematurely, or before thirty-eight weeks' gestation. Besides being obviously smaller, they experience immaturity of various organ systems. Infants born as early as fourteen to fifteen weeks before their due date have a chance of surviving today in a modern intensive care unit.

Depending on how early a baby is born and what type of problems she is experiencing, a premature infant may be cared for at her hospital of birth if sufficient expertise is available there. Otherwise, she will be transferred to a regional center where she will receive highly specialized care for several weeks or more before returning to your community for further convalescent care. Common problems encountered by premature infants include the following:

Cold Stress: Because premature babies (preemies) have little fat stores, they have trouble keeping warm on their own. A preemie will burn many calories trying to stay warm, and cold stress can make respiratory problems worse. For this reason, a premature infant is routinely kept in an incubator or warmer for weeks or longer, until she has enough fat to maintain a normal body temperature in a regular crib.

Feeding Difficulties: Nutrition is very important to a premature infant who is born too small and needs adequate calories in order to grow, remain healthy, and keep warm. Most premature infants will require some nutrition and fluids to be provided intravenously for a time. It is also common to feed them by mouth through a little tube passed into their stomach at mealtimes. This is known as gavage feeding. The nurses caring for your baby will help determine when she is ready to try to suck and swallow, partly by watching her suck on the gavage tube or a pacifier. An infant's sucking and swallowing reflexes aren't coordinated until at least thirty-four weeks' gestation. It is important to switch premature infants to bottle or breast feeds gradually, as suddenly taking all her feedings by nipple can rapidly tire her out.

Respiratory Distress: Immaturity of the lungs and lack of the substance that helps keep the little air sacs in the lungs open causes difficulty breathing, known as hyaline membrane disease (HMD). Infants with HMD need additional oxygen and sometimes require assisted breathing with a respirator. To do this, a tube is passed into the baby's windpipe and taped securely in place. HMD tends to get progressively worse over the first few days of life before gradual improvement begins.

Often a premature infant with severe HMD will develop scarring of the lungs, known as bronchopulmonary dysplasia (BPD). An infant with BPD may require oxygen therapy for several weeks or months as the lungs heal. Occasionally parents will take home their otherwise well premature infant while she still requires oxygen therapy. Home oxygen is arranged, with portable tanks for traveling, and close medical follow-up is provided until the child outgrows her need for additional oxygen.

Heart Failure: The way a baby's blood circulates while in the uterus is different from how it circulates after she is born and can breathe on her own. Very soon after birth, the fetal circulation pathways close off and normal infant circulation begins. In preemies, one of the fetal pathways sometimes persists and can place additional stress on the heart and lungs. This fetal circulatory pathway is known as a patent ductus arteriosus (PDA). If PDA places serious stress on the baby's heart and lungs, an operation can be performed through the left side of the baby's chest, and the PDA can be closed off outside the baby's heart.

Hemorrhage into the Brain: Very small prematures, such as those born at less than thirty-two weeks' gestation and/or less than three pounds weight, have very soft brains and skull bones. Sometimes a blood vessel in the brain will rupture and leak, causing a blood clot within the brain, known as intracranial hemorrhage (ICH). The abnormal bleeding can lead to hydrocephalus, or water on the brain. If hydrocephalus occurs it can be treated by an operation that shunts excess brain fluid out through a thin tube buried under the skin above the skull.

Bowel Disease: Occasionally a premature infant will develop a serious bowel infection, known as necrotizing enterocolitis (NEC). When this occurs, the baby's abdomen becomes distended, she passes blood in her bowel movements, and appears very ill. The treatment is to stop all feedings and to rest the bowel while giving the baby antibiotics until the infection clears. Meanwhile, intravenous fluids are administered. We don't fully understand NEC, but it does seem to occur in clusters, with several cases appearing at once in a premature nursery.

Jaundice: A premature infant is at particular risk of developing jaundice because of immaturity of the liver and several other contributing factors. Many preemies receive phototherapy (see pages 99-101) during the first week of life until their bilirubin level falls to a safe value.

The care of premature infants is extremely specialized and intense, and the doctors and nurses who care for these babies are admirable indeed. But please remember that your baby also needs your presence, touching, voice, and love. She will begin to recognize your visits and respond to you in a special way. You can decorate your baby's incubator with mobiles and pictures of your family and make your presence known to her as best you can. There are now several books available to help you better familiarize yourself with medical terminology, various aspects of your baby's care, ways you can participate, and tips about taking your baby home. Two of these are *The Premature Baby Book: A Parent's Guide to Coping and Caring in the First Years,* by Helen Harrison, and *Premature Babies: A Different Beginning* by Drs. William Sammons and Jennifer Lewis.

If you had planned to breast-feed your premature infant, you can use an electric breast pump to express your milk and bring it to the hospital to be fed to your baby. You will want to hold her up to your nipple, even if she cannot yet suck and swallow her feedings. Learning to grasp your nipple is crucial to breast feeding later.

All the time I spent in neonatal intensive care units during my pediatric training has left a special place in my heart for the parents of prematures. The long weeks of worrying and waiting will someday pay off and you will have your baby home with you at last. I admire your courage and love and patience.

Infection

Because a newborn's immune system is immature, any possible indication of an infection is cause for worry. An infection can rapidly spread to the bloodstream and become life-threatening. For this reason, prompt investigation and treatment are begun as soon as an infection is suspected. Cultures are taken of the blood, urine, and other sites, and antibiotics are given, usually intravenously. Antibiotics are continued during the forty-eight hours while the cultures are growing. If the cultures confirm that an infection is indeed present, treatment usually is continued for ten days or more. If the cultures are negative and the baby looks well, the antibiotics are discontinued.

Jaundice (See page 86.)

Prior to the 1950s, when there was no treatment for jaundice, very high bilirubin levels occasionally caused brain damage or death. Fortunately, today jaundice is readily treatable, and permanent problems are exceedingly rare.

Sometimes jaundice is treated with fluorescent lights, which have been shown to effectively decrease bilirubin levels. Infants receiving this phototherapy usually are kept naked, with their eyes covered, lying under a bank of special lights that cause the breakdown of bilirubin within the baby's skin. Babies receiving phototherapy may act sleepy or feed slowly. To prevent dehydration while under the lights, infants are fed extra water. It is important for breast-feeding infants to continue nursing frequently and remain familiar with the breast at a time when they may be receiving supplements by bottle. The eye patches are always removed for feedings to allow infants to look around.

Now closely monitored home phototherapy is becoming a safe and practical alternative to prolonged hospitalization for neonatal jaundice. Over the next several years, home phototherapy may become available on a broad scale. Meanwhile, if your infant requires phototherapy, you should make every effort to remain as close as possible. Feel free to ask for explanations about the cause of jaundice in your baby's case, and inquire about actual bilirubin levels.

The level of bilirubin rarely rises so high that it poses an immediate danger. When it does, an exchange transfusion is performed in order to rapidly decrease the bilirubin level. Small volumes of the baby's blood are removed and replaced by amounts of fresh donor blood. This gradual exchange of blood is repeated for approximately an hour until most of the bilirubin has been safely removed from the baby's system. My first baby required an exchange transfusion for severe jaundice, which resulted from our incompatible blood types. My fears of brain damage have long since disappeared; he graduated second in his high school class and won a full tuition college scholarship!

The following guidelines may prove helpful to you if your baby is being treated for jaundice:

- ✓ Bilirubin levels up to 12 or 13 milligrams percent (mg%) between the third to fifth day of life are not uncommon among healthy full-term infants and pose no danger.
- ✓ Bilirubin levels of 15 mg% or higher will often be treated with phototherapy to prevent further rise in bilirubin to dangerous levels. A level of 15 mg% does not always require phototherapy, however.
- ✓ Bilirubin levels greater than 20 mg% will usually require exchange transfusion, since levels this high pose a risk of brain damage to the infant.

Many other factors contribute to the decision to treat jaundice, including the infant's age, condition, and prematurity; the rate of bilirubin rise; and the underlying cause of jaundice.

Breast-milk Jaundice: The breast milk of 1 to 2 percent of mothers has been found to contain a substance that can lead to prolonged jaundice in their nursing infants. This type of jaundice usually begins after the first week of life and is diagnosed only after all other causes of jaundice have been eliminated. Breast-milk jaundice may last several weeks and is harmless unless bilirubin levels approach 20 mg%. Some physicians will recommend interrupting breast-feeding for one to two days if bilirubin levels reach the upper teens. If formula feeding during this interval results in a marked fall in bilirubin level, it confirms the suspected diagnosis and usually solves the problem.

Unfortunately, breast-milk jaundice, which is rare and usually benign, all too often leads to permanent disruption of breast feeding because of inadequate maternal information and support. If breast-milk jaundice is diagnosed in your infant, remember that breast feeding is still highly desirable. If you are asked to interrupt breast feeding for one to two days, be sure you maintain your milk supply by pumping your breasts regularly. Periodically offer your breast after pumping so your infant doesn't forget how to nurse. Then resume breast feeding enthusiastically once the bilirubin level has fallen. The problem should not recur and your baby will benefit from long-term breast feeding.

Birth Defects

Approximately 3 percent of infants are born with a birth defect, such as cleft lip or palate, a heart problem, clubfoot, Down's syndrome, spina bifida, or other problem. If a birth defect is discovered, specialists will be consulted promptly to plan the repair and/or long-term team management. Your initial shock and disappointment will gradually be replaced by acceptance and energy to tackle the problem. Spend as much time as possible with your baby and learn her special care needs, so you can provide them yourself, first with the help of the nursing staff, and soon on your own. Ask questions, both of your baby's pediatrician and the consultants involved. Talk together as a couple and request team meetings if necessary to be sure you fully understand the problem and the plan. A geneticist can meet with you and determine whether the problem occurred randomly and is not likely to happen with another pregnancy, or if it is genetic and has a known inheritance risk.

Remember, the unknown is always more frightening than the known and familiar. The more knowledgeable you are about your baby's problem the easier it will be to deal with. Numerous parent-support groups are available in which parents who have coped successfully with their baby's problem can help you manage with the same one in your infant.

Finally, don't forget to emphasize all the normal, perfect, and positive aspects of your baby and remember that the defect is just one part of a whole child who needs you now more than ever. I'll always recall a certain mother's touching story about her experience delivering her daughter with a birth defect. At first stunned, saddened, and guilty, her whole attitude reversed when her husband embraced her in the recovery room and said, "Thank you for giving me a daughter." He saw a wonderful baby, not just the defect. He thanked her for carrying and giving birth to his child when she worried about "letting him down." I think the most rewarding part of being a pediatrician is witnessing such incredible strengths among parents.

PARENT-INFANT BONDING

Twenty years ago, medical experts believed that infants at birth could not see, feel pain, or interact with their environment. Some parents believed these "facts," while others quietly noticed their infant's obvious responsiveness and ignored the medical opinions. During the past few years, the exciting study of newborn behavior has resulted in the recognition that newborns are capable of a variety of responses to their world and that each of these behaviors can generate powerful reactions in their parents.

This interaction between parent and newborn has appropriately and accurately been linked to the process of parental attachment to their infant. For every time your baby turns to your voice, calms when lifted into your arms, or gazes into your eyes as she nurses, you become hooked on her anew.

Unfortunately, the bonding process, which really begins before birth and can take weeks to complete, has been commonly thought of as taking place in the first few minutes or hours of life. A false concept of "epoxy bonding," effected by holding an infant immediately after birth and allowing some magical exchange to occur between parent and child, has been popularized. The large number of parents who are separated from their infants at birth because of medical reasons, who had Caesarean births, or who adopted babies have recently come to doubt whether they "fully bonded" to their infants. In fact, true bonding is a long-term process. It almost never goes awry among well-intentioned, committed parents, even in the worst of delivery circumstances. Almost all of our mothers gave birth to us under general anesthesia and had very limited contact with us during the first week of life, and still they

BONDING

managed to "bond." Bonding can be made more difficult when an infant is sick or premature or has a birth defect, and it can occur more easily when the birthing experience is enjoyable, the infant remains with the parents immediately after birth, and the family has easy access to the infant during the entire hospital stay.

Bonding is the emergence of profound love between a parent and child, the surge of affection that calls a parent to respond to every infant need despite their own physical sacrifice. It simply cannot be guaranteed nor lost in the first five minutes of life. Nevertheless, where bonding can be nurtured by more sensible and supportive hospital policy, it makes good sense to offer such options, and you should ask for them.

Meanwhile, never fear. You will fall in love with your baby and take her home with an irresistible urge to care superbly for her. Just trust your instincts. If she cries, comfort her. If she is hungry, feed her. When she looks adorable, feel free to kiss her. Remember, you cannot spoil an infant who has no will of her own yet and no other motives except comfort and security. Your regular response to her early needs will allow her to begin to build trust in her world. This early trust in adults to care for her needs will allow her the confidence and independence to later separate and function well as a secure adult herself someday. It all begins in infancy when you generously share your love with your baby.

5 BASIC BABY CARE

BEFORE YOUR BABY IS BORN you will naturally create a mental image of him and fantasize about your future life with him. But most of us have found that the reality of having a new baby is far different from our fantasy. Once your baby arrives and actual parenthood unfolds, you will find yourself on a journey filled with surprises. Most of them are joyful, many are challenging, and some are even startling. Realistic expectations will be helpful as you try to imagine your new life-style.

Fantasy #1, Sleep: You believe newborns sleep most of the time. In the beginning the baby will need to be fed at 2:00 A.M., but soon he will sleep through the night.

Reality: In the beginning, sleep does not come in a predictable pattern. Some newborns sleep a great deal, while others sleep very little. There is no way to predict how much or how regularly your individual baby will sleep. Your newborn may sleep in ten-minute snatches, then for two hours, then for thirty minutes, then for five hours.

Don't be surprised if your baby wants to be fed several times during the night. New babies are simply not meant to be isolated from human contact for eight-hour stretches, and their empty stomachs just may be nature's way of ensuring some closeness every few hours.

Face it, "real babies" don't sleep through the night. You may feel terminally fatigued during the early months of your baby's life, but your body will adjust to several short intervals at night and daytime naps. You'll eventually start to feel rested.

Fantasy #2, Feedings: You envision your baby needing to be fed every three to four hours.

Reality: Newborn babies are rarely regular in their eating habits and become hungry more often than you expect. Their hunger is not scheduled, predictable, or well defined. Your baby may want to nurse every half hour and then every four hours for no apparent reason; that is a normal newborn eating pattern. How many adults do you know who are hungry at evenly spaced intervals for identical amounts of food?

Fantasy #3, Crying: You expect that if your baby is fed and dry, he won't cry. When he does cry, you don't intend to jump up and run to him. After all, you don't want to spoil him.

Reality: Your baby may cry very little if he is fed on demand, held a great deal, and escapes infantile colic. On the other hand, even if your baby's obvious needs are satisfied, he may cry for reasons unknown to you. A great deal of an infant's crying is puzzling to his parents. He may be colicky, overstimulated, bored, or unhappy and uncomfortable in ways we cannot fathom. Although TV babies rarely cry, and of course magazines always depict happy babies, real-life babies do cry more often than we expect.

You may have imagined that ignoring your "future" baby's crying would be the appropriate thing to do, but your real-life baby will so strongly trigger your parenting instincts that ignoring your baby's cry will feel neither appropriate nor possible. Being unable to console a crying baby is probably the most difficult and frustrating part of new parenthood. But our babies do grow older and cry less, and the reasons for their tears become more comprehensible, making life a great deal easier.

Fantasy #4, Advice: Once your baby is born, you expect those around you will give you credit for being capable parents and respect your individual parenting style. You even imagine being praised for your informed, caring, and modern approach to parenting.

Reality: Actually, those around you will feel strangely obligated to offer you endless well-meant advice, perhaps because you are new parents, or because a helpless new baby just prompts a nurturing response in all of us. Whatever the reason, be prepared to hear lots of child-rearing advice, some of which is unsolicited. You can listen to it politely and then continue to do what you feel is best. Conserve your energy; don't defend your child-care practices or argue with anyone else's. People are deeply committed to the way they handle their children.

Fantasy #5, Feelings of Confidence: You have read every book in the library's parenting section; you have attended every available class; you have quizzed your more experienced friends to exhaustion; you feel confident that you know all that you need to be a parent.

Reality: The birth of your baby is often accompanied by tremendous feelings of inadequacy. "Will I be able to care for my baby properly? Will I be able to meet all his needs? I don't know how to fold a diaper, or buckle the belt in the car seat, much less how to safely give him a bath or comfort him during a two-hour crying spell." There is simply a great deal to learn about parenting that comes only with experience. Books and classes cannot fully prepare you. But, after a brief period of feeling inadequate, true confidence and capability will emerge.

Fantasy #6, Couple Time: You and your partner are very committed to each other and to your relationship, and you won't allow it to change with the birth of your baby.

Reality: Inevitably "couple time" takes a back seat to "baby time" early in your baby's life. The all-consuming needs of an infant take precedence over adult desires. This adjustment can be very difficult for some couples and may cause resentment in one partner. Redefining your relationship in light of your new parenthood may help. Once your baby is a little more independent, your couple relationship will once again be prominent in your lives.

Fantasy #7, Time for Yourself: You imagine that since newborns sleep so much and you'll be home more, that you'll have more time to yourself than ever before. You'll catch up on reading, clean out some closets, and take that sculpture class you've been postponing.

Reality: In fact, one of the most difficult adjustments you make in the transition to parenthood is the lack of time for yourself. In the beginning, your days and nights are monopolized by your baby's care. Your are pleased if you have time both to eat lunch and take a shower in the same day. Fortunately, just about the time you're adjusting to a life that feels like total self-sacrifice, your baby begins to fall into a more predictable pattern, to entertain himself, to tolerate some separation from you, and time for yourself slowly returns.

Fantasy #8, Older Sibling: Your older child loves babies and seems to be looking forward to the arrival of his sibling. You are sure your child will be thrilled with his new baby and love him dearly.

Reality: If your older child is normal, he probably won't adore his new baby at all. His feelings will be very mixed, but you can be sure that one of the strongest will be jealousy. It will be very difficult for him to share you. It is natural for you to love the new baby intensely, but it is natural for the older child to be jealous.

Fantasy #9, Loving the Second Baby: You are so filled with love for your first child that you can't imagine being able to love another baby the same way.

Reality: Each time a new baby (including the first) is added to a family, all the relationships change, but they are not diluted as you have feared. When your new baby arrives, so does a new abundance of love. You never love your first child less, but the same kind of love flows easily to your new baby.

Fantasy #10: Who Is Your Baby? You have spent your childless years formulating child-rearing ideas, watching your friends completely "blow it" with their children, and you now have definite views about what kind of child you will have. Your child will not whine or be overly demanding. He will not bite or hit other children, and he will obey you (the first time) and treat you with respect. He will be good-natured, beautiful, intelligent and athletic.

Reality: Without a doubt, the biggest surprise you face after the birth of your baby is his emergence as a person. Although you thoroughly anticipated determining who he would be, the truth is that you will discover—not determine—who your child becomes. You will watch in awe as your baby reveals himself to you. He may be passive, he may be easily excited, he may cry often in frustration. He might be a genius and he might be ordinary—but he comes to you as a unique person. And nobody asks for a whiner!

This is not to imply that you have no influence on your

child. You will contribute to your child's sense of self-esteem, feelings of security, and establishment of values. But you will also recognize that your child is an individual, with many factors genetically predetermined at birth. He arrives with some of his personality and temperament already established.

NEWBORN CARE

Your baby's basic care is a responsibility that hits you immediately after his birth. Although you no doubt provided some of his care while still in the hospital, assuming full responsibility for your baby's care may feel overwhelming. Caring for a newborn feels foreign to everyone at first. His small size, unsupported extremities, inability to verbalize, and apparent fragility all make his routine care feel awkward and even a little frightening until you gain some experience.

Certain newborn features call for a brief period of special attention. Follow a few guidelines and you should find these tasks to be fairly simple.

Navel

After the newborn's umbilical cord is cut at birth, a stump remains that will fall off sometime between one and three weeks of age. Until it falls off, you need to keep it as clean and as dry as possible to prevent infection.

Sponge bathe your baby and do not give a tub bath until the cord falls off. Some recommend not putting your baby to sleep on his stomach until the cord falls off to avoid irritating the umbilical stump. However, I always found my own babies slept better on their tummies and none had a problem with their cord.

Each time you change your baby, clean the cord base with a clean cotton ball soaked in alcohol. Alcohol prevents the growth of organisms and dries the cord so it will fall off sooner. You can also use a Q-tip soaked in alcohol or a packaged alcohol-soaked swab. I prefer the cotton-ball method because it holds more alcohol. It is important to squeeze the alcohol all around the base of the cord by gently lifting the dried stump. Don't be afraid to lift the blackened stump to clean beneath. Wipe away any dried drainage that may have accumulated. Since there are no nerve endings in the cord, the alcohol does not cause your baby any discomfort. He may cry, however, when cold alcohol touches his tummy.

Continue to apply alcohol for several days after the cord falls off to assure complete healing of the umbilical stump and reduce chances of infection. This is even more important with "innies," where you can't see the cord base, than with "outies."

You may notice a little spot of blood on the diaper near the time the cord is about to fall off. This is normal and no cause for alarm as long as the blood is not freshly accumulating. Never pull the cord off or attempt to loosen it, even if it seems to be hanging by a thread. Leave it alone, and let it fall off naturally. Report to your pediatrician any unusual drainage from the umbilical cord.

With proper cord care, your baby's umbilical cord will likely heal without problems. Although uncommon, the most serious cord problem is infection, or omphalitis. An infected cord is usually foul-smelling and oozes yellow pus. The surrounding skin may also be red and hard. A cord infection could rapidly spread into the bloodstream and so requires prompt medical attention. (See page 385 in "Illnesses and Disorders.")

A second infrequent problem is active bleeding from the cord, usually due to accidentally pulling the cord off before it has completely healed. In this case you notice active bleeding from the cord; every time you wipe blood away, a fresh drop appears. Report this to your pediatrician immediately.

The final problem is the least serious but most common. Instead of completely drying up, the cord base can develop a pinkish lump of scar tissue that oozes and drains a light yellow material. This is known as an umbilical granuloma, and it usually resolves in a week or two with frequent applications of alcohol. Occasionally the pediatrician may choose to cauterize the umbilical granuloma in the office to speed its resolution.

Penis

If you choose to have your baby boy circumcised, you will need to care for the head of the penis carefully for about a week. Ask your baby's doctor for suggestions on how best to manage this.

Several methods of neonatal circumcision are commonly used. In the Plastibell method, a small plastic bell-shaped device remains on the head of the penis for about five days, while other methods of circumcision do not leave any device in place.

Little special care of the circumcised penis is really necessary. Although urine is sterile as it leaves the body and serves to wash the penis, I also recommend that parents gently rinse the circumcision at each diaper change by squeezing a cotton ball soaked with lukewarm water over the head of the penis. Then, if a Plastibell was used, you can gently lift the plastic ring away from the penis for a second or two to prevent it from sticking to the head of the penis and causing irritation. Call your pediatrician promptly if you ever notice the Plastibell has slipped below the glans onto the shaft of the penis.

For three or four days after circumcision, you can apply petroleum jelly or an over-the-counter antibiotic ointment directly to the head of the penis when you put on a diaper. This is not necessary, but it may help prevent the glans from sticking uncomfortably to your baby's diaper.

After a circumcision, there should be no active bleeding. If you notice more than a few drops of fresh blood, call your baby's doctor. The head of the penis may show signs of irritation and appear whitish or yellowish in places as it heals. If a Plastibell was used, the remaining rim of skin in front of the string will blacken and fall off with the bell. The shaft of the penis should always appear normal, however, after any type of circumcision. Consult your pediatrician if you notice any redness or swelling progressing toward the body.

If you didn't have your son circumcised, no special care of the penis is necessary in infancy. The foreskin is too tight to be retracted yet, and there is no reason to do so. In fact, during infancy the foreskin protects the glans from frequent exposure to the ammonia in urine. Vigorous at-

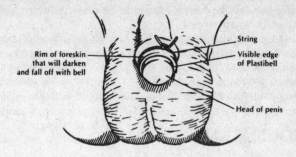

Rim of foreskin that will darken and fall off with bell

String

Visible edge of Plastibell

Head of penis

PENIS WITH PLASTIBELL IN PLACE

tempts to retract the foreskin can be painful to your baby, and premature forceful separation of the foreskin from the glans can cause the foreskin to later tightly readhere to the head of the penis.

To check periodically if your son's foreskin can be retracted, hold the penis with one hand and with the other hand push the foreskin back gently—never forcibly—until you feel resistance. Try again in a few weeks or months. If the retraction is easy and your baby seems comfortable, you can push the foreskin back farther each time.

Spontaneous erections that occur naturally in all male infants serve to gradually loosen the foreskin around the glans. Eventually the foreskin will be completely retractable, exposing the entire glans. This occurs by three years of age in many boys and in virtually all males by adolescence. Occasional retraction of the foreskin and cleaning beneath is adequate at first. Later, as your son learns to bathe himself, you can teach him how to retract his foreskin and clean his penis as part of his routine hygiene.

Fontanel

The fontanel is the soft spot on the top of the baby's head that is present until the four surrounding skull bones grow together. The area is covered with a membrane that is about as tough as canvas. Common sense tells us that normal handling, such as washing and shampooing, are safe, but that the baby's head must be protected from hard blows or sharp objects.

If the fontanel dips inward, it may be an indication that the baby is dehydrated. If it appears tense or bulging, it could indicate illness, and your physician should be consulted promptly. It is not uncommon to notice the fontanel pulsating with each heartbeat. This is quite normal.

ROUTINE CARE

Bath

Your baby should be bathed every few days. A daily bath is unnecessary, since young babies generally do not have many opportunities for getting dirty. You'll want to wash your baby's face and bottom frequently, however.

For the first one to three weeks, until his cord falls off, sponge bathe your baby only. Place him naked on a nice soft towel. Have two additional towels, two bowls of warm water, baby soap, baby shampoo, a washcloth, and his change of clothes nearby.

Cover half of your baby with a towel to prevent chilling. First wash his face with an unsoaped washcloth. Then gently wash the exposed half of his body with a soapy washcloth (or hand), rinse off, and dry. Alternate the bowls of water, using one for the soapy cloth and the other for rinsing. Next reverse the covered and exposed halves and wash, rinse, and dry again. You can shampoo your baby's hair either first or last depending on how well he likes it.

Once the cord falls off, you can bathe your baby in either a dish tub, a baby bathtub, or a sink. If you bathe him in a sink, watch that he doesn't grab the faucet and turn on the hot water or bump his head on the faucets. Carefully position the tub at a height that does not strain your back as you bathe your baby. Don't bend over; put the tub on a high surface instead. Some parents enjoy taking the baby into the bathtub with them, and this feels especially secure to your baby. Remember that a comfortable water temperature for you may be too hot for your baby. Here are some guidelines to follow when you bathe your baby:

√ Never leave your baby unattended in any bathtub, not even for a second.

√ Always check the water temperature before immersing your baby. Make sure it's not too hot or too cold. Your baby will like cooler bathwater than you do.

√ The room should be warm (about 75°F).

√ Remove any jewelry that might scratch the baby.

√ A towel on the bottom of the tub will keep the baby from slipping.

√ Hold onto your baby firmly, so he feels secure in the water.

√ Try to keep bath time calm and pleasant.

√ Have a towel handy so you can wrap your baby in it immediately after he leaves the water.

√ Use a mild baby soap and tear-free shampoo.

√ Scrub his scalp with a soft brush to avoid cradle cap (scaly skin) and rinse well.

√ Be sure to clean and rinse all his folds and creases.

√ Do not probe any of the baby's orifices in an attempt to clean them. A wet washcloth is sufficient for the eyes. Wash only the outer ear with the washcloth; leave the wax in the ear canal alone. Also do not unnecessarily probe your baby's nose.

√ Bath time provides dads with an excellent opportunity to have some wonderful skin-to-skin contact with baby.

√ It is not good for your baby's skin to goop him up with oils or lotions after his bath. If you and the baby enjoy the sensual aspect of rubbing him with a good cream, it probably won't hurt. But do refrain from oiling his hair, as this has no benefit and can cause cradle cap.

It is a good idea to bathe your baby before a feeding so you can feed him afterward and let him fall asleep. Feeding prior to the bath may result in a bowel movement in the water. A very hungry baby, however, will probably not be happy in the bathtub, either.

Some babies enjoy their bath from the beginning, but for others it is an acquired joy. Your calm, confident handling will help the baby who initially dislikes the bath. Bathe this type of baby less frequently until he enjoys it more. Try other methods of bathing; taking him into the tub with you can be very pleasant for both of you and may be the most acceptable form of bathing to a fearful baby.

As babies grow older and gain more control of their bodies, it is unusual to find a baby who does not enjoy the bath. Most kick and splash with wild abandon. You might want to wear an apron once kicking becomes an integral part of the bath-time ritual.

Remember that bath time may be officially a cleaning process, but the skin-to-skin contact, the exploration of his own body and its movements, and your social interaction are all equally important components of your baby's bath.

Dressing

Dress your baby with the same gentle touch you use whenever you handle him. Your baby's startle reflex is strongest in the early weeks, making it especially important to move him slowly and hold him firmly, so he doesn't feel insecure and frightened.

Have the baby's change of clothes handy, so you won't be tempted to leave him unattended on the changing table. If you're in no hurry and the temperature is warm enough, you can give your baby an air bath. A little time without clothes is a special treat to some babies, and is good for their usually-moist bottoms.

Stretch out the collars of shirts before putting them on, so they'll go over his head more easily. Be sure there are no loose strings in the feet of your baby's stretch suits to bind his toes and cut off circulation.

Do not overdress your baby, because babies can easily become overheated. New babies do have less capacity for keeping warm than adults, so don't go to the other extreme, either. While your baby is a newborn, it is a good idea to keep your house at least 68°F to 70°F and avoid placing the baby in a draft. Newborns are usually wrapped in a receiving blanket over their clothing. If it's a sweltering summer day, however, you can forego that custom.

DISPOSABLE DIAPER

Diapering Your Baby

Diapering a baby is a dreaded aspect of baby care for many prospective parents, but it is not really an unpleasant chore. Here are some guidelines to help you develop your diapering skills.

Disposable Diapers: A common mistake is putting on disposable diapers too loosely. Pull the diaper around the

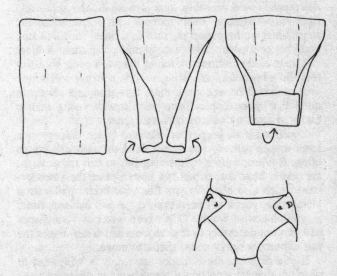

FOLDING AND PINNING A CLOTH DIAPER

legs and attach the tapes snugly to prevent leaking and to keep his clothes dry.

Cloth Diapers: Put cloth diapers on snugly, too, being very sure that the pins are fastened securely. As you put the pin into the diaper, hold your fingers behind the part of the diaper to be pinned. If you should miss, you'll hit your finger instead of the baby. If your baby screams as if in great pain, do check his diaper pins. Occasionally one may open and stick him. Point the diaper pin toward the hip, so if a pin does open it will scratch his side rather than pierce an organ. To keep your diaper pins sharp, stick them into a bar of soap, and store them there between uses.

Although plastic pants are often needed with cloth diapers, try to leave them off when you can. The plastic holds moisture against the baby's skin and makes him more prone to diaper rash. Without plastic pants on, you are more apt to notice when he is wet and to change him more often.

How to Wash Cloth Diapers: The idea of washing diapers may intimidate you, but remember you can just wash them like any other clothes, using a low sudsing detergent. You'll probably want to wash diapers separately from other laundry. Most parents add a few additional steps when washing diapers, such as a rinse, soak and spin cycle before washing, and a second rinse cycle after washing.

You can add chlorine bleach to the wash cycle to disinfect and whiten diapers. Using a fabric softener will soften your diapers but may make them less absorbent. Keep in mind that many babies have very sensitive skin that is easily irritated by various laundry agents.

You'll want to keep your wet and soiled diapers in a large diaper pail, so you won't need to wash diapers so often. Buy one with a tight-fitting lid, to contain unpleasant odors. Most diaper pail lids have a place for a deodorizer, which also helps. If you line your diaper pail with a plastic bag, you won't need to rinse the pail out each time, as you otherwise would. Don't keep water in your diaper pail; it's not necessary to soak diapers and water makes the pail extremely heavy and difficult to move.

If you're not using a diaper service, you will want to rinse out diapers with bowel movements in the toilet. Just dunk the diaper and slosh it up and down as you flush (hold on tight!), then wring it and place it in the diaper pail.

A minor yet annoying problem many mothers complain about is the lingering odor on their hands left from rinsing out diapers. Washing with soap just doesn't get it all out. The only product I know that does remove the odor is a liquid cleaner, L.O.C. by Amway.

Changing Wet Diapers: Changing your baby's diaper frequently is your best insurance against diaper rash. It is not necessary to wash the baby's bottom when changing a diaper that is only wet. Do not use baby powder, as it is not beneficial and the baby may inhale some of it. If he seems to be getting a diaper rash, apply either Desitin, zinc oxide, or A&D Ointment. Be sure to air dry his bottom well before applying ointment.

Once your baby is not having bowel movements during the night, you needn't awaken him for nighttime diaper changes. Use a double cloth diaper, a disposable diaper pad, or a nighttime disposable diaper at bedtime. You can put a coating of Vaseline, Desitin, A&D, or another waterproof ointment on his bottom before he goes to sleep at night to keep urine away from his skin. If your baby has a diaper rash, however, you will find that it clears up faster if you awaken him for nighttime diaper changes for a few days.

Changing Soiled Diapers: Baby wipes are handy, especially when away from home, but a warm wet washcloth works just as well and may be less irritating to your baby's skin. I know one woman who kept a stack of washcloths and warm water in a thermos with a pump on the changing table. That way, if she was surprised by the condition of her baby's diaper, she was prepared.

ELIMINATION

Many new parents focus undue attention on their baby's bowel movements, usually because of their unfamiliarity with normal infant elimination patterns.

Breast-fed Babies

Breast-fed babies pass stools very frequently during the first several weeks. The infant may stool with each feeding, or have eight or more bowel movements in a day. In fact, infrequent stooling in a breast-fed baby under one month suggests inadequate milk intake. The normal, loose stools of a young breast-fed infant may resemble diarrhea. The typical stool will be somewhat liquid, yellowish in color, and contain small soft curds. A mother once described her breast-fed baby's stool as looking like mustard and cottage cheese. The color can vary and may be greenish at times. Don't worry, this is normal. Breast-fed babies' stools have very little odor, and the mild odor they do have is not at all offensive.

Many breast-fed babies continue the frequent stooling pattern, while others gradually pass stools at less frequent intervals. In fact, it is not uncommon for a breast-fed baby several months old to pass only one stool every few days. This is not constipation. True "constipation" is very rare among breast-fed infants. Your baby may strain and grunt when passing a soft stool because of his poor ability to control the muscles he uses to push out the bowel movement. I often ask parents to imagine trying to pass a bowel movement while lying flat on their backs. We'd all grunt and strain if we couldn't plant our feet firmly on the ground!

Bottle-fed Babies

A bottle-fed baby will typically stool once or twice a day and the stools, while soft, are more formed and darker than those of a breast-fed baby. Iron-enriched formula may give the stools a greenish color.

Abnormal Stools

Diarrhea is defined as an increase in the number and water content of bowel movements over the baby's normal pattern. Diarrhea stools are very loose and often leave a ring of water on the diaper. Young infants with diarrhea need to be monitored very carefully since serious dehydration can occur rapidly. Diarrhea can be due to an intestinal infection, formula intolerance, or a variety of other causes. (See "Illnesses and Disorders," page 340.)

Many parents inaccurately define constipation as decreased frequency of stooling. If a day passes without their baby having a bowel movement, they believe he is constipated. This is not necessarily so. Constipated bowel movements are hard and dry and passed with difficulty. The consistency of the stool is more important than the frequency in determining constipation. Some babies pass a normal stool only once every several days. (See "Illnesses and Disorders," page 330.)

BURPING YOUR BABY

Whether you breast or bottle-feed, you will want to burp your baby during and after each feeding. Most babies swallow some air during feedings, and a bubble of air in his stomach can make a baby feel full too soon, cause him to spit up milk when the bubble is brought up, or make him uncomfortable after eating. Some babies need to be burped several times during a feeding, while others burp with ease.

Breast-fed babies should be burped between the first and second breast. This also helps awaken the baby to take the other side. Bottle-fed infants should be burped after every couple of ounces. There are several ways to burp your baby:

Sitting. Sit the baby up on your lap, with your hand cupped under his chin to support his head. Lean him slightly forward and gently pat or rub his back as described.

Shoulder. Prop the baby upright against you, with his head resting on your shoulder. Gently rub or pat his back as described.

Lap. Lay the baby across your lap face down, with his head turned to one side. Gently pat or rub his back.

You'll want to keep a diaper in front of your baby's face, in case he spits up some milk when he burps. If one of these methods hasn't worked after several minutes, you needn't keep trying. Babies don't always need to burp. If your baby acts fussy during or after a feeding, however, do try burping him again.

NORMAL NEWBORN BEHAVIORS

New parents often have questions about a variety of newborn behaviors that occur quite normally, including hiccups, sneezes, and startles.

For some reason, newborns develop hiccups often. If you think about it, you probably can recall your baby having hiccups while still in the uterus. It felt like he was kicking you rhythmically, once every second. Many parents will offer glucose water or a feeding to try to stop their baby's hiccups. There's certainly no harm in doing so, but there's no need to either. Although it bothers us to have hiccups or to watch someone else hiccupping, young infants don't seem to mind at all.

Newborns commonly sneeze as a reflex action to clear dust, milk, or dried mucus from their noses. Parents usually assume a sneeze means their baby is getting a cold. This is seldom true, unless a runny nose or other symptoms are also present. (See Cold, "Common Illnesses and Disorders," page 328.) Since newborns breathe through their noses and not their mouths, nature has provided a reflex to keep the passages clear.

A sudden movement or loud noise will cause a baby to experience a startle reflex, known as the Moro reflex. If the baby is lying on his back when startled, he will fling his arms outward and flare his fingers, then bring his arms toward his body and cry. It is also not uncommon for a newborn who is undressed and lying on his back to have fine, symmetrical tremors of his extremities and quivers of his chin, lasting a few seconds. These movements are normal. On the other hand, coarse jerking of one arm and leg or the whole body might signal a medical problem and should be reported to your pediatrician.

Observant parents often notice their newborn's irregular breathing pattern and wonder if it is normal. Young babies tend to have periodic breathing, several seconds of short shallow breaths, followed by several seconds of not breathing, during which their color remains just fine. This is perfectly normal.

Regardless of the feeding method, young infants commonly spit up a small amount after eating. The circular muscle between the esophagus and the stomach tends to be lax in early infancy, allowing stomach contents to come back up. About a teaspoon of milk may roll out of the baby's mouth, often after he has just been fed and placed down in a horizontal position. Burping the baby both during and after feedings will help minimize spitting. Spitting up, or regurgitation, is different from true vomiting, which is usually a large amount expelled forcefully. (See pages 303 and 390.) Mild spitting is almost universal, but a few babies with severe spitting will need medical attention to prevent growth problems or other medical concerns. (See page 353.)

CRADLE CAP, PRICKLY HEAT, AND NEONATAL ACNE

A newborn's skin is a frequent cause of parental concern, yet most newborn rashes have little significance. Many babies will have dirty-appearing, crusty or oily patches on their scalp, known as cradle cap. Simply washing the scalp daily with soap and water will clear up most cases of cradle cap. Regularly applying oil to the hair and scalp will clog the baby's pores and make the condition worse. You can apply oil, however, just before shampooing in order to loosen the patches and brush them out with a soft baby brush or fine-toothed comb. For persistent cases of cradle cap, your pediatrician can prescribe a cream, and you can use a mild dandruff shampoo. Cradle cap seldom lasts beyond the first few months.

Many young infants will develop prickly heat in hot weather, especially if they are overdressed. The rash looks like tiny pink raised bumps on a red base; sometimes the teeny pimplelike bumps contain a clear fluid. Prickly heat tends to be distributed around the neck, the upper chest and back, along the scalp line, around the ears, and on the scalp. It results from sweat retained in the young infant's immature pores. The rash resolves on its own, although your baby may be more comfortable after a cool bath and if dressed in light, loose-fitting clothing.

In the first few weeks of life, a few infants will develop an oily, pimply facial rash that resembles acne, and is known as neonatal acne. No treatment is necessary apart from gentle washing of the face with a mild soap. It usually resolves in a few weeks. Adolescent acne treatments should NEVER be used for this type of acne. It is self-limiting, resolves quickly, and never scars.

TAKING BABY OUT

Opinions on the subject of when you can safely first take your newborn out vary considerably. Your grandmother may have warned you to keep him home for six weeks, while your neighbor took her three-day-old baby to the shopping mall.

I would advise neither extreme; just use common sense. You should limit the number of people who handle your new baby, but you don't need to be overprotective. Visiting with a few relatives and friends is fine. Taking your newborn out to visit Grandmother is sensible, but leaving him in the bowling alley nursery or taking him camping would be stressful and foolish. Don't let anyone who has a cold or other illness or cold sore on their face hold or kiss your new baby. I've always felt it was considerate of visitors to wash their hands before handling a newborn.

Even new babies enjoy movement and fresh air, so as long as the weather is nice, don't hesitate to get out for short walks. When you take your newborn out, dress him appropriately. If it's winter, he needs to be protected from the cold. Warm the car first and have him dressed in at least a stretch suit, receiving blanket, and snow suit. Be sure his head, hands, and feet are well covered. If it's summer, shield him from the heat and avoid direct sunlight, since babies burn very easily. Don't overdress him; booties aren't necessary. You may need to cover him with a light blanket to keep the sun off him. Put a hat on him and use sunscreen with SPF 15 if he must be in direct sunlight. My own first child received a blistering sunburn when I foolishly took him to the beach unprotected at a year of age.

Many parents inquire about traveling long distances to introduce their new baby to other family members. Such visits can provide important support for new parents who are often separated by many miles from their own parents. Again, let common sense prevail. If the baby is healthy and you keep him comfortable, travel usually poses no problems. Breastfed babies are especially easy travelers, since their food source is readily available regardless of location. If you are bottle-feeding, you can bring ready-to-feed formula or use bottled water to avoid the possibility that your baby may not respond well to the local water. Single-feed, ready-to-use formula is convenient for travel, although expensive.

When traveling by plane, nurse or give the baby a bottle or pacifier during takeoff and landing to prevent uncomfortable changes in middle-ear pressure.

HOW BABIES SLEEP

Parents often assume that infant sleep is the same process as adult sleep only in a smaller package. This underlying misconception leads to unnecessary problems for everyone. Infant sleep is, in fact, far different from adult sleep. It is a mystery how the phrase "sleep like a baby" ever came to mean a long, sound, peaceful sleep. Any parent can tell you that adults are far better sleepers than babies. Why shouldn't we be? Over time, our sleep patterns have developed and stabilized. And we have learned how to fall asleep.

You will undoubtedly be quizzed about your baby's sleep habits and made to feel like an inadequate parent if your baby isn't sleeping through the night. Since it is unlikely that your baby will be sleeping through the night in the early months (by the way, this usually refers to sleeping from 12 A.M. to 5 A.M.), you need to know the facts about normal infant sleeping.

Research indicates that sleep patterns are biologically determined; you can't "teach" your baby to sleep differently. Sleep patterns vary from one baby to another. A young baby sleeps exactly as much as he needs to. He cannot keep himself awake or put himself to sleep at will. Even if his sleep pattern is not what you expected, it is right for him.

An average newborn sleeps sixteen hours out of twenty-four. Some babies, however, may sleep as many as twenty or as few as twelve. Generally newborns will sleep for two to four hours at a time.

Waking up during the night is normal for babies. It is usual for an infant to awaken one, two, or three times a night. By the age of a year, one third to one quarter of babies are still waking up during the night. (Yours isn't the only one!) Many babies awake during the night simply because they need human contact. As babies grow older, it is natural for them to be awake more. If they sleep a great deal during the day, you can expect them to be awake more at night.

Adding solid foods to a baby's diet does not affect the length of time a baby sleeps at night. Although parents may claim that solids help, there is no evidence to confirm that they really do.

You will more cheerfully accept your baby's greater wakefulness if you don't feel that you need to accomplish all your tasks when the baby is asleep. Parents learn to perform most activities while enjoying the company of their baby. It is also a good idea for you to nap when the baby naps.

Helping Your Baby Sleep

Although you can't determine your baby's sleep needs or patterns, there are things you can do to help a baby who has difficulty falling or staying asleep.

Make it clear to the baby when it is day and when it's night, the time for the longest stretch of sleep. The distinction may be registered more clearly if you keep the baby in light all day, even during nap time. By associating darkness with night, the baby's "internal clock" is set more accurately, leading to a rhythm of more day wakefulness and more nocturnal sleeping. It is not necessary to be absolutely silent when your baby is asleep. Babies can learn to tune out noise.

Some babies sleep very little during the day and less than their parents wish at night simply because it is their nature. Other babies sleep poorly, especially at night, because like any mammal, they are lonely when they sleep alone. Parents often overlook their baby's very real and legitimate need for human contact.

Few parents in our society feel they should sleep with their babies. Sleeping with our babies is a practice that is out of vogue and usually discouraged by our own parents, pediatricians, or friends. Parents often discover bringing the baby into bed with them out of desperation. The baby cries on and off all night; the parents doubt the baby can be hungry so often; no one gets adequate sleep; and everyone is cranky. The mother wonders if she has enough breast milk, or if cereal should be added to the last bottle in the evening. Finally, the parents bring the baby into their bed. The baby, feeling safe and secure, goes promptly to sleep. The parents are assured about their baby's wellbeing and find snuggling their infant to sleep to be an endearing experience. Soon it is an established bedtime practice and everyone is sleeping better.

Some families are sold on the "family bed" and expound it like a newfound religion. Some families wouldn't dream of having one. Others keep a closet family bed and never share their secret with their friends. Although they avoid criticism by maintaining secrecy, many parents are left feeling like they are doing something wrong and must be the only ones who bring their baby into bed at night.

Babies need closeness. It is natural for babies to sleep better when close to another person. There is nothing wrong with this practice if it works for you. If your baby does not sleep well alone, but sleeps contentedly with you, you do not have a spoiled, manipulative baby. You have an emotionally healthy baby who loves you and feels safe with you.

Sandy Jones, in her book, *Crying Baby, Sleepless Nights*, writes, "The baby is not mature enough yet to console himself with the concepts of 'safe bedroom,' or 'safe crib,' because for him safety is a body feeling that comes from the sense of warmth and enfoldment of an adult." If your baby is very fussy or has difficulty sleeping, you will want to read this book.

If the idea of bringing your baby into bed with you is not comfortable for you or your partner, or if you feel you need additional strategies for getting your wakeful baby to sleep, here's a collection of ideas that have worked for others. Perhaps some will help you, too.

Most babies respond well to singing. The quality of your voice has no relationship to the comfort it provides. Time-tested lullabies are effective. Simple monotonous songs like "ABC," "Twinkle, Twinkle, Little Star," and "Old MacDonald" are also good bets.

Rocking is another age-old method of putting a baby to sleep. If your baby is very fussy and restless, he'll probably squirm and cry, resisting your efforts as you sit down to rock. Stick with it a little longer, perhaps sing too, and see if the motion affects him. You might have to stand and sway a little while until he's calmer, then return to the rocker and try again.

Walking your baby may be the most reliable (and one of the most tiring) ways to put a baby to sleep. Walk up and down a room or hall at an even pace, singing or humming as you walk. It will be less tiring to walk your baby in a baby front pack. You can take shifts and share the walking with your partner or someone else. On the other hand, some babies like to be bounced or jiggled to sleep. A baby carriage with springs works well for this. Other babies will drift off if you simply pat them on the back once they are in the crib.

Strangely enough, the sound of a vacuum cleaner has lulled many fussy babies to sleep. You can either vacuum with the baby in the front pack (a sure bet), or put the baby in his crib and turn on the vacuum in the hall; or record the sound of the vacuum and play it in his room. You can buy recordings of the human heartbeat or a Crib Cuddle (see Chapter 3, page 67), which has a recorded heartbeat in it. Very young babies especially are soothed by the sound of the heart.

Some parents purchase a lamb skin for their infants and always put him to sleep on it. The familiar association of the feel and smell of the lamb skin may help your baby sleep even when you're away from home.

Since awareness of your absence may be the source of your baby's waking, place one of your unlaundered nightgowns in bed with him near his face, allowing him to smell your very familiar scent.

If your baby is breast-fed, always offer the breast as a first effort for putting your baby to sleep even if he last nursed ten minutes ago! Nursing is usually your most effective tool. If your baby is bottle-fed, and you are sure he's full, try giving him a pacifier as you rock him. The added comfort of sucking will sometimes make the difference. For a very young baby, a small, soft pacifier is most likely to be accepted.

If all else fails, it's a rare baby who can resist a drive and it's a rare parent who can't tell stories about long drives in the night to get a devout nonsleeper to nod off. More than once, I have met a sheepish couple in the emergency room at night whose "unconsolable" infant finally fell asleep in the car on the way to the hospital.

When Your Baby Doesn't Sleep

What about those rare instances when your baby wakes up during the night and just doesn't fall back to sleep?

First, ask yourself if you offered too much stimulation when you fed him. Did you turn on the light, change his diaper, talk to him, and otherwise encourage wakefulness?

Your attitude will make a great deal of difference. Try and put this sleepless night in perspective. This is a brief period in your life; you will be caring for an infant for just the tiniest flash in relation to your whole life. Look at it from his point of view. He hasn't planned to ruin your night; he simply cannot get himself back to sleep, and he may not be any happier about it than you are.

Since you're up, you might as well enjoy his company during this quiet, peaceful time. You can make yourself some noncaffeinated tea, turn on the TV or radio if you like, remind yourself how brief this time in your life is, and vow to nap tomorrow.

If your baby's sleeplessness is accompanied by crying and he seems to be in distress, suspect a physical cause such as an ear infection or other medical problem requiring attention.

The Older Baby

Although babies usually begin to sleep more as they mature, nocturnal waking still occurs in many babies between six months and one year (and even older). From around the age of nine months, an infant is capable of keeping himself awake. From that point on, a variety of causes including overstimulation or his unhappiness at being away from you may give him difficulty falling asleep.

If your baby goes from a stimulating environment straight to bed, he may be unable to relax enough to fall asleep. Since your baby is now more sensitive to his environment, even small changes may be enough to disturb his sleep. Redecorating his room, a move, or even a vacation could temporarily cause trouble.

Help your baby unwind before you put him into bed. Sandwich a "calming period" between playtime and bedtime. Some parents use a quiet bath or a peaceful period with one parent in a quiet room. As the child gets older, a bedtime story serves this purpose well.

Then, instead of just putting your baby right into bed, incorporate some sort of consistent routine that the baby can associate with bedtime. This helps him accept the fact that bedtime is here. He will probably become attached to his "routine," so be sure to teach it to anyone else who puts him to bed. An example of bedtime routine might be: 1) a bath or quiet playtime, 2) changing into pajamas, 3) closing the shades in his room, 4) going downstairs to get a good-night kiss from the rest of the family, 5) getting the teddy bear or favorite stuffed toy, and 6) being kissed, laid down, and covered.

Keep a small night-light on and leave the door open a little so the baby doesn't feel as cut off from you. Perform the bedtime routine the same way each evening (as much as possible), including the calming period. This will help your baby unwind and relax in preparation for bedtime. Encourage the use of comforting behaviors or objects such as a stuffed animal, special blanket, or thumb sucking. These are your baby's tools for calming himself and he can use them when you're not there to do the comforting. Babies who use self-comforting behaviors are usually better at putting themselves to sleep.

The most common cause for bedtime difficulties at this age is your baby's reluctance to be separated from you, commonly referred to as separation anxiety. The bedtime ritual is a help because it provides a more gradual separation from you. Your leaving may still be upsetting to him and he may cry and want you to come back. Since the last thing you want to do is compound his separation anxiety, never leave him to cry alone. On the other hand, you want him to accept his bedtime and learn to fall asleep on his own, so don't take him back out of bed either. Simply come to him when he cries, talk to him in a comforting way, pat him on the back, say good-night again, and leave.

In order to feel safe enough to fall asleep he needs to learn that you have not vanished, but are just in another room. You may need to make several visits (no longer than a few minutes each) until he feels secure about being away from you. Eventually he will understand that you have not abandoned him, but you are not going to remove him from his crib either. After a while, your voice from another room alone may suffice. If you follow the (1) don't leave him crying alone, (2) briefly visit and reassure, (3) but don't take him out of bed method, you will provide the psychological safety your child needs for comfortable bedtimes.

In addition to having trouble falling asleep, older babies frequently experience night waking. If your baby is waking during the night, try to make the bedtime routine more pleasant and loving; pick him up when he cries during the day and help him to feel loved and secure; cover any diaper rash with petroleum jelly or Desitin so night wetting won't sting; make sure he's not too hot or too cold; and try to keep his sleeping area quiet. If he does wake and cry, ignoring him will only fuel his worst fear—that you have deserted him. Try to calm and reassure him without picking him up and then tuck him in again as described earlier. Play peek-a-boo with your baby during the day to reinforce the concept that something or someone that is out of sight still exists.

Many parents have lived through a period of night waking and you will survive it, too. Remember, though, that building his feeling of trust in you is the way to prevent night waking. This period is temporary and is indicative of his developmental phase, not a permanent behavior. Work with your baby and his needs to lay the foundation for a lifelong pattern of easy sleep.

COLIC

If your baby has a regular "fussy period," usually starting around supper time and lasting several hours, and if he screams like he's in pain, often pulling up his legs, he probably has been labeled as "colicky." The questions most parents ask after this diagnosis are: "What is colic?" and "What can I do about it?"

Colic is a fairly vague and undefined condition even among pediatricians. Colic broadly refers to unexplained, excessive crying in an otherwise healthy baby. Colic usually begins after an initial "honeymoon" period of two to three weeks. It seldom lasts longer than three months. Although the cause of colic has not been proven, among those believed responsible are:

√ a very sensitive nervous system
√ evening reaction to a full day's stimulation
√ a neurologic or digestive system that is overly sensitive to environmental stimulation
√ overactive muscular movements in the colon
√ difficulty moving food downward through the intestines
√ gas trapped in the lower loops of the bowel
√ sensitivity to infant formula or infant vitamin and iron drops
√ sensitivity to certain foods in the breast-feeding mother's diet
√ solid foods introduced inappropriately early

Although not all colicky babies suffer from digestive disorders, colic is frequently attributed to "gas," or other intestinal causes. It may be hard to pinpoint the exact cause of your baby's excessive crying, but one thing I would firmly assert is that colic is NOT caused by a nervous mother. Unfortunately, in the past, doctors often blamed "nervous mothers" for colic, yet there is no basis at all for this accusation. I sadly recall a patient who described to me her then nine-year-old daughter's severe colicky behavior as an infant. This woman clearly suffered lingering emotional pain as a result of her pediatrician's claim that her "nervousness" had caused the baby's symptoms. I'll always wonder if her traumatic, unnecessary feelings of inadequacy contributed to her decision not to have more children. In fact, subsequent babies are as likely to have colic as firstborn; breast-fed infants are affected as often as bottle-fed; and boys are involved as frequently as girls. The myth that a nervous mother causes colic in her infant originated when doctors observed the nervous, even frazzled state of mothers who brought colicky babies into their offices. If any of these doctors had been living with colicky babies, they too would have been nervous and frazzled.

If your baby seems to have colic, consult your doctor to rule out any medical condition that may need treatment. Colic should not be diagnosed over the telephone. It should be considered only after a thorough exam has confirmed that your baby is normal and thriving. Your doctor will probably not prescribe medication for colic, but will offer you measures to help you cope with colic until it disappears, at around the age of three months.

While you are trying to survive your baby's colic, lean on the following strategies and remedies.

Never leave the baby to cry alone in his pain. You cannot always console him during a colic attack, but he needs your presence and reassurance. The exception to this rule would be a time when you felt you were losing control due to your frustration over your baby's crying. It is preferable to leave your baby alone briefly than to risk hurting him.

Try the "colic hold." Place the baby facedown on your forearm. His face should be near your palm, his abdomen against your forearm, and his legs draped over either side of your elbow. Your other arm can be used to stabilize or pat him. Walking with the baby this way seems to offer relief from abdominal discomfort. Some babies receive the same type of relief from being held with their abdomen against your shoulder. You can also roll up a cloth diaper

COLIC HOLD

and put it under the baby's tummy when he's lying down, so that he has something to push against when he gets a gas cramp.

Place a baby-sized hot-water bottle against the baby's tummy. Don't get it too hot, though.

Use the strategies offered for getting your baby to sleep, like walking, rocking, singing, the vacuum, and so on.

Consider whether your baby might be hungry. Try feeding him on demand instead of following a schedule. Remember, he needs more milk as he gets bigger. When you do feed him, offer smaller, more frequent feedings instead of fewer regular-sized feedings. Burp him before, during and after feedings, especially if he is a "gulper." Try holding the baby in an upright position for thirty minutes after each feeding. In those instances when you are sure your baby is not hungry, you might offer him the emptiest breast or a pacifier to suck on.

If you have a family history of allergies, consider the possibility of a cow's milk allergy, either to his formula or cow's milk you are drinking if you are breast-feeding.

Don't overstimulate your baby; handle a colicky baby in an especially calm, gentle fashion. Don't bounce or jostle him unnecessarily. Some babies are happier when wrapped tightly; others hate it. Determine which is better for your baby. Change your usual evening routine. Perhaps an evening stroller ride or warm bath will interrupt a crying cycle.

Remember, despite all the crying, a colicky baby is a completely healthy baby. His parents may be harried, but the baby still thrives! In fact, some pediatricians believe there is a link between babies with colic and higher intelligence. Take one day at a time. Colic does end.

Keep in mind that some of these suggestions may work well for your baby and others won't. Stop anything that seems to make him less happy and use the methods that seem to bring relief.

It is increasingly recognized that various foods in the diet of breastfeeding mothers can cause allergic or sensitivity reactions with gastrointestinal symptoms in their nursing infants. Clear documentation exists for some of these offenders. In other instances, anecdotal reports by mothers incriminate various substances. If your baby is not colicky, you certainly should not eliminate anything from your diet. And, if your baby has colic, don't eliminate all these substances at once. If he gets better, you won't have any idea which substance was the offender and what you can safely add back to your diet. Suspect first those foods that you eat every day.

The most common cause of digestive problems in a breast-fed baby is an allergic reaction to cow's milk in the mother's diet, especially milk intakes greater than sixteen ounces per day. Try cutting out milk and dairy products for a week. If this works, add back yogurt and cheese to see if your baby can tolerate that much dairy. You need to experiment a little with his tolerance level.

Other common allergens in the maternal diet are peanut butter, fish, eggs, and berries.

Gas-producing vegetables and an excess of fruit sometimes cause uncomfortable gas in the breast-fed baby. Carbonated beverages and an excess of caffeine have been implicated in some cases.

If your baby is bottle fed, changing formula can sometimes be the answer. Discuss this with your doctor first. Don't rush to soy formula, however, as soy is also a common allergen. A predigested formula, Nutramigen, has been shown to relieve colic symptoms in many formula-fed babies. Although it is more expensive than standard formulas, most parents of a colicky baby find the extra expense well worth it.

Parents of a colicky baby often ask their pediatrician whether a drug can be prescribed to relieve their infant's symptoms. I want to stress that the precise cause of colic is unknown, and numerous causes probably exist. There is no single drug that "cures" colic the way penicillin cures strep throat. My own bias is that drugs are overprescribed in the management of colic, probably because it is easier to write a prescription than to patiently listen to a distraught parent and offer suggestions for coping.

The drugs often prescribed for colic are medications that relieve spasm of the intestinal muscles and/or sedatives. The idea of sedating a bright-eyed, responsive infant has always bothered me. I'd almost rather sedate the parents! Drugs that relieve muscle spasm in the gastrointestinal tract might work, provided the baby's colic is indeed caused by disturbed intestinal activity, rather than one of the other suspected causes. Overdosage with either type of drug can pose a grave danger in a young infant. Don't insist on a prescription drug for your baby's colic and don't use a medication unless your pediatrician has a valid reason for expecting it to work. Believe me, if there was a miracle drug for infantile colic, we'd all be using it!

Having a colicky baby can put a real damper on new-parent euphoria. There are few experiences as distressing to a parent as being unable to comfort their crying baby. Try every idea you can come up with. Stick with your baby and at least hold him through this uncomfortable period, and most of all keep reminding yourself that colic is brief and self-limiting. See Basic Parent Care (page 167) to help you through this trying period.

SPOILING YOUR BABY

You can't.

What does spoiling your baby mean? You'll hear that giving your baby what he wants will spoil him. In fact, "spoiled" is how people refer to children they don't like.

It is extremely important to realize there is no difference between an infant's needs and his wants. Not only will you not spoil your baby by loving him and giving him what he wants—but it is your job as a parent to do just that. Giving your baby what he wants—almost always you—teaches your baby to trust. When he has a need and it is satisfied, he learns that the world is a safe place and that he is loved. By trusting, he begins to learn to communicate.

When your baby wants to be held, what happens if you follow the oft-heard intrusive advice, "Show him who's boss" and leave him to cry? His need is unfulfilled; he feels abandoned and frightened and begins to develop either mistrust, or worse yet, hopelessness. Was this really your goal?

Unfulfilled needs do not go away; they remain. Needs go away only when they are fulfilled. Think of hunger. When you are hungry, do you get that feeling to go away by ignoring it or by satisfying it? Emotional needs are just as legitimate and urgent.

Human development depends on physical and social contact. Your baby's instincts make him cry out for it; lots of holding and affection are essential to his survival. Do not make the mistake of thinking that a "good baby" is undemanding and that a demanding baby is "bad." A demanding baby is a healthy baby.

Follow your instincts and hold, hug, talk, and attend to your baby without limits. You CAN'T overdo it. If you are excessively affectionate, you'll end up with a responsive, secure, happy baby who knows he is loved and will love in return. Turn a deaf ear to anyone who advises you to let your baby cry. There is no reason to ever leave your baby to cry. Perhaps the worst prediction you'll hear is that if you continually respond to your baby, he will cry even more and that he'll be "clingy." Both statements are completely wrong. Studies show that babies who were picked up as soon as they began to cry, cried less often and for shorter periods than babies whose parents did not respond quickly. Crying did not become as common a behavior for babies whose parents responded promptly.

The surest way to produce an independent child is to satisfy his dependency needs during infancy. Children whose needs are met are free to put their energies into healthy growth and development, and can become truly independent.

Don't be intimidated by other people's insecurities and fears of a baby controlling them. A baby can't control you. All he can do is ask for what he needs. Listen to your baby, not your neighbors. See your baby's cry not as a challenge to a power struggle, but as an opportunity to teach your baby that he is loved and that he can count on you.

Remember, no one gets through life without learning that "we don't always get what we want." Life teaches this to every child soon enough. You don't need to go out of your way to make it his first lesson.

CHOOSING A BABYSITTER

Every couple differs in their need to go out together after the birth of their baby. Some couples wouldn't think of going anywhere for many months without taking their infant along. Others feel the need to have a few hours alone together within several weeks of adding the new family member. In my own case, my husband was stationed at sea for six months before our first child was born, making little communication possible during our countdown to parenthood. We had only six days of reunion before Peter was born and had scarcely become reacquainted before we turned our full attention to the new baby. About six weeks later, an intuitive older couple who we admired offered to babysit one evening, insisting that Larry and I go to dinner alone. It was one of the nicest things anyone did for us during that difficult adjustment period.

Newborns are so portable that you may find little need for a babysitter at first. Eventually everyone, however, encounters some occasions when they need to leave their baby with another caretaker for several hours. You will want to give careful thought to the selection of the person to whom you entrust your infant's care. Full-time childcare options for working parents are discussed in Chapter 16, while considerations for occasional babysitters are addressed here.

Ideally, if your extended family lives nearby, you may feel most comfortable leaving your baby with a trusted family member: your mother, mother-in-law, sister, or other relative who is already familiar with your baby and who has child-care experience. Don't assume your relative is eager to babysit on a regular basis, however, and try not to overuse their services. Many new grandparents are thrilled to babysit, but others may be uncomfortable around young infants or have busy schedules of their own that make frequent babysitting an imposition. Remember, they already raised you!

If you are a working parent and have day-care arrangements worked out, you might ask your day-care mother if she would be interested in evening babysitting. Most full-time day-care mothers, however, prefer to keep their evenings free for their own family's needs.

You may have a neighbor or friend who you already know and trust and could ask to babysit, either for pay or in exchange for watching her own children sometime. Many parents find a neighborhood babysitting co-op to be a very effective way of providing competent, low-cost babysitting.

Your church, community center, or other organization may be a source of potential babysitters. Or, if you are socially isolated and without word-of-mouth referrals, you might try contacting a formal babysitting service. Avoid choosing your child's babysitters from ads at the laundromat or supermarket, unless you insist on several references.

Most of us probably have used teenage babysitters from our neighborhood regularly to cover our evenings out or afternoons away. Remember that it is unwise to leave your child in the care of a youngster under twelve years of age, and in some states it's illegal. The following guidelines should aid you in selecting and using a reliable babysitter of any age, but especially when the caretaker might be an adolescent.

Get recommendations by asking around the neighborhood and select someone who has a good track record or who you already know and feel is a responsible teen. Remember that the babysitter might need to handle an emergency, so ask yourself how you think this individual would react in a crisis. A teen with younger siblings for whom they have had some responsibility is often a good choice. If they lack babysitting experience, it is preferable if one of their parents will be home for the first time or two to back them up.

Invite the teen over on an afternoon when you will be home with the baby. Familiarize the person with the baby's routines, where his things are kept, how you feed and handle him, and the mechanics of diapering. Let the teen-ager hold and change the baby. Do pay them for the time spent that afternoon.

Whenever you go out, leave a number where you can be reached and an accurate estimate of how long you will be gone. Write down your address in case they need to summon help. Also leave the name, address, and phone number of someone in the neighborhood who could be contacted in an emergency. Be sure sitters know how to call the police, fire department, paramedics, and poison control center. Post a simple first-aid chart by the phone. Tell them to keep the doors locked at all times. Indicate how you want telephone messages recorded and remind sitters not to reveal that they are alone or to give out your address over the phone. Similarly, review how you want them to respond if someone comes to the door.

Before leaving, review child-safety measures, since teens often are not familiar with developmental abilities of infants at different ages. Remind the sitter that the baby cannot be left alone on the changing table, that gates must protect stairways, that the toddler cannot chew nuts, and so on. Remember, you have been living with your child and have grown accustomed to safety issues, but the sitter may not have recent experience with a baby this age and will need reminders about common hazards.

Explain the baby's anticipated schedule: how long he might sleep, when he might awaken to eat, how much he usually takes, specific bedtime routines, and other details, such as if you want him to be taken for a stroll or given a bath. The less complicated your expectations, however, the better. It's probably preferable not to request that the dinner dishes be done, for example, at the risk of taking the sitter's attention away from the baby.

For older children, you can minimize conflicts and attempts to manipulate the sitter by clearly stating ground rules in everyone's presence: for example, they are not allowed in the computer room, they can have a bedtime snack, they can watch specific TV shows, they are expected to brush their teeth, and they go to bed at 8 P.M.

Clarify what the sitter is allowed to do, such as eat certain snacks, watch TV, play videogames. Also specify that you do not want them to call friends on the telephone, have anyone over, smoke, and so on.

Ask the sitter what they usually charge and pay a fair price. The care of additional children should cost more, and marathon days deserve a special tip. Plan ahead to have cash on hand. Although a check is better than an IOU, it's still not quite the same as the immediate reward of crisp greenbacks. Consider paying the sitter something if you need to cancel at the last minute. She may have altered her own plans to sit for you and should be compensated for being available if you canceled on short notice.

Listen to your children. If they "don't like" Susan but look forward to Chris coming over, they may have a good reason. On the other hand, it's also possible that Susan can't be manipulated and Chris lets them run free. Try to find out the reason behind their feelings.

When you get home, ask how the evening went and whether any problems arose. An honest admission of difficulties or a confession about a broken rule suggests maturity on the part of the teen, while unexplained cigarette butts or a beer can in the trash, or your child's revelation that a boyfriend came over should prompt you to discontinue using that particular sitter.

With the increased recognition of the magnitude of child sexual abuse, many parents are reluctant to hire male babysitters, since males are more often the perpetrators of sexual abuse. While caution should be exercised in the selection of *any* babysitter, the refusal to ever select a male sitter may cause our children to miss special opportunities to model adolescent males and unnecessarily deprive teenage boys of valuable caretaking experience. My older son once spent a most insightful summer providing full-time daycare for a school-aged boy and girl, learning the world's hardest job, parenting, firsthand.

Always accompany the babysitter home, even if he or she lives across the street. This may be a burden for single parents who may have to bundle up a sleeping baby to drive the sitter home, but it should never be overlooked.

Ask your sitter to let you know if they are ill, so that you can contact a substitute sitter instead of exposing your baby. You will be less inconvenienced by arranging for another sitter or canceling your plans than having a sick baby on your hands in a few days.

Following these guidelines should allow you to have some relaxed time away from your baby with a measure of peace of mind, knowing he is being cared for by a responsible and competent sitter who you have properly prepared and educated.

TEETH AND TEETHING

I often wonder why the universal and unalterable process of eruption of teeth attracts so much attention. We hail the cutting of the first tooth and view it as some sort of developmental landmark. Indeed, teething often coincides with the baby's readiness for solid foods and encourages her natural inclination to explore everything with her mouth. It's important to understand that erupting teeth is as natural, and usually as uneventful, as growing hair. Although teething can produce excessive drooling and chewing, mild discomfort, and fussiness, by and large, the process requires very little special treatment.

It's commonly believed that teething causes fever, diarrhea, excessive irritability, and a host of other symptoms. Unfortunately, symptoms of unrelated illness are often inappropriately attributed to teething, thus delaying diagnosis unnecessarily. Misinformation about teething also causes undue alarm and concern among parents about how to manage the teething process. In general, teething causes teeth. Period. To dispel some common myths and help you better understand teeth, teething, and dental care, let's review some dental facts.

Everyone gets two sets of teeth—twenty baby teeth and twenty-eight (thirty-two counting wisdom teeth) permanent teeth. The baby teeth begin calcifying during fetal life; the permanent teeth begin calcifying after the first several months of postnatal life and are fully formed, although not all erupted, by seven years of age.

A baby has no teeth at birth because he needs none. Nature planned it so that he gets his first teeth around the time he will begin to eat solid foods, in the middle of the first year. The first tooth erupts around six months of age, but many normal babies will have a tooth by four months, while others don't get one until a year of age.

Once the first tooth comes in, a baby gets about one tooth a month thereafter. In order to erupt twenty teeth, you can see that he will be "teething" for nearly two years. That's a long time to fuss over teething symptoms if you don't really have to.

Teeth erupt in an orderly and predictable fashion. The two lower central teeth are usually first, followed by the upper matching pair. Then come the upper teeth on either side of the central ones, so that around a year of age a baby has six teeth. The lower teeth next to the central ones come in next, followed by the first molars. Then the pointed canines appear next to the central group. The last baby teeth to erupt are the second molars, which come in behind the first ones between two and two and a half years of age.

Breast feeding can continue uninterrupted during teething. Occasionally a nursing mother will be bitten by her infant, but you should remember that a baby cannot bite while actually nursing. When biting does occur, it is usually toward the end of the feeding when the child stops sucking. You can eliminate biting by saying "no" and removing your nipple. It is rare for biting to continue. Contrary to popular belief, you will be unaware of your baby's teeth while he is nursing.

While teething usually causes little difficulty, many babies do experience some minor gum irritation when certain teeth are erupting, especially the first molars, between a year and eighteen months of age. Babies drool excessively when teething and thus swallow excess saliva. Some people think this causes temporarily looser stools. A few babies are fussy and irritable with teething and may have trouble sleeping at night, when the discomfort is more noticeable. A baby's gums may be uncomfortable when sucking or nursing, causing his appetite to decrease during

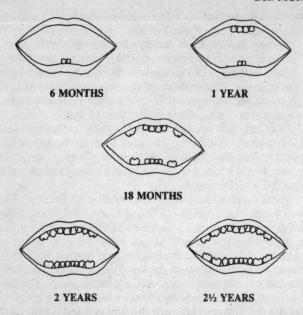

6 MONTHS   **1 YEAR**

18 MONTHS

2 YEARS   **2½ YEARS**

teething. He likes to rub his gums against cold smooth objects and seems to chew incessantly. The following suggestions will help you safely deal with your baby's teething symptoms:

√ Provide him with a cool, safe object to chew on, such as a teething ring, chilled pacifier, or firm, smooth toy. Popsicles are not a good idea, however, unless you hold them yourself and take care not to let them touch his cheeks, since they can cause thermal injury to his delicate facial skin.

√ Consider giving a dose of acetaminophen at bedtime, but don't do this on a regular basis. Remember that teeth will be erupting for nearly two years, so you certainly don't want to make the giving of medication a daily habit!

√ A variety of over-the-counter preparations are sold specifically for teething. They contain a topical anesthetic that temporarily numbs the gums when rubbed

on. Of course, such preparations should be used spar-
ingly and only when necessary, not routinely or for
long periods. Babies can develop a sensitivity to the
ingredients. Home remedies, such as frequently rubbing brandy or other liquor on the gums, should be
discouraged. Babies can easily be overdosed on alcohol.

√ If your baby has symptoms greater than drooling and
slight fussiness, consider that he may have an illness,
and just happens to be teething, too. Don't ever attribute a high fever, cough, rash, vomiting, or other
specific symptom to teething, even if friends or relatives try to convince you teething causes these.
Call your baby's health care provider and report the
symptoms.

Dental Care

Once the first tooth has erupted, you will need to begin
regular dental hygiene, either with a Q-tip, washcloth, or
gauze pad, then gradually switch to a soft toothbrush.
Don't use toothpaste until your baby is about two, and
then use only a tiny amount. Cavities can occur within a
few months among infants with soft enamel or those who
have the habit of taking a bottle of milk to bed with them.
When a baby nurses a bottle of milk all night, his upper
teeth are bathed in milk, which can cause severe bottle-
mouth caries, or cavities, in susceptible children. Sugary
drinks like soda pop are even worse. The typical pattern of
decay with bottle-mouth caries involves the upper teeth,
since the tongue lies over the lower ones and helps protect
them. Another common cause of cavities is regular snacking on sugar-containing sticky foods, such as raisins or
chewy candies, that cling to the rough surfaces of the
molars. Cavities are caused when sugars are broken down
by enzymes in saliva to produce acids; these acids destroy
the enamel of the teeth, and then bacteria normally present
in the mouth enter the tooth and "digest" it.

If your baby's teeth are healthy and his habit is to drink
a bottle and toss it out of the crib, you may not need to
discontinue the nighttime bottle. If, however, your baby
likes to suck on the bottle intermittently all night, you

really should discontinue the night bottle or fill it with water instead of milk. This is especially true if weak enamel runs in your family or your baby shows any signs of cavities already.

Please do not believe that cavities in the baby teeth don't matter! I have seen so many preschoolers with untreated caries that it breaks my heart. It hurts to eat; it causes loss of teeth and shifting of the other teeth; it causes bad breath and fosters the growth of the cavity-causing bacteria that will attack the permanent teeth; and it ruins a beautiful smile. Yes, dental care is expensive and seldom covered by insurance, but it is worth every penny spent. Obviously, preventing cavities by monitoring snacks, brushing regularly, and discontinuing the nighttime bottle is optimal.

You will need to supervise your child's brushing for many years. When he is old enough, stand behind him and hold his hand with your own as you brush his teeth. That way he can better understand the correct motions. It is very difficult to learn to brush correctly, and a child probably needs to be at least seven years old before he can do it effectively on his own. Don't forget to also use dental floss with your youngster, once all his baby teeth have erupted. Flossing helps prevent gum disease that plagues so many of us as we get older. Another excellent habit to learn is to rinse the mouth with water after meals or simply drink water after eating.

Preventive Care

You should begin regular dental checkups around the age of three years and continue them at least yearly, and preferably every six months. Decades of research have shown that daily exposure of developing teeth to optimal levels of fluoride (0.7-1.2 parts fluoride per million parts water) can reduce tooth decay by 50 percent to 60 percent. If your water supply is not fluoridated, your pediatrician may decide to start your child on a daily fluoride supplement. In addition to dietary fluoride, your child can receive added benefits from topical fluoride, in the form of fluoride toothpaste, fluoride mouthwash (in older children), and periodic fluoride treatments applied directly to the teeth. Later, when the permanent teeth erupt, deeply pitted and cavity-prone molars can be covered with an invisible sealant, a thin plastic coating that will protect the tooth from decay. Thus our children need not experience the inevitable cavities that accompanied our own growing up.

LEGS AND FEET

Most babies' legs and feet don't look "normal" until the child has been walking for several years. Bowlegs are normal from infancy until around two years of age, largely due to the baby's position in the uterus. You can't cause bowed legs by pulling your baby into a standing position or letting him walk "too early." Referral to an orthopedic surgeon is indicated if your child's legs are bowed beyond two years of age, the bowing is increasing instead of decreasing, or only one leg is bowed.

Occasionally one or both feet are curved inward at birth because the front of the foot itself is turned inward, compared with the back of the foot. If you can move the foot into a "normal" looking position, and if the foot moves freely when your baby kicks and squirms, it is almost certainly a normal foot influenced by his intrauterine position. Your pediatrician can give you some stretching exercises to hasten the straightening of the foot. If a baby has a turned foot that is fixed in its abnormal position, then referral to an orthopedic surgeon is necessary for casting or other treatment.

Young children are frequently pigeon-toed. This condition is often caused by a slight rotation of the leg between the knee and the ankle, and can be made more obvious when the knee ligaments are lax. Pigeon toes due to rotation of the lower leg gradually resolve around one year of age, but can persist longer in some children who sleep on their tummies with their feet turned in.

"Toeing in" beyond age two or three is usually due to a slight rotation of the upper leg, between the hip and the knee, and tends to resolve on its own by eight years of age. The condition is common in youngsters who sit and play or watch TV in a squatting position, with their knees together and their lower legs turned out. They can be encouraged to sit in a crosslegged position instead. If toeing-in is causing your child to trip often and his legs are not gradually straightening, then your pediatrician may want to refer him to an orthopedic specialist.

Many infants will turn their legs outward when first learning to walk, in order to increase their stability. This "toeing out" gradually resolves as a child begins to walk and run capably.

From two to about eight years of age, children tend to be knock-kneed due to lax knee ligaments. As they grow older, their ligaments strengthen and they assume an adultlike alignment of the legs and feet. A child whose degree of knock-knees is increasing should be referred to an orthopedist.

All young infants appear flat-footed until about two to three years of age. In infancy the arch is hidden by a fat pad on the baby's foot. Later the lax ligaments binding the bones of the arch cause the arch to collapse under his standing weight. By four years of age, the ligaments have strengthened enough to support his weight, and the "flat feet" correct themselves.

ROUTINE INFANT AND CHILD MEDICAL CARE

Routine medical checkups are a very important part of your infant's basic care. These health maintenance, or health supervision, visits should begin within the first two weeks after birth and continue throughout childhood. The visits are most frequent during the first year of life, when your baby is changing most rapidly. Between one and two years, several checkups will occur. Between two and six, annual appointments for routine health care are scheduled, with regular checkups occurring every two years thereafter.

Growth Parameters

At each health supervision visit, your child will be carefully weighed and measured, then plotted on his own growth curve to determine whether his rate of growth is appropriate. Ask to see your baby's growth curve at each visit. Since boys are slightly taller and heavier than girls, even in infancy, different growth curves are used for each sex. The graphs for boys are often blue, and girls pink, so we are less likely to mix them up in the office.

We know that normal children and adults range widely in height and body build. Much of this variation is related to the genetic background we inherited and have passed on to our children.

Growth curves have been established among populations of healthy children to indicate normal rates of growth. Lines are drawn on these graphs to demonstrate a child's growth at the 50th percentile (half of children would be taller, and half would be shorter), the 75th percentile (25 percent would be taller, and 75 percent shorter), 25th percentile (75 percent taller, and 25 percent shorter), and so on. Similar curves exist for weight and head circumference. Some people are naturally taller or heavier than average, while others are shorter or lighter. One child's normal pattern of growth might be along the 95th percentile, while another's normal rate of growth is along the 25th percentile. Your doctor measures your child and plots his growth to look for any unexplained changes in the rate of growth that could signal a problem.

For example, if a baby was born at the 50th percentile for weight, and has gained so slowly that he is at the 5th percentile at four months of age, this dramatic change in growth percentiles should be carefully investigated. It would be important to determine whether this baby was consuming enough calories for adequate growth. Perhaps he has chronic vomiting or diarrhea that is causing him to lose nutrients. He may have a chronic infection or an undetected medical problem that is impairing his growth. Another baby the same age who had been gaining along the 5th-percentile curve since birth would raise no concern, even though both infants weighed the same amount at the same age.

In another example, a child might have been born at the 25th percentile for weight, and now at four months of age, is over the 95th percentile. His parents may be overfeeding him. Perhaps they are misinterpreting his cues and think

BOYS: BIRTH TO 36 MONTHS
Weight and Length for Age

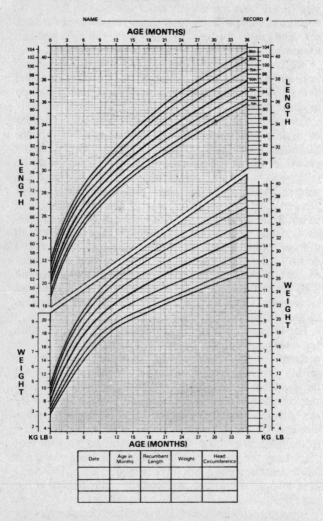

NAME _____   RECORD # _____

AGE (MONTHS)

LENGTH

WEIGHT

Date	Age in Months	Recumbent Length	Weight	Head Circumference

Department of Health, Education, and Welfare, Public Health Service, Health Resources Administration, National Center for Health Statistics, and Center for Disease Control

GIRLS: BIRTH TO 36 MONTHS
Weight and Length for Age

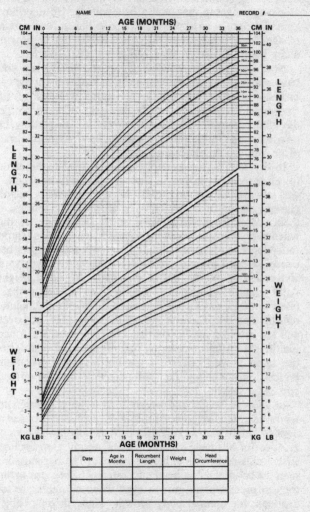

Date	Age in Months	Recumbent Length	Weight	Head Circumference

Department of Health, Education, and Welfare, Public Health Service, Health Resources Administration, National Center for Health Statistics, and Center for Disease Control

that every time he cries they should feed him again. He might be at risk for childhood and adult obesity if such overfeeding continues. Another baby may have been large at birth, weighing nine and a half pounds. He may have gained weight at an appropriate rate, so that at four months of age, he is still heavier than most babies but is growing along his own normal curve and is not being overfed.

Now you can see how weighing and measuring your baby and plotting his growth on infant growth curves can provide valuable information about his well-being. His "normal" growth curve might be at the 50th percentile, the 95th percentile, or the 5th percentile. By plotting his measurements in the office regularly, his own normal rate of growth can be established.

In my family, for example, children tend to be at the lower percentiles in height throughout early childhood. I was always the shortest child in my elementary school classes, and most of my children are now the shortest in their classes. I entered puberty later than average, so that when everyone else began their growth spurt, I was temporarily left even further behind. Then, when the others had nearly stopped growing, I finally entered a growth spurt and ended up within the normal range for adult height. After years of calling me "Shorty," my friends realized one day that I was as tall as most of them! No one pointed out this normal pattern of growth to my mother, however, and she worried needlessly that I would never attain normal height. After discovering that my husband manifested the same growth pattern, I am not surprised when my preteens grow along the 3rd percentile on the growth curves for height.

In general, height and weight tend to be proportionate, while head circumference follows its own curve independent of height and weight. If a baby is not getting enough calories for adequate growth, rate of weight gain declines first, followed by rate of height increase. The last measurement to be affected is head circumference, because nature tries to protect brain growth even when nutrients are unavailable for optimal body growth. Thus, if your baby's growth has been inadequate, don't panic or fear that he has experienced irreparable harm. Most likely he will recover quickly once he gets enough to eat.

Physical Examination

In addition to the important growth measurements that will be made at each health maintenance visit, a complete physical examination will be performed to assure that no previously undetected illness exists and no new medical problems have arisen. If your baby is known to have a heart murmur or other medical condition, this will be carefully followed at every well-baby visit.

Developmental Screening

Formal or informal developmental screening takes place at each checkup. This will include the doctor asking questions about your baby's development or the administration of a specific developmental screening test, such as the Denver Developmental Screening Test (DDST). Part of developmental screening also includes vision, speech, and hearing screening as soon as your child is old enough to cooperate.

Immunizations

Vaccines will be administered to your infant at his health maintenance visits, when indicated by the routine immunization schedule. It will be important for you to bring an immunization record (shot book, card, et cetera) to each appointment, especially if you move or change health care providers. This will prevent your child from skipping immunizations or repeating immunizations needlessly. Also be sure to mention any adverse reactions to an immunization, so the particular vaccine can be avoided in the future if necessary. If your baby gets behind in his immunization schedule, he does not have to restart the series from the beginning.

Laboratory Screening

At various ages, specific laboratory screening is recommended, such as a urine test, a blood test for anemia, et cetera. These tests are performed to uncover common conditions that might go undetected because symptoms are not apparent.

Anticipatory Guidance

One of the nicest parts of a regular checkup for your child is the sharing of information by your baby's physician or health-care provider. This counseling may be in answer to your direct questions, as well as in anticipation of inquiries and concerns that may arise before the next visit, and might include feeding recommendations, discipline suggestions, behavior counseling, safety tips, and other matters. Come prepared with a list of concerns to be sure all your questions get answered.

Schedule of Visits

The following outline of routine health supervision visits during the first five years of life will acquaint you with the expected frequency and content of your child's medical checkups.

Two-week (or earlier) Visit: This is a most important appointment, as it is usually the first checkup after hospital discharge. You probably will have lots of questions and will appreciate the reassurance that this visit should provide.

Your doctor will review your baby's feeding routines and assure you that he has regained his birth weight. In fact, your infant will probably be well above birth weight and averaging an ounce per day weight gain by now. Your doctor will carefully inspect your baby for any signs of jaundice, which should be completely resolved by two weeks. The cord will probably have fallen off, or be drying nicely and expected to fall off soon. If a circumcision was performed, it will be well healed by now.

The PKU test is usually rechecked at this visit, by obtaining a few drops of blood from your baby's heel. The doctor will probably inquire about your own physical health and the family's adjustment to the new baby. He or she should leave ample time for your questions about feeding, safety, elimination, sleeping, sibling rivalry, and other concerns.

Two-month Visit: This visit marks the beginning of routine immunizations. Your baby's growth parameters will be measured and plotted and a complete physical examination performed. Weight gain should still average an ounce per day.

Again, feeding suggestions will be made, safety guidance offered, and developmental expectations given. This may be the visit to discuss topics such as the adjustments involved in returning to work or selecting day care.

The oral polio vaccine (OPV), a few drops of a pink liquid, will be administered and your baby will probably like it. The DPT (diphtheria, pertussis, tetanus) vaccine will be given as an intramuscular injection, probably in the well-developed thigh muscles. Your baby's leg will be tender for a day or two, so keep this in mind when you change his diapers or handle him. Most likely your baby will react very little to the DPT injection. Be prepared to call your doctor for any unusual reaction to the immunization, such as a fever above 103°F that doesn't respond to acetaminophen, incessant crying, a convulsion, or extreme lethargy.

Your doctor should check to be sure you own a thermometer and have acetaminophen (Tylenol, Panadol, Tempra, St. Joseph's Aspirin Free, Anacin-3, Liquiprin) on hand in case your baby reacts to the injection by running a fever for a day or two. Be sure you know the correct dose of acetaminophen to give. (See page 300 for acetaminophen dosage.)

Four-month Visit: Your baby will have nearly doubled his birth weight by four months of age. The second series of immunizations are given, after ascertaining that your baby did not react unfavorably to the first set. Check to be sure the dose of acetaminophen hasn't changed with your baby's increased weight. Your infant will probably interact with and coo at his doctor during the physical examination, making this a most delightful visit for all.

You may have questions about starting solid foods in the interim before the six-month checkup. Your doctor may recommend beginning an iron supplement at this age.

Safety counseling will probably be given, as your infant is becoming much more active.

Six-month Visit: A third DPT immunization is given during this visit; the third OPV is not yet necessary. The examination is still probably well tolerated, although your baby may need to have you nearby. You can help out by distracting him with toys, or parts of the exam can be performed on your lap, if necessary.

Specific instructions for starting solid foods should be offered at this visit. If your baby was premature, his blood count may be checked to be sure he is not anemic. Safety counseling is very important at this age, as your baby will soon be crawling. I like to give parents a sample of syrup of ipecac to take home with them from this visit, just to have on hand in case their baby ever swallows a poisonous substance. Syrup of ipecac can be used to induce vomiting, but only after first consulting with your regional poison control center. (See page 427, "Emergencies!")

Be sure to bring up any questions you have about thumb sucking, awakening at night, beginning stranger anxiety, or teething.

Nine-month Visit: No routine immunizations are given at this visit, although screening for anemia is commonly performed at this age. The physical examination now takes a bit of ingenuity on the part of your baby's doctor. You will enjoy watching the doctor amuse, distract, and reassure your infant while trying to complete the examination. You can help out by providing reassuring looks, toys, a bottle, pacifier, or other distraction. Formal developmental screening, such as the Denver Developmental Screening Test (DDST), may be administered at this visit, and vision and hearing should be evaluated. Share any concerns with your baby's doctor.

Ways to stimulate your baby's development, specific safety guidelines, and beginning table foods are important anticipatory guidance provided at the nine-month visit.

One-year Visit: Your baby probably will have tripled his birth weight by one year of age. He may be starting to walk while holding onto furniture, and you might have questions about his legs and feet. Your baby will probably be apprehensive about strangers and hesitant to be examined, but you can help in the ways previously described.

A screening test for tuberculosis is commonly administered at this age. Be sure to tell your baby's doctor if your infant could ever have been exposed to TB. The test, in the form of a superficial skin prick, will be placed on his forearm, and you will be asked to check his arm for any reaction in forty-eight to seventy-two hours.

Feeding, development (especially language, which is rapidly progressing), safety, and early principles of discipline will probably be discussed.

Fifteen-month Visit: At this visit, an immunization is given to protect against measles, mumps, and rubella (German measles) (MMR). It is usually administered into the soft tissues of the thigh. Remember to bring your shot record to record the immunization. In addition to the complete examination, anticipatory guidance about weaning (if your child is ready), safety, development, discipline, and toilet training may be provided. Ask about your specific concerns arising from your baby's growing independence.

Eighteen-month Visit: DPT and OPV boosters are given at this visit, so bring your immunization record. Review the correct dose of acetaminophen, in case your baby reacts to the vaccine. In addition, it is common to screen again for anemia by taking a few drops of blood from your baby's fingertip. Formal developmental screening, such as the DDST, is also typically performed at this age.

Weaning, preparation for toilet training, discipline, and safety are usually discussed.

Two-year Visit: Your baby has probably quadrupled his birth weight by now. He may still object to parts of the examination, but is beginning to cooperate somewhat. It is common to start weighing and measuring the child in an upright position at this age. You can demonstrate by standing on the scale first.

The fairly new vaccine against *Hemophilus* influenza type b (Hib vaccine) is now recommended for routine administration at two years of age. Anticipatory guidance usually emphasizes toilet training, nutrition, weaning, safety, and behavior.

Three-year Visit: This is the first visit when your child's blood pressure is routinely taken, since he will probably be able to understand a simple explanation of the procedure. He should also be able to cooperate for formal vision, hearing, and speech screening, and the DDST is commonly repeated at this age.

At last, your child should enjoy participating in the physical examination. Since no routine immunizations are given at this visit, it can serve as a time to reassure your child about trips to the doctor. He may want to try out the instruments and will probably be eager to please. Remember, NEVER threaten your child when at the doctor's. When I hear a parent say, "Be good or I'll tell the doctor to give you a shot," I'm tempted to give the parent one! Such comments make it very difficult for health professionals who want to dispel fear and make the visit as pleasant as possible.

Regular dental care should begin around age three. Unfortunately, cavities are often already present by this age. A urine sample is sometimes obtained from girls to screen for unsuspected urinary tract infection.

Anticipatory guidance includes information on discipline, toilet training, nursery school, safety, development, and nutrition.

Four-year Visit: Your child can begin to participate in answering some of the questions in the medical history about preschool, friends, chores, et cetera. Try to encourage him to contribute even if it didn't occur to the doctor to include him.

Many children this age are modest about exposing their bodies, so try to be sensitive and ask for a gown if the doctor hasn't thought of it. Your child will probably enjoy cooperating for the exam and will appreciate reassurance about his good health and strong body. The DPT and OPV school boosters can be given now or at age five or six. Blood may be taken to screen for anemia.

Anticipatory guidance includes information on counseling about strangers, street safety, sexuality, and discipline.

Five-year Visit: In addition to the routine physical examination, this visit is important for assessing school readiness. Vision, speech, hearing and development are usually screened at this time. The DPT and OPV boosters are given, unless they were already administered at age four. NEVER tell the child not to cry, or to be a "big boy," for the shot. NEVER say it won't hurt. I always tell the child that it will hurt briefly, and that I want him to hold very still, although we always restrain him securely anyway. I encourage him to yell loudly while the needle is in. Afterward, I always congratulate him on holding still and giving such a great yell. I give him a fancy Band-Aid and a spare one to take home.

Anticipatory guidance includes information on car, bicycle, water, and fire safety, discipline, and growing responsibility.

Immunizations and Informed Consent

The issue of routine immunizations is one example of how parenting today is more difficult than in past generations. My own mother never questioned the indications, side effects, or efficacy of immunizations, although as military dependents, we were more frequently vaccinated than any other segment of the population. Parents today are forced to examine the issues and make a conscious decision about routine immunizations. The indications and side effects of immunizations are presented to parents, either verbally, in writing, or by both means, before routine immunizations are administered. The concept of informed consent is an admirable one. Indeed, parents should be more informed about all aspects of their child's care and function as joint partners in medical decisions. Unfortunately, however, partial information about the issue of immunizations has resulted in an alarmist attitude about current medical recommendations that have been carefully weighed by knowledgeable and concerned professionals. Let's look at some of the facts.

Routine immunizations protect children from three strains of paralytic polio, diphtheria, pertussis (whooping cough), tetanus, hard measles, mumps, German measles, as well as meningitis, cellulitis, and other serious infections caused by Hemophilus influenza. All of these diseases still occur. For some, there is no cure. All can cause permanent disability. Some can cause death.

Polio: Polio is caused by a virus that attacks the central nervous system and can cause permanent paralysis, leading to crippling, and occasionally death when the muscles used in breathing are paralyzed. There is no specific treatment for polio, and antibiotics are not effective against the virus. Prior to the availability of polio vaccine in the 1950s, thousands of cases of polio occurred each year in the United States. Now that children are routinely vaccinated against polio, the disease has almost disappeared in this country. Polio continues to occur in parts of the world where immunization is not available, however, and it is believed that polio could become reestablished in this country if routine vaccination were discontinued.

Diphtheria: Diphtheria is caused by a bacteria that infects the nose, throat, and vocal cords. Diphtheria can cause death by interfering with breathing, attacking the heart, and paralyzing muscles. Even if antibiotics are given, at least one out of ten people who gets diphtheria dies of it. Routine vaccination has almost eliminated the disease in this country.

Pertussis (Whooping Cough): Pertussis, or whooping cough, is caused by a bacteria that leads to severe spells of coughing. The coughing can be so frequent and violent that it interferes with eating, drinking, and even breathing, and can lead to hemorrhage into the brain. Three in 1000 unimmunized children who get pertussis will have encephalitis, or inflammation of the brain, as a complication. Pertussis is still a real threat in the United States, especially among young infants who may be unimmunized or only partially immunized. Nearly two thousand cases occur each year in this country; I see several every year.

Tetanus (Lockjaw): Tetanus, or lockjaw, results when wounds or burns are infected with tetanus bacteria, commonly found in dirt and animal and human excrement. The bacteria manufacture a poison that causes uncontrollable muscle spasms. Eventually the mouth cannot be opened, and swallowing becomes difficult or impossible. The spasms can be agonizingly painful. Four of ten people who get tetanus die, usually from spasm of the respiratory muscles or by choking on their own mucus or vomit. In underdeveloped countries tetanus is a common cause of neonatal deaths. The organism usually enters the infant's body through the umbilical cord due to unhygienic practices. Widespread immunization in the United States has almost eliminated the disease here.

Measles: Measles is the most serious of the common

childhood illnesses (no longer so common in the United States). It is caused by a virus and begins with several days of unexplained high fever before the onset of the typical rash. The child also has a cough, runny nose, and watery eyes. The illness lasts one to two weeks. About one out of every 1000 children who get measles will develop an inflammation of the brain, known as encephalitis. This can lead to convulsions, permanent deafness, and mental retardation. In underdeveloped countries measles frequently causes death when it strikes a malnourished child. Routine immunization has nearly eliminated measles in the United States, and many young pediatricians have never seen a case.

Mumps: Mumps is usually a mild illness causing fever, headache, and inflammation of the parotid, or salivary, glands. It can also affect other glands, including the testicles and ovaries, pancreas, and breasts. Mumps encephalitis and meningitis can also occur, and permanent deafness is a recognized complication. My own sister is permanently deaf in one ear due to mumps.

German Measles (Rubella): German measles, or rubella, is a usually mild illness causing slight fever, rash, and swollen lymph glands. Sometimes it causes temporary arthritis in women, and rarely it is associated with encephalitis. The most serious risk of rubella is to the unborn child of a pregnant woman with the disease. If a woman gets rubella in early pregnancy, her baby is likely to be miscarried or to be born with heart defects, deafness, blindness, or mental retardation. A simple blood test will tell if a woman of childbearing age is protected against rubella. Routine immunization of young children and unprotected women has almost eliminated the occurrence of damaged "rubella babies."

Hemophilus Influenza Type B: The Hemophilus bacteria is the leading cause of serious infections in young children in industrialized countries. Approximately 20,000 to 30,000 cases occur each year in the United States, and these infections result in spinal meningitis, cellulitis, pneumonia, epiglottitis, and other diseases. Five percent to ten percent of those with meningitis die and 30 percent are estimated to be permanently damaged. The newly developed vaccine is not effective in children under eighteen months of age but is very effective beginning around age two. Current recommendations are to administer the vaccine to all two-year-olds and to children between eighteen months and two years of age who are in day care, and therefore at higher risk of infection. Unimmunized three-, four-, or five-year-olds should also receive the vaccine.

For many of us, the risks of these diseases confirm the value of continued routine immunization of our children. Unfortunately, however, the vaccines themselves are not totally without risk. In fact, nothing in life is totally without risk. Taking aspirin for a headache can cause a rare allergic reaction or a bleeding ulcer. Pregnancy poses medical risks to both mother and baby. Riding in an automobile, especially on a holiday weekend, carries a small, but definite, risk. So it is with immunizations. Just as I occasionally take aspirin, elect to get pregnant, and travel extensively, I acknowledge and accept those small risks involved with routine immunizations. Just what are these risks?

Oral polio Vaccine: Although there are no immediate reactions to oral polio immunization, such as fever or fussiness, rare severe reactions can occur. About once in every 8.1 million doses, the weakened virus used to give immunity actually causes paralytic polio. About once in every 5 million doses, a close family contact of the immunized person gets paralytic polio from the virus, which is passed in the immunized person's stool. These risks can be minimized by not immunizing a person with abnormally low resistance to infection or someone who lives with such a person. Immunization against polio can also be accomplished by giving an injection of a dead vaccine. There is no risk of polio by this method.

DPT (Diphtheria, Pertussis, and Tetanus) Injection: DPT is three vaccines combined into one shot to make it easier to provide protection. Most children will have some type of reaction to the injection. This is usually a mild fever, irritability, or increased sleepiness within two days of getting the shot. Half of all immunized children will have some tenderness and swelling in the area where the shot was given. In one out of twenty cases the fever will go above 102°F. One out of 1000 times, unusual high-pitched crying will occur. One out of 1750 times, a child will have a convulsion or go limp or appear pale. One out of 110,000 times, inflammation of the brain (encephalitis) may occur, with permanent brain damage resulting in one out of 310,000 shots. All these reactions are thought to be due to the pertussis component of DPT, as few reactions occur when pertussis is left out of the vaccine, and these reactions are only soreness and slight fever. For this reason, any child who has had a previous high fever, high-pitched crying, limpness or paleness, convulsion, or other severe reaction to a DPT injection should not receive the pertussis part of the vaccine again. In this case, the risk of the pertussis vaccine is believed to exceed the risk of contracting and being harmed by the disease.

MMR (Measles, Mumps, and Rubella) Injection: One to two weeks after the injection, about one out of five children will get a faint rash or slight fever for a few days due to the measles part of the vaccine. Occasionally the salivary glands will swell mildly due to the mumps component of the vaccine. About one out of seven children will react to the rubella vaccine one to two weeks later with temporary swelling of the lymph glands in the neck or development of a rash. About one out of twenty children will have some aching or swelling of the joints one to three weeks later. There is no proof, but it is suspected that VERY RARELY a child may have a more serious reaction, such as inflammation of the brain (encephalitis), convulsions with fever, or deafness. Because the MMR injection is a weakened but live virus vaccine, it should not be given to anyone who has weakened immunity to disease, such as a person with cancer, or to a pregnant woman. Because the vaccine is prepared in chicken eggs, it should not be given to someone who has had a severe allergic reaction to eating eggs.

HIB Vaccine: Although this vaccine is just newly available, it has been tested for over ten years with more than 50,000 children. So far, no bad reactions have been reported, except for one severe allergic reaction, which was treated promptly. Fewer than 2 percent of vaccinated children have had a fever greater than 101°F or redness and swelling where the injection is given. It appears to be a very safe immunization and to offer 90 percent protection against serious Hemophilus infections.

Medical personnel regularly review the risks of routine immunization to assure that the benefits derived from immunizations far outweigh the risks. We all weigh risks in life every day and elect not to do some things, like smoke cigarettes, try hang-gliding, have a homebirth, or use illicit drugs. The issue of routine immunizations is very similar. I acknowledge that immunizations carry certain small risks. I do everything possible to minimize such risks by taking a careful history before prescribing an immunization, giving the correct dosage by the correct route and technique, withholding the immunization if a child is ill, or he reacted badly in the past, et cetera. Then I rely on periodic review of the data to determine when the benefits of an immunization no longer outweigh the risks.

RECOMMENDED IMMUNIZATION SCHEDULE	
AGE	FOR INFANTS AND YOUNG CHILDREN
2 mos.	DPT #1, OPV #1 (Diphtheria, Pertussis & Tetanus; Oral Polio Vaccine)
4 mos.	DPT #2, OPV #2
6 mos.	DPT #3
15 mos.	MMR (Measles, Mumps & Rubella)
18 mos.	DPT #4, OPV #3
	HIB: if high-risk group, i.e. in daycare (Hemophilus Influenza B)
2 yrs.	HIB
4-6 yrs.	DPT #5, OPV #4

For example, in the late 1960s, Dr. C. Henry Kempe, an eminent pediatrician under whom I later had the privilege to train, proposed that we discontinue routine smallpox immunization. There had not been a reported case of smallpox in the United States for over twenty years, but a handful of children died each year from the vaccination. With this information, he believed we could no longer justify preventing a now-rare disease at this expense of children's lives. Such arguments make sense to me. I find it gratifying that periodic review of the risks and benefits of each immunization continues among experts in the field of infectious disease. Recently, the polio vaccine given at six months of age was discontinued because it was found to be unnecessary for maintaining adequate immunity. The current schedule of immunizations recommended in pediatric care represents carefully weighed risks and benefits.

OTHER MEMBERS OF THE HEALTH-CARE TEAM

Your child's primary health-care provider will probably be his pediatrician or family practitioner. Eventually, however, you may seek out or be referred to other health professionals. Following is a brief survey of other professionals you might encounter and factors to consider as you select them.

Child Psychotherapist

If you or your child's physician believes your child has a behavioral or personality problem, professional counseling might be recommended for him. If your child suffers a severe emotional trauma or life change and has difficulty adjusting to it, counseling can often help. Counseling can be especially beneficial after a death or divorce when the parent is too depleted or emotionally involved to be helpful to the child as he tries to sort out his feelings.

Look for a licensed practitioner, either a social worker (M.S.W.), a psychologist (Ph.D.), or a psychiatrist (M.D.), who works primarily with children. If cost is a factor when seeking help, try a university hospital, a training facility, or a mental health center that has a program where visits are billed on a sliding scale according to income. In a teaching clinic your therapist might be a trainee working under close professional supervision.

Dentist

At about three years of age, your child should begin receiving regular dental examinations. Choose a dentist who is known for working well with children. Some dentists do not treat children at all, and some do not relate to them very well. Again, ask friends for recommendations.

You might want to use a pedodontist, a dentist who specializes in treating children. Many general dentists are also qualified to treat most children. A pedodontist is preferable for a young child, a child with medical problems, or one who needs to be sedated or anesthetized.

Learning Disorders Specialist

Sometimes a parent has a feeling that something is not quite right with their child's mental development. Yet every time a parent expresses concern, it is discounted or dismissed by well-meaning relatives and physicians. You know your child better than anyone, so trust your instincts. If you suspect that your child might have a learning disorder, have him evaluated by a trained specialist such as a psychologist or a special-education teacher. Early and proper diagnosis can make a major difference in resolving an educational problem that could seriously affect your child's life.

When seeking diagnosis, begin with your school district. In all states, school districts are required to provide an evaluation of any child from birth to age twenty-one in their jurisdiction and report their findings to the parent. If you're not satisfied with what you learn from that evaluation, then you can seek private testing from someone who specializes in learning disabilities and has had training in this area. Universities often have serices through education departments, and sometimes hospitals have developmental or neurological clinics and will do some learning-disability testing.

Nutritionist

If you desire specialized advice about your child's diet, you can consult a nutritionist. Common reasons for seeking a nutritionist's help include chronic skin, digestive, or weight problems and difficult eating habits or food allergies. Nutritionists are frequently available at multispecialty clinics, or your physician can refer you to one.

Speech Therapist

Children who experience repeated ear infections in the early years of life are at risk for later speech problems, because their hearing may have been impaired while early speech patterns were being established. A parent may be the last person to recognize a speech problem, because parents usually learn to understand their own child's speech regardless of how unintelligible it may be. Two clues for you are:

How does your child's speech honestly compare with that of other children his age? Children's speech should be intelligible by age three.

Do other people seem to have difficulty understanding him? Do you often translate for him to others?

I failed to realize that one of my own children had inarticulate speech at age three because I could understand, albeit with difficulty, what she was saying. Fortunately, my neighbor bluntly told me one day that the child could not be understood by others and needed a speech evaluation. After eight months of therapy, she spoke quite normally and by kindergarten no one could tell she'd ever had a problem.

If you or your child's physician decide that your child may have a speech problem, you can be optimistic. Most speech problems respond well to therapy, and your child will probably find speech therapy pleasant and even fun. Correcting abnormal speech patterns before school age will help prevent your child from being unfairly stigmatized by teachers and classmates.

In addition to the above health professionals, your pediatrician or family doctor might refer you to a physician certified in a subspecialty for a specific problem. Below is a list of specialists a child might encounter and some common reasons for referral. Hopefully this guide will make the world of medical specialties more understandable.

ENT (ear, nose, and throat), or Otolaryngologist

Treats: ears, nose, throat, sinuses, vocal cords
Why Referred: chronic ear infections and impaired hearing

Urologist

Treats: kidneys and bladder
Why Referred: recurrent urinary tract infections

Plastic surgeon

Treats: medical problems with cosmetic impact
Why Referred: birth defects, birthmarks, and injuries affecting appearance

Pediatric Surgeon or General Surgeon

Treats: conditions requiring abdominal surgery and other general surgery, specialized surgery in children
Why Referred: hernia repair, appendicitis, burn treatment, birth defects

Orthopedic Surgeon

Treats: bones and joints
Why Referred: hip dislocation, malformations of extremities, fractures, scoliosis

Ophthalmologist

Treats: eyes
Why Referred: crossed eyes, cataracts, nearsightedness, farsightedness

Cardiologist

Treats: heart and major blood vessels
Why Referred: heart murmur, heart defect, heart failure

Gastroenterologist

Treats: esophagus, stomach, small and large intestines
Why Referred: chronic diarrhea, chronic constipation, chronic vomiting, blood in stool

Neurologist

Treats: brain and spinal cord
Why Referred: epilepsy, developmental problems

Hematologist

Treats: disorders of any of the blood components
Why Referred: chronic anemia and abnormalities in red cells, white cells, or platelets

BASIC PARENT CARE

Perhaps the most overlooked area of baby care is parent care. How can you continuously offer care to your baby if you are completely depleted yourself? One of the nicest things you can do for your baby is to take care of yourself! Pay attention to your physical, mental, and emotional well-being.

You can easily find yourself physically run-down and fatigued during new parenthood: To some extent this is unavoidable in the early period of your baby's life. But to minimize your depletion, remember to eat. Keep nutritious snacks in your house and please don't try to diet at this time. Sleep when your baby sleeps. Nap instead of catching up on the housework: Go to bed early; those late movies will still be on when your baby is older and you're rested. Never stand when you can be sitting, never sit when you can be lying down, and never just lie down when you can be sleeping.

Physical help is important at this time. If you can, hire someone temporarily to help with the house. Or perhaps your partner will take on the major share of house maintenance. If someone comes to help you, such as your mother or a relative, it is crucial that they help with the house, not the baby. Resist the temptation to be the hostess, serving those who come to help you.

Mentally, you may be stressing yourself by believing you can do it all. You can't. Nobody can. Your old "production schedule" just won't fit into your new lifestyle. Slow down for a while and reorder your priorities. Some things will have to go. Keep caring for your baby (and other children if you have them), maintain some semblance of a relationship with your partner, and do only whatever else is truly essential. Everything else can wait. Your social life, work, hobbies, and obligations will all still be there in a few months. But your baby's care and your energy level are the only immediate concerns that cannot be postponed. Don't be hard on yourself; set only realistic expectations.

Your emotions will be in some turmoil as well. On the third day postpartum most mothers feel overly emotional and cry for little or no reason. Be reassured; there is nothing wrong with you. It happens to all of us and is due to hormonal changes and facing the reality of becoming a parent. Once you come home, there are other emotional hurdles to clear. Many women feel let down. They imagined an idyllic existence with their perfect baby and find instead much work, a baby who cries and needs to be fed and cared for around the clock. In addition, after enjoying all the attention you received during your pregnancy, you must step aside while all that attention is now showered on your baby. The temporary depression that often accompanies the early days with your baby is sometimes called "baby blues," or postpartum blues, and is experienced strongly by some women and not at all by others. It is generally short-lived. By six weeks, most parents feel they have adjusted to life with the new baby and experience a renewed sense of well-being. If your depression is either severe or prolonged, please seek counseling to help you make this adjustment.

The hardest part of new parenthood emotionally is that suddenly your life is all giving. Of course your baby brings you pleasure and caring for him gives you satisfaction, but you are on call twenty-four hours a day, every day of the week. You are putting out all the time—no lunch breaks, no days off. Giving so much can leave you feeling emotionally drained if you don't build a little receiving into your life. Do something for yourself every day. In the beginning it will probably be something very small. Give yourself time to read the paper, soak in a bath, or take a walk. One of the most important things you can do is surround yourself with a support system. It will probably be comprised mostly of friends. They are important. Having a baby doesn't mean you can't get together with friends. Invite them over or take the baby visiting.

Classes and organizations may be helpful to you, too. The YMCA and community centers often offer parenting classes. Parent and baby swim classes or gymnastic programs can be fun. If you are breast-feeding, don't miss out on the support of your local La Leche League group. You'll find like-minded friends and support for responsive parenting at their monthly meetings.

Find what it takes to keep you feeling sane and happy as you adjust to parenthood. Babies don't want martyrs for parents; they want happy people who are fulfilled themselves so that they can give freely and without resentment.

6 Nourishing Is Nurturing

EVERYONE LOVES TO FEED BABIES and other little creatures. We buy a new puppy doggie treats or toss him table scraps. Kids allow a purring kitten to lap leftover milk from their cereal bowl. We toss seeds and nuts to the birds and squirrels in our yard. On a picnic in the park, my kids will feed their entire sandwich to the eager, demanding ducks, aiming crumbs in the direction of those they think have not received a fair share. Everyone is so compelled to feed other creatures that signs in every zoo must warn us "Please don't feed the animals!" This irresistible desire to feed cute little things stems from the association we make between the act of feeding and love and affection.

Infant feeding, whether by breast or bottle, also involves more than just providing nutrition. It is a very rewarding and social activity, both for the baby and for the person feeding her. Feeding an infant allows one to feel the pleasure of satisfying another person's needs. For the baby, feeding satiates hunger and provides security, trust, and love.

BREAST FEEDING

Throughout history, the social and emotional experience of infant feeding has changed little, although the practical aspects of providing nourishment to babies has evolved. Until this century, no safe alternatives to breast feeding were available. Attempts to artificially feed infants were hampered by the lack of a nutritionally adequate food substitute and the inevitable contamination of infant foods with dangerous microorganisms, since neither pasteurization nor refrigeration existed. Infant death usually resulted from a combination of malnutrition and infection. We know that artificial feeding of infants has been attempted since ancient times, often because the mother had died during or shortly after childbirth. Artificially-fed infants, however, seldom survived until the advent of pasteurized commercial formulas that closely resembled the composition of breast milk.

Once the availability of safe and economical infant formula made it a feasible alternative to breast feeding, the popularity of breast feeding began to decline in the United States. This trend started in the early decades of this century due to a combination of social and cultural factors, including the growing numbers of women in the work force and the medical profession's initial enthusiasm for formula feeding. It was then believed that breast feeding and bottle feeding were comparable sources of infant nutrition. Perhaps women chose to formula-feed simply because infant feeding options had never previously existed. By the 1950s and 1960s, only one in five mothers elected to breast-feed her baby and bottle feeding was the norm.

Beginning in the early 1970s, the incidence of breast feeding began to increase once again, in that back-to-nature and health awareness era when natural childbirth experiences, sound nutritional habits, and physical fitness were all being emphasized. Breast milk was literally rediscovered by the medical profession, and its benefits to the infant were widely publicized to both lay and professional people. With this new knowledge, many mothers chose to breast-feed. The majority of new mothers now elect to breast-feed, so that nursing one's baby has again been established as the norm.

Advantages of Breast Feeding

Breast feeding is nature's design for feeding human babies. After millennia of evolution, the milk from each of the thousands of species of mammals is specially suited for the optimal growth and development of its young. Although infant formulas are made to closely resemble breast milk, new constituents in breast milk are discovered each year and there are others as yet undiscovered. Thus it remains impossible to successfully alter cow's milk, or any other formula, to perfectly match human milk composition.

Colostrum

Colostrum is the thick, premilk fluid that appears in the breasts in late pregnancy and is present for the first few days after delivery, until the milk "comes in." Colostrum is higher in protein, vitamins, and minerals than breast milk and lower in fat and the milk sugar, lactose. It contains large amounts of antibodies and other immunological properties, including white blood cells. A newly discovered property in colostrum increases the gut's absorptive capacity for nutrients, and colostrum's natural laxative effect helps clear the intestinal meconium that has formed in utero. Colostrum is a perfect, easily digestible first food for a new infant. It helps protect her from infections and prepares her intestines for breast-milk feedings.

Because colostrum is present in such small quantities, however, many health professionals advocate giving supplemental water or formula to a newborn during the first few days after birth. But consider for a moment a newborn's tiny, "virgin" stomach, her neurological system still unskilled at the complex task of sucking and swallowing while breathing, and her digestive system, which has not yet processed food or produced stool regularly. In this light, the scant volumes of colostrum that gradually increase seem less like a starvation diet and more like the perfect way to introduce a newborn to obtaining her postnatal nutrition. Furthermore, healthy infants are born with sufficient water and sugar stores to last until the milk comes in.

Even if a mother does not plan long-term breast feeding, her infant can benefit greatly from early colostrum feeds. Since "dry-up" medicines are no longer routinely prescribed for bottle-feeding mothers, some bottle-feeding women choose to nurse occasionally during the first postpartum week. This helps them dry up more comfortably, while allowing their infant to receive some of the benefits of the precious early milk. Occasionally a mother who begins with colostrum feedings finds that she and her baby enjoy breast feeding, and she decides to nurse after all.

Nutritional Benefits of Breast Milk

The three major components of food that provide for growth and energy are protein, fat, and carbohydrate. The ratio of these nutrients in breast milk and the percentage of calories that an infant receives from each is optimal for infant growth. Although formulas now contain these major nutrients in proper ratios, they are unable to duplicate their exact composition in breast milk. Thus, the *type* of protein, fat, and carbohydrate differs in breast milk and formula, even though the *amount of* protein, fat and carbohydrate is similar.

The American Academy of Pediatrics and other experts on infant feeding agree that optimal infant nutrition for the first four to six months of life is provided by exclusive breast feeding.

Other elements in breast milk, including vitamins, minerals, enzymes, and water, are present in the exact amounts that a newborn needs and can best utilize. It is the complicated way in which these components work in combination with one another that makes breast milk impossible to duplicate. Let's look at two of the many components in breast milk: lactoferrin, a protein, and iron, a mineral. Although babies need iron to make red blood cells, iron is also a necessary ingredient for the growth and multiplication of bacteria in the gastrointestinal tract, some of which can cause disease. Lactoferrin is a protein that binds to iron in the intestines and prevents bacteria from using iron, while still allowing the baby's system to absorb it.

A baby reaps the greatest benefits of breast milk during that period of her life when she is exclusively breast fed. We are beginning to learn that the addition of other substances to a baby's diet affects the interaction of ingredients in breast milk. Obviously, additional foods are necessary after four to six months of age when breast milk no longer supplies all a baby's growth needs. But until that time, the addition of unnecessary supplemental foods or formula will compromise and diminish the maximum benefits of breast feeding.

Although babies may be allergic to infant formulas, it is impossible for a baby to be allergic to mother's milk. Breast-fed infants can react to foods in their mother's diets, such as cow's milk or peanut butter, but breast milk itself is nonallergenic. Also, it is difficult to overfeed a breast-fed baby, thus placing her at less risk of infant and childhood obesity.

Immunological Benefits of Breast Feeding

When formulas first came into use, it was soon recognized that artificially fed infants experienced more gastrointestinal and upper respiratory infections than breast-fed babies. The risks of formula feeding are greatest in underdeveloped countries where contaminated water may be used to mix formula and insufficient quantities are fed to an undernourished infant. In the United States, where sterile formulas and pure water are available and almost everyone can afford to feed adequate amounts, health differences between breast- and bottle-fed infants are harder to detect. Most would agree, however, that breast-fed infants do experience fewer bouts of diarrhea than artificially-fed infants.

Many immunological components have been identified in breast milk to explain how it protects against illness. Breast milk contains antibodies against organisms to which the mother has been exposed. In fact, antibodies often will appear in breast milk even before they can be detected in the mother's own blood, as if nature were more concerned about protecting the young infant from illness than the mother herself. Breast milk also contains white blood cells that produce antibodies or ingest bacteria. A host of enzymes and other protein substances help protect against infection in a variety of ways. A breast-fed baby's stool is more acid than that of a formula-fed baby. This acid intestinal environment favors the growth of a harmless germ instead of disease-producing ones, and is one of the reasons that gastrointestinal infections are rare in breast-fed infants. These immune properties are absent in formulas, and no one has yet discovered a way to add them.

Other Benefits of Breast Feeding

Although bonding is important, its magic has been exaggerated in many descriptions. What science has recently labeled as "parent-infant bonding," new parents have known about all along, only they simply called it "falling in love." Breast feeding won't guarantee bonding. But the early, loving, skin-to-skin contact that breast feeding affords may enhance the process. Obviously, you will fall in love with your baby regardless of how you feed her.

Breast feeding is the easiest, most convenient way to feed a baby. Breast milk is highly portable; it never needs heating or refrigeration. The container is sterile, self-cleaning, and unbreakable. There's no mixing, no mess, no trips cut short because you didn't bring along enough to feed your baby, no cold kitchen floors to walk at 3:00 A.M. while you prepare a bottle of formula.

Furthermore, breast feeding is inexpensive! What new parent can't appreciate a savings of money? Six months of not buying formula can save enough to purchase a major household appliance.

An incidental advantage of breast feeding is the pleasant fragrance of breast milk. It leaves no unpleasant scent when spit up, and a breast-milk stool has a tart, inoffensive odor, unlike the hold-your-nose type of stool of a formula-fed infant.

Oxytocin, a hormone released during breast feeding, helps the mother's uterus contract back to its normal size. Breast feeding also temporarily alters the hormonal balance in a woman's body and suppresses ovulation. The return of menstrual periods is delayed while a woman breast-feeds, thus reducing the risk of anemia from blood loss and decreasing the possibility of conception. However, BREAST FEEDING IS CERTAINLY NOT A FOOL-PROOF METHOD OF CONTRACEPTION. If you plan to incorporate this anovulatory time into your birth-control planning, you can read about it further in *Natural Family Planning: The Ecology of Natural Mothering* by Sheila and John Kippley. Consult with your physician to assure that you fully understand the relationship between breast feeding and your reproductive cycle.

Finally, breast feeding uses calories that most postpartum women are happy to give up. The fat stores laid down during pregnancy were meant to subsidize breast feeding and usually will melt away gradually during months of lactation.

The Decision

Knowing these advantages of breast feeding may help you decide how you will feed your baby. The majority of women decide about infant feeding well before the end of their pregnancy. Most of us have a mental image of ourselves as a mother, including imagining ourselves feeding the infant, by the time we feel the baby move. Our past exposure to breast feeding, our comfort with our bodies, whether we think we were breast fed, and a host of other conscious and subconscious factors contribute to the infant feeding decision.

How the infant will be fed should also be a joint decision made by both partners. An enthusiastic father should not impose breast feeding upon a mother who does not want to nurse. On the other hand, a woman motivated to nurse her infant should never be discouraged by a partner who dislikes the idea.

My concern is that each of you make an informed decision, based on accurate information. I encounter many parents who are interested in breast feeding, but who decide against it because of misconceptions. I urge you to read and become knowledgeable about breast feeding. The chart below shows some commonly expressed breast-feeding myths and misconceptions and the facts that dispel them.

How to Breast-feed

"If breast feeding is so natural, why do I have to read about how to do it?" That is one of the first questions I'm

MYTH	FACT
Breast feeding is too much bother.	Although only you can feed the baby, many women find breast feeding is less bother than preparing formula and feeding with bottles, especially in the middle of the night.
Breast feeding ruins the shape of your breasts.	Your breasts fill with milk after delivery whether or not you intend to breast-feed. Pregnancy alone changes your breasts, and such changes are largely dependent upon heredity.
Breast feeding is uncomfortable.	Your nipples may be slightly tender in the first few days, but thereafter breast feeding does not hurt. Even when your baby gets teeth, breast feeding will not be uncomfortable, since her tongue covers her lower teeth when she nurses.
Breast feeding ties you down.	Although only you can feed the baby, a breast-fed baby is so portable that she easily goes anywhere you do. There is no fuss preparing bottles and no chance of being caught unprepared to feed her.
A nursing mother's milk supply is very fragile and can easily "dry up."	Hormonal responses in your body condition your breasts to produce the right amount of milk in response to your

MYTH	FACT
	baby's sucking. This supply-and-demand mechanism allows your baby to stimulate a milk supply to meet her needs.
Breast feeding is impossible if your breasts are too small (or too large).	Differences in breast size primarily result from fat tissue (not the number of milk-producing glands) and thus breast size has little effect on your ability to nurse.
Breast feeding makes the father feel left out.	Fathers of breast-fed babies are likely to feel proud and supportive of breast feeding, and they can find many warm and special ways to be involved in the care of their babies.
Breast feeding makes it hard to lose weight.	On the contrary, breast feeding utilizes calories, in both the milk itself and the energy spent to produce it.
Breast feeding requires that the mother follow a very restricted diet.	Most breast-feeding mothers do not find any reason to change the types of food they eat.
Breast feeding is impossible if you go back to work.	Many mothers continue to nurse very successfully after returning to work, if they are provided with accurate information. Working and nursing need not be mutually exclusive.

MYTH	FACT
Breast feeding won't work if you are too nervous and high-strung.	It is a rare woman who cannot condition her let-down reflex to occur, no matter how wound up she feels the rest of the day.
Breast feeding won't work for you if your mother failed at it.	Many of our mothers failed because of lack of accurate information and their physicians' eagerness to switch to formula, not because of any genetic or physical incapability.

asked when I recommend that patients learn about breast feeding.

Breast feeding is natural. But until recently, it was also natural for a girl to grow up watching her mothers, aunts, sisters, and neighbors breastfeed their children. Girls casually learned about breast feeding from childhood on. Today, most of our mothers and aunts have bottle fed their babies, our sisters probably live in other states, and many of us don't even know our neighbors. So we miss out on that handed-down knowledge from our mothers and grandmothers, and the easy acceptance of breast feeding as a tidy package of feeding, loving, and caring for the baby.

Fortunately, with some advance knowledge, and patience and commitment, the chance that nature will take its course—that breast feeding will succeed—is vastly increased.

How Milk Is Made: It is helpful to understand how milk is produced and released from the breast. During pregnancy, your breasts enlarge with the development of a network of milk-producing glands and ducts to carry milk to the nipple openings. You may have noticed a small

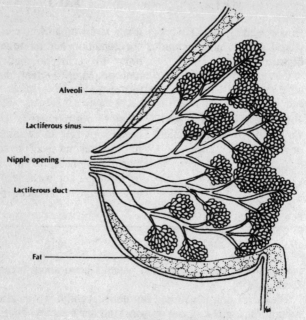

Alveoli

Lactiferous sinus

Nipple opening

Lactiferous duct

Fat

ANATOMY OF THE BREAST

amount of thick, yellowish colostrum appearing from your nipples. After delivery, colostrum is your baby's first food. By the second to fourth day, colostrum increases in volume and begins to change to a whitish appearance, as your milk "comes in." Your breasts become quite full and milk may drip and leak spontaneously.

Prolactin, a hormone secreted from the pituitary gland whenever your baby nurses, is the primary hormone involved in milk production. The more your baby nurses, the more prolactin is released and the more milk you make.

Oxytocin is another hormone released in response to nursing. It causes tiny muscle cells surrounding the milk glands to contract and eject milk into the ducts and down to storage areas called sinuses, near the nipple openings. The release of oxytocin and the ejection of milk from the glands is known as the "let-down reflex." This is perceived by many women as a "pins-and-needles" or "tightening'' sensation in both breasts as milk begins to flow. Other women with a normal let-down response don't seem to notice the sensations. Sometimes just thinking about your baby or hearing her cry will make your milk let down.

Correct Breast Feeding Technique: Many women believe that breast-feeding is pure instinct for both mother and baby. This is not true. Each mother's breasts and nipples are slightly different and each baby's mouth is uniquely shaped, and so every mother-baby couple has to spend a "learning period" getting accustomed to nursing. It is best to start as soon as possible after delivery, when both of you are alert, and before your baby has had too much exposure to the rubber nipples on bottles.

Most of us imagine initiating nursing by holding our new baby on her back, with her head cradled in the crook of our arm. But that position leves the baby's mouth aimed at the ceiling and the nipple aimed at the wall! In this position we are told to stimulate her cheek so that she will turn her head toward the breast. Have you ever tried to drink and swallow with your head turned to one side?

To correctly position your baby to nurse, lie her on her side, with her entire body facing you. Be sure you are comfortable, with back support, and that your baby is elevated to the level of your breast so that you aren't hunching over to reach her. Hold her securely, with the *side* of her head in the crook of your arm and her abdomen against yours. Tuck your baby's lower arm (the one nearest your body) around your side to keep her hand out of the way.

Since most women have rather flat, soft nipples, it will be much easier for your infant to grasp your nipple correctly if you aid her by making your nipple more erectile. You can do this by supporting the breast with your third, fourth, and fifth fingers of your free hand; then place your thumb at the upper outer margin of the areola and your index finger at the lower outer areolar margin. Gently tickle your baby's lip with your nipple until she opens her mouth *wide* (she'll do it—it's a reflex) and then pull her close, center your nipple within her mouth (see page 185), and allow her to latch on. When done correctly, she'll be directly facing the breast, with her mouth open very wide and her bottom lip curled out. You will feel her gentle tugging motions as she sucks, but there should be no discomfort.

Your nipple and areola will be stretched far back into your baby's mouth during nursing. Sore nipples often occur because the nipple is not centered within the baby's mouth, causing one area of skin to be excessively stretched or to rub against the roof of the baby's mouth.

The suction created while nursing is very strong; don't ever try to pull your nipple out of your baby's mouth without breaking suction first. In order to remove your baby from the breast before she releases naturally, break suction by sliding your finger into the corner of her mouth along your breast.

Breast-Feeding Routines: Begin by nursing for five minutes at each breast at each feeding on the first day. Nursing for fewer than five minutes may not be long enough for the let-down reflex to occur. On the second day, you may increase to 10 minutes at each breast at each feeding, and by the third day, you will probably be comfortable nursing for 10 to 15 minutes on the first side and as long as the baby wants on the second.

After nursing for 10 or 15 minutes at one breast, pause to burp your baby to bring up any air bubbles and to arouse her to nurse on the second breast. You should burp her after the second breast as well so that she will sleep comfortably after feeding.

Since the most vigorous sucking stimulation is at the first breast, be sure to alternate sides on which you start feedings. You can use a safety pin on your bra strap to indicate which breast to offer next.

Expect to nurse every 2-3 hours round-the-clock, or 8 to 12 times a day, during the early weeks of breast-feeding. This schedule helps assure that your baby gets plenty to eat and a generous milk supply is generated. Most young breast-fed infants will sleep one 5-hour stretch each day, preferably at night. Remember the law of supply and demand: The more often your infant nurses, the greater milk supply you will produce. I encourge my patients to pour themselves a glass of juice or water before sitting down to nurse. This will guarantee adequate daily fluid intake for a nursing mother, and drinking often triggers the let-down reflex.

Infants vary considerably in their nursing styles; some are loud squawkers who demand to nurse every few hours whereas others are placid and quiet and may sleep through feeding times without indicating they are hungry. In the early weeks, it is a good idea to awaken a non-demanding infant after 3½ hours during the daytime and encourage her to nurse until she is demanding more predictably. Some infants stop nursing once they have emptied most of the milk, whereas others linger at the breast for many extra minutes of comfort and security. Soon you will recognize your baby's style of nursing and know what to expect from her. Remember that your baby is an individual, and will develop her own preferences and routines, as the two of you become a "nursing couple."

Because your sleep will be disrupted for several weeks or longer, it is crucial that you nap periodically throughout the day whenever your infant falls asleep. In this way you will be more physically able to cope with the frequency of the early feeding schedule. There is nothing wrong with bringing your baby to your bed to nurse during the night feedings, where you can rest or nod off to sleep yourself.

Perhaps the best advice a breast-feeding mother should remember is: When in doubt, nurse. Nursing is not simply a way of getting food into a baby's stomach; it is also a way of nurturing. Nursing is meant to pacify, to comfort a fussy baby, to offer close contact, to provide social interaction, and to put babies to sleep.

It's hard at first. We feel compelled to time, weigh, and measure everything that relates to our new baby. Many new mothers I see have questions like: "She's fussy and seems hungry, but it's only been an hour and a half. Should I nurse again already?" (Yes.) "My breasts are full and tender—she's been sleeping almost five full hours. Is it okay for me to wake her up and nurse?" (Yes.)

Maternal Diet: Maternal diet is another topic that prompts many questions among nursing mothers. That's not surprising since maternal weight loss, optimum infant nutrition, and the effect of components of the mother's diet on the nursing baby are all of concern to a new mother. You can be assured that the quality of milk you produce is uniformly excellent, but the amount varies with the frequency of feeding and your physical well-being, nutrition, and rest. Now is not the time to start a strict diet, as a sudden decrease in caloric intake may dramatically diminish your milk supply.

Maintain your health and stick to the good eating habits you practiced when you were pregnant. You should continue taking your prenatal vitamins, and since nursing requires approximately 500 extra calories a day, you'll want to have nutritious snacks on hand. Try to eat a variety of foods in as natural a form as possible. Limit your caffeine intake (coffee, tea, and cola) to three cups a day. It has been noted that excess ingestion (over 16 ounces per day) of cow's milk by nursing mothers may be associated with symptoms of colic in their infants. If after one or two trials you notice a particular food in your diet that seems to upset your baby, try to avoid it. But unless you make specific observations, it is not necessary to restrict any foods from your diet just because you are nursing.

Is My Baby Getting Enough To Eat? Because it is impossible to see exactly how much milk a breast-fed infant is taking, parents often wonder how to tell if their baby is getting enough to eat. There are several things you can look for. Your baby should act hungry and demand to eat approximately every 2-3 hours, with one longer night interval. She should nurse well from both breasts, swallow audibly during the feeding, and appear satisfied for the next few hours. Your breasts should feel full before each feeding and softer after nursing. You might notice milk dripping from one breast while your baby feeds from the other. Your baby should have a wet diaper with each feeding and her urine should be clear, not dark. For approximately the first month, a well-nourished breast-fed infant will pass a soft, yellow, curdy bowel movement six or more times each day. After the first several months, breast-fed infants may have a bowel movement only once or twice a week, but in the early weeks, infrequent stooling is a strong clue to inadequate milk intake. Whenever you doubt the adequacy of your baby's intake of breast milk, it is always best to check your baby's weight at her doctor's office. Breast-feeding problems that are detected

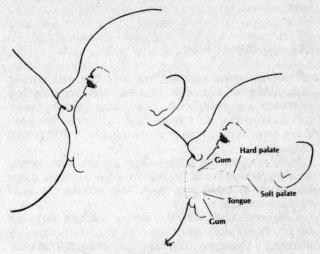

NIPPLE POSITION WHILE NURSING

early are much easier to remedy than those overlooked for many weeks.

Supplemental Bottles: Although it is common for a nursing mother to offer her infant bottles of either water or formula, regular supplementation may actually disrupt the success of breast-feeding. Due to the close balance of breast milk supply and the infant's demand, it is important to nurse an infant as often as she appears hungry in order to stimulate the breast milk supply that is right for her.

If your baby's father or grandparent wants to be able to feed the baby at times, you may want to hand express or pump some of your milk and put it in a bottle so the baby occasionally can be fed by another caretaker. Also, if you know that you will be going back to work, you will want to keep your baby familiar with the bottle nipple so that she will readily accept the bottle in your absence. Offering a bottle twice a week after the first few weeks of breast-feeding should be sufficient to keep your baby familiar with the artificial nipple. Many mothers prefer to use an orthodontic nipple when they offer a bottle, since this nipple shape resembles the shape of the breast nipple in the baby's mouth.

Solving Breast-feeding Difficulties

Our body systems usually function pretty well, with an occasional quirk that needs some attention. We learn how to prevent minor problems, and/or to remedy temporary malfunctions like constipation or a stiff neck. We don't really expect our bodies to perform perfectly 100 percent of the time.

Few breast-feeding problems signal failure or necessitate the disruption of breast feeding. Most problems are minor and can be managed quite easily. Here are some areas of common concern:

Caesarean Birth: Although mother and baby may be a bit groggy early on, breast feeding can progress smoothly following a Caesarean birth. Many Caesarean mothers nurse in the recovery room. While the incision is healing, a little extra patience may be required to find a comfortable position for nursing. If you feel that you need the pain medication you're offered, by all means don't think you have to refuse it because you are nursing. Nursing will be much easier if you are comfortable and a few doses of pain medication pose no risk to your infant.

Nipple Confusion: Some perfectly normal infants and motivated mothers still have difficulty getting started as a nursing couple. After repeated exposure to the rubber nipple on bottles, some infants become accustomed to a long, stiff artificial nipple as early as the first or second day of life. They readily accept the bottle, but when put to the breast they fret and fuss and don't seem to know how to draw the mother's nipple into their mouth to nurse effectively. This common problem is known as "nipple confusion," and can be frustrating to overcome. The best approach is to nurse your baby soon after birth and as often as she shows interest, so that she readily becomes familiar with the breast nipple. If nipple confusion occurs, try to discontinue all artificial nipples (including pacifiers) and patiently help your baby learn to grasp your nipple. Using a breast pump before feedings will start some milk flowing and draw your nipple out. You might manipulate your nipple a little to make it as protractile as possible.

Offer your breast whenever your baby is sufficiently alert to nurse instead of waiting until she is frantically hungry and upset. The "football hold" often facilitates infant grasp of the nipple. Avoid using a nipple shield, or rubber nipple placed over your own nipple, as this practice only reinforces the artificial nipple. If you must turn to a nipple shield as a last resort, then try at every feeding to wean from it. As soon as the baby is nursing contentedly, slip out the nipple shield and offer your nipple directly. Until your infant learns to nurse well, express your milk regularly with an electric breast pump in order to maintain a generous milk supply. You may have to supplement the baby bottle as you continue trying to teach her to nurse. If you have any doubt that your baby is getting enough to eat, have her weighed at the pediatrician's office and seek professional help with your breast-feeding technique.

Engorgement: On the second to fourth day after the birth of your baby, you will notice your breasts have become larger, very firm, and slightly tender, as abundant milk production begins. Scant yellowish colostrum changes to creamy white milk in generous amounts. Sometimes the breast swelling may make the nipple more difficult to grasp, and the baby may cause nipple tenderness by latch-

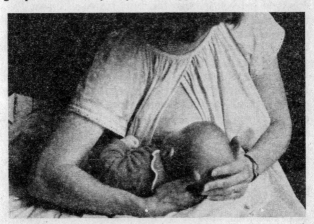

FOOTBALL HOLD *(Phil Stietenroth)*

ing onto the tip of the nipple only, rather than also taking some areola into her mouth. To ensure that she is able to get your nipple far enough into her mouth to nurse properly, hand express a little milk before you offer her the breast. This will make the areola softer and easier to grasp.

Even bottle-feeding mothers become engorged when their milk "comes in," but if engorgement is not relieved, the pressure causes the glands to stop producing milk. It is important to relieve engorgement by nursing frequently, around the clock in order to maintain milk production.

If engorgement becomes uncomfortable, you can either gently pump or hand express a little milk. Don't empty your breasts completely; just reduce the firmness enough to relieve the discomfort. Heat will enhance blood flow and hasten the let-down, so a warm shower or a warm washcloth may help relieve engorgement.

Sore Nipples: Although sore nipples are fairly common among breastfeeding mothers, soreness can be minimized by proper positioning of the baby at the breast. As you begin to nurse, pay close attention to the guidelines on pages 181-86. Soon positioning your baby will be so automatic that you won't even think about it.

Sore nipples may be more common among women with dry skin. If you do get sore nipples, the tenderness will probably last only a few days. Here are some do's and don'ts to get you through this brief period of discomfort: Don't wash your nipples with soap or apply lotions containing alcohol; this will dry them out. Don't pull your baby off the breast without breaking suction. Finally, don't give up. They'll feel better soon!

Do attend to your baby's nursing position; you can also try the "football hold" (see page 187) to change the pressure points on the nipple. Keep your nipples dry, change nursing pads often, and apply a thin layer of lanolin to the nipples after nursing. Frequent shorter feedings are often better tolerated than lengthy nursings.

Drugs in Breast Milk: Almost any drug a mother takes will appear in her breast milk in some amount. Fortunately, the amount in the milk is usually too small to be of any consequence to the infant. But since there are some drugs that should not be given to infants in any amount, it is important to notify your doctor about all medications that you need to take. Don't decline treatment for an illness simply because you are nursing, however. Most medications can be taken without harm, and often a safe alternative to an objectionable medication can be found.

Drugs that pose a problem for a nursing baby include radioactive compounds, anticancer drugs, lithium, marijuana, and alcohol in excessive amounts.

Nicotine can affect infants more significantly than you may imagine. Although nicotine does not pass into breast milk to any significant degree, whenever you smoke in the presence of your baby, the infant passively smokes, too. Children of smokers develop bronchitis and pneumonia more often than children of nonsmokers. If you smoke, you would be doing your baby and yourself a great favor by quitting or cutting down as much as you can. Never smoke while nursing or holding your baby, or even while in the same room with your baby.

Drugs that mothers often worry about but that do not really present a problem include most antibiotics, pain medications, and antihistamines. Although standard birth-control pills are not recommended for breastfeeding mothers, some authorities think that the minipill is acceptable during lactation if it is delayed four to six weeks until breast feeding is well established. Any time you need to take a specific medication, you can check its safety for your baby by calling your regional drug consultation center or your baby's physician.

Mastitis: Occasionally a breast-feeding mother will develop a breast infection, known as mastitis. The symptoms of mastitis are a "flu-like" feeling, with fever, chills, and achiness. There is usually a reddened area of the breast that is warm, firm, and painful. Years ago, doctors routinely prescribed weaning for maternal mastitis, but it is now recognized that continued nursing helps resolve mastitis sooner. Obtain antibiotic treatment promptly from your physician if you suspect mastitis. Hot packs, pain medication and rest will also help you feel better sooner.

Special Circumstances

Premature or Sick Infant: If you had planned to breast-feed but your infant is sick or premature and unable to nurse for a period of time, you can still breast-feed with some extra effort. It will be important for you to obtain an efficient breast pump, preferably an electric pump, in order to stimulate your breasts regularly to produce a generous milk supply. You will need to empty the milk from your breasts just as if you were nursing. You can save the expressed milk to be fed to your baby by bottle or tube until she is able to nurse. By regularly expressing milk, you will ensure a supply for your baby when she is ready to nurse. Talk to the nurses caring for your baby about the details of breast-feeding a hospitalized newborn.

Although pumping and storing milk for a sick or premature infant takes a great deal of time and effort, it is well worth the investment to contribute to your baby's care in this important way. Even if your baby receives your expressed milk for only a short period, you will have given her a gift of love that only you can provide.

Twins: It is possible to nurse twins. If both infants are nursed often, the breasts get twice as much stimulation and

BREAST-FEEDING TWINS

so produce twice as much milk. Obviously this involves many round-the-clock feedings, and a mother usually requires outside help and support during the early weeks to keep up with the frequency of feedings. After a month or so, nursing twins can be easier than bottle feeding, since there is no bother with formula or bottles.

In the beginning, it may be best to feed each baby separately until you are familiar with the feeding style of each infant. Later, you may find you can position both infants to nurse at once. If one infant is bigger and nurses more vigorously than the other, it is usually best to rotate the breast you nurse her on so that she can help stimulate a generous milk supply in both breasts. When nursing twins together, the bigger twin can generate the let-down reflex for the smaller twin at the same time. Nursing twins is a big effort, and even if some supplement is required, the babies can still enjoy the special closeness that nursing provides.

Cleft Lip and/or Palate: If your infant is born with a cleft lip and/or palate (in which the upper lip and/or roof of the mouth failed to fuse normally, leaving a gap in the structures), it may still be possible to partially breast-feed. Since an infant with a cleft lip or palate has difficulty sucking effectively, it is likely that you will have to pump your breasts after nursing in order to keep up a generous milk supply and to obtain milk to supplement your baby after she attempts nursing. You can first offer your breast, then supplement your baby with formula or your expressed milk by cup, bottle, or syringe. Infants with cleft lip alone can sometimes breast-feed successfully, but those with cleft palate will usually be unable to effectively obtain milk by nursing. They can still enjoy the close security of breast feeding and the comfort it offers even if most of their nutrition is obtained by cup or bottle. Because of their special feeding problems, infants with cleft lip and/or palate need close follow-up to monitor their weight gain and ensure that they are getting enough to eat.

Hospitalized Infant or Mother: In the event that either you or your baby needs to be hospitalized while you are still nursing, you will want to avoid being separated for long periods if at all possible. You might request that your baby room-in with you if you are hospitalized and are still capable of caring for your baby. Or you might have a relative bring the baby to you for as many nursings as possible.

If your baby is hospitalized, you may be able to room-in with her, or at least be present for a large part of each day. Continuing to nurse will help your baby cope with hospitalization.

If you must be separated from the baby for more than a few hours at a time, you will want to express milk from your breasts to maintain your supply and to keep your breasts comfortable. Follow the nurses' instructions for storing the expressed milk so that it can be fed to your baby in your absence.

Hand, or manual, expression is comfortable and simple and can be performed anywhere. To hand express milk, cup your breast with the third, fourth, and fifth fingers of one hand, and grasp the areola with the thumb and index finger. Gently roll your thumb and finger toward each other, compressing the areola between them. Many women can effectively empty their breasts in this way, especially if they experience a spontaneous let-down reflex. Manual, battery-operated, and electric breast pumps are all available commercially (see page 69) if desired. Whenever you express milk, it is imperative that you use good hygiene and follow carefully all cleaning instructions for your breast pump.

Employed Mother: If you plan to return to work after your baby is born, it is possible to continue breast feeding, and nursing will add a wonderful continuity to your relationship with your baby. During your absence, your baby can be fed either formula or expressed breast milk.

It is important to nurse often whenever you are with your baby. Night nursings are often the key to success for an employed mother. Nursing at night keeps your milk supply up and offers extra time for closeness with your baby. If you can nurse comfortably with your baby in bed with you, you'll be more rested.

If you will be expressing breast milk during the work day, the details of pumping, transporting, and storing breast milk can be found in *The Breastfeeding Guide for the Working Woman* (Wallaby Books/Simon and Schuster). *Breastfeeding Success for Working Mothers,* by Marilyn Grams, M.D. (Achievement Press) also contains valuable tips for combining employment and breast feeding.

Some general guidelines about breast-milk storage are:

√ Store in the refrigerator and use within forty-eight hours.
√ If milk needs to be kept for longer than forty-eight hours, store up to three weeks in a refrigerator freezer without a separate door, or
√ Store up to three months in a refrigerator freezer with a separate door, or
√ Store up to six months in a deep freezer that maintains zero degrees.
√ Quick-thaw frozen milk under tepid running water.
√ Once thawed, breast milk can be kept refrigerated for up to twenty-four hours.
√ Milk that has been offered to the baby but not finished can be refrigerated promptly and used within four hours.

When Breast Feeding Doesn't Work Out

Although most women can breast-feed successfully, a few women are unable to produce a full milk supply despite their most conscientious efforts. After all, every organ in the body experiences malfunction, and so does the breast. A small percentage of women, for example, have insufficient glandular development to produce enough milk for a baby's needs. Other women need to take a medication that is contraindicated for a baby and are forced to choose their own health over breast-feeding their babies. Other women have a variety of medical or psychological problems that make breast feeding impossible for them. A few babies have medical problems that will preclude breast feeding.

If breast feeding does not work for you, for whatever reason, do not view this as a failure. If you breast-fed for even a short time, you gave your baby valuable antibodies in colostrum. You have also learned a close intimate style of mothering and you can continue that when you bottle-feed. Each of us must do the best we can with the circumstances we have. There are many ways to nurture, love, and comfort an infant apart from breast feeding.

FORMULA FEEDING

Although breast feeding is rising in popularity, formula feeding is still common. Parents choose formula feeding for a variety of reasons, including the desire to share feedings jointly by both parents or other caretakers; the personal feeling that breast feeding is immodest; the need to return to work soon after delivery (although it is still possible to continue breastfeeding); the belief that formula feeding is easier or more convenient; previous bottle-feeding experience that was positive and enjoyable; previous breast-feeding experience that was difficult or unfulfilling; maternal illness, breast abnormalities, or breast surgery that prevents breast feeding; infant adoption; multiple births; and other practical and personal reasons. Many women who initiate breast feeding switch to partial or complete formula feeding sometime in the infant's first year of life. In fact, the vast majority of parents give their infants bottles occasionally or regularly.

Formula feeding is safe and healthy. Despite the nutritional superiority of breast milk, it's not possible to distinguish among a class of preschoolers who was breast fed and who was formula fed. What's important is that adequate volumes of milk be prepared correctly and fed lovingly.

Formula Preparations

Infant formula is readily available in supermarkets and drugstores under several brand names and in numerous preparations. The formula your baby starts out on in the hospital probably depends upon which brand a formula company provided to the nursery. Many parents prefer to keep their baby on that formula, but there is no harm switching to another brand that is more readily available or that you used with your last baby. There are minor differences among the major brands, but they are basically very similar, and each provides sound nutrition.

Concerned and conscientious parents often ask me whether a homemade formula, or goat's-milk formula, or other special preparation would be preferable to commercial infant formula. I must reply with an emphatic *NO!* Making an infant formula is no small matter. There are well over a hundred presently identified ingredients in human milk and more being discovered all the time. Each must be present in formula in an exact amount, since milk is your baby's only source of nutrition in the early months. The absence of even one nutrient in your baby's exclusive milk diet could have devastating results. The major infant formula companies routinely conduct research and continually modify their products to resemble breast milk as closely as possible. If an infant is not breast fed, prepared infant formula provides the best nutritional substitute.

Each brand of infant formula can be found on your grocery shelf in a variety of preparations. In general, the more convenient the preparation, the higher the price of the formula.

Ready-to-feed: Ready-to-feed formula is available in thirty-two-ounce cans. It must *not* be mixed with water, or your baby will not get enough calories. It is convenient to use, since it requires no mixing and you pour it directly from the can. Unopened cans of formula can be stored on your pantry shelf. Once opened, however, formula must always be refrigerated and used within forty-eight hours.

Concentrated Formula: Concentrated formula comes in thirteen-ounce cans and *must* be mixed with water before being fed to your baby. You mix it in a 1:1 ratio with water. Thus, if you wanted to make a four-ounce bottle, you would add two ounces of concentrate and two ounces of water. Concentrated formula is less convenient but also less costly than ready-to-feed.

Powdered Formula: Powdered formula comes in a large can with a scoop inside. You mix it by adding one scoop of formula to every two ounces of water. Powdered formula is the least expensive form, and it is convenient for traveling. You can just bring bottles with premeasured powder in them without worrying about the milk spoiling. When you are ready to feed the baby, you just add water.

Each of the above preparations comes in two forms: with and without iron, clearly marked on the label. Your baby's health-care provider will let you know whether or not they recommend iron-fortified formula for your baby. Full-term, healthy babies don't need extra iron for several months, but some pediatricians like to start them out on it so you won't need to switch later. Premature infants, or those with low blood counts, need iron sooner.

Each of the major formula brands also offers a soy formula preparation, in which soy is the protein source. Soy formulas also differ from regular formulas in the type of sugar used as the carbohydrate component. The type of fat is slightly different, too. The overall amounts of protein, carbohydrate, and fat are still the same as in regular cow's-milk formula, however.

Soy formula may be recommended for your baby if you have a strong family history of milk allergy, though soy is potentially allergenic also. Soy formulas are also commonly used temporarily following a bout of infant diarrhea, since they are thought to be more easily absorbed by the healing intestinal tract. Since the greatest experience in formula-feeding babies has been with regular formula, I don't recommend using soy milk routinely, just when one of these indications exists.

Other formula preparations can make formula feeding more convenient. For example, you can buy ready-to-feed milk in eight-ounce cans designed for travel. By opening only eight ounces at a time and pouring it into a bottle, you don't need to worry about storing opened cans of milk or mixing formula with a different water supply. Formula can also be purchased in those convenient four-ounce ready-to-feed bottles found in hospitals. I know one mother who used these for the middle-of-the-night feedings during the early weeks home. She simply opened a bottle at her bedside and felt the extra expense was definitely worth it!

You may want to have several different types of formula preparation on hand and use a combination of them, such as concentrated formula at home, powdered formula for running errands with your baby, or keeping on hand at the sitter's, and eight-ounce ready-to-feed cans for travel. Gone are the days when preparation of an infant formula involved elaborate sterilizing, mixing, and measuring.

Now that you are comfortable with what you are going to feed your infant, let's discuss other supplies you'll need and the actual mechanics of bottle feeding.

Many principles of breast feeding are worth incorporating into bottle feeding. For the first four months or so, always hold your baby when you feed her and whenever possible thereafter. Never prop the bottle. An infant too young to hold her own bottle is at risk of choking if the bottle is propped. Besides, propping the bottle eliminates the social interaction of feeding. Although many infants learn to hold their own bottle by four or five months of age, I know one baby who refused to do so. She figured out it was more stimulating and enjoyable to be fed by one of her parents than to eat alone. Switch the side you feed from periodically to give your baby the benefit of two-sided stimulation.

Common Questions about Formula Feeding

Among the new parents I see in my office, I find the following basic questions about formula feeding are consistently asked.

Q: *How many bottles should I own and what type should I buy?*

A: Buy about a dozen bottles each in the eight-ounce and four-ounce sizes, an equal number of nipples, and a bottle brush. If you are going to use the disposable bag-and-holder type, buy at least four bottle holders. Any type of bottle is fine. Plastic is lighter than glass but may be harder to clean, especially when made into cute shapes. You may need to experiment a little to find the nipple your baby prefers. However, most bottle-fed infants rapidly become accustomed to the nipple first introduced in the hospital. Some babies like the orthodontic nipples, while others don't. A very small baby may feed better with a soft preemie nipple.

Q: *Do I have to sterilize my baby's formula or bottles?*

A: No, you don't need to sterilize providing: (1) you live in a city with sanitized water, (2) you prepare only one bottle at a time, (3) you wash your bottles in hot soapy water, using a bottle brush, or in a dishwasher, and (4) you refrigerate opened formula no longer than forty-eight hours. As soon as your baby finishes her bottle, rinse it out. Dried milk supports the growth of germs and is very hard to wash off after it hardens. Milk left standing also supports organism growth, another reason for prompt rinsing.

Q: *How do I know how much formula to feed my baby?*

A: After the first couple of weeks, infants consume about a quart of formula a day, but some babies may need more. Use the principle of demand feeding as much as possible, rather than adhering to a schedule of times and ounces. It's a good indication if your baby leaves a little formula behind in her bottle. Then, when she starts finishing it completely, you know it's time to increase the amount in each bottle. This guideline may not be appropriate if you have a very obese baby who consistently wants to overeat. Babies with a strong sucking urge make it harder to read their cues.

Q: *If my baby doesn't finish a bottle, can I save it, or do I have to throw it out?*

A: If your baby has consumed part of a bottle, you can leave it out at room temperature and offer it again up to one hour later. If you put the bottle back in the refrigerator promptly, you can keep it approximately four hours until the next feeding. Never add formula to a partially finished bottle; rather, prepare a fresh bottle each time. Bottles for nighttime feedings *cannot* be prepared in advance and left at room temperature.

Q: *If I've opened a can of formula but haven't used it all, how long can I keep it?*

A: You can consider refrigerated formula "good" for forty-eight hours after opening the can. Be sure to wash the top of the can before you open it. Breast-feeding mothers who supplement occasionally with formula and can't use up a can within forty-eight hours usually prefer to use powdered formula.

Q: *Should I heat formula before I offer it to my baby, or can I just give her the cold bottle?*

A: Many babies will accept a cold bottle. The bottles offered in the hospital nursery are room temperature. But I always like to look to breast feeding for the model. We know that nature provides babies with milk at body temperature, so that must be ideal for them. I recommend that you heat the bottle under hot tap water, with a bottle warmer, or in a pan of water on the stove. Test the temperature by sprinkling a few drops onto your wrist. The formula should feel neither hot nor cold. If you think it's too warm, cool it before you serve it. It is much better to err on the cool side than to risk burning your baby's mouth.

Another easy way to bring your baby's feeding to an appropriate temperature if you are using concentrate is to mix it with hot tap water. This should bring refrigerated concentrate to a warm temperature. If you use powder, just mix it with warm tap water. It can be dangerous to heat your baby's bottle in a microwave oven, because the milk can easily become too hot. Also, plastic bottle bags may burst after microwave heating. If you ever use a microwave to heat a bottle, use the "defrost" setting instead of "high" and carefully check the temperature of the formula before feeding it to your baby.

Q: *How will I know if a formula disagrees with my baby's system?*

A: If a formula is upsetting your baby's digestive system, she may: vomit frequently; cry excessively; have chronic congestion, excess gas, diarrhea, constipation, or a rash. If any of these symptoms are present, consult your pediatrician about changing formulas. Be sure to follow guidelines for switching formulas. Wait about a week on the new formula to decide whether your infant has improved. If your baby is gaining and thriving, it usually means she is tolerating her formula well.

Q: *Must I use a commercially prepared formula, or can I make my own?*

A: Commercially prepared formulas are nutritionally superior to all but breast milk. In fact, many homemade formulas can be dangerous. Although inferior to prepared formulas, one acceptable alternative formula can be made from whole evaporated milk if desired, but it must be supplemented with infant vitamin drops.

Recipe for One Quart of Evaporated Milk Formula
    13 oz. can whole evaporated milk
    1½ cans water = 19 ounces
    2 Tbl. light corn syrup

Recipe for Five-ounce Bottle
    2 oz. whole evaporated milk
    3 oz. water
    1 tsp. light corn syrup

Do not use regular undiluted cow's milk—whole, 2%, or skim—during the first six months of life and preferably not before one year of age. This caution also goes for goat's milk, which is low in iron, Vitamin C and folic acid, but high in protein. It is difficult for your baby to process the much higher mineral and protein content in regular cow's milk or goat's milk. Remember, cow's milk was designed for a calf and should not be served to your baby without significant alteration, making it more like breast milk. When you begin to switch her from formula to cow's milk, at about the age of twelve months, do it gradually—one bottle at a time. Rapidly switching to cow's milk can cause constipation. And do not add chocolate, strawberry, or any other flavoring to your toddler's milk.

Q: *Do I need to give my formula-fed baby vitamins?*
    A: Prepared infant formulas contain all the necessary vitamins, so you shouldn't give additional vitamins unless your doctor specifically orders them.

Q: *Is there a preferred position for feeding my baby?*
    A: One precaution I always like to make is not to feed your baby while she is lying flat on her back. Milk gets into her eustachian tubes and can make her prone to ear infections. If you don't like the idea of your baby becoming attached to her bottle and carrying it around, always feed her yourself, while holding her, and then put the bottle away.

STARTING SOLID FOODS

Your baby has been thriving on milk alone now for several months, and you are beginning to wonder when and how you should introduce solid food to her diet. Beginning solid foods marks the end of a very convenient period of infant feeding, but also brings advantages of its own. For one, it's fun to introduce your baby to the pleasures of new tastes and textures. It's also easier to pacify and occupy a baby in a public place, like a restaurant, when you can offer her something to eat. A breastfed baby can now more easily be left in someone else's care. Solid foods are a new adventure for your baby.

When to Start

You need to observe your baby for signs of readiness for solid food. Most babies need solids at about five to seven months. Some babies need solid foods as early as four months, while others show no interest in solids and grow quite satisfactorily until eight or nine months. Either end of the spectrum is fine, as long as your baby is growing well and you are taking the cues from her rather than looking to a chart or someone else's baby.

By about six months a baby's digestive system and coordination, especially in the tongue, have matured sufficiently for handling solid food. If you begin solids much earlier, you simply replace the food from which your baby derives the most nutrition, breast milk or formula, with less nutritious sources. Additionally, beginning solids too early can be stressful to your baby's digestive system, contribute to obesity by providing excess calories for her age, and make her prone to food allergies.

Beginning solids means adding food to your baby's diet, not replacing milk in your baby's diet with solids. Continue to nurse as your baby wishes, which will probably be about the same as before you started solids. Also continue to give your baby formula throughout the first year of life before switching to regular milk. Your baby also still very much needs the holding and closeness associated with nursing or being given the bottle.

If solids are started at an appropriate age of four to seven months, keep in mind that you can use many of the foods that you typically feed the rest of the family. Many parents mistakenly believe that they need to bring along jars of commercial baby food when they go to a restaurant. Actually most restaurants have foods suitable for a baby who has started solids. Ask for a side order of applesauce, rolls, cottage cheese (if the baby is at least nine months old), a baked potato, fruit cocktail (pour off the syrup), and other soft, plain foods.

If you do use commercially prepared baby foods, there are a few guidelines to follow.

- √ Check the lid. It should be indented a little in the center and "pop" out audibly when you open it. If this doesn't happen, throw the jar away and don't use it. Smelling the food will not tell you if it's safe. Dangerous contamination of food can be both odorless and tasteless.
- √ Use predominantly single foods, such as plain fruits, meats, cereals, and vegetables. Combination dinners are less nutritious and should be used as a vegetable, not the meat, in your baby's meal. They have the nutrient content of a vegetable and do not contain enough protein to meet your baby's requirements, unless they specify "high meat" dinner.
- √ Always spoon the food into a bowl and feed from the bowl, not the jar. If you feed directly out of the jar, saliva from the baby's mouth will digest many foods and leave a watery mixture in the jar. This is especially true of foods with a lot of starch, like combination dinners and puddings.
- √ Always refrigerate jars after opening.

How to Start Solids

When introducing solid food to your baby, keep several basic principles in mind. Most mothers find success offering the new solid food after a familiar nursing. After nursing or taking a bottle, the baby is usually in an agreeable mood. If you offer a cold spoon and a new food to a

ravenous baby, can you really expect cheerful cooperation? For the early feedings, keep the amount scant. Offer
a tablespoon or so of food per meal until the baby seems to
want more; then you can let her be your guide.

You do not need to use commercially prepared "baby
foods." They are fairly expensive and lack texture, although they are convenient. Several hundred varieties of
commercial strained baby foods became necessary only
when solids were started inappropriately early, before teeth
or necessary motor skills were present. Since your baby is
probably around six months old by the time you are offering solids, she can handle mashed food and small pieces,
and does not require the pureed versions. Or you can use
your blender on a coarse speed to finely chop food for
your baby. Feeding your baby from an Infa-feeder (a
device like a bottle for feeding pureed solids) bypasses the
development of the mechanical skills that are essential to
self-feeding and encourages overfeeding by "plunging"
large volumes into the baby.

Another form of baby food is dehydrated baby food.
One advantage of dehydrated food is that you can mix only
a small amount at a time without concern about the remainder spoiling. You can also increase its caloric content,
if you want to, by mixing it with formula or breast milk
instead of water. Dehydrated baby foods are convenient
for travel, lightweight, and unbreakable.

It is important to introduce only one new food at a time
so you can monitor any allergic reaction. You can introduce a new food about every three to five days. During
that period, watch for diarrhea, vomiting, constipation,
fussiness, rashes, or other unusual reactions.

Anticipate messy feeding sessions. It's unrealistic to
expect a baby just learning how to eat to do so neatly. Put
a large bib on her and place newspapers or plastic on the
floor under her high chair to minimize the inevitable mess.
Experimenting with her food, by testing its texture, its
taste, its response to the law of gravity, and her own
ability to handle it are as important to this process as
consuming the nutrients. So put things in perspective and
watch proudly as your little scientist experiments and learns
with her food.

Be flexible. You don't like all foods equally well, do

you? Well, neither will your baby. If some food is not to
her liking, stop offering it for now and try again later.
Some babies do not seem to like any foods until they have
sampled your offerings for weeks. In this case, back off
and try solids again in a couple of weeks. I can promise
you this—all babies do eventually eat solid food!

The Food Order

Foods are usually introduced in a certain order to corre-
spond with the baby's growing nutritional needs. Although
this order is often made to sound very rigid, it is really
quite flexible.

The first food group I introduce is fruits and vegetables.
Your goal is to provide your baby with vitamins A and C.
Although citrus fruits are good sources of vitamin C, they
are highly allergenic and should be delayed until the age of
one year. Suggestions for first fruits include: applesauce,
pureed apricots, pears, cantaloupe, bananas, peaches, and
plums. Among vegetables, corn is hard to digest, and peas
and beans are allergenic. Well tolerated first vegetables
include carrots, squash, potatoes, and sweet potatoes.

The second food group to introduce to your baby's diet
is breads and cereals to add B vitamins, carbohydrates,
and bulk. Many parents start with baby cereals. You could
also give your baby crackers, toast strips, or dry unsweet-
ened, unpreserved cereals. If you want to give your baby
hot cereal, you can offer oatmeal, Cream of Wheat, Malt-o-
Meal, Cream of Rice, or Familia rather than the very
processed, textureless "baby cereals." Avoid the coarse-
grained cereals like Wheatena or Roman Meal cereal in the
beginning, as your baby will not be able to digest them
well. When you offer hot cereal, use expressed breast milk
or formula instead of cow's milk to thin it. Don't add any
sweetener. Babies will eat foods without added sugar but
they will rapidly develop a preference for sweetened foods
if they are offered. You can add pureed peaches, bananas,
or applesauce if you like.

Third, I suggest protein sources to meet your baby's
increasing protein requirements to maintain growth. Protein also contributes iron to your baby's diet. Meat, poul-

try, fish, and eggs are good sources of both protein and iron. When introducing meat, start with chicken and lamb, then beef, and last pork and liver. Only the yolk of the egg should be offered before one year of age, because the white is allergenic. Fish should also be delayed until late in the first year, because it is allergenic.

Babies are usually unenthusiastic about their first meat. Until your baby acquires a taste for it, you can disguise meat in sweet potatoes, bananas, or something else she likes. Egg yolks are usually well accepted. You can either fry the yolk alone (using a vegetable spray to grease the pan) and let her eat it with her hands like a little patty, or you can also hard-boil it and take the yolk out and mash it with some breast milk or formula. Peanut butter (smooth, not crunchy) on toast is another handy way to offer some protein, but peanut butter should be delayed until about a year because of its allergenic tendencies.

Your baby's meats should *not* include those containing nitrites or nitrates, like hot dogs, bacon, salami, bologna, and other processed products.

At this point, you have discovered many foods your baby can tolerate and likes. For variety's sake, feel free to offer soups, casseroles, or other dishes containing several ingredients that agree with your baby.

The fourth group I recommend is dairy products. Your baby will enjoy the foods in this group, but since cow's milk is such a common allergen, wait until late in the first year before introducing dairy products, such as yogurt, cheese, and ice cream.

Your baby's meals will evolve from a single food per meal at six months to a meal that resembles (or is) your regular meal by a year of age.

Around twelve months, babies typically begin to eat proportionately less. This is because the rapid rate of growth your baby experienced during the first year slows down considerably during this second year. It is natural for her to be less hungry and at times it seems that exploring the food is more important than consuming it. At this point, think of your job as simply offering your toddler healthful foods, not forcing her to eat them.

Introducing your baby to solid foods offers an opportunity for exploration and greater social interaction. Make it pleasant and relaxed. The attitude your child develops toward food and eating is more important than the exact number of calories and the specific nutrients she consumes. Eating is a social and developmental experience. Make it fun!

Foods to Avoid

As already emphasized, some foods should be avoided during the first year because they are highly allergenic. These are citrus fruits (including tomatoes, oranges, and grapefruit), egg whites, milk, fish, berries, peanut butter, and chocolate.

Other foods are just not good for us and should be avoided for as long as possible (it's always longer with the first than with subsequent children!). Foods in this category are sweets, soda pop, salted snacks, highly processed foods, and foods that contain additives and artificial colors.

Safety requires that another group of foods be avoided. Some foods, like carrot sticks, can choke babies and toddlers. If the baby has only front teeth and lacks molars for grinding, she can bite off a chunk big enough to cause choking. Nuts, popcorn, and hard candy can also lead to choking and should not be fed to a child under four years old. Allowing a child to eat or chew gum while running is another potential cause of choking. Use common sense before offering food to your baby and ask yourself if it could possibly lead to choking.

Honey poses a problem for infants under one year. It can contain the bacteria that causes botulism in infancy. After a year, honey does not pose a danger.

Drinking from a Cup

At around nine months of age, your baby can begin learning to drink from a cup. The cup will not immediately replace the breast or bottle, but your baby will enjoy mastering the necessary skills involved in this task. Gradually she will take a greater percentage of her fluids by cup.

At first you can hold the cup for your baby and offer her small sips. Once she seems able, let her hold the cup herself. It is best to begin with the type of cup that has a lid and spout and is weighted on the bottom. Don't fill the cup with more than an ounce at first.

Despite these precautions, much of your baby's early cup liquids will end up on her rather than in her. For this reason, I like to pass on a tip I learned from a very practical patient. Let your baby practice cup feeding while she is in the bathtub. The mess will fall into the bathwater and you'll be able to readily clean her up. You can simply refill her cup from the faucet as often as necessary.

As your baby becomes more proficient, let her drink from her cup in her high chair with a plastic tablecloth underneath. Drinking from a cup is a skill all normal children acquire with age; the messes are temporary. By fifteen to eighteen months most babies can drink efficiently without the lid and spout.

NUTRITION FROM THE AGES OF TWO TO FIVE

Once your baby is past the age of about one year she will, for the most part, join your family eating patterns. Some new issues arise now that you're feeding a child.

The first issue is formulating your "food philosophy," or at least your "food attitudes." As you become more food-conscious on behalf of your child, you have the perfect opportunity to revamp your own eating habits. Good eating habits are the foundation of good health, so it's important to begin early. Decide what specifics and habits of good nutrition will be important in your family.

Always offer water for a first choice when your child asks for a drink. This communicates that "water is for thirst" and also reinforces the habit. The advantages of giving water with meals (except breakfast) are that the child does not fill up on a drink like milk or juice, leaving no appetite for the nutritious meal you prepared. In addition, milk or juice adds several hundred unnecessary calories to the child's diet each day, possibly leading to a future weight problem.

Never allow eating to become a power struggle. The few extra bites you coax down are not worth risking a serious eating problem later on. Children should eat because they are hungry, not because they are coerced to do so. We all equate food and love to some extent, but perhaps we equate them too strongly at times. When that urge to celebrate with or share "fun food" emerges, consider offering an activity instead, or an activity connected with the food, like baking cookies together, or walking for an ice cream cone, rather than food alone.

Eating is universally a social activity and mealtime can often be a special family time. Sometimes if our family has had a particularly hectic week, I'll make a nice meal, then take the phone off the hook (provided I'm not on call) to protect our special family time, while we have a long social dinner. We find spending this time together to be wonderfully relaxing.

Avoid foods that contain additives, preservatives, or excess salt. Almost any food can either be found in a natural state or made from scratch.

Be flexible about the form of food your child prefers. For example, if she hates the cooked vegetables you serve with the meal, but will eagerly consume a bowl of raw vegetables you offer her just before supper, let them replace the hot ones.

Your child may go on a "food jag" when she seems to want nothing but one certain food all the time. You can usually relax and go along with her desire. Food jags normally fade quickly and she'll soon return to a more balanced eating style.

Snacks may be as important a contribution to your child's overall nutritional picture as her meals. To a toddler, snacks are not a luxury, they are a necessary source of energy. Make them count. Offer real food for snacks, not sweets. The needed energy boost will come from cheese, yogurt, peanut butter, fruit, frozen peas or blueberries, to give a few examples.

Most children experience at least a brief period of being a finicky eater. In keeping with the warning not to allow eating to become a power struggle, minimize arguing with and prodding the finicky eater. An approach I have seen work well is a balance between respecting the finicky eater's right not to eat foods that she dislikes and the right of the parent who cooked supper to provide only one meal. When the finicky eater declares that she cannot possibly eat the dinner you are serving, tell her that she can either find something acceptable to eat herself (i.e., a carton of yogurt, or an apple and a slice of cheese), or she can wait for you to finish eating your supper and you will fix her something cold, like a sandwich.

Another way to deal with the chronically fussy eater is to build choices into the meal. A salad or sandwich bar is a good idea. Tacos or pitas with a variety of available ingredients is another choice-oriented meal.

Some children are not generally finicky eaters, but hate a certain common food, like tomatoes. These children should know that it is appropriate for them to pick out and not eat the offending food, but that they cannot expect their portion of food to be served without it.

There are times when an easy meal must be prepared for your toddler either because you're not eating with her or because you're sending the meal with her to day care. Some quick meal ideas for toddlers are:

- √ a carton of yogurt
- √ cottage cheese mixed with fruit
- √ cheese cubes, crackers, and a piece of fruit
- √ a minipizza
- √ macaroni and cheese
- √ pita bread filled with ingredients your toddler likes
- √ fish sticks and a vegetable
- √ American cheese and fruit cocktail

Another feeding issue for the growing child is table manners. Some basic manners, like asking for food to be passed rather than reaching for it, may be learned by example. Other manners will need to be taught more directly. It works well to teach manners just a lesson at a time and to do it in a pleasant conversational way at mealtime. Encourage your children from a young age to act appropriately in a restaurant.

Feeding our children, from that first nursing or bottle in the recovery room, through introducing solid foods, to finally establishing sound lifelong eating habits, is one of the most time-consuming endeavors of parenthood. It is not only a way of showing our children love, but it is a lifelong investment in good health, and well worth all the time, energy, and care we put into it.

WEANING

The next major step in your child's maturing eating pattern is weaning. Weaning can be quite a controversial subject in our culture. In other cultures weaning is a natural event occurring on its own like the eruption of teeth or the first steps. This more casual attitude toward weaning will serve you and your baby well. A few guidelines are important to healthy weaning, but beyond that, much will depend on your baby's nature and your own.

First, plan to allow your baby to simply stop nursing or give up the bottle on her own, rather than imposing a weaning schedule. Read your baby's needs. A mistake parents sometimes make, after noting how strongly their baby or toddler needs the bottle or breast, is to conclude that this need will only increase unless the child is abruptly weaned. Actually, if you observe a great need in your child for bottle or breast, it is more helpful to allow your child to satisfy that need—not to deny it. After it is fulfilled, the need will diminish and then disappear. If you deprive your child of the breast, bottle, or pacifier during a time when her very legitimate need is strong, the behavior may be eliminated, but the need may not disappear. Rather, it may surface in other ways because it was not satisfied and outgrown naturally.

Don't be in a rush to take the breast or bottle away from your little one; all babies give it up eventually on their own. If you feel pressure from friends and relatives who offer disapproving comments, feel free to ignore their advice, since it is probably based on lack of information. Instead, take pride in the sensitive way you are parenting.

If you decide to initiate weaning, do it gradually. Try to anticipate a month or two in advance of the time you feel you need to wean, and then slowly (perhaps one feeding per week) begin replacing the breast with a bottle of formula if the child is under one; of juice (not a sweetened beverage) if the child is under two and seems to need it; or the breast or bottle with a cup if the child is over two. Omit the feeding your child is the least attached to first. The nighttime bottle is often the hardest to give up. You can put less in that bottle or put water in it if you've been using milk. The bedtime nursing is also usually the favorite. When encouraging the child to give it up, a story (read at first by the father) can serve as a substitution.

If you feel confident that your child is ready to give up the bottle or breast but hasn't, you can offer her some guidance. If your toddler is verbal, you can talk about the idea that "big girls" or "big boys" don't nurse or drink from a bottle, but "big girls and boys" do many other wonderful things that babies can't do. Fill in the discussion with fun "big kid" activities that will appeal to your child, such as swinging at the park, riding a trike, going camping, and so on. After talking together about weaning as a sign of growth for a couple of weeks, set a goal, like an upcoming birthday, holiday season, or some other date in the future. Then, as that date approaches, continue the gentle discussions about "getting big," and keep her posted on the approaching time. It may be helpful to acknowledge to your child that you know there is some sadness associated with weaning.

Weaning is an important process in emotional and psychological terms in addition to its nutritional significance. Weaning usually goes well if you make it a gradual process (unless you are faced with an emergency) and if you put your child's needs above the opinions of your neighbors, friends, and relatives.

7 Your Child's Development

AS ORDERLY AS his prenatal maturation, as exciting as the anticipation of his arrival, and as miraculous as his moment of birth is the wondrous unfolding of your baby's development. Like the gorgeous blossoming of the tiniest rosebud, each new milestone contributes to his transition from newborn to infant, from infant to toddler, from toddler to preschooler. Your parental role in this fascinating process will be:

√ to aid your baby in acquiring new skills by your knowledge of predictable patterns of development;

√ to protect him from harm as his environment expands and his mobility increases;

√ to guide him in gradually separating from you and assuming greater control over his own body and thoughts;

√ to help him distinguish between right and wrong, and to ultimately choose to do right;

√ to relish each new accomplishment and cherish the whole developmental process that confirms your baby's own individuality.

Some of you will conscientiously record each memorable event in your baby's record book and preserve important moments in organized photograph albums or on videotape. Others maintain dust-covered books with empty pages and only a child's name on the inside. Instead of albums, some will keep drawers filled with pictures that capture someone's first smiles and first steps. However we manage to preserve our baby's milestones, each of us will have indelibly imprinted on our minds countless scenes from our little ones' babyhood and childhood, permanently recording their individual development.

OVERVIEW OF DEVELOPMENT

There is no other period in one's life when knowledge and skills are achieved as rapidly as in the first few years. This rapid learning process can be enhanced by your knowledge of what your baby can do at each age and what abilities will come next. This information comes only from reading, knowledgeable advice, or previous experience with young children.

I recall once leaving one of my newborns with a teenage babysitter while I went for my six-week postpartum checkup. I had just nursed the baby and expected to be back before the sleeping infant awakened. Just in case he appeared hungry before my return, I left a bottle of sterile water to tide him over a short while. "Do you have any questions?" I inquired of the relatively inexperienced babysitter before I departed. I was alarmed when she asked, "Can he hold his own bottle?" Her question made me realize how little she knew about infants and how dangerous her ignorance could be.

And· yet, many parents have unrealistic expectations of babies, simply based on their lack of experience. Most of us have no idea how helpless and dependent new babies are or how their development occurs. At the very least, this lack of knowledge makes child rearing unnecessarily uncomfortable, and at the worst it leads to child abuse. Parents who have inappropriate expectations of their babies may project unrealistic thoughts, motives, and abilities onto the infants, such as, "I told him to stop crying, but he wouldn't."

In fact, it is relatively easy to understand child development, since it proceeds predictably and logically. A baby won't run before he walks, or walk before he sits, or sit before he rolls. He won't speak sentences until he says single words, or pronounce words until he first experiments with sounds. He won't manipulate toys until he reaches for objects, and he won't reach for things until he first grasps something placed against his palm. He won't want to be out of your presence until he is confident of your return, and he won't believe you will return until he has been totally dependent upon you and learned you can be trusted. He won't develop a conscience or inner sense of right and wrong until he first accepts your standards of right and wrong, and he won't recognize your standards until you point them out to him by setting firm limits for him.

In general, early development proceeds from head to toe, from trunk to outer limbs, and from gross motor movements to delicate maneuvers. For example, a baby acquires head control and the ability to push over from his tummy to his back before he learns to sit alone or pull up to standing. He learns to reach for something he wants before he is able to manipulate it with his fingers. He learns to walk shakily before he can hop on one foot, and to scribble indiscriminately before he can draw a circle.

In medical school, I learned a simple developmental scheme that generally applies to the first year of life and nicely illustrates these principles. One milestone is associated with each month of age to point out the orderly progression of a baby's development. The ages given here are only approximations of when each milestone is accomplished, but the sequence provides a useful overview.

    1 month: smiles
    2 months: coos
    3 months: holds head steady when sitting
    4 months: reaches for object
    5 months: rolls over
    6 months: sits up
    7 months: crawls
    8 months: uses fingers in pincer grasp
    9 months: holds on and pulls up to a standing position
    10 months: walks holding onto furniture
    11 months: stands alone
    12 months: walks alone

Actually, evaluating a baby's development involves the examination of several major categories of activity. *Gross motor* is the area of development related to physical milestones, such as rolling, sitting, walking, running, hopping, and skipping. These tend to be the areas that receive our greatest attention because they are so obvious. Although gross motor accomplishments are actually poor predictors of ultimate intelligence, parents of youngsters who walk early are still easily convinced of their children's intellectual superiority.

Fine motor development relates to physical accomplishments requiring delicate coordination, such as transferring a toy from one hand to the other, picking up a small object with a pincer grasp, building a tower of cubes, or drawing with a pencil. These important items are often overlooked in favor of the more obvious gross motor milestones.

Language development refers to the acquisition of speech and language comprehension. Language ability includes both "receptive" skills, or the ability to comprehend what is spoken to you, as well as "expressive" skills, or the ability to articulate thoughts effectively to others. Naming objects, pointing to body parts, obeying simple commands, and understanding abstract concepts, such as being tired or hungry, will be some of your child's early language accomplishments.

Personal-social development refers to those behaviors that involve a baby's interaction with others and his gradual assumption of responsibility for his day-to-day care. Babies' games like peek-a-boo and pat-a-cake are part of early socialization, and are followed by gradually learning to feed and dress oneself, play interactive games, and imitate adult activities.

Often development proceeds in spurts. A baby may make dramatic progress in gross motor activities, learning to pull up, stand alone, and walk all in the span of a few weeks, although he may say only a single word or two. Another baby may continue to cruise around, holding onto the furniture for months before taking a step alone, while he learns to name a dozen objects during a language spurt.

An important distinction needs to be made between "normal" and "average" development. A wide range of normal behavior is present on either side of the average performance. For example, the average baby walks at a year of age, but babies normally learn to walk anywhere from nine months to eighteen months of age. For every developmental milestone, there is a span of several months during which the earliest infants start to accomplish the task and when the majority of babies are able to perform it. Unfortunately, parents often mistakenly assume that milestones should be achieved at specific ages, such as sitting at six months or walking at a year. It is important to recognize the range of normal around these estimated time frames and to realize that your entirely normal baby may be average in some areas, earlier than average in others, and later than average in a few.

Delayed development may occur in one or more major categories and may be due to untreated medical problems that require attention. For example, a commonly over-looked cause of abnormal language development is impaired hearing, which requires early detection and intervention. Neglected or abused children who have not enjoyed normal interactions with loving adults may have delayed personal-social development. Infants with impaired motor function, due to cerebral palsy or muscular dystrophy, for example, may have delayed gross motor and fine motor development even though their intelligence may be normal.

If your child's performance seems delayed in one or more categories, bring your concerns to your pediatrician's attention so that formal developmental screening can be performed. One important reason for the early evaluation of your infant's development is to detect any treatable medical problems that might be interfering with his performance. Obviously, development should be assessed at every well-baby visit, either by formal testing, astute observations, or careful parental interviewing. Babies are not expected to give their best performances when they have an ear infection or other illness, so sick visits are not suitable times to evaluate an infant's development.

DEVELOPMENT AND SAFETY

The odds are that your baby is developmentally normal. By knowing what to expect next you can help him acquire new skills, and more importantly, protect him from the potential dangers that each new ability brings. As his increasing mobility rapidly expands his world, he will have ever-changing "safe" zones, "exploration" zones, and clear "danger" zones. Much exciting learning and challenging will occur under your close supervision within an exploration zone, but you will need to set protective limits.

For example, as a small infant, your baby will be safest in your arms or in his crib, but his development would be limited if he never left those sanctuaries. His learning is enhanced by your allowing him to lie on a blanket on the floor with toys nearby, with you encouraging him to reach, push up with his arms, and ultimately roll over. This exploration zone requires supervision, however, since he cannot protect himself from the family dog, older siblings, or rolling into an uncomfortable position.

An eight-month-old may be safest in his playpen, but he will enjoy being allowed to crawl about the living room exploration zone, pulling up on furniture and cruising about with your supervision. He should not be permitted near an unprotected stairway, however, as his exploration will surely take him on a bumpy, dangerous fall.

The preschooler might be safely left to play in his own room or fenced backyard, but roaming in the unfenced front yard under your close observation may be even more challenging to him, since he can watch neighbors and cars go by. He should never be left alone, however, where there is any chance he could wander into the street or come to other harm. Thus, for each age, your child's most rapid learning may occur in those settings where maximal exploration is permitted and his environment has expanded. He will continue to need "safe" areas where he can play unsupervised without fear of harm, and there will always be "danger" zones whose limits you will have to define and strictly enforce. Your defining the danger zones will be your baby's first introduction to any form of discipline or setting of limits.

It is always best to assume that today your baby will begin to perform the next anticipated milestone and to protect him accordingly. For example, as early as two months of age, some infants can roll over from their tummies to their backs. To be safe, therefore, you should treat your own two-month-old as if he may roll over for the first time at any minute. Don't leave him alone on any high surface, even if he has never rolled before. Similarly, before your baby is crawling about, you should remove all hazardous materials from his path, protect stairways, cover electrical outlets, remove toxic substances from or lock floor-level cupboards, et cetera.

Sometimes we mistakenly assume that the passing of a new milestone automatically makes a baby safer in certain situations. For example, once your baby can sit, we may falsely believe that he can now be left alone sitting up and playing in the bathtub. Babies have slipped and drowned in an inch of water and should *never* be left alone in the tub under the age of four.

The following outline will give you a bird's-eye view of your child's abilities at various ages. This knowledge will help you protect him appropriately. Also, by knowing what milestones to expect next, you can enrich his play by providing toys and introducing games that allow him to use newly developed skills. Mostly, the information should help you enjoy your baby more as you appreciate and delight in his expanding world.

If you would like to read in more detail about your baby's development, several good references are available. For the first year, when your baby changes most rapidly, you might want to read either *Infants and Mothers*, by T. Berry Brazelton, M.D. (Dell) or *The First Twelve Months of Life*, by Frank Caplan (Grosset & Dunlap). Each provides a month-by-month developmental overview of your baby's first year.

For the toddler years, I suggest *Toddlers and Parents* (Brazelton, Dell) and *The Second Twelve Months of Life* (Caplan, Grosset & Dunlap). For an in-depth discussion of the psychological maturation of a child from birth to six, Selma Fraiberg's *The Magic Years.: Understanding and Handling the Problems of Early Childhood* remains a classic.

Newborn

Gross Motor: Your newborn can move his arms and legs symmetrically and withdraw from an uncomfortable stimulus. He can lift his head and turn it from side to side. He displays a variety of newborn "reflexes" in which he has a spontaneous motor response to certain stimuli.

Fine Motor: He can focus on and briefly follow your face or an object held eight to twelve inches away. He can occasionally get his fingers or hand up to his mouth to suck.

Language: He responds to sounds and will usually be calmed by a soothing voice, particularly his mother's or another female voice. He cries in response to all needs and discomforts.

Personal-Social: Your newborn actually has a visual preference for a human face over an inanimate object and can soon recognize your facial contours. He may smile spontaneously, but these smiles will have no social significance until your lively input makes him smile responsively. He immediately responds to being picked up and will probably cuddle against you.

Play: A stuffed animal with a simulated heartbeat may calm or soothe your newborn. He will enjoy watching a mobile hung over his crib, and a musical wind-up toy also briefly holds his attention. He is still unable to interact with any toys, however, and enjoys human contact most.

Safety: A newborn requires your protection in every setting. His weak neck muscles make it necessary for you to support his head when you pick him up. He should be secured properly in an infant safety restraint whenever he travels by car. Place him on his tummy or side to sleep, since he could spit up and choke if lying on his back. He should never be left alone on any high surface, since his newborn "crawl reflex" could cause him to scoot off.

Discipline: No form of discipline is appropriate at this age. Your newborn has no willpower of his own and only desires to be warm, dry, fed, and allowed to feel secure.

Physical Features: You need to protect your newborn's soft spot and regularly clean the healing umbilical cord and circumcision, if one was performed. Babies have a greater percentage of body fat than adults, proportionately a much larger head, and shorter legs. These features are what make them so cute!

Your newborn is entirely dependent upon adults for his care and well-being. He has well-developed senses of

NEWBORN

hearing and sight, and desires and needs human contact. His motor activities are largely restricted to reflex motions, and he indicates his needs by crying. He requires love, food, and protection.

Two Months Old

Gross Motor: When lying on his stomach, the two-month-old can push his head and chest up with his arms. Soon he will push completely over and start rolling front to back. When held in a sitting position, his head is much steadier and bobs little.

Fine Motor: By now your baby can follow your face or an object in a 90 degree arc and is beginning to bring his hands together for later useful purposes. He may be able to suck his own thumb or fingers, but may accidentally spit his pacifier out when he really wants it. He still has a tongue-thrust reflex that makes him spit things out of his mouth, such as solid foods introduced too early.

Language: The two-month-old is beginning to coo and vocalize using vowel sounds (''ooh,'' ''aah''). He tries to ''talk back'' to you when you talk to him. He is starting to laugh out loud with you and to associate your presence with response to his cries.

2 MONTHS

Personal-Social: Your two-month-old now smiles regularly when you smile and talk to him. He also smiles spontaneously to try to elicit a response from you. Now no one can say it's just "gas."

Play: Your baby enjoys the same toys he did as a newborn, but he now derives lots more pleasure from them. Mobiles, musical toys, and anything with a smiling face on it will attract him. He is still too young to manipulate toys on his own, however, except to explore them with his mouth. He enjoys having you entertain him with rattles he can't hold onto by himself.

Safety: You must assume your baby could start to roll at any time and never leave him unattended on a high surface, such as a changing table or the examining table at your doctor's office. Be sure all his toys are safe, without small, removable parts that might choke him.

Discipline: No discipline is indicated yet. Your two-month-old simply craves the same creature comforts, love, and security as a newborn and has absolutely no desire or knowledge of how to upset you.

Physical Features: Your baby now seems less fragile and is thriving, gaining about an ounce each day. His cord has been healed for weeks, and his soft spot is growing smaller. He still may appear bowlegged, due to his position in the uterus. His eyes may be turning their permanent color.

Your two-month-old is still entirely dependent upon you, but is growing more effective in indicating his needs by the nature of his cries and his overall responsiveness. He is beginning to develop preferences and a personality of his own. He is becoming highly sociable and is developing a more predictable schedule. He likes being propped up in an infant carrier so he can view the world.

Four Months Old

Gross Motor: Your four-month-old can probably roll over both front to back and back to front. He is beginning to support some weight with his legs when held upright. He can completely control his head when pulled up to a sitting position from lying down. He enjoys movement, such as bouncing on your lap.

Fine Motor: Your baby can hold onto a rattle placed in his hand and tries to grasp an object within his reach. He can follow faces and objects with his eyes a full 180 degrees, and bring his hands together in the midline. He may enjoy just looking at his hands or playing with his own feet.

Language: He laughs and squeals with delight and tries to vocalize, primarily still with cooing vowel sounds and new combinations (''aahgoo'').

Personal-Social: He is absolutely delightful, smiling responsively to you and other adults. He shows excited anticipation by moving his arms and legs when he sees you, his bottle, the breast, or a favorite toy. He willingly goes to strangers, smiling and trusting others. This is my favorite age for a well-baby visit!

Play: Your four-month-old enjoys rattles and toys he can hold in his hands and bring to his mouth. He can't pick them up when they drop, however. He still enjoys mobiles and may reach for them. He can amuse himself for short

4 MONTHS

periods with rattles and small safe toys. He loves to kick and splash in the bath, but also enjoys just sitting and watching you or his own reflection in a mirror.

Safety: Your baby is now at great risk of rolling off high surfaces, including the examining table at the doctor's office. He can also wriggle and flip out of an infant carrier left on a high surface. He might chew off small, loose objects from unsafe toys. If you are spending more time with him outdoors, remember that he sunburns easily. Although he loves bouncing and rapid movements, *don't* toss him about or swing him by his arms. You could cause hemorrhaging into his brain or dislocate his elbow.

Discipline: Your four-month-old is still too young to discipline and has no knowledge of right or wrong. A stern voice will frighten and upset him without his understanding what caused it. His only desires continue to be food, warmth, and the security of your presence.

Physical Features: He is beginning to drool, chew on things, and to teethe, but it may be another month or two until he actually gets a tooth. He may be sleeping through the night and take two regular naps each day. He has nearly doubled his birth weight already!

This is an absolutely delightful age, and usually chosen by the media to depict a happy baby. Your infant is gaining mobility and starting to manipulate his environment. He is adorably sociable, slightly predictable, has outgrown his colic, and makes you love being a parent.

Six Months Old

Gross Motor: Your six-month-old can sit up briefly without support. He can bear weight on his legs and probably likes to stand momentarily, holding onto your hands. He rolls both ways with ease now and may roll from one place to another or begin to crawl or creep around.

Fine Motor: Your baby can pick up two toys now, one in each hand. He uses his hand like a rake to obtain a small object. He can transfer a toy from one hand to another and bang a toy on the floor or table. It is still far too early to tell whether he will be right- or left-handed, as he uses both hands equally.

Language: If his name is called, your baby will turn in the direction of a voice. He is just beginning to make babbling consonant sounds, such as "ma," "da," "ba," and is discovering that these sounds bring a response from you.

Personal-Social: He now resists your pulling away a toy he wants and will close his mouth if you try to feed him more than he wants. He works to get a toy that is out of his reach. He can feed himself a breadstick or teething biscuit and can hold his own bottle. He is beginning to be shy around strangers and may no longer go to just any welcoming adult. He may reach out his arms to let you know he wants to be picked up.

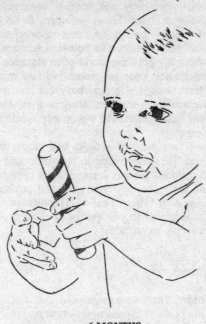

6 MONTHS

Play: A six-month-old loves his toys and can much more effectively manipulate them with banging, dropping, and picking up. He enjoys mirrors and laughing at and patting his reflection. He can amuse himself for longer periods, but he is also more reluctant to be left alone. He is so active that he dislikes holding still even for diaper changes. Peek-a-boo games make him laugh and help reassure him that people out of sight do come back.

Safety: Rolling is still a danger, and soon anything that he can use to pull up on can potentially be pulled down onto him. Small items will go straight to the mouth, where they could cause choking. Although he can sit in a high chair, he is in danger of pulling up to a stand and falling out. Don't hold him while drinking hot liquids, as his constant, unpredictable movements may cause a spill.

Discipline: No specific disciplinary measures are yet

appropriate, but your baby will have to be regularly re-moved from danger zones. He is beginning to understand your tone of voice, even if he can't comprehend your meaning. Small knickknacks and potential hazards should be removed from his growing world of exploration.

Physical Features: Your six-month-old has more than doubled his birth weight. He may have cut his first tooth by now, most likely a lower central incisor. He continues to chew, drool, and teethe. He's probably weathered his first cold by now.

Your baby is a bundle of activity and seems to be in constant motion. He is beginning to recognize and display his likes and dislikes. He has learned ways to manipulate his world with his voice, by feeding himself crackers, and choosing among toys. The typical development of stranger anxiety makes it appear to you that he is more dependent, despite his growing independence.

Nine Months Old

Gross Motor: Your nine-month-old can not only sit well, but he also gets to the sitting position on his own. He can pull up to a standing position and will try to grasp almost anything to do so. He may already be taking a few steps while holding onto furniture and other props. When he wants to get from one place to another rapidly, however, he crawls, scoots, or creeps efficiently.

Fine Motor: A nine-month-old can bang two objects together and can use a thumb-and-finger grasp. He loves to practice this new feat on Cheerios and other small edibles. He is also just learning to release things from his grasp.

Language: He babbles in imitation of your speech sounds, and talks animated "baby talk." However, he probably still has no real words yet, although he seems to carry on a whole conversation with himself and can com-bine syllables ("ba-ba," "ma-ma," "da-da").

Personal-Social: He likes to sip from a cup and may reach for your drink. He is also showing an interest in table foods. He can play pat-a-cake, peek-a-boo, and wave bye-bye and loves these early interactive games. He will resist your removing a toy he wants from his hand and

9 MONTHS

purposefully go after a coveted toy out of his reach. He displays his beginning understanding of cause and effect by such acts as covering his face to prevent you from washing it, repeating a performance that his audience laughed at, or pulling the clothes of someone to get attention.

Play: Your nine-month-old can amuse himself for longer periods alone with his toys and, if he has a playpen, he may be content there for a while. When he begins to fuss, be sure to let him out, however, so he won't feel confined. He likes to crumple paper, drop things from his high chair, stack things, and take things apart.

Safety: Your baby is at great risk of trying to pull himself up to a standing position using the ironing board, coffee pot cord, or other hazardous item. He may try to eat adult foods, such as peanuts or popcorn, and is at risk of choking. Be sure you have turned your hot water thermostat down to a safe level, as your baby may accidentally

turn on the hot water faucet in the bathtub. He is likely to
fall trying to stand up in his stroller or high chair. Everywhere he can crawl, potential hazards need to be removed.

Every home with a child this age should be equipped
with syrup of ipecac to be administered in case of accidental ingestion of a poisonous substance. The number of the
regional poison control center should be posted near the
phone and always called first before giving ipecac.

Discipline: When your nine-month-old approaches danger, say "no" and remove him from the danger. More
importantly, however, minimize his dangers by baby-
proofing the house and never turn your back on him when
he is outside the playpen. Remember, it is your responsibility to remove dangers from his path, since he is still
completely unable to consciously avoid them.

Physical Features: Your nine-month-old probably has
several upper and lower front teeth now, so you should
begin daily brushing. As he is now standing up and learning to walk, you may notice that he is still bowlegged,
or that one foot turns in or out a little. This is quite
common and is almost always outgrown.

Your baby is extremely mobile, inquisitive, and ever
more sociable. He may be clingy and prefer Mommy to
anyone else. He may be awakening at night for reassurance of your presence, but he generally sleeps through and
may be eliminating one of the daytime naps. He is gaining
more control over his ability to feed himself, to indicate
wants, and generate responses in you.

One Year Old

Gross Motor: Your one-year-old can probably walk
well holding onto furniture and may be able to stand alone,
stoop and pick up something, or even take some steps on
his own. He resists being confined and may try to climb
out of the crib or playpen.

Fine Motor: He has a neat pincer grasp using his thumb
and index fingers. His increased coordination makes stack-
ing rings or blocks challenging and fun. He is less likely to
explore something with his mouth and likes to manipulate
things with his hands.

Language: Your baby can probably say "mama" and "dada" with specific meaning and may have another two or three single words. He continues to talk baby talk, often modulating his voice and using adult inflections. He can understand simple questions ("Where's your shoe?") and directions ("Get your ball").

Personal-Social: He continues to enjoy interactive games and will roll a ball back to someone who has rolled it to him. He can drink from a cup without spilling much. He is beginning to make his needs and wants known by pulling, pointing, or verbalizing instead of just crying. He is willing to separate from Mommy briefly and still enjoys peek-a-boo games to see if you will reappear.

Play: Your one-year-old enjoys music and will rock to it. He likes different textures and exploring "texture" books. Anything he can manipulate, stack, or arrange will amuse him. A busy box on his crib may help keep his interest when he awakens in the morning. He likely has a favorite stuffed animal or other "lovey" that he carries from room to room now in place of Mother herself.

Safety: Your baby is now so mobile that you must be on continuous guard to safety-proof the house. Electrical sock-

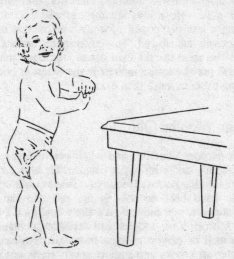

1 YEAR

ets must be covered, stairs protected, kitchen cupboards emptied of dangerous materials, and medicines locked up. Since a few toddlers have fallen head-first into the toilet and drowned, make a habit of keeping the toilet lid down and the bathroom door shut. Outdoor safety is important, too, as your baby will be exploring the yard. If you have diligently used a car seat from birth, he will continue to accept it naturally at this age without complaining about being restrained in the car. He should *never* be permitted to travel without being properly secured.

Discipline: A one-year-old can understand "no-no" and generally wants to please you. Continue to remove him from danger as you say "no," and minimize the hazards in his environment. If he has a temper tantrum, ignore it (see page 287).

Physical Features: He is gradually losing some of his infant proportions, getting longer legs, and having a lower percentage of body fat. His head has completed much of its growth, and he has tripled his birth weight. His hair is finally beginning to get longer.

Your one-year-old has learned to manipulate his environment in a number of ways and has expanded his world tremendously with his mobility, curiosity, and emerging language skills. He enjoys feeding himself, but eats proportionately less per pound of body weight now that his rate of growth has slowed. To you, it seems he eats like a bird and you need to take care not to start daily mealtime battles. He may be losing interest in the breast or bottle, or may cling to them more than ever.

Eighteen Months Old

Gross Motor: Your one-and-a-half-year-old is walking more smoothly and with better balance. He also can walk backwards, pulling a toy. He may be able to walk up stairs with one hand held or holding the rail. He can kneel without support, seat himself in a chair, and kick a ball.

Fine Motor: Your toddler can scribble spontaneously with a pencil or crayon grasped in his fist. He can stack small cubes or blocks into a short tower. He is just beginning to reason and can figure how to dump an object out of

18 MONTHS

a bottle instead of trying to reach his finger inside to get it.

Language: An eighteen-month-old can say several words and may be able to combine two words together, such as "cookie now," "want milk," "go bye-bye." He can point to one or more named body parts, obey simple commands, and recognize common objects. He often says "no" without meaning it.

Personal-Social: Your baby is gaining more control over his daily activities and can remove a piece of clothing. He uses a cup and spoon well and enjoys eating with the rest of the family. He likes to imitate you performing household tasks and is actually able to help in putting toys away or fetching an object for you. He may let you know he has soiled diapers and wants them off.

Play: He now explores with zeal and wants to look, touch, and try everything. He likes other children but doesn't know how to take turns with them yet and won't share. He may cling to a security object and take it every-where. He enjoys bath toys and may be found playing in the toilet. He likes push-and-pull-toys, balls, noisemakers, and soft cuddly toys.

Safety: Safety-proofing must now extend to the garage and yard. Streets and your own driveway pose a major danger. Your toddler still can't be left alone in the bathtub, and pools and ditches are grave hazards. Choking on peanuts and popcorn is still possible, and such foods must be kept from him.

Discipline: Continue to use "no" for dangers and ex-pect him to obey more. Tantrums are common and will be reinforced if they provoke a big response from you. He is old enough to spend a minute in a "time-out" chair for misbehavior, but if he doesn't seem to understand yet, don't insist (see page 248). Remember to reinforce posi-tive behavior, too.

Physical Features: Your toddler is beginning to resem-ble a little boy or girl now, instead of a baby. He has up to a dozen teeth, including his first molars. His hair is getting longer, and may prompt his first haircut.

Your eighteen-month-old is generally fun to be with and is fitting in smoothly with the family. He is separating from his mother briefly and asserting himself through tan-trums and saying "no" even when he doesn't mean it. He has mixed feelings about his growing independence and may regress to clinging at times.

Two Years Old

Gross Motor: Your two-year-old is quite agile. He can throw a ball overhand, jump in place, walk tiptoe, kick a ball, and run. He may be able to pedal a tricycle if his legs are long enough, and he balances momentarily on one foot. He goes up and down stairs alone, two feet per step. He can stoop and retrieve an object from the floor without falling.

Fine Motor: He can build a higher tower of small cubes or blocks. He likes to scribble, and can copy a vertical line and hold a pencil in his fingers instead of his fist. He can unscrew a lid and turn a doorknob.

Language: Your toddler's language skills have rapidly advanced in the past six months. He can follow simple commands, name pictures, combine several words into short sentences, and is beginning to use plurals. He can point to four or more body parts. He knows his name and can ask for his simple wants. It seems he talks incessantly and often repeats what others have said.

Personal-Social: Your two-year-old can partially dress himself and wash and dry his hands with little help. He likes to play near other children and watch them, but doesn't really play with them yet. He plays imitatively with dolls, wrapping them up and putting them to bed, for example.

Play: He likes toys with lids and parts and messy activities, like finger painting and playing with clay. He loves to work simple puzzles, look at books, and hear short stories. Music, songs, and rhythms entertain him. He enjoys joining you in daily activities, such as trips to the store.

Safety: No household with small children should contain loaded firearms. Two-year-olds have accidentally fired

2 YEARS

weapons or been accidentally shot by older siblings. Pools, ditches, and even bathtubs are still dangers. This is the most common age for poisonous ingestions—remember, even his vitamins with iron can be dangerous!

Discipline: Discipline can be expanded beyond simple safety issues at this age. He comprehends commands well, but he may protest at times with tantrums or other negative actions. He may anticipate your disapproval, saying "no-no" for himself as he approaches something he knows is off limits. The time-out chair can be increased to two minutes at a time. Reward good behavior and try to ignore most misbehavior. He should help put his own toys away.

Physical Features: His head is nearly adult size, and he has quadrupled his birth weight. He is about half his adult height, and his legs are proportionately longer than in infancy. He still has a slightly protuberant abdomen. By two and a half, your child has all twenty of his baby teeth, including his second molars.

Your two-year-old identifies strongly with the same-sex parent and wants to mimic Mommy or Daddy. He enjoys imitative play with toy power tools, vacuums, mowers, and tea sets. He is proud of his growing independence and expresses an interest in some adult activities, such as beginning toilet training.

Three Years Old

Gross Motor: Your three-year-old can ride a tricycle well, jump in place, broad jump, and balance on one foot for several seconds. He can go up stairs, with one foot on each step, and down stairs, two feet per step.

Fine Motor: He can copy a circle and likes to color, although he cannot stay in the lines. He can build a tall tower of small cubes and can imitate making a simple three-piece bridge with them.

Language: Your three-year-old can probably give his first and last names and uses plurals regularly. He uses pronouns, but with some errors ("I want she to play with me"). He comprehends some prepositions and concepts like "tired" and "cold." He can recite some nursery rhymes, can probably count up to ten, and may be able to name one or two colors.

Personal-Social: He can dress himself with supervision and is beginning to manage buttons. He separates from you more easily to go to a babysitter or preschool. He can pick up his toys and likes to help you with simple chores.

Play: Your three-year-old enjoys other children and can begin to take turns but probably doesn't understand sharing yet. He enjoys imitative play with cars and little people and may have an imaginary friend. He enjoys hearing stories repeatedly and looking at books or doing puzzles.

Safety: He is at continued risk of street dangers and getting lost, since he is tempted to wander beyond his own yard. Strangers are also a great danger, as he is highly verbal and wants to please adults. Drowning, car accidents, and poisonous ingestions continue to pose threats.

Discipline: Your three-year-old is beginning to understand right from wrong, but is more interested in avoiding

3 YEARS

your disapproval than in good behavior for its own sake. He may test you at times but really wants the assurance that you have firm limits for him. He is beginning to understand consequences of his behavior; the time-out chair can be increased to three minutes. He likes being told when he is a good boy.

Physical Features: He has lost much of his baby fat and is taller and leaner and assuming more adultlike proportions. He thinks he can play all day, but he may still need a daily nap and gets cranky if he stays up past his bedtime. He is probably toilet trained or making good progress, but he may still wet the bed at night.

Your three-year-old is somewhat self-centered, proud of himself, and tells tall tales. One little boy told me his name was "Super Boy," and that's just how he viewed himself! He wants muscles and to be like his same-sex parent, but at other times he wants to curl up in your lap. He asks questions constantly. He loves preschool, new games, learning, and challenges.

Four Years Old

Gross Motor: Your four-year-old can balance well on one foot, hop in place, and throw a ball overhand without losing his balance. He may be able to catch a bounced ball and to walk heel to toe. He can go down stairs, one foot on each step.

Fine Motor: He can copy a plus sign and pick the longer of two lines. He can draw a primitive person with up to three parts. He can use round-pointed scissors to cut out a picture.

Language: Your four-year-old understands "cold," "tired," and "hungry" and prepositions like "on," "under," "in front of," and "behind." He understands simple opposites like "hot and cold," "man and woman," and "big and small." He recognizes a few basic colors, can count four objects and can tell a story.

Personal-Social: He can do buttons and requires only minimal supervision with dressing. He separates well from you and accepts an explanation. He plays well with other children.

4 YEARS

Play: Your four-year-old enjoys other children immensely and can now share and take turns well. He likes parties and can anticipate events, with his developing sense of the passage of time. He likes action figures and dolls with safe parts to manipulate and anything that lets him use his imagination.

Safety: Street safety should be stressed, including one's own driveway. Your child should be taught not to touch stray animals. Strangers, pools, firearms, and automobiles continue to pose hazards.

Discipline: He is generally well behaved, and can understand the consequences of his misbehavior. He is learning to postpone his gratification, to control aggression, and to do what is ''right'' with less nudging from you. Most four-year-olds will tell lies without realizing this is wrong, and they may take something at a store without paying for it. You need to insist that such behavior is wrong, without making the child feel unnecessarily guilty. Accompany your child to return the item and have him retract any lies. You'll find that positive reinforcement for telling the truth, instead of harsh punishment for the confession, will reinforce future truth telling.

Physical Features: Your child may still need a daily nap. He is fully toilet trained by day, but may still wet at night. He is taller, leaner, and now has a flat abdomen, but he may appear pigeon-toed or knock-kneed.

Your four-year-old is rapidly gaining independence, but may also have imaginary fears, such as monsters, the dark, dogs, or death, and needs frequent reassurance about these. He may have an imaginary friend, and loves to play solitary fantasy games involving different people and roles. He may display signs of an Oedipal conflict where he imagines that Daddy dies or goes away and he marries Mommy and takes care of her. Your four-year-old enjoys selecting his clothes and may change outfits several times a day, much to your consternation. His friends are becoming more important to him, and he enjoys preschool or regular activities with his peers.

Five Years Old

Gross Motor: Your five-year-old can walk backward heel to toe, catch a ball, hop on one foot, and skip.

Fine Motor: He can copy a square or triangle, draw a person with at least six parts, and can probably tie his shoes. He can manipulate small toys, dress and undress figures, color, and draw.

Language: He can define words in simple terms and tell you what objects are made of. His articulation is good, with the exception of a few difficult sounds, such as double consonants (bl, th, br, sn, et cetera). His sentences are fairly complex, and he probably can count ten objects correctly and recognize four colors. He asks about the meanings of words.

Personal-Social: Your five-year-old can dress and undress without supervision and enjoys picking what to wear.

5 YEARS

He still needs help brushing his teeth effectively and combing his hair. He can make himself a sandwich or fix a bowl of cereal and milk, and likes to prepare things for you and join you in your chores: shopping, setting the table, making cookies, and so on. He is sensitive to your feelings and will try to console you if he thinks you are unhappy.

Play: Your child is very interested in friends, enjoys preschool or kindergarten activities, including singing, stories, coloring, craft activities, group games, and records. He may enjoy a weekly group activity like gymnastics or swimming. Of course, he still enjoys toys that he can manipulate and fantasize with, including little people, vehicles, and accessories.

Safety: Bicycles, tricycles, and scooters pose hazards, especially with regard to street dangers. Playing with matches can be a real risk at this age. Allow him to light candles with your supervision and stress that he is never to do this without an adult being present—explain why. Be sure he never comes home after kindergarten to an empty house.

Discipline: In addition to understanding delayed gratification, your child can now comprehend later consequences for previously committed infractions, although delayed discipline is less effective than immediate negative reinforcement. His conscience is emerging, and he is beginning to do what is "right" because of his own internal controls.

Physical Features: Your child may erupt his first permanent molars around six years of age, before he loses any baby teeth. His appetite is increasing rapidly, and he probably no longer needs a nap. His legs are longer and his proportions more adultlike. He may still be slightly pigeontoed or knock-kneed.

Your child is growing in independence in so many ways that he is ready to begin spending part of every day away from you in kindergarten. He probably has a best friend and strongly identifies with other children of the same sex. He is resolving his Oedipal feelings and now strongly wants to grow up and be like his same-sex parent. He is interested in differences in the opposite sex and how babies are made. He would probably like to have a pet and is able to take some responsibility for it. Having a few simple daily chores helps build responsibility and confirm his importance in the family. Overall, your five-year-old is anxious to please, to mimic adult behavior, to interact with other children, and to learn new skills.

However universal the growth and development of the world's babies may be, your own baby's development is intensely unique. We delight in the unsolicited sharing of her first smile, first tooth, first steps, and first words as if no other infant ever achieved those milestones. Not-yet-parents often find such conversations mundane and wonder how we can be so engrossed by such trivia. Years later, we may actually smile at our early preoccupation with our baby's routine activities.

Although I sometimes chuckle silently at another mother's accounts of her baby's amazing antics, I can still recall my own wonderment at my children's landmark performances. In fact, I was truly stunned when my firstborn failed to win the Hawaii Beautiful Baby Contest. Surely the judges must have been blind! Never had an infant looked so beautiful or developed so precociously. I was the luckiest mother in the world!

Actually, every baby whose adoring parents view her through rosecolored glasses is really the luckiest baby in the world. For it is our doting attention, our celebration of each milestone, our marvel at the predictable that turns a spontaneous curling of the lips into a social smile, disjointed vocalization into meaningful language, and faltering first steps into responsible independence.

8 The Challenge of Parenting

I FINALLY TOOK some time off from medicine the first summer after I completed my pediatric residency training. At that point, I had a new baby and four other children ranging in age from two to seven. Despite my professional credentials, parenting proved to be my greatest challenge. One particularly poignant scene occurred that summer at the grocery store. My toddler was having a rotten day, now culminating in a full-fledged tantrum for all to witness at the check-out counter. A woman, older than I, and from her attitude certainly a "better" mother, walked by surveying the pandemonium of miscellaneous young children, a newborn baby, and me—all trying to manage the tirade of a miserable toddler. She looked at the screaming child, at me, at all the other children, then at me again, and walked by, nose in the air, with a deadly "tsk, tsk."

I wanted to run up to her to exclaim, "Wait! I'm a pediatrician!"

No matter how conscientious you are, no matter how many other children you have raised, even if you have a doctorate in child-rearing, parenting is a daily challenge. The difficulty is compounded by confusion, since opinions on discipline range as widely as those on politics or religion, and are just as avidly defended by their various proponents. You probably have strong feelings about how you will discipline your child, and although your instincts are to be valued, they may not be enough. Good discipline is based on appropriate expectations, and is inextricably tied to development. A toddler wandering toward a busy street is not "bad," she is too young to know how dangerous the street is.

Chapter Seven reviews appropriate expectations for your child. Discipline begins as attention to safety, and can only progress at the same rate as the child's growing awareness of boundaries, increasing self-control, and emerging conscience. Although she'll gradually distinguish the difference between "right" and "wrong," first she'll do what's right only in your presence, and often do wrong the minute your back is turned. Eventually she'll not only know right from wrong, but her own conscience will guide her to make "right" choices because they are right, regardless of your presence, much like the adult who stops at a red light at a deserted intersection at 2:00 A.M. Consistent, loving, and age-appropriate discipline in early childhood helps us raise children we can "trust" when they are out of our sight. I am so convinced of my children's internal standards and controls that I don't worry every minute about them "getting into trouble."

Whatever your own style or philosophical bent, a clear understanding of the meaning and purpose of discipline should help you evaluate your parenting techniques. Too often, the words "discipline" and "punishment" are used interchangeably, and worse yet both are incorrectly used to mean "spanking." In truth, neither "to discipline" nor "to punish" means "to hit." A closer look at the literal definitions of these connotation-laden words offers valuable insight to parents.

To punish is to inflict a penalty for an offense, fault, or violation. The word "discipline" has somehow come to be used negatively in relation to children, as in "Johnny needs to be disciplined for throwing mashed bananas on the carpet." But to discipline is to teach. Discipline is training that corrects or molds mental faculties or moral character. Interestingly, it has as its semantic base the word "disciple," one who so loves and respects another that she models herself after that person.

To parent is to take responsibility for. Our regular everyday behavior shapes our children's value systems, models acceptable behavior, fosters their self-esteem, and implants subconsciously the parenting techniques that they'll employ with the next generation.

The semantics are revealing: To parent is to protect, to discipline is to teach, but to punish is to inflict. It's easy to pick out which of the trio is the least appropriate child-rearing technique. But parents often believe that their major job is to punish, which they equate with disciplining.

Ideally, parenting (protecting) is made up of a great degree of discipline (teaching) and as little punishment (inflicting penalties) as possible. Of course, we can't just model ideal behavior and expect perfect little imitations of ourselves to develop. But we can model behavior that we would like our children to emulate, interact and communicate with them openly and generously, and offer them the trust that penalties will be meted out only in deserving situations.

Effective parents dedicate as much as 90 percent of their time with their children to disciplining/parenting, and less than 10 percent to punishing/reprimanding in appropriate ways.

PARENTS' EMOTIONAL INVESTMENT IN PARENTING

Parents discipline and punish for the good of the child, but we are fulfilling lots of our own needs too. Because we have strong feelings about how we were parented and about what kind of parents we will be, we come to parenthood heavily loaded with subconscious memories of our own childhood. In fact, as parents we may even "reparent" ourselves in the way we wish we had been raised.

But occasionally there are some less healthy emotional needs operating, an example of which is the parent's need to have a child who always appears to be "good." When the need to appear to be a good parent overrides the concern with your child's needs, a problem exists. For example, on the first day of preschool you're hoping that your child will make you look good by walking in, kissing you good-bye, and acting well adjusted. If instead she is frightened, cries, and clings to you, you need to overcome your disapproval of your child's relative dependence and offer her what she needs (even if you feel slightly embarrassed to ask the teacher if you can stay with your child).

Perhaps the most unhealthy emotional need felt by many parents is the need to exhibit power, to be the one who is in control (usually a result of not having had power as a child). Sadly, most parent-child power struggles occur around events much less significant than the power struggle itself. Every time I hear "You know, it isn't that . . . (whatever the problem is) . . . is so terrible, but she needs to learn that she has to mind," a little voice inside me wants to ask that parent why their need to prove their power over that child is so great. You *are* more powerful than your child, so avoid trying to prove it to yourself or your child at all costs.

Obviously power struggles are most unhealthy when they become physical. I wanted to cry for the physical and emotional pain of a three-year-old girl as her father told me,

> "Emily is just so stubborn and strong-willed I don't know what to do with her. The other day she hit her five-year-old sister, Lisa, so I spanked her and told her to apologize. Lisa doesn't need to see Emily get away with hitting, and Emily needs to learn not to do it. But she looked me right in the eye and said 'No!' So I spanked her again, and told her to say she was sorry. 'I'm not sorry. She's mean to me!' Even after the third spanking, she was too stubborn to give in. I had to spank her four times before she would, in tears, apologize to her sister for hitting her."

Even the way he tells the story speaks of his need for power. Phrases like "give in" and "I *had* to spank her" give away his motive of power. Yet this well-meaning, educated man thinks he is really teaching her obedience and self-control. The only lesson apparent to me is that it is okay to hit someone else provided you are stronger, bigger, have more power, and can last long enough to win.

SPANKING

Hitting another person is not socially acceptable in any situation other than parent to child. It is so unacceptable, in fact, that parents disguise it with a different word— spanking. After thus civilizing this violence, we see child abuse all around us and wonder how a parent could do such a thing!

Many parents who spank have lost their tempers and hit longer or stronger than they intended. Filled with guilt, these basically good parents wonder just where the line is drawn between spanking and child abuse. I offer the following guidelines for spanking.

- ✓ Spanking should be reserved for behavior that is dangerous to the child or others. Frankly, spanking should be avoided altogether.
- ✓ Spanking is hitting your child on the bottom or thigh only. Hitting a child anywhere else is child abuse.
- ✓ Spanking occurs with the child clothed. If the child's pants are down, it is child abuse.
- ✓ Spanking is hitting the child with your open hand. If you use a belt or paddle or any other weapon, it is child abuse.
- ✓ Spanking does not leave a welt or bruise where you have hit. If any mark is left where you have hit, it is child abuse.

Before ever spanking, stop first and ask yourself a few questions. Why do you hit your child? What is the purpose in inflicting pain upon the one you love? Even if it does "work," is obedience worth the price of your child's very real pain? When it doesn't work, many parents hit harder. If this is you, ask yourself why you feel such a need to increase the level of pain your child will endure. Another good question—since children model our behavior so well—is do you want your child to model this response in other relationships? Toddlers who spank their dolls are already practicing this learned interaction.

After years of parenting with and without spanking, and after years of counseling parents on discipline and treating abused children, I am convinced that

It Is Preferable for Parents Not Ever to Hit Their Children.

ALTERNATIVES TO SPANKING

Many parents, especially those raised with spanking, know no other way to manage children. There are several alternatives to spanking, depending on your child's age.

For toddlers who are too young to absorb rational thinking yet old enough to find fascination in every aspect of their ever-widening environment, substitution is quite effective. For this age group, the best approach is to alter the offending situation instead of attempting to manage behavior. Rather than spank or reprimand your toddler for pounding a spoon on the restaurant table, simply slip the spoon away and quickly replace it with a quieter toy. If she is tempted toward the tall, precarious bookshelf in your aunt's home, steer her to the safer magazine caddy.

As she grows, your child will become more verbal, as well as more open to rational thinking. Talk as a method of action management is vastly underemployed. You understand why the edge of the table is not the best place for her glass of milk, but does she? When she was a baby, you simply moved the glass (or cup on the high chair tray). At some point, add the comment "I'll put the glass back here, so we don't spill milk." Eventually, you ask your toddler to move the glass herself, and before you know it she tells Uncle Bill to move his glass from the edge, so it won't spill.

Talking rarely works the first time; it will consume lots of time and energy. But parents will find few better ways than patient explanation to teach and guide their children. But what about the times when an infraction has occurred that truly warrants a penalty? If I shouldn't spank, what else can I do?

First, understand the basics of punishment. A very ineffective behavior modification technique, punishment usually only stirs resentment in the offender. The subconscious motive in some parents is often pure revenge. Excessive or inappropriate punishment could lead to emotional damage. Acceptable punishment meets the following four criteria.

√ Educational: Since the purpose of punishment is to eliminate an undesirable behavior, mete out penalties that help your child learn acceptable from nonacceptable

✓ actions. (Thirty minutes without the trike for riding it
in the driveway.)

✓ Age-Appropriate: A popular punishment, a time-out
chair or room, is often used inappropriately with young
children. One minute per year of age conveys to the
child a clear message of punishment; longer only stirs
either anger or boredom. Always use a timer.

Helpful: Of course your intended long-term benefit of
punishment, a change to appropriate behavior, may
not be realized for some time. But punishment should
also help your child in the short term. Although they
may not verbalize it, young children will appreciate
your help in regaining self-control and recognizing
limits.

✓ Relative and Responsible: Rather than imposing arbitrary penalties only in the name of making the child
suffer, choose punishment that relates as closely as
possible to the crime. (If Megan colors on the walls,
she has to help clean them.)

Remember this fundamental rule: The less you punish,
the more profound will be punishment's effect on your
child.

MODELING

In addition to not modeling negative characteristics,
parents should concern themselves with modeling positive
behaviors for their children. Make a continuing effort to
bring to the conscious level all of what you have stored in
your subconscious about how you were raised so that you
don't merely make a mental tape of all the behaviors (good
and bad) your parents used and hand it to your children to
play for their children. (This subconscious modeling is the
way in which the tragic problem of child abuse is passed
down through generations.)

Pay attention to your everyday actions—your preschooler,
toddler, even infant is recording everything. They see how
you deal with anger and express your feelings. They observe how you handle relationships. Their recordings are
also incredibly accurate; they'll know if your words and

body language give conflicting messages. There are some specific abilities and attitudes to model that not only enhance our own lives, but are among the most valuable skills we can offer our children.

Some people say that the only thing direct action management (discipline/punishment) teaches a child is how to directly manage the actions of others. In other words, whatever technique we use to get them to do what we want them to, they'll use to make other people act the way they want, as evidenced by the youngster who says, "No, no! Bad girl!" while shaking and spanking her doll. So model skills that you'll be proud to see flourish in your children, traits like consideration, understanding, and open communication.

The fundamentals of modeling for our children are still best laid out in the well-known poem by Dorothy Law Nolte:

If children live with criticism, they learn to condemn.
If children live with hostility, they learn to fight.
If children live with ridicule, they learn to be shy.
If children live with shame, they learn to feel guilty.
If children live with tolerance, they learn to be patient.
If children live with encouragement, they learn confidence.
If children live with praise, they learn to appreciate.
If children live with fairness, they learn justice.
If children live with security, they learn to have faith.
If children live with approval, they learn to like themselves.
If children live with acceptance and friendship,
They learn to find love in the world.

I have discovered that the ability to say "I'm sorry" is a very valuable one to pass on. It is never easy to acknowledge mistakes, and somehow less easy from parent to child. But your children won't think less of you if you err, and will appreciate, and thus learn, the strength to admit errors, apologize, and go forth. Having apologized many times to my family, I am warmed each time one of my children voices an apology, confident that it will be accepted.

One of the strongest messages to come across to children of even very young ages is your basic outlook on life. Do you set out to make every day a good day, or do you live for Friday, so you can do less? Do you freely acknowledge that each of us is responsible for our own actions, or do you often moan about what someone else, or life, has done to you? Do you let the circumstances of the day determine your attitude? Do you live with a constant list of "if-onlys"? If you find yourself with a constantly unhappy child who always looks to you to solve every problem, ask yourself who she is modeling after.

There is a story that illustrates that feeling of positivity, of looking on the bright side. Which child are you raising?

> Two children came home from summer camp and were told they had presents waiting in their rooms. One opened the door and saw a beautiful, brand-new blue ten-speed bicycle, and sat down sobbing because it wasn't the hoped-for red one. The other opened the bedroom door to a giant, smelly pile of dung.
>
> "Yippee! Where there is horse manure, there has got to be a pony!"

SELF-ESTEEM

Well-adjusted youngsters have a healthy sense of self-esteem. These children are comfortable with who they are. They have been well loved, so they feel worthy of love. They like themselves and it seems only natural that others will like them, too. To more fully understand how to enhance your child's self-esteem, read *Your Child's Self-Esteem: The Key to His Life,* by Dorothy Corkille Briggs.

Self-esteem, or one's own positive opinion of oneself, stems from feeling both loved, and lovable, or worthy of love. We may tell our children that we love them, but they come to their own conclusions about our love for them, based on our words, actions, body language, and parenting style. In *How to Really Love Your Child*, author Ross Campbell, M.D., asserts that "Most parents love their children, but most children don't feel as loved as they really are."

To a young child, adults—particularly parents—are all-powerful and all-knowing. Thus, your child will assume that your opinion of her is an accurate representation of her true nature. Toddlers who hear "bad girl!" enough times ultimately believe in their badness. Even infants begin to sort out their sense of value according to the way they are handled. They use every encounter as a basis for evaluating their place, and more importantly, their significance, in this world.

One of the most effective ways of demonstrating another's significance to you is to give them what is called focused attention. The woman whose husband vacantly nods a "yes, dear" to her narration of an issue gets the message that she is not important to him. And baby Michelle, whose mother absentmindedly jiggles the infant seat whenever Michelle cries, begins to form a picture in which she is far less important than most of the other things in the parent's world.

That baby, though, molds her self-image in another direction entirely each time her mother smiles and coos to her, lovingly stroking that adorable little curve in her nose. In those moments, in the mirror of her parent's expression and attitude, she sees herself as something of value, as if saying to herself, "Wow! I must be pretty important if this powerful adult person takes herself away from other important activities to look at me like that!" Parents don't have to employ focused attention in every encounter with their child; a pattern of consistency will convey to a child her worth.

Focused attention is an extremely powerful force in the establishment of self-esteem, since it communicates worth so effectively. For this reason, it is a valuable tool in all personal relationships. Even parents who are familiar with this skill find it hard to make these encounters a habit and admit they don't offer focused attention often enough. When my youngest was about two years old, he developed a habit of getting my attention by taking my face between his two hands and turning my head toward him. Then, when we were face to face, he would tell me what he had been trying to say, now with my full attention.

With your new baby, compare the number of times that your child has 100 percent of your attention with the number of times you go through semi-attentive motions in a vacant manner. If encounters of the esteem-building variety predominate, you are forming healthy habits for good family relations.

Beware: As your baby reaches toddlerhood a third mode of attention is added, that of negative focused attention in the form of reaction to misbehavior. ("Blaine! Don't throw mashed potatoes at the cat!") As you deal with repeated small but direct moments of action management, which tend to be negative, you move from a balance between two modes (focused and vacant) to a balance of three (positive focused, negative focused, and vacant). Predominance is the key. Keep most of your encounters positive, and your children will feel as loved as they really are.

Another powerful skill that you can develop is the ability to separate your feelings about the child from your feelings about her behavior, and to communicate them clearly. If your toddler pulls all the magazines off the shelf, she is not a "bad girl" as you might be tempted to exclaim. She is really still the delightful, good girl that you love, but her behavior has angered you. Look at the way most of us communicate with our young children:

"Sarah! Bad girl! Don't do that!"

The problem with the above pattern is that it ties a single event (pulling magazines off the shelf) to the child's very character ("bad girl!"). If this connection is made too frequently the child's self-esteem is likely to suffer.

Someone I know was raised by his divorced mother, who repeatedly admonished him with, "You're just like your father!" whenever he misbehaved. Such statements can be profoundly devastating to a child's self-esteem because they offer no hope for salvation: The very character of the child is bound inextricably to that of the father who has been rejected by the child's mother. Through "guilt by association," the child (who is "just like his father") feels rejected as well. Such blows to self-esteem have a long-lasting impact. While the immediate result might be the elimination of an undesirable behavior, the long-range effects are likely to be low self-esteem coupled with resentment toward authority figures.

Parents should react to misbehavior without labeling, judging, or referring to the character of their children. A preferable approach would be to:

1. Describe the specific unacceptable behavior;
2. Tell the child how it makes you feel (and why it makes you feel that way); and
3. Provide a description of the appropriate replacement behavior that you expect—in other words, the limit.

Using the above formula on our magazine-tossing toddler yields the following: "Sarah, when you throw magazines on the floor, it makes me angry because I don't like to pick them up. Magazines belong on the shelf."

In response to this kind of statement, children have nothing to feel resentment toward, nor do they feel controlled. Their self-esteem is not battered, because there is no reference to their character. But, since children generally like to please, they will begin to find their own internal controllers, ones that will ultimately work well whether or not you are around to see the magazines go flying.

The value of communicating in this way is that children eventually get the message that your love for them is a separate entity from your feelings about the way they act. Their personal value is not conditional, nor is your love for them. This conviction will greatly enhance their feelings of security and trust.

It is one thing to react to behavior or to try to mold a child's behavior to fit what you desire. It is another thing entirely to react to a child's feelings and try to change them. Many parents inappropriately try to negate children's feelings, ignore them, or even decide how children should feel!

"Tell her you are sorry."

"Don't be mad."

"Of course you love your sister."

But those children probably did not feel sorry, did feel mad, and didn't feel too loving. Children only become confused when we decide for them that they feel differently. The lesson for those children should be that they have the right to their feelings, that it is okay to have a wide range of feelings and that you love them no matter how they feel. But, while all feelings are okay, the child's behavior stemming from those feelings must be acceptable. It is understandable to be mad at your brother, it is not acceptable to hit him when you are mad. Your responses in these instances can communicate this, effectively modify behavior, and nurture self-esteem if handled according to the following two rules:

1. Be an empathetic, active listener. When you say "Don't be mad," you are saying that the child's feelings are either bad or wrong. Instead, draw out and accept feelings. "I can see that you are really mad" simply acknowledges the feelings, and is often a potent diffuser.

2. Let the child "own" both the feelings and the problem. Often you can diffuse a situation by disclaiming ownership for the child's problem and thus his associated bad feelings about the problem.

For instance, Ben and his dad have been playing at the park.

"Come on, Ben. It is time to go home now."

"No! I don't want to go home. I want to slide some more."

"Of course you want to go home, Ben. Mom will be there soon, and you want to see her, right? Let's go!" (Ben feels one way, but Dad says he feels another. How confusing.)

"I won't go!" Ben runs back to the slide.

Ben's father has to pick him up and carry him to the car, and both are angry. But the scene could be very different if Ben's father had used the two rules for bad feelings.

"I know you don't want to go, Ben. The park is sure a fun place, isn't it?" This is active listening, telling the child you hear what is being said. Ben has no reason to be mad at Dad now, because he understands that Dad is not the foe; he is on Ben's side because he empathizes. It is entirely plausible that at this point Ben will mope to the car, then forget the incident and chatter all the way home.

But if he is still reluctant to go, the most effective response is simply to disclaim parental responsibility for the problem. "I know it feels rotten that we have to go now, Ben, but we do." If Dad says that they have to go because he says so, Ben can again be mad at his dad. But when stated as a condition that Dad does not own, Ben's resentment is minimized.

In fact, Ben's total possible reactions have been minimized:

√ He can't be mad at Dad, because empathy has put Dad on his side.

√ He can't refuse the request to go, because it has been stated as a fact instead of as a parental request.

√ He can't fight for power, because Dad claimed none, so the deadly power struggle is avoided.

These two basic rules provide a very useful tool for dealing with feelings, and everyone wins. Parents avoid exasperating conflicts, and children's self-esteem is left intact.

BEHAVIOR MODIFICATION TECHNIQUES

There are three basic occurrences that modify behavior: positive reinforcement, negative reinforcement, and shaping. Each of these has the same effect on adults and children, and even animals. We cannot choose to enforce them or not; they are laws of behavior that are always at work. The only choosing involved is whether or not you consciously use them to your advantage, and that of your child. For a thorough description of the laws of behavior modification, read Karen Pryor's *Don't Shoot the Dog*.

Positive Reinforcement (used to encourage a desired behavior): Positive reinforcement is something that increases the likelihood that a behavior will be repeated, by providing anything desired in concurrence with the subject behavior. Social reinforcers like smiles, hugs, and praise are the most effective kind with young children. Nonsocial or material reinforcers include candy, toys, or stars on a chart. Mixed reinforcers combine a social with a material reinforcer, like a favored lunch out with a parent. Any positive reinforcement will fit two qualifications: it must be something the subject wants or likes, and it must appear concurrent with the desired behavior. For instance, babies smile for the reinforcement of parental attention, and adults perform work for both social and material reinforcers. Once learned, appropriate behavior is best maintained by a variable schedule of reinforcement.

Negative Reinforcement (used to discourage undesirable behavior): This term is often inaccurately defined, making it the most often misunderstood of the three behavior-modification techniques. Many parents incorrectly consider yelling or spanking to be negative reinforcement: "If she doesn't want to get yelled at or spanked, she won't do that again." However, two qualifiers must coexist to determine what is truly negative reinforcement: something occurring concurrent to the behavior that (a) the subject wishes to avoid, and (b) will end as soon as the behavior ends. So a spanking after the act is not negative reinforcement. But watch any barefoot toddler on hot pavement. They learn not to walk on hot pavement quite easily, because as soon as they step off, their feet feel better.

Shaping (used to produce a new desired behavior): Shaping is a kind of one-step-at-a-time positive reinforcement in which you reinforce even the smallest move in the direction of a behavior you want to develop. You continue to reinforce each partial success until the child has produced the whole behavior that you can reinforce as a unit. E.T. wouldn't have just trooped right into the house for a whole bag of Reese's Pieces, but he went one step at a time for each morsel. Offering a three-year-old a reward for cleaning her room won't work if she has never done it. You can, however, reinforce each step (toys on shelf, clothes in basket, bed made) until she masters the whole series.

Ironically, the most crucial element in all three processes is also probably the least understood and most often misused—timing. It will make or break your efforts. Positive reinforcement is the most effective tool for changing behavior, provided the timing is correct. If you offer the "reinforcement" too early, in hopes of producing the behavior, it becomes a bribe. A late "reinforcement" at best will become a reward, which may have a diluted effect, if any, on the behavior.

Secondly, a late "reinforcement" can confuse the poor child, who has to try to figure out just what was done right. The worst and very likely outcome could be that you reinforce the wrong behavior—the one occurring closer to the time of reinforcement.

To feel the real chasm of difference between well-timed reinforcement and a late reward, imagine that you've just finished a big project and you present it to your boss. She either says, "Wow! It's great! Take the rest of the day off," or she says, "Thanks" and then two weeks later, she offers you the afternoon off. Can you feel the different impact those two reactions have on you?

Timing is also crucial in the effective use of "negative reinforcement." Late negative reinforcement is not negative reinforcement at all; it is pure punishment (which is ineffective, esteem-shattering, and resentment-provoking). The most effective negative reinforcement disappears as soon as the behavior does. The pressure on the reins of a horse disappears the moment it turns in the right direction. It could take forever to train a horse to turn if we punished it after every wrong turn. It is the immediacy of the relief that provides the horse the right information to quickly produce the correct behavior.

Another common error is talking about the behavior modification either before or after it takes place. Advance notice turns positive reinforcement into a bribe (I'll get us ice cream on the way home if you be quiet) and negative reinforcement into a threat, both of which are far less effective than any kind of reinforcement. And after-the-fact admission of having "trained" a behavior in your child will only stir resentment, so you are best off if you simply act and keep your mouth shut.

It is also a mistake to continue reinforcing after the new behavior is mastered. If you have been reinforcing your four-year-old for putting her cereal bowl in the sink after breakfast, you should stop reinforcing after the habit has taken hold. (You praise baby's first steps, but do you praise every step?) Reinforcement is for learning, not maintaining.

Effective parents work hard to fit lots of positive reinforcement into their day-to-day interactions with their children. They find that it enhances the natural self-confidence and feelings of worth in their children and fosters good feelings between parent and child. It also replaces punishment as a more effective method of action management, one that does not incite resentment. The laws of behavior dictate that positive/negative reinforcement is always in action. See that it works for you.

PARENTING GOALS

Our ultimate goal as parents is to prepare our children for eventual membership in society as responsible, well-adjusted adults. We help our children attain this goal by instilling in them a strong sense of ethics and a value system that will help them make independent decisions in later life. By teaching our children personal responsibility for the consequences of their choices and actions, we foster self-sufficiency and positive self-esteem.

Parents need to encourage growth and exploration in their children, while simultaneously clearly defining limitations. Children do not live in a vacuum. In order to function as members of society, they must learn social responsibility as well as personal responsibility.

It is the natural inclination of children constantly to test their environment. It is the responsibility of parents to make their children aware of the limitations beyond which they should not step. The parent who provides little or no structure for his/her child is every bit as irresponsible as the parent who is overly punitive and/or rigid.

Regardless of your parenting style—strict or lenient, rigid or relaxed—the common denominator for successful parenting is guidance and unconditional love.

ESTABLISHING NEW SKILLS

Every parent feels the frustration of trying to get children to act the way we want them to act. Why does it seem to be so hard when the fundamentals I've just laid out are so simple? Well, how do you build a mountain? Simple. Put some dirt in a pile, then keep adding dirt until it is as big as a mountain. Simple, yes. Easy? No!

The fundamentals are few:

√ As you discipline your children, understand your investments in parenting and model positive attitudes and appropriate characteristics.

√ Avoid Hitting Your Child!

√ Communicate with esteem-building skills such as separating the child from the act, using focused attention,

expressing your reaction (not judgment) to misbehavior,
and employing active listening
√ Use the laws of behavior to your advantage by encouraging existing good behavior with positive reinforcement, discouraging undesirable behavior with negative
reinforcement, and producing new desired behavior
with shaping.

Imagine a scenario: A toddler, in the grocery cart for an
hour, begins to squirm and whine for candy she sees.
Mom says no and tries to finish the shopping, but the
whining increases in volume and intensity. Mom implores
her to be quiet, just long enough to finish, and promises an
ice cream cone if she behaves. Three minutes later (in a
bored toddler's mind an eternity easily encompassing enough
time to have completed the shopping) the whining resumes,
and Mom, exasperated, retorts, "Can't you ever be good!
All I wanted was a few minutes, but you *always* make a
mess of a trip to the store!" Once in the car, the already
frazzled toddler is blasted again. "Well, we *were* going to
have ice cream, but you can forget that. Rotten children
don't get ice cream."

Now replay the scene, but imagine a mother with appropriate expectations, knowledge of self-esteem fundamentals, and some skill at behavior modification. Knowing this will be a particularly long trip, Mom packs a few toys in her purse. She has also prepared a good shopping list and works through the store as quickly as possible. Throughout the shopping, she nonchalantly battles boredom by chatting with her daughter about what she is buying and what she will cook with it on which night. Noticing the first ten minutes of nonboredom, she remarks, "Christie, I love to be at the store with such a happy daughter."

About halfway through the excursion, they stop at the in-store deli for cups of potato salad, and Christie gets out of the cart to eat and stretch her legs. Allowed to walk around for one more aisle, Christie is asked to help Mom by putting some items into the basket. For the rest of the trip, Mom sporadically carries Christie for a few minutes, offering at least bits of attention as the boredom mounts. Finally in line, they play finger games together, then celebrate a job well done with some fruit leather in the car.

It is very hard to learn effective parenting. No matter how simple a new way might be, the old way is so firmly implanted in our subconscious that it takes very specific and very consistent effort to change. The change will be a continuing, gradual one, but it will occur if you nurture it. Remember that the old ways are fraught with hidden messages that eat away at your children's sense of self-esteem and also mask your true love for them. So take the time to learn what you can about effective parenting and practice the skills I've outlined for you. I also recommend *Redirecting Children's Misbehavior*, by Bill and Kathy Kvols-Riedler, and the Parent Education Text from the series "What Shall We Do with This Kid?" by Foster W. Cline, M.D.

I think it was Ann Landers who first said that we should treat family like company and treat company like family. There is a corollary in parenting. If we take the time to practice and learn new skills, then use them and treat our loved ones with the kindness, respect, and consideration we afford acquaintances, we'll be doing the best we can do to raise happy, healthy children who will grow up to be stable, productive, and happy adults. We'll certainly be meeting the challenge of parenting.

9 Toilet Learning

EXPERTS HAVE LONG INSTILLED in parents fear and awe of the toilet learning process. You have been warned that this is the time when you'll make or break your child's psyche, when you'll determine if he is to become a neat or messy person, and whether he will suffer lifelong personality quirks. A more realistic perspective on the importance of toilet learning agrees it is indeed one of the sensitive and important steps in a child's development. But since the manner in which parents impart toilet learning is just one more manifestation of their entire parenting style, it is unfair to place so much emphasis on this one lesson. It is certainly at least as important to be age appropriate, sensitive, and understanding when teaching toilet skills as it is with any other lesson parents teach their children.

Perhaps toilet learning receives so much frightening PR because even well-intentioned parents can panic and become overzealous about the subject. Many parents feel the age at which their child can use the toilet represents a major developmental milestone. Actually, toilet competency is not an item on most developmental tests because it is influenced more by cultural and social factors than by your child's innate intelligence. So, relax and approach toilet learning realistically. It is an important, essential part of your child's education and it will be far easier and more effective if you approach it as learning rather than as discipline. And, remember, eventually all normal children learn to use the toilet.

HISTORY

Toilet learning has a depressing history. Misguided experts in the first third of this century ludicrously recommended that toilet training begin between birth and three months of age. Modern parents are probably quite curious how newborn infants of the twenties were so precocious as to accomplish toilet "training" at such young ages. Infants of that time were "trained" by having a suppository inserted into their rectums and a porcelain cuspidor held against their buttocks until the stool was passed!

Mothers of that time were motivated largely by the arduous chore of washing diapers by hand and hanging them out to dry. A mother trained herself to anticipate, maneuver, and catch her baby's excrement. In addition to the modern convenience of disposable diapers, a cultural change has also occurred. In the past, parents believed in the importance of instilling regular and orderly habits in their children. Today most parents let realistic age expectations guide them, and flexibility and individuality are more desirable values than orderliness for its own sake.

WHEN AND WHY START TOILET LEARNING?

Sounds like a pretty obvious question, right? It isn't. Your purpose for instilling toilet habits will differ depending on the age of the child. If you are "toilet training" your baby around a year, your reason is probably to wash fewer diapers, since that's about the greatest benefit you might reap. I distinguish between "toilet training" and "toilet learning" to highlight the difference between a parent who is simply conditioning a response and one who is educating the child to act, for his own motives, and with full understanding of his actions.

If you are trying to teach your child to use the toilet before the age of two, you may hope to train a new behavior in your child, but since it is really not voluntary, it will probably be temporary. In the next year or two, as he replaces simple reactions with voluntary control, "accidents" may reign supreme. Your work begins anew.

If, however, you wait until your child is between two

and three to begin toilet training, the "why" will really make sense. At this age your purpose will be to effect an integration within the child of the process of elimination, the use of the toilet, and the ability to perform these tasks from beginning to end independently—just because he wants to (like all the rest of us).

Getting an early start on such a desirable behavior sounds like a good idea to some parents. But in reality, too-early toilet learning is fraught with trouble. The nervous system development essential for elimination control is not complete until around two. A child cannot voluntarily control the sphincter muscles (the ringlike muscles that close both anal and urinary openings) until the nerve fibers are covered with a sheath made of a fatty substance called myelin. This process of covering the nerve fibers that will transmit messages to the brain is not completed until about the age of twenty-one months. A younger child is therefore neurologically unable to voluntarily control the sphincter muscles. In addition to this physiological unreadiness, psychological development is also insufficient for toilet learning under the age of two.

A young toddler needs to feel capable, more grown up, and confident about his emerging control over himself. Starting toilet training too early sets up the child for inevitable failure, and you for frustration.

Dr. Fitzhugh Dodson is convinced that early toilet training can lead to later bedwetting. Most authorities agree that early toilet training will at least be more problematic and less effective. Additionally, it has been shown that the later you start toilet learning, the less time it will take. An interesting study with twins exemplifies this point. One twin began "toilet training" at the age of seven months and was using the toilet fairly well by the age of two. The other twin began toilet learning at the age of two and was almost immediately competent. Again we see that children are most able to learn to control elimination and use the toilet after the age of two.

When is the best time to begin toilet learning? Of course, the answer varies a little from one individual child to another. Most children achieve physical and psychological readiness between the ages of two and three. Two and a half is a good time to begin if your child shows signs of readiness. An occasional child under two will be truly ready and some children will pass three not quite ready. You will find it difficult to judge your child's neurological and muscular development, not to mention his bladder capacity. It will be a little easier to assess your child's psychological readiness, which usually parallels the physical development. A reflection of this psychological readiness would be his understanding of what you expect him to do, why it is a good idea, and how to do it.

Some experts tell us that girls are ready to learn to use the toilet earlier than boys. Other experts claim that there is no physiological reason for this discrepancy. Mothers usually do most of the toilet teaching, thus offering girls an excellent role model. Mothers tend to allow their toddlers to follow them into the bathroom and observe them in the process of using the toilet. If fathers participated more in toilet teaching, especially with their sons, boys would have an "equal opportunity" with appropriate models, possibly eliminating the observed age difference in toilet learning.

Readiness signs to look for include:

- √ an understanding of the concept that it is preferable to urinate in the toilet and have dry pants
- √ an understanding of the connection between dry pants and using the potty
- √ the ability to communicate his need to use the toilet
- √ recognition of the sensations of a full bladder and the urge to have a bowel movement
- √ the ability to briefly delay the urge to go to the bathroom (i.e., waking up from a nap with a full bladder, telling you he has to go, and getting to the potty before urinating)
- √ the ability to walk to the toilet and pull his pants down and back up

HOW TO TEACH THE USE OF THE TOILET

The next step is to figure out how to go about this toilet teaching in the best possible way.

1. Example is the first important step. Allow your child to observe you using the toilet, adding an educational commentary as you go. Also let him practice flushing the toilet so he becomes accustomed to the sound.

2. Help him become aware of when he has wet or soiled his diaper. Always change him promptly so he won't like being wet or soiled. Give each function a name and be sure to use a word you will not mind hearing for years to come. Do you really want him to publicly announce, "I have to make yucky"?

3. Next, help him become aware of being in the process of moving his bowels or urinating and label it. State that "Billy is going poo poo or pee pee."

4. Help him express it just before he moves his bowels or urinates. If you see by his behavior or expression that elimination is imminent, verbalize it for him: "Billy needs to go poo poo/pee pee."

5. Suggest to your child that being nice and dry feels good and that feeling wet and messy feels unpleasant. This will be your child's motivation for using the toilet.

6. Explain what elimination is, how it comes out of his body, and where it goes after it's flushed.

7. Introduce the idea of underpants. Point out that they're just like Mommy's and Daddy's. Use thick absorbent ones; there is no need to have your child feel any more uncomfortable than necessary during accidents.

8. Tell him that when he needs to go to the bathroom, you'll help him. Take him into the bathroom and help him pull his pants down all the way. Help him feel secure on either a little potty chair or on the toilet. Show little boys from the beginning how to stand (on a stool if they can't reach) to urinate. Help your child wipe (teach girls to wipe from front to back), pull up his pants, flush, and wash his hands. He will need help with wiping after bowel movements for years to come.

9. Explain to your child that toilets are everywhere. When you go out, show him that toilets are in restaurants, movie theaters, and other places and that everybody uses them.

10. Explain that he may not always make it to the bathroom on time when he's learning, and if he doesn't, you will change him into nice dry clothes. Offer him encouragement that he'll get better and better at this all the time.

11. Don't overdo praise, since it will cause anxiety over accidents. Offering treats or promoting the idea that he is pleasing you or someone else by his behavior will not be as successful as his learning to use the toilet because he wants to. He wants to grow up and be like everyone else, he likes to feel dry, and he feels proud of his ability to control himself. Of course you can communicate to your child that you are very pleased for him.

12. Take clues from your child to help him make it to the bathroom on time. If he is squirming and dancing around, ask him if he needs to go to the bathroom. It helps him identify and respond to the urge.

13. If you put your child on the potty, perhaps after she wakes up dry from a nap, make these times brief and pleasant. You might read her a short story, for example. Please never strap her onto the seat. If she doesn't urinate fairly soon, let her get up and leave without a lot of cajoling.

14. Teach your child how to go to the bathroom outside, just in case. Sometimes this is essential. For little girls, it is easiest to pull their pants down all the way and then have the parent hold them in a supported squatting

TOILET LEARNING

position. To protect them from social disapproval, help your children urinate outside as discreetly as possible.

15. A young child's "waiting time" is very brief. When it is apparent your child needs to go the bathroom, get him there as quickly as possible. Remember that most children wait until it feels painfully urgent before they announce it. Don't admonish your child with "Why didn't you tell me sooner?" Kids don't plan ahead like we do.

16. Expect accidents. Between the ages of three and four they will be frequent; between five and six they will still happen occasionally. Feel sorry for your child; an accident is embarrassing, unpleasant and discouraging. Never reprimand or punish. Some parents evaluate success by the number of accidents a child has. Accidents should not be your guide. Instead, measure success by how much of the investment in toilet learning is the child's. Parents often place too much pressure on some young "toilet students." A three-year-old boy I know was wearing big-boy pants and had a successful day with a great deal of attention focused on the toilet. The next day he announced, "I don't want to be a big boy today." Despite his "success," the pressure was exhausting.

17. Don't try to toilet train in a day or even a week. There's a lot to learn; be patient, go slow, always be encouraging, never discouraging. Children want to please their parents.

A newly trained youngster may temporarily regress for a variety of reasons. Or they may simply test out other toilet options once they gain control over this important bodily function. One little girl, Jennifer, was easily potty trained shortly after turning two. She appeared to be adjusting well to her new sister, with only occasional "accidents." One day her mother was surprised to find Jenny alone in the living room, barebottomed, her dry training pants in her hand. Her toy lunch box nearby contained a familiar yellow liquid. "What's that?" her mother asked accusingly. "It's pee pee," Jenny replied, matter-of-factly. "That's not where you're supposed to go pee pee," her mother reprimanded and tried reasoning, "Where do Mommy and Daddy go pee pee?" "In their lunch box," Jenny suggested, much to her mother's dismay. I persuaded the woman to ignore the incident, and Jenny abandoned her novel idea for the more conventional potty chair.

Common Mistakes Parents Make during Toilet Learning

√ starting too early
√ using scolding and punishment
√ using excessive rewards and creating pressure
√ imposing long unpleasant times sitting on the potty
√ making toilet learning a power struggle
√ inappropriate timing (birth of a sibling, move, et cetera)

A highly recommended book for pleasant and effective toilet learning is *Toilet Learning* by Alison Mack (Little, Brown). It contains an informative introduction for you and a wonderful section to read to your child. This book usually becomes a child's highly prized possession.

NIGHTWETTING

Night wetting generally does not disappear just because daytime control is established. It takes more maturity to become dry at night. Night wetting is usual until the age of five and common until seven. Daytime wetting, however, is not normal once the child is really using the toilet competently. Daytime wetting might suggest a physical problem and should be reported to your pediatrician.

A variety of reasons have been ascribed to night wetting: a new baby, a trauma or a stressful event, a recent illness, or an emotional problem. But most authorities agree that the majority of night wetting actually results from small bladder capacity.

One factor contributing to bed-wetting, often missed by parents, is fear of getting out of bed in the dark. Keep a night-light on for your child. Let him know that he can call you and that you'll come and take him to the bathroom. This won't last forever. But for a toddler, it is probably too frightening to get up and walk into the bathroom alone in the dark.

Some facts on night wetting:

√ Night wetters seem to be sounder sleepers than those who wake up dry.

√ More boys wet the bed at night than girls.

√ Except for sex, bed-wetting is apparently unrelated to other traits, such as size, position in the family, or intelligence.

√ Although some diseases, such as kidney infections or diabetes, can be signaled by bed-wetting, the most common cause of night wetting is a combination of small bladder capacity and a deeper sleep pattern.

√ It is possible for emotional problems to be the cause of bed-wetting, but it is far more common for emotional problems to result from the criticism and frustration associated with night wetting. If the child was once dry at night and suddenly is wetting the bed, an emotional problem is more likely.

√ Bed-wetting is often familial.

Under the age of seven, bed-wetting is still common enough that physical or emotional causes are unlikely. Bed-wetting after the age of five should be mentioned to your pediatrician at the annual checkup. Share this information when your child is out of the room. Bed-wetting is difficult for your child, so be as helpful to him as you can. If either parent or another family member was a bed-wetter, such information will be reassuring to him.

Keep him in diapers at night if he's wetting until he objects. At least he'll sleep more comfortably. Don't put a diaper on him, however, if he complains of feeling babyish.

Do not restrict fluids. This only prevents your child's bladder from the necessary stetching for eventual nighttime capacity. Also, the restriction of fluids will seem like a punishment. Do, however, make a point of having your child empty his bladder before he goes to bed.

Do not buy special pajamas, sheets, a bed, or a blanket as a motivation for a "big boy/girl who can keep it dry."

This creates too much pressure. Please remember that night wetting is not done on purpose.

Do not praise dry beds and remain silent for wet ones. This is a very close cousin to scolding. If your child does not wet the bed on purpose, then he also does not stay dry on purpose. It happens to him. React to both wet and dry mornings neutrally.

Think twice before turning to a drug like imipramine for help. Several cases of fatal and near fatal imipramine poisonings have been reported. Many of these children deliberately took overdoses because they desperately wanted to stay dry for a special reward or overnight at a friend's.

Do not get your sleeping child up in the middle of the night, carry him to the toilet, and have him urinate in a half-sleeping state. This prevents the child from developing a larger bladder capacity and any involuntary behavior like this will not really be habit-forming. Parents who do this generally have dry sheets as their goal.

Encourage your child's independent management of his bed-wetting. Once your child is old enough, place a felt-covered rubber sheet on top of his regular sheet and lay out a spare pair of pajamas at night. That way, when he wets he can easily remove the wet rubber sheet, change pajamas, and crawl back into a dry bed all by himself. He will appreciate feeling in control of the situation and he won't worry about disturbing you to take care of his wetting.

If your child is invited overnight or if you are traveling, accommodate the night wetting discreetly. A sleeping bag, perhaps with a rubber sheet inside, can be brought along for your child. That way in the morning the wet bag can simply be rolled and stuffed away with no explanations needed.

Never punish a child for bed-wetting. It is never purposeful. Your child needs your loving reassurance that a time will come when he'll wake up dry every morning. A hug will go much farther than a reprimand.

Toilet learning is a large developmental step for your child. It is a step toward his independence, a step he'll be proud of. Help him learn both day and night control. Teach him, reinforce it, reassure and encourage him. Above all, recognize that this learning process must proceed at a pace that is all his.

10 Understanding Common Behaviors

ONE GLANCE AT THE LIST of habits described in this chapter is enough to convince some childless persons to remain so for life! "Do you mean that it is common for a child to be a picky eater, bite, whine, fight, swear, wet the bed, throw a tantrum, and masturbate?"

Well . . . yes.

"Oh no. So how do I stop such behaviors?"

Well . . . you don't.

Many adults view these behaviors as ills to be exorcised at all cost, but they really are not. They are normal phases that children outgrow.

SELF-COMFORTING BEHAVIORS

If your child had a bad habit, you would naturally be eager to break it. But you would not for a moment deny your child a true need, would you? Of course not. Unfortunately, there is no dividing line between behavior that is habit and one that fills a need. If needs are at one end of a scale and habits at the other, many self-comforting behaviors fall between the two. In fact, children develop and change so rapidly, anything that begins as a true need can over time become a habit.

Unfortunately, many parents believe that the more their child needs something, the more important it is to break the attachment. How many times have we heard "I just must take away the blanket/bottle/bear. She just *has* to have it, like she *needs* it, so we'd better put a stop to

271

it.'' Such parents are missing the point: she *does need* it.

Society often mislabels needs as "bad habits" and then pressures us to eradicate them. Your probable panic at the opening list of "offending" behaviors resulted from societal expectations to extinguish them. But you don't always have to stop these behaviors; they serve a purpose.

All babies and young children develop a variety of self-comforting behaviors that are part of a very healthy mechanism. Young children need lots of comforting until they learn to manage the big, scary world. Even loving, attentive parents cannot provide them with that all the time. So children learn to find ways to help themselves feel better until an adult comes to take over. (When a trusted adult is seldom present, the self-comforting can take over in a damaging way, like the child who bangs her head, rocking against the crib slats for hours on end.)

Your child will probably do some of the things described but not all of them. Remember, evidence of some self-comforting behavior in your child is a sign that all is well.

Although children exhibit these behaviors normally, any behavior present in excess could suggest problems. If your child seems to manifest a behavior to the exclusion of normal healthy activities, or beyond its age appropriateness, or to endanger herself in any way, do not hesitate to seek professional help.

Nursing Habits

The breast-feeding relationship is a delightful one, filled with special habits and behaviors all its own. Many, if not all, babies, develop small habits associated with nursing at some point during their breast-feeding life. Some babies pat their mother's tummy, or stroke a spot on her face or neck. They may twiddle with or tug at the other breast while they nurse, or twirl a lock of their mother's hair. Older babies may develop a favored position or a favorite side for nursing. There is really nothing wrong with any of these behaviors, as long as they are comfortable to both mother and baby.

Problems arise when an unacceptable behavior becomes

established as a habit. Quite commonly, a once-endearing behavior eventually becomes intolerable to the mother after being established as a firm habit. One mother told me, "Jessie has always loved to touch or tug at the other breast while nursing. When she was tiny, it seemed so sweet. But now that she's older, it's become a real problem. I can't nurse her in a restaurant or anywhere public because she insists on pushing my blouse out of the way so she can get to that other side. And it doesn't feel so sweet anymore either. It's become a physical and emotional irritation. What can I do?"

Well, her options depend on the age of the child, how deeply rooted the habit has become, and how invested the mother is in diverting the behavior. Usually the most effective method of eradicating an unwanted behavior is to gradually replace it with a more desirable one. Keep the process positive: encourage the new behavior instead of discouraging the old one, and you'll meet less resistance. Hold the offending hand in yours, stroke her palm with your thumb, lay her hand on your side and caress it there, or do anything else with it that you can subtly enforce by your involvement and positively reinforce with your loving touch. Don't say "no" to the old behavior or even mention it, or you'll draw more attention to it and risk a power struggle. Since she can't do both at the same time, simply continue to offer and reinforce the new habit and the old one will melt away.

Better still, be on the lookout for nursing habits that are forming when your baby is very young. If she puts her arm around your side and pats you, you may find that behavior endearing for as long as it lasts. But what about hair twirling? Will it be endearing for many months, or might it become an irritant? If there is a chance that something will bother you later, start immediately to reinforce another habit.

Nursing language is another very common area for problems. In a well-intentioned desire to encourage clear speech and discourage baby talk, many new mothers refer to nursing by name, "nursing" or "breast feeding," instead of the substitute words like "nummies" or "mukie." As long as the words are used only among Mom, Dad, and baby, any of these expressions conveys the message "I want to nurse" once the baby is old enough to verbalize this need.

However, this is one area in which I do recommend the use of code words over anatomically correct expressions. When your nursing toddler becomes tired and cranky, would you really want to hear at the grocery store: "Can I nurse now, Mommy?" One clever mother I know used the word "snuggle" to mean nursing with her two sons. On-lookers were touched to hear her toddler request, "Wanna snuggle, Mommy." And it gave her obvious cause to excuse herself to be alone with her baby—a discreet solution to nursing an older baby.

Thumb-Sucking and Pacifiers

Babies need to suck, and some need sucking more than others. Most have been sucking a thumb, finger, or hand while in utero. Sucking is as real a need as food to a baby. Please acknowledge and accept that fact before you even begin the debate over thumb-sucking and pacifiers.

Some babies will satisfy all their sucking needs at the breast (or bottle), but many will need additional sucking time. For some babies, an occasional cuddle while sucking on a parent's finger (place the pad of your finger against the roof of her mouth) will be all that is needed. Or a breast-fed baby may enjoy some extra, nonnutritive time at the breast. But many babies have such a strong urge for additional sucking that thumb or finger-sucking or a paci-fier is warranted, and in fact may be essential for every-one's peace of mind. A pacifier is as important to me in examining an infant as my stethoscope. It always saddens me to hear a new parent exclaim, "No baby of mine is going to have a plug in her mouth." The fear of having a four-year-old with a plug is simply not reason enough to deny a pacifier to a newborn, and only a rare baby will hang onto this behavior until a late age anyway.

Although thumb-sucking may conjure up unwarranted fears of braces, it has its advantages over a pacifier. Thumbs are free, generally much cleaner than pacifiers, and far less likely to be lost. They are more easily manipulated by babies, and don't break or wear out. Parents don't even have to fret about which model is best!

However, pacifiers can offer babies a chance to interact with one small part of their environment. In a world soon to be filled with bumps and bruises, this positive interaction is a nice way for a baby to learn that the world feels good. Although most babies give up pacifiers at a young age, concern about "breaking the habit" pushes many parents to decide in favor of pacifier over thumb: you can't just throw a thumb away.

Babies are often very opinionated on this topic, and many have "outstubborned" their parents in deciding for or against a thumb or pacifier. I am convinced that the baby's need is independent of her parent's wishes. Three of my children were avid thumb-suckers, while two used a pacifier only briefly.

If you choose a pacifier (and if your baby complies), there are do's and don'ts for safe and appropriate use. First of all, your baby must learn to nurse without added confusion. Any extracurricular sucking will compete with breast feeding during the first weeks. Let breast feeding become comfortably established before introducing anything else. Pacifiers serve a real purpose under normal circumstances, but should be avoided if your baby is gaining weight slowly. Nonnutritive sucking on a pacifier may be interfering with effective nursing.

Well-intentioned parents often put a pacifier on a loop of yarn around the baby's neck so that when she spits it out (and she will), it won't drop to the floor. Don't do it. There's clear danger of strangulation any time a string is around a baby's neck. If you feel compelled to attach the pacifier, do so with a very short single strand pinned at the chest of your baby's stretch suit.

Another practice I discourage is the use of a surrogate, or homemade, pacifier in the form of a bottle nipple with cotton stuffed inside. These makeshift pacifiers are unsafe. In addition, saliva passes through the nipple opening and eventually soaks the cotton, encouraging the growth of germs. I have seen some pretty foul ones. Please get a real pacifier.

Babies like pacifiers for the sucking and don't need the added enticement or dangers of honey or corn syrup on the nipple. (Honey poses the danger of botulism in babies under a year, and both substances cause tooth decay.) To encourage a reluctant baby, try different pacifiers, or tickle the roof of her mouth with it. If she shows no interest, perhaps she doesn't need or want it.

Blankets and Bears

Adopting a favorite soft animal or blanket is another way a small child manages to soothe herself. Although most of the world holds a dim view of such "dependencies," I applaud very young children who find such ways to allay some of the many fears the big world presents. Initially, an infant seeks comfort from her parents and soon she learns to interact with others. But gradually she is called upon to find comfort on her own for lengthening periods. A soft and cuddly parent substitute is a healthy way to temporarily handle things herself.

Try to understand that this fondness for one special item is not just a childish dependency, and be sensitive to your child's real need for "blankie" or "teddy" or "lambiekins." Have a duplicate ready in the closet for the day the real one is lost or damaged. No, it won't fool the child (unless you regularly alternate between the two for cleaning), but it will be better than nothing. Acknowledge the very real purpose for this item and don't deny your child the comfort of having it at the nursery, in the grocery store, at a restaurant, in the bank. All the places some parents want to deny the object are the very places the child needs it the most. Do encourage her to take it to Grandma's, an overnight, or on other outings.

By the age of four or five, your child can begin to take responsibility for blankie. You needn't accommodate your every waking thought to ensuring that blankie follows her. She can learn that if it is important to have blankie with her at the grocery store, she must remember to bring it along. By relieving yourself of this responsibility, you'll also relieve a great deal of "blankie stress."

As the child begins to grow older, the social acceptability of a blanket or soft animal begins to wane. She may voluntarily leave it at home or in the car. Rather that trying to abruptly or forcefully break the habit, take the time and patience to very gradually help the child phase out this behavior as she learns to manage her environment in other ways. One way to diminish the use of the "lovey" is to gradually restrict its use by first eliminating only one low-stress place it can be taken, then another, until it is accepted only in the home. (However, this can all occur at a much later age than you may think.)

Another way to diminish use of a blanket is to begin, *with* the child's permission, to cut away at the blanket. Cut it in half, in half again later, and again later. Soon you'll have a small square that is far less offending to the public eye but just as comforting to the child. Eventually there will only be a very tiny square that the child can carry in her pocket: socially acceptable, portable, and very inoffensive. You'd be surprised at how many young ones face that first frightening day of kindergarten with a hand in one pocket clutching their blanket!

PICKY EATERS

When your baby starts eating solids, it is the beginning of eating independence. Initially, she opens her mouth like a baby bird as each bite approaches. Later, as she feeds herself, you are sure there's more on her clothes, in her hair, and on the floor than ever entered her mouth. She may go through stages of being picky just to learn where the limits are, but mostly, babies and children seem to go through periods when they have strong preferences about what they want to eat. (I do too; don't you?)

Remember that a tiny baby eats a great deal for her body size and initially grows rapidly. She doubles her birth weight by four or five months, triples it by a year, and quadruples it by two years. If her rate of growth didn't keep slowing, she'd soon outweigh an elephant! Generally, between the ages of one and two, as your baby feeds herself, she'll eat less than you think she needs, and she'll go through spurts of increased or decreased appetite. As long as her appetite is not overly influenced by sugar and salt, she is usually her own best judge of what to eat and how much.

A common pattern for a toddler is to eat lots of one type of food at a meal instead of the well-balanced menu you prepared. For example, she may eat mainly meat or protein food one meal and almost nothing else, then lots of fruit or vegetables at the next meal, and so on. Over a period of a day or two, however, you'll see that she manages to eat a good variety of all the things she needs. If that is her pattern, don't fight it and remember that it will change with time. Some toddlers will even eat in these food group spells for a day or two at a time, before switching to another food group. Your job is to offer a variety of nutritious foods at each meal, not to assure that they are all eaten. Over the course of a whole week, you'll usually find that your toddler did consume a "balanced" diet.

Toddlers often refuse one food or even a whole group of foods for a period of time. (Many twelve- to fifteen-month-olds seem to abandon meat for a while.) For the short term, succumb to their desires, find other sources of the nutrients they need (cheese is a real winner), and don't set up a struggle. Many instances of adolescent obesity or anorexia are found to be related to early control and attention issues concerning food. The long-term benefits your child will reap from a relaxed attitude about food are well worth your brief anxiety about the absence of meat or another food in her diet. Even food jags—the insistence upon the same food for every meal—are best handled with a calm and relaxed attitude. The outer limits of acceptable nutrition are much broader than you realize. These guidelines should help establish lifelong healthy eating patterns.

BEDTIME BATTLES

I think parents complain more about difficulties in getting their children to sleep than they do about any other problem. But this is an area that parents seem to struggle with far more than is necessary, and certainly far more than the children with the "problem" do. Most parents' rigid expectations about bedtime and children's sleep requirements produce far more difficulty than is warranted.

If you expect that a child (this is a beyond-babyhood issue) should only go to sleep at 8:00 P.M. sharp, alone in their own bed and tucked between the sheets, you have set up many conditions to be met for success. Ultimate success in bedtime matters is really simply sleep, and only a very disturbed child would be able to avoid sleep for prolonged periods. All children will eventually fall sleep. What they struggle against are imposed, unnecessary conditions to that sleep. After all, Billy will be just as rested after a night in his T-shirt as he would be had he worn pajamas. I suspect that the families with the most bedtime problems are those with the most rigid rules and conditions for sleep. If you are having bedtime struggles, see if there are areas where you can be more flexible.

Toddlers love ritual. Although it may not matter a bit to you whether she brushes her teeth before or after donning pajamas, it feels comforting to her to follow the same pattern every night: pajamas, teeth, story, kiss, wink, lights out, and door left open exactly four inches. Boring as it will become, don't discount her ritual; heed it and she'll sleep more readily.

Do you insist on pajamas? Does it matter what your children wear? If they prefer a T-shirt, a nightshirt, or only underwear, all you gain by insisting on pajamas is a battle.

Must they sleep in their own bed? If they want to join a sibling (and the sibling agrees), fine; if they prefer a sleeping bag, fine. I know of young brothers with bunk beds who trade and share and switch so regularly they'd be hard-pressed to tell you which bed is whose. If one of them needed the security of knowing that he had his own bed, the arrangement would not work. But since they are both happy with their musical-beds system, their parents need not impose.

Most adults like to sleep between the sheets, but children have been known to prefer the feel of top sheet below and blanket above, or blanket below and bedspread above, or bedspread below and nothing above. You can insist on the standard if you don't mind a fight, but kids can sleep fine in any of the other "deviations."

If you relax your expectations to allow for your child's preferences, but continue to have problems, maybe your child is just not tired. Does she nap too long? Is bedtime too early? Many couples acknowledge that bedtime is too early, but are unwilling to interrupt their couple time by allowing the children to stay up later. One compromise is to enforce bedtime (or room-time), but not demand sleep. Even a three-year-old can entertain herself alone for a while; tell her she must get ready for bed at eight and then stay in her room (or in bed) after that. She can choose to play or sleep, but no calling out or coming out after bedtime. In the early novelty phase, she may stay up too late a time or two and be tired the next day. Shortly, though, the new routine will be established and she'll fall asleep at an appropriate hour. This plan has averted countless bedtime battles.

BITING

Some toddlers go through a biting phase. I've not yet figured out just why. Usually a biting toddler is between one and two years old, younger than the typical age for other kinds of aggressive behavior. A three-year-old may kick her playmate because she really wants to kick her preschool teacher or her baby brother. Although some authorities view biting in that genre, I believe it is not quite the same. Perhaps biting is an expression of aggression, perhaps it's an overflow valve on a child's frustration tank, or maybe biters have just had their fill of being powerless babies and have discovered this way to feel powerful. Biting starts out being exploratory, but when it gets a guaranteed big reaction, it blossoms quickly into a fullfledged well-reinforced behavior problem.

Whatever the cause, the parents of a biter suffer tremendously. What could be more embarrassing than having your precious baby bite into the forearm of your best friend's son? It is usually this very strong, real, and frustrating embarrassment that misguides many parents to initiate the horrible tactic of biting back. I am continually amazed that parents think that they can teach anything with the nonverbal message "I'm inflicting pain on you so that you will learn not to inflict pain on others." They insist the child doesn't realize how much it hurts to be bitten, which is probably true. But would they teach their child that the stove is hot by burning the child's hand?

Please don't bite your baby. Talk about how much it hurts, about how angry she is feeling, about feelings being okay but hurting people not being acceptable, about other ways to express bad feelings. All of this talk may seem a bit futile if your baby is very young. But much of what you say will sink in, and your attitude will certainly be understood. If your tone is very angry, her frustration and anger will rise. Try to be understanding of her feelings and nonaccepting of her behavior. The difficulty of this stance in such a frustrating situation will be doubled if you are also faced with the "victim's" parent demanding apology or harsher reprimand, which often happens.

If you have a biter, give extra attention to emotional nourishment. Double up on focused attention to boost self-esteem and increase skin-to-skin contact and hugs of every sort. Help your child feel powerful in any area you can, and diffuse or minimize areas where power cannot yet be attained. Offer a vocabulary of feeling words, like "angry," "mad," "frustrated," "mean," "unfair," et cetera, and help her figure out and talk about her feelings.

Let her observe you being angry and handling it appropriately. Offer alternative ways to "blow a fuse" like clapping hands as loud as she can, or jumping high and stomping loud when landing. Teach the other children in your family to immediately withdraw the part being taken toward the mouth. Watch your little biter constantly when she is in the presence of other children, and be prepared to jump in quickly to prevent a bite.

It won't stop immediately, and it will be terribly frustrating. It is a phase and it will end, so please don't bite your baby. (Biting past age three may suggest an underlying psychological problem and require counseling.)

WHINING

The words "whining" and "three-year-old" go together so naturally one wonders if *every* three-year-old whines. I think so. Every child goes through a whining stage, so that means whining is normal behavior in small children. Nothing to solve, nothing to treat: normal behavior. But it is guaranteed to drive parents absolutely crazy! And that creates the problem.

Children whine because they want something, usually attention. If they ask politely for a drink of water, that is what they get—water. But if they whine, voilà! The parent pops a cork, and heaps on attention, albeit negative attention. Or let's say they don't want attention, they want a pack of gum. If they just ask, and we say no, it's over—no gum. But then they whine. First they get a load of (negative) attention as we implore them not to whine, probably countless times, and with increasing intensity. But the ending? "Oh, all right! But *stop* that whining!" A perfect example of reinforcing a behavior: gum for whining will surely encourage whining for gum.

Whining is normal, and you will hear your share of it, and you will hate it. But you can minimize it by *not* reinforcing it. Start with an initial statement of "I don't like to hear whining." Then ignore whining, even in public if you can. Respond only when your child speaks in a regular voice. Remember that lack of attention is a strong negative reinforcement that will be effective if you offer attention again as soon as the whining stops. It's most effective if you follow the reinforcement "don't-talk-about-it" rule: resist the temptation to say "stop whining and I'll listen to you." (See Chapter 8, under Behavior-Modification Techniques.)

While the whining persists, it is helpful to offer nonverbal attention to the child, not to the behavior. Holding, touching, tousling hair, all convey to the child that you love her yet allow you to still ignore the offending whine. As a last resort, try repeating to yourself: "This is a temporary phase that will end soon."

FIGHTING AND SIBLING RIVALRY

Fighting and sibling rivalry are kinds of behavior different from those previously explored, but they are often mishandled the same way: by denial. "Take that thumb out of your mouth!" "No, you cannot take that blanket to the grocery store!" "Stop fighting with your sister this instant!"

I recognize needs like a blanket and thumb-sucking, as legitimate. If I were to take the same stance on the issue of fighting and sibling rivalry you might, rightly, protest that children simply don't have the same need to fight as they do the need for comfort. But what I want to validate for children is their feelings. People all have feelings—love, anger, jealousy, fear, joy, guilt, hate, sorrow, resentment. Children have all those feelings, too, even though they cannot label them and often don't understand them. Telling a child "Don't be mad" is like saying "Don't breathe." It's impossible. I hear your protests again: "Do you mean that I'm supposed to accept their fights of rage?" No. I mean that you are supposed to accept the rage. The harder part, of course, is teaching the child that although the feelings are normal and okay, excessive fighting is not.

Your job as a parent begins before the fight erupts. Basically, children who feel they are good, usually act good, and children who feel they are bad, usually act bad. So fill your child up with your belief in their goodness, value, and ability to act appropriately. Children with healthy self-esteem simply will not have as much to fight about.

You will have eliminated at least some fights that would have erupted for the purpose of feeling strong or getting attention.

The next piece of fine-tuning to attend to is your own attitude. One mother expressed to me her concern about the amount of sibling fighting at home. Only later in the conversation did I discover that she had a misconception about how much fighting normally occurs. She was raised as an only child in a very strict and religious home where no one raised a voice and there were no siblings to fight with. She simply had no idea that fighting among siblings normally occurs in almost every home. Expect your children to fight and you'll be less distraught by the fighting that occurs.

Another consideration is the attitude of children. The mother of three young children revealed to me that their frequent sibling fighting was a source of anger and frustration for her and her husband. Preparing the children for a three-day stay with grandparents, the mother pleaded for limited fighting. "But, Mom," her young daughter's voice sing-songed, "fighting is fun!" Sibling fighting often bothers us more than the kids are bothering each other.

Obviously you have to insure that your children don't hurt one another. But beyond that, ignore as much fighting as possible, and let the children mediate some issues. Don't always punish the older child or in any way designate one child as a scapegoat. Accept the feelings, nurture self-esteem, don't set up power struggles, and expect fighting. After all, kids can have personality conflicts, test out domineering behavior, take out frustration, or simply get on each other's nerves like any other set of roommates. And in the end, they'll probably be better friends for it.

SWEARING

There are two distinct phases of swearing that children may go through. The first is during language acquisition at about age two, and the second is at a later point, after age four, when the child has mastered basics of verbal communication.

The two-year-old who swears usually does so initially

out of pure imitation of you or another adult. Babies at this age really have no way to tell good words from bad words, but they are amazingly adept at picking up perfectly "appropriate" language for the situation. So the "damn it!" you exclaim upon dropping an egg may well be mirrored (correctly) when your toddler drops a toy out of reach from the high chair. In this case, as in much of parenting, your best defense is a good offense. Train yourself to exclaim something you'd like imitated; try to exclude as much profanity as possible from your vocabulary.

Be prepared for the eventual appearance of some inappropriate language in your child's vocabulary. When it does happen, the milder your reaction the better. Your negative outburst is certain to confuse the struggling language student, who has accurately appropriated verbal skills heard elsewhere. Having heard only praise from you for each precious step mastered in language acquisition, she'll really have no idea what she has done wrong. Beware of positive reinforcement, too. An outburst of laughter is something your child loves, so she'll repeat anything to provoke it again, be it a funny face, a silly gesture, a new word.

Lack of attention is a negative reinforcer that can work against you here. For instance, you are at the bank filling out important papers and your toddler wants to show you the little hole she discovered in the paneling under the counter. You put her off and ignore her as you try to finish the forms. She pesters more, you put her off again. Finally she bursts out with "Damn it, Mom, look!" She gets your attention immediately (because you could die of embarrassment) and a pattern is in motion. If she wants your attention, she knows swearing will get it.

Endure a few embarrassments; don't overreact to swearing and it will go away. In a time and place separate from the offending incident, offer a couple of comments about some words not being right to use when anyone else is listening. Keep it low key and nonjudgmental, then drop the subject.

An older child swears for very different reasons. The toddler is trying out language, but the over four-year-old is trying out being grown-up, or cool, or rebellious, or is testing limits. Although swearing is undesirable, and inappropriate, it is not the worst sin that a five-year-old can commit. To all children, it feels wonderful to do anything that is usually reserved for anyone bigger. At five, your child cannot go to work, or drive, or even go to a movie alone, but she can swear. She does it because it offers some kind of power she doesn't even understand. Usually some calm, straight talk will help a lot. The more urgent your tone, the less effective you will be. Let her know that no one should swear, because no one wants to hear it. Reassure her that she will seem smarter and more grown-up if she finds other ways to express herself. Then drop the subject.

BED-WETTING

In a book for parents of children from birth to age five there is actually no reason to even discuss bed-wetting as a problem behavior. Night wetting is normal at age three, still common at age five, and although less frequent, should not be a source of great concern at age seven.

However, many parents seem to regard nighttime bladder control as a crucial developmental milestone, and become quite concerned if it does not develop concurrently with daytime control. In fact, the timing of nighttime control will be independent of daytime control (probably later) and usually is of less concern to the child than to the parent responsible for attending to wet sheets and pajamas. (See "Toilet Learning," page 261.)

MASTURBATION

Masturbation is a common social phenomenon. Almost everyone has done it. As children we almost all felt both terrific and guilt-ridden about it. Virtually all experts say it is normal and healthy, and yet much of the population thinks masturbation is immoral, unhealthy, dirty, or bad in some way. As universal and normal as this behavior is, a very negative opinion of it somehow persists.

Your child's developing sexuality, of which masturbation is just one aspect, is influenced greatly by your own attitudes about sexuality, sex, and sexism. If we think of genitals as a nameless "down there" and refer to them as such ("You shouldn't touch yourself down there"), our children readily learn that "down there" is so bad we can't even name it or talk about it. Offer both girls and boys all the vocabulary—vagina, urethra, clitoris, penis, testicles, scrotum—and show each child her or his own parts. If we fail to accept that self-discovery, self-play, and masturbation occur naturally in our children, we will raise yet another generation of men and women who don't feel good about their bodies and who are cheated out of sexual pleasure with and without partners.

It is no surprise that this is a troublesome area for many parents, considering how previous generations were raised on myths and misconceptions about masturbation.

Masturbation in young children, however, is merely the innocent repetition of what they have found feels good: tugging at his penis in the newfound freedom of "big boy" underwear, or rubbing her clitoris in time to the music on the radio.

The best reaction is no comment at all. As soon as the child can comprehend, the case can be made for modesty. Just as with nudity, or genital scratching, a matter-of-fact "This is something we don't do in front of other people" conveys acceptance yet offers some social training.

Children are delightful, sensual little people. Let them enjoy their developing sexuality in this normal childlike way and they are likely to enjoy healthy adult sexuality as well.

TANTRUMS

Tantrums have been wrongly labeled temper tantrums for too long. The proper name should be frustration tantrums. A tantrum is not the result of temper; it is a pure flow of frustration. It is as scary and overwhelming for her as it is maddening or embarrassing or frustrating to you.

You cannot teach a child not to be frustrated, nor should you punish her for such feelings. The only possible prevention is to minimize or alleviate frustrations, and provide other appropriate vents for the frustrations that do build up.

The first natural reaction for many parents is to get sucked into the anger and frustration. Avoid that trap. By all means, don't punish or reward. She hates the tantrums as much as you do, and your reaction could spawn intentional tantrums for attention. Hold her if it helps. Otherwise just ignore the tantrum.

Perhaps the most effective way of extinguishing tantrum behavior is to listen carefully whenever your child calmly expresses her frustrations to you. Listening behavior on your part promotes positive self-esteem in your child and also fosters an environment in which open two-way communication can occur. Tantrums are most often a result of children feeling powerless to make their desires known. Acknowledging those desires (without necessarily acceding to all of your child's demands) creates a greater opportunity for the calm, rational resolution of a frustration.

Sometimes the relationship of a behavior to its initiating event is not appreciated at first viewing but becomes quite obvious in retrospect. There was a period of time when my firstborn, Peter, began twirling his hair while sucking his thumb. He had been an avid thumb sucker from the time he first managed in the hospital nursery to insert his thumb in his mouth with the four remaining fingers splayed across his nose and face. Around eighteen months of age, he began twirling his hair with fervor while thumb sucking. Before long, his hair above his ears was broken off, patchy, and irregular.

The more distressed I became about the practice, the more he twirled. We finally gave him a close-cropped haircut and tried to ignore the habit, which ceased several months later.

I never had thought about the cause of the hair twirling until sometime later when I came across a picture of Peter sitting on the sidewalk in Hawaii, thumb in mouth, finger wrapped around hair, staring at me cradling his new sister in my arms. Suddenly I realized that the onset of the nervous habit coincided with her birth. I had missed the significance of his behavior change, since he then lacked the verbal skills to protest about his new sister as articulately as Paige would do later when Tricie was born.

11 Care of Your Sick Child

NO MATTER HOW HEALTHY your baby is at birth, how meticulous you are about his physical care and diet, how vigorously you protect him from the outside environment, he will inevitably experience occasional childhood illness. The average child gets approximately six colds, or upper-respiratory infections, each year. Many infants will have a bout of diarrhea during the first year, and few children will reach school age without having at least one ear infection. Although routine immunizations have nearly eliminated measles, mumps, and other formerly typical childhood illnesses, most children still get roseola, mono, chickenpox, and others before adulthood.

Bacteria and viruses are the two types of germs that cause most common illnesses. Viruses are tiny organisms that are difficult to grow in culture and against which there is no available antibiotic therapy. They cause colds, most stomach "flus," chickenpox, and many other illnesses. Fortunately, your body is usually quite capable of combating a viral infection on its own. Sometimes over-the-counter medication is used to relieve symptoms, such as acetaminophen to control fever or relieve aches and pains, a decongestant to dry up a runny nose, or a mild cough medicine to diminish the frequency of cough.

Bacteria cause infections like strep throat, impetigo, urinary-tract infections, and other illnesses that require antibiotic therapy for effective treatment. Without antibiotics, symptoms may persist longer, and serious complications of a bacterial infection might occur, such as spreading to other organs.

SUPPLIES

Most minor illnesses are caused by viruses, are self-limiting, and can be managed safely at home by your comforting presence, your careful observations, and over-the-counter or home remedies. You should be prepared for minor illnesses by having some commonly used supplies on hand. Of course all medications, whether prescription or over-the-counter, need to be kept safely out of reach of infants, toddlers, and preschoolers. The following supplies are recommended for the home care of your sick child:

- √ Thermometer, rectal or oral, depending on the age of your child.
- √ Acetaminophen (commonly sold as Tylenol, Tempra, Panadol, St. Joseph Aspirin-Free, Anacin-3, Liquiprin, and other preparations) for fever and minor discomforts. Acetaminophen comes in a variety of preparations ranging from infant drops, elixir given by spoon, chewable tablets, junior tablets, and adult dosage tablets and capsules. At first you'll want to buy infant drops until your baby is old enough for one of the other preparations.
- √ Syrup of ipecac (one-ounce bottle) to be kept on the shelf and used to induce vomiting in case of poisoning. Post the Poison Control number next to your phone.
- √ Cool-mist vaporizer or humidifier to moisten secretions in the upper airway and help relieve nasal congestion. Do not buy a hot-air vaporizer; many young children have been accidentally scalded by them.
- √ Antibiotic ointment, such as Bacitracin, and Band-Aids for minor wounds.
- √ Desitin ointment for ordinary diaper rash
- √ Sunscreen (SPF #15) to protect infants and children from sunburn (though it is best to keep infants out of direct sun altogether, if possible).
- √ Benadryl (now available over-the-counter) in case your child ever has an allergic reaction.
- √ Emetrol for nausea and vomiting.
- √ Bulb syringe to suction a baby's oral and nasal secretions.

Other over-the-counter medications, such as decongestants acquired during a minor illness, can be kept on your shelf for future use. Always watch the expiration date on medications and safely discard them when they have expired. Outdated medications are ineffective at best and can cause complications at the worst. Furthermore, their presence poses the risk of accidental ingestion by your child. NEVER save unused antibiotics or administer them when your child gets sick again. Only a physician should authorize antibiotic therapy and only after examining your child. Giving several doses of leftover antibiotic won't help your child and could mask more serious illness. Discard any unused antibiotic (flush it down the toilet) after giving the prescribed course.

EVALUATING YOUR CHILD

You are no doubt the best observer of your child's behavior and degree of illness. You will want to carefully assess your sick child before calling his pediatrician, so that you can give detailed descriptions of specific symptoms. In evaluating your sick child, thoroughly assess his symptom as follows:

Fever: How high is the temperature? Does the fever come down after he takes acetaminophen? If the fever does come down, does your child look and act much better?

Vomiting: How many times has your child vomited? What does the vomited material look like? Is the vomiting forceful? How soon after eating does vomiting occur?

Diarrhea: How many bowel movements is your child having each day? I smile inside when I get an answer like "every time I change him." I still can't tell how much diarrhea the child is having! Try to be specific; three times per day? six to eight times? over ten times a day? What does the stool look like: green, yellow, brown? Is it very watery, pea-soup consistency, semisolid, or solid? Is there any pus or blood visible?

Coughing: Is the cough hoarse, barky, loose, frequent? Does it cause vomiting, keep him up at night? Does he cough repeatedly without taking a breath, turn blue?

Trouble breathing: Is your child's breathing labored,

difficult, or faster than usual? Is he tugging in between his ribs or where the breastbone joins the neck? Do his neck muscles stand out with each breath? Is his breathing noisy? If so, is the noise coming from his nose or deeper down in the chest? Is it a noise when he breathes in or when he breathes out?

Rash: What does the rash look like? Is it raised? (Can you feel it with your eyes closed?) Are there blisters or "hickey marks"? (These can be associated with serious illness.) How did it start and what was the pattern of spread? What parts of the body does it cover now? Does it include the palms and soles, mouth, or lips? Is it itchy? Weepy or oozy, like it might be infected?

Behavior: Has your child's behavior changed with the illness? For example, is he irritable, listless, lethargic, hard to console, sleeping past feeding times, eating less, awakening at night?

TELEPHONING YOUR PHYSICIAN

After evaluating your sick child, you should call your pediatrician and describe your child's symptoms so the two of you can decide whether his illness requires an office visit. After you become more experienced, you will find that you don't need to call for every illness. With a young infant, however, it is best to call with even minor concerns. The following suggestions should prove helpful:

√ In a dire emergency (i.e., child unresponsive or not breathing), begin cardiopulmonary resuscitation (CPR) if necessary (see page 400) and have someone call paramedics at 911.

√ If your child ingests a poisonous substance, call your regional poison control center. Experts at a poison center are usually available twenty-four hours a day every day of the year, and they have up-to-date, readily available information about drugs and other poisonous substances. They will tell you whether or not to give syrup of ipecac and will call your doctor if follow-up is necessary. If you do not have access to a regional poison control center, call your baby's pedia-

✓ trician. Be sure to keep the container of the ingested substance; read the label to the poison control personnel and take the bottle with you if you are told to take your child for medical care.

✓ For questions of a routine nature, try to call during office hours or your doctor's telephone consultation hour. It is annoying to physicians to be disturbed during off-hours for calls of a routine nature that could more conveniently be handled during the regular work day.

✓ DO call whenever you are uneasy about your baby's condition. Yes, even at 3 A.M., especially if your baby is under three months old or his condition is deteriorating rapidly. Often parents whose infant became sick in the middle of the night have waited until morning because they didn't want to "disturb" the doctor, only to find that their child's condition had seriously worsened overnight. Every physician would rather treat a serious illness immediately, even if it means being disturbed, than to allow it to progress because a parent hesitated to call. Use your good judgment.

When you do make a call to your baby's physician, use the following guidelines for the conversation:

✓ If the situation is an emergency, interrupt the receptionist as she is answering to prevent getting put on hold.

✓ Mention your doctor's name, give the child's name and age, and leave your phone number in case you get cut off.

✓ Have a pencil and paper handy when you make the call in order to write down the doctor's suggestions.

✓ Keep the number of your pharmacy by the telephone in case your physician decides to call in a prescription. Several mothers I know keep the pharmacy number next to their physician's number in their address book.

State your reason for calling as clearly as possible and be prepared to answer the following questions about your child:

✓ How old is your child? The significance of specific symptoms can vary with the age of the child. For example, a temperature of 101° F rectally might occur with a minor illness in a two-year-old but would be extremely worrisome in a two-week-old.

✓ How and when did the problem start? How have the symptoms progressed? Is the baby's condition changing rapidly? A child whose symptoms are progressing rapidly needs to be seen right away.

✓ How much does your child weigh? If a medication, even acetaminophen, is prescribed, the dosage will usually be based on the child's weight.

✓ Does your child have any special health problems? For example, if your baby has had four ear infections in the past year and is showing similar symptoms now, it is likely he has another ear infection. If he has a heart defect or other medical problem, the doctor might prefer to see him in the office even if the illness sounds relatively minor.

✓ Does your child have any allergies, especially to any medicines? The physician will not want to prescribe anything that has given the baby a reaction in the past.

✓ What is your child's temperature? Even though temperature itself is a poor indicator of how serious an illness is, knowing the temperature pattern can help the physician. Does the temperature come down after acetaminophen is given? Does the child's appearance and behavior improve when the temperature falls? Such expressions as "he's burning up" or "he feels really hot," are not very helpful. You cannot accurately estimate a child's temperature by feeling the child. Tapes that measure forehead temperature by color change can also be inaccurate. If your child is ill, take his temperature with a thermometer (see pages 296-98) so you can report it accurately. Also tell the physician whether you took the temperature by mouth, under the arm, or rectally, since normal temperatures vary at each location.

✓ Has your child been exposed to anyone else who has been sick recently, either in your family, the neighborhood, or at the babysitter's?

The person who knows the most about the baby's illness should make the call or be present during the call. For example, often a mother will call after picking her child up from day care, where the baby has been sick all day. The mother may be unable to answer specific questions about the baby's symptoms. In this case, it would be better to call from the sitter's house so she can provide necessary details about the baby's behavior during the day.

If you call about an illness and something later changes in the baby's condition, DO call back and describe the change. The advice you received at the time of the first call was based on the doctor's impression then. The doctor has no way of knowing the baby's condition has changed unless you call back.

SYMPTOMATIC CARE

The majority of childhood illnesses can be managed satisfactorily without office visits or prescription drugs. A general approach to the management of specific symptoms will enable you to handle most of these minor illnesses with confidence and keep your child as comfortable as possible. However, you need to be aware of possible danger signs that indicate when medical intervention is necessary. The following symptoms are common to a wide variety of childhood illnesses and you will probably manage one or more of them by the time your child is a year of age.

ORAL THERMOMETER

Fever

Although we all learned that 98.6° F is a "normal" temperature, in fact, our own body temperature may be a little higher or lower. Temperatures are usually lowest first thing in the morning and highest in late afternoon, or after

vigorous exercise. A rectal temperature up to 100° F in a
child is considered normal. An elevated temperature, known
as fever, occurs with infection, dehydration, drug reactions, and other conditions. Fever is one of the most
common symptoms in childhood illnesses. In general, a
rectal temperature between 100° and 102° F (around 38° C)
is considered a low-grade fever. A moderate fever is between 102° and 103° F (about 39° C), while a temperature
of 104° F (about 40° C) or greater is considered a very
high fever. Children tend to have fevers with illness much
more commonly than do adults.

Fever Phobia: Parents often fear that high fever itself
can cause permanent damage to a child. This is not true
unless the temperature gets over 106° F, which is highly
unlikely with an infection. A few children are prone to
have convulsions, or febrile seizures, in the presence of
temperatures over 103° F. In such children, fever control is
more important than in others (see page 310, ''Illnesses
and Disorders''). In general, fever itself is not harmful to a
child, though the illness causing fever may be dangerous.

Although parents usually carefully follow the degree of
fever in a sick child, fever alone is not a good indicator of
how severely ill a child is. Serious illness can occur without a high fever, and some children typically run a high
fever with even minor illnesses. While a high fever can be
one predictor of serious illness, fever needs to be considered in light of many other observations about the sick
child.

Taking Your Child's Temperature: Before deciding what
a fever means, it is important to take and interpret the
child's temperature accurately. Temperatures can be taken
orally, under the arm (axillary), or rectally. Oral temperatures can usually be taken safely in children over four
years of age, and most this age will resist a rectal ther-

Read this, ''One hundred point two.''

Read this, ''One hundred and two.''

RECTAL THERMOMETER

mometer. Children younger than four may harm themselves by biting and breaking a thermometer. Axillary temperatures are commonly used but are less accurate than the oral or rectal readings.

Before taking the temperature by any method, shake the thermometer down first to below 96° F (35.6° C). Both oral and rectal thermometers have the same temperature scale and are read the same way. The only difference is that a rectal thermometer has a round, short bulb on the end, while an oral thermometer has a slim, long bulb.

To take your child's temperature orally, place the bulb end of an oral thermometer under his tongue. Tell him to close his mouth but not to bite the thermometer. Leave the thermometer in place for two minutes. If your child just drank hot or cold liquids, that could falsely affect the oral temperature.

Rectal temperatures are very accurate, but an improperly taken rectal temperature in a fighting, squirming youngster may cause injury to the rectum. As soon as a child is embarrassed to have his temperature taken rectally, around four years of age, you should discontinue this method. Even if he doesn't seem to mind, I think rectal temperatures shouldn't be taken in children over six.

The best way to take a rectal temperature is to lay the infant across your lap and quiet him with a pacifier or by patting his back. Gently spread his buttocks and insert a rectal thermometer tip lubricated with petroleum jelly no more than one inch. Then hold the thermometer in place and the buttocks together for two to three minutes.

To take an axillary temperature, lift your child's arm and insert either an oral or rectal thermometer under the armpit. Be sure the bulb is not sticking out the other side and recording the room temperature instead of the baby's! Hold the arm against the infant's side and distract him while holding him on your lap for three to four minutes.

After taking the temperature by any method, read the thermometer by slowly rotating it in good light until you see the mercury. Read the temperature where the mercury column ends. Write down the temperature and time of day and whether you gave acetaminophen. Then clean the thermometer with warm soapy water (not hot) and wipe it with rubbing alcohol. Keep the thermometer stored in its

TAKING AN AXILLARY TEMPERATURE

original container to prevent it from breaking. Digital thermometers are now available to simplify reading a thermometer.

Definition of a Fever: The definition of a fever varies according to where the temperature is measured. Rectal temperatures are normally higher than oral, and oral temperatures are higher than axillary. Thus, a child with normal body temperature may have an axillary temperature of 98° F, an oral temperature of 98.6° F, and a rectal temperature of 99.6° F.

Thermometers that measure in degrees Centigrade, or Celsius, are also now commonly available in this country, and many physicians' offices use Centigrade thermometers. A simple conversion table is provided here to help you change between degrees Fahrenheit and Centigrade. Briefly, 37° C corresponds to 98.6° F. There are roughly 2 degrees Fahrenheit for each degree Centigrade above 37, so that 40° C is approximately 104° F.

TEMPERATURE CONVERSION CHART
FROM CENTIGRADE TO FAHRENHEIT

Degrees Centigrade	Degrees Fahrenheit
34.0	93.2
34.5	94.1
35.0	95.0
35.5	95.9
36.0	96.8
36.5	97.7
37.0	98.6
37.5	99.5
38.0	100.4
38.5	101.3
39.0	102.2
39.5	103.1
40.0	104.0
40.5	104.9
41.0	105.8

Although no strict criteria exist for defining when a "fever" begins, the following guidelines should be helpful to you:

Axillary temperature	greater than 99.2° F or 37.3° C
Oral temperature	greater than 99.5° F or 37.5° C
Rectal temperature	greater than 100.4° F or 38.0° C

Treatment of Fever: Since fever tends to make a child feel uncomfortable and may aggravate symptoms such as headache, vomiting, and listlessness, it is a good idea to treat a rectal temperature above 101° F or 38.3° C with appropriate doses of acetaminophen. Acetaminophen is prescribed by weight, so that a large six-month-old might receive the same dose as a small one-year-old. Because acetaminophen is available in so many different concentrations and preparations, be sure that you follow the directions for the specific preparation you are using. A dosage chart for acetaminophen is included to help you figure the correct dose for your child.

Overdoses of acetaminophen are very dangerous, so be sure to give the correct dose and to keep the medicine out of the reach of children. After giving an appropriate dose of acetaminophen, check your child again in thirty to sixty minutes. In general, if a fever comes down following acetaminophen and the child perks up, looks better, and acts well, the fever is probably being caused by a minor illness.

The effects of acetaminophen last approximately four hours. If the fever returns, you can repeat the dose at four-hour intervals. Don't give unnecessary doses of medication if the fever has not returned, as repeated doses of acetaminophen can build up in a child's system and eventually cause toxicity. Since acetaminophen (and aspirin) are common ingredients in over-the-counter medications such as cold remedies, check to be sure that no other medicines you are giving your child also contain acetaminophen.

ACETAMINOPHEN DOSAGE CHART

Child's Age	2* to 3 mos	4 to 11 mos	12 to 23 mos	2 to 3 yrs	4 to 5 yrs
Weight in pounds (lbs)	6 to 11 lbs	12 to 17 lbs	18 to 23 lbs	24 to 35 lbs	36 to 47 lbs
Weight in kilograms (kgs)	2.7 to 5 kgs	5.5 to 7.7 kgs	8.2 to 10.5 kgs	11 to 16 kgs	16.4 to 21 kgs
Dose in milligrams (mg)	40 mg	80 mg	120 mg	160 mg	240 mg
Infant drops: 80 mg per dropperful = .8 milliliters (mls)	½ dropper	1 dropper	1½ dropper	2 droppers	3 droppers
Elixir: 160 mg per teaspoon (1 tsp = 5 mls)	—	½ tsp	¾ tsp	1 tsp	1½ tsp
Chewable tablets	—	—	1½ tablets	2 tablets	3 tablets

*If you believe your infant under 2 months of age has a fever, call your pediatrician before you administer acetaminophen, to determine whether the baby should be examined first. Remember, illness in a baby less than two months of age is uncommon and can be serious, so discuss her symptoms with her doctor right away.

When fevers respond poorly to medication and children continue to look ill after being given acetaminophen, a more serious illness may be present. Call your doctor to discuss your child's illness if any of the following is present:

- √ ANY fever in a child under three months of age. (In this case, don't give acetaminophen unless your doctor recommends it. Your pediatrician will probably want to promptly examine a young infant with fever and may prefer that you bring the child in while the fever is still present.)
- √ ANY fever present for more than three days
- √ A fever of 101° F (38.3° C) that has been present for more than twenty-four hours
- √ A fever associated with specific symptoms, such as fever and cough, fever and earache, fever and rash, fever and abdominal pain
- √ A persistent fever that is not responsive to correct doses of acetaminophen
- √ A fever in a child who looks quite ill, regardless of the duration of fever, height of fever, or associated symptoms
- √ A fever associated with abnormal movements, such as twitching of the face or arms and legs
- √ A fever in a child who has not been eating or drinking normally for twenty-four hours

When a child has a fever, he will need about 10 percent more fluids for each degree Fahrenheit of temperature elevation in order to prevent dehydration. Thus if your child has a 103.6° F temperature, or 5 degrees Fahrenheit above normal, he will need 150 percent or 1½ times his normal fluid intake. This is why it is important to encourage your feverish child to drink extra fluids, even if this means he eats fewer solids. The liquid intake is more important.

In the past, aspirin was commonly used to treat fever and minor discomfort in children. However, the use of aspirin during chickenpox, influenza, and other viral illnesses in children has recently been linked with the development of Reye's syndrome, a rare and poorly understood serious illness that often leads to coma. (See page 376-77, ''Illnesses and Disorders.'') Now many health professionals are discontinuing the use of aspirin therapy in children and using acetaminophen exclusively instead. Whether aspirin is really related to Reye's syndrome remains unclear, but until further information is available, I do not recommend aspirin for children. Check ingredients in over-the-counter medications to be sure you aren't giving aspirin inadvertently.

Diarrhea (See page 340, Illnesses and Disorders.)

Diarrhea can be caused by an infection in the gastrointestinal tract or occur as an associated symptom of other illnesses or disorders. It is defined as an increase in the number and water content of bowel movements. Diarrhea can be associated with vomiting or other symptoms, or may occur in an otherwise well-appearing child.

In general, breast-fed infants with diarrhea should discontinue any solids they may be on, but should continue to breast-feed. Formula-fed infants should discontinue both formula and solids for twenty-four to forty-eight hours. In the meantime, the baby should be fed generous amounts of clear liquids, such as Jell-O water (made with twice the amount of water indicated on the directions), flat soda pop, and juices. The baby should be given a variety of clear liquids, but not a lot of new drinks.

Young infants under six months of age are usually placed on a balanced solution of sugar and electrolytes, which looks clear like water. Some brand names for these solutions are Pedialyte and Lytren. These products will assure that your young baby will get the proper balance of minerals he needs to replace losses in the stool, as well as sugar for energy. Babies with diarrhea usually lose weight for a couple of days because of their frequent stools and restricted diet. The dietary changes usually allow faster recovery and sooner return to a regular diet, however, with less overall weight loss than if diarrhea persisted for many days.

If the diarrhea has slowed down after twenty-four to forty-eight hours on clear liquids, the baby can gradually be returned to his regular diet. If the baby is formula fed, it is a good idea to return to his regular formula gradually by first feeding a soy milk, such as Nursoy, Prosobee, or

Isomil. The sugar in soy milk is easier to digest than the sugar in regular formula.

Sometimes diarrhea occurs when a child is taking antibiotics, because the antibiotic temporarily eliminates many normal bacteria that live in the gut in balance with other organisms. You can reintroduce these normal bacteria by feeding your child natural yogurt during antibiotic therapy. The dietary changes described earlier can also be used. It is important NOT to change the diet for more than forty-eight hours without contacting your physician. I recall one mother who kept her infant on clear liquids for several weeks, which led to malnutrition and "starvation diarrhea," which can be a serious problem.

When there is blood in the stool, or when diarrhea has been present for over two days, has not improved on a clear liquid diet, is associated with high fever or signs of dehydration (see page 307), the child should be seen by a physician.

Vomiting (See page 390, Illnesses and Disorders.)

Vomiting can be caused by an infection in the gastrointestinal tract or can be a symptom of a variety of other illnesses. For example, many children will vomit whenever they have a fever.

Vomiting should be managed by trying to bring any fever under control. In addition, it is important that only tiny amounts of clear liquids be offered to drink at a time. Give a teaspoon of 7-Up, for example. If the child keeps it down, then slowly increase the volume offered. Only clear liquids, such as juice, flat soda pop, broth, and Jell-O water, should be offered. Pedialyte or Lytren are preferable with younger infants. This regimen will allow the stomach to rest but prevent dehydration. Milk and solid food should not be given to a child with vomiting, as these will almost certainly cause the child to vomit again. I do make an exception to the milk rule for breast-fed babies and allow them to continue to nurse.

Any child who has vomited blood or yellowish material should be seen by a physician. Vomiting associated with abdominal pain. signs of dehydration. high fever, lethargy, extreme irritability. or following a head injury should also prompt a visit to the physician.

Coke syrup. or an over-the-counter preparation known as Emetrol. can be used to settle the stomach in children with vomiting. A teaspoon can be given initially and sips of clear liquids offered about twenty minutes later. The dose can be repeated in twenty minutes if necessary.

Cough

Cough has been called "the watchdog of the lungs." It plays an important role in clearing mucus from the respiratory tract and in warning of serious illness. For this reason, it is not a good idea to try to suppress a cough in an infant. The cough is needed to get mucus out, and it is a good sign to use to observe for worsening of disease.

Children over two years of age with nagging coughs can be given an over-the-counter expectorant. An expectorant helps loosen mucus in the upper chest and makes coughs due to simple colds less frequent but more productive. In addition to expectorants, numerous cough medications contain combinations of cough suppressants or decongestants. These preparations should not be used in children under two years of age. Do not exceed the recommended dosage for age, and if you are using other over-the-counter cold remedies, read the labels to be sure they don't contain ingredients in common. Since some coughs are produced by irritation in the back of the throat, a spoonful of honey or Karo syrup or unmedicated cough drops (in a child old enough to eat hard candy!) may coat the throat and bring relief. (Don't give honey to children under one year of age, because there is a risk of botulism.)

Whenever a cough is present, it usually means mucus is being cleared from the respiratory tract. You should give lots of clear liquids to drink so the mucus will be thin and easy to cough up.

When a cough has been present for several days, is associated with high fever, difficulty or rapid breathing, or comes on abruptly after "choking" on something, the child should be seen by a physician.

Rash

Rashes are common with many illnesses. Most are associated with viruses, cause no problems in the child, and require no intervention. Rashes tend to be readily noticed by parents and cause them to worry. It is helpful to call your baby's doctor whenever a rash occurs and describe it instead of automatically taking the child to the office. Some guidelines about rashes are as follows:

- √ A large raised, red, itchy rash similar to giant mosquito bites (hives) suggests an allergic reaction and should be seen by a physician so that a diagnosis can be made. An antihistamine may be prescribed for the child's comfort and to hasten improvement. Calamine lotion may also provide temporary relief of itchy rashes. (See "Allergy," page 314, and "Allergic Reaction," page 405.)
- √ Any rash with blisters in any stage should be seen by a physician. The exception to this is chickenpox. (See page 326, "Illnesses and Disorders.") Routine, uncomplicated chickenpox cases should NOT be taken to a physician's office, because chronically ill children who might not be able to fight off the infection will be put at risk of exposure.
- √ Any rash that resembles hickey marks, bruises, or purple marks that do not fade away briefly when you press on them can be associated with serious disease and should be seen promptly by a physician.
- √ A faint, flat, red rash that briefly disappears when you press on it, when present in a child who is mildly ill, usually does not need to be seen and will probably disappear in a day or two. This type of rash is usually caused by a viral infection.
- √ Any rash present more than three days should be seen by a physician.
- √ Any rash that bothers the child in any way or is associated with other symptoms should be seen by a physician.

Runny Nose

A runny nose usually accompanies a cold or other upper-respiratory infection. Since most children under two years don't understand how to blow their nose, they may be uncomfortable with a lot of mucus in their nostrils. You should use a soft tissue to wipe their nose often to try to keep it clear. You can also use a bulb syringe purchased from a drugstore or brought home from the hospital after your baby was born to suction mucus from the nostrils. To use the bulb syringe, compress the bulb and close one nostril. Place the squeezed bulb gently inside the other nostril and release the bulb. This will create mild suction and clear out the nostril. Then repeat on the other side.

Occasionally the child will have thick mucus that is difficult to remove. In this case, you can use a clean eye dropper to instill a few drops of saltwater nosedrops into each nostril before suctioning with the bulb syringe. This will loosen up the thick mucus and make it easier to remove. You can purchase saltwater, or saline, nasal sprays (Ayr or Ocean) and use them as nosedrops, or you can make your own solution by mixing ½ teaspoon noniodized salt in an eight-ounce glass of lukewarm water. Make a fresh solution daily. Your baby will fuss and cry while his nose is being cleared, but he will feel better afterward.

Running a vaporizer is another way to help keep nasal mucus thin and easier to remove. Children with colds usually breathe more comfortably if a cold-water vaporizer is running in their room

Mild decongestant nosedrops or sprays, such as ⅛% (0.125%) NeoSynephrine, can be purchased over-the-counter and used to relieve a stuffy or runny nose. Medicated nosedrops should not be used in children under six months of age because of possible side effects. They should never be used for more than three consecutive days at any age because they can be "addictive." After chronic use, the nostrils tend to swell tightly shut after each dose wears off, so that the user requires more medication. Therefore, it is best to avoid medicated nasal sprays or drops in children.

Finally, oral decongestants or antihistamine-decongestant combinations can be purchased over-the-counter. Common combination products are Sudafed Plus, Actifed, Triaminic,

Novahistine, and many others. You will note on the bottle that their use in children under two years of age, and in some instances under six years of age, should always be supervised by a physician. An antihistamine-decongestant can make a child with a mild cold more comfortable, and often a single nighttime dose will enable the child to breathe through his nose more easily. Children differ in their reactions to antihistamine-decongestants; some get drowsy from the antihistamine, and others become hyperactive from the decongestant. You should be careful not to use more than one "cold remedy" at a time, since most of them contain ingredients in common, making it easy to accidentally overmedicate a child.

Dehydration (See page 390, Illnesses and Disorders.)

Dehydration is the dangerous loss of body water, usually due to several factors in combination. Common factors leading to dehydration include diarrhea, vomiting, low intake of liquids, and fever. Infants are at much greater risk of dehydration than older children. Severe dehydration can lead to shock and ultimately to death. Mild dehydration can be treated with increased liquid intake by mouth, whereas severe dehydration must be treated in the hospital with intravenous fluids.

The first signs of dehydration are lethargy and decreased urination. You should note your child's frequency of urination and appearance of the urine. Scant, dark yellow urine suggests dehydration. Another helpful sign to observe is the amount of moisture in the baby's mouth. If the saliva is thick and sticky and the mouth looks dry, the child is probably dehydrated. The absence of tears is another indicator of dehydration, and sunken-appearing eyes is a late sign. In a young infant, the soft spot, or fontanel, may become sunken if the child is dehydrated.

To prevent serious dehydration, offer your sick child frequent clear liquids and contact his physician whenever any of the signs of dehydration appear.

GIVING MEDICATIONS

One and a half billion prescriptions are dispensed each year, and up to half of these are taken incorrectly, with resultant prolonged illness, side effects, and harmful drug interactions. It has been shown that few parents actually give medications in the correct schedule and for the full course. Perhaps this is because most patients don't ask questions about their medicines and most physicians fail to educate patients about the purpose of a prescribed drug, its correct dosage schedule, possible side effects, storage requirements, and other details of its use. A new organization, the National Council on Patient Information and Education, was created to improve communications about prescription medicines. It recommends that all patients ask and all health professionals answer these five questions:

1. *What is the name of the medication and what is it supposed to do?*

I am amazed how often patients don't know whether they are taking an antibiotic to cure an infection or another drug to relieve symptoms. They just take it blindly. How many times have you given your child a drug without knowing its indication or exact purpose?

2. *How do I take it and for how long?*

Have your physician tell you the dosage and schedule when a drug is prescribed. That way you can verify the prescription label when you pick up the drug from the pharmacist. In one instance, a miscommunication with the pharmacist occurred when the physician telephoned in the prescription. Because the physician had explained the medication schedule to the mother, she detected the mistake by reading the label before she left the pharmacy.

Very often, a prescribed medication will be an antibiotic. The purpose of the antibiotic is to kill the infecting germs. For this reason, the drug will have to be given at regularly spaced intervals around the clock in order to maintain a killing level of the drug twenty-four hours each day. If an antibiotic is to be taken three times a day, you should attempt to give it approximately every eight hours. Without this knowledge, many of us would give it at breakfast, lunch, and dinner. This might leave an interval of twelve to fourteen hours at night, during which adequate drug levels might not be maintained. It would be preferable to give the drug first thing in the morning, early afternoon, and just before bedtime. Although it is tempting to discontinue an antibiotic when the child is feeling better, always give the full prescribed course to be sure the infection has been adequately treated.

Be sure you know whether the drug is to be taken by mouth or instilled into the eyes or ears. Many naive parents have tried to instill the oral antibiotic prescribed for an ear infection into the ears instead of giving it by mouth! Never put any medication into the eyes unless the label says *ophthalmic* on it.

3. *What foods, drinks, other medicines, and activities should I avoid while taking this medicine?*

Your pharmacist is often helpful in providing details about a drug, such as whether to give it with a meal or on an empty stomach. Some drugs are irritating to the stomach and will be better tolerated with a meal. In other instances, milk or other foods may limit the absorption of a drug. For most drugs, it probably doesn't matter when you take them in relation to meals, but if you aren't sure, ask the pharmacist when you pick up the prescription.

4. *What are the side effects and what should I do if they occur?*

You might inquire whether another drug with fewer side effects can be used instead. Try to recall whether your child has had a previous reaction to any drugs used in the past, so you can avoid them later. If your child has a drug allergy, get him a Med-Alert bracelet. It could save his life someday.

5. *Is there any written information available about this medication?*

Some pediatricians have prepared parent information sheets for commonly prescribed drugs.

I would add a sixth question about medication storage. Most antibiotics in liquid form need to be refrigerated to maintain their potency. In such cases, the bottle is usually labeled "Refrigerate." Pills and capsules will keep well on the shelf in a cool, dry place.

Finally, I would caution all parents against insisting on medication when it may be unnecessary. While physicians are certainly guilty of overmedicating their patients, a pill-for-every-pain attitude is prevalent in our culture today. Parents who insist on a penicillin shot for every cold can be frustrating to physicians. Even after a lengthy explanation about why an antibiotic is unnecessary, I often hear: "Well, I'll just go to Dr. So-and-So; they'll give him a shot like they always do." These same parents own every over-the-counter drug on the market and offer their children a smorgasbord of medications for every tiny sniffle. A dangerous side effect of this overmedication is conveying to our children the attitude that drugs are an answer to life's problems. I find it refreshing when parents request a full explanation of their child's illness and the recommended medication. It's good to have more parents actively participate in their child's health care by appropriate questioning of prescribed medications.

Giving Your Child Medication

Typical antibiotic dosages for children are a teaspoon or half a teaspoon. Instead of estimating these measurements with an ordinary kitchen spoon, you can ask your physician or pharmacist to give you a syringe or other measuring device and to show you how to measure the dose correctly. For some medications, such as heart medica-

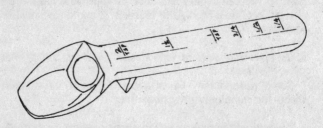

MEASURING SPOON FOR LIQUID MEDICINE

tions, asthma medications, and others, a calibrated dropper or syringe is used, since extreme accuracy is required to prevent dangerous overdosage.

It is best to give your child medication with a matter-of-fact approach. If you maintain a positive attitude, the child will probably accept it readily. Don't make a nasty face or act like you expect the child to refuse the medication. Don't plead with the child or try to coerce him. With babies, smack your lips and act like you are eating too.

If your child tries to spit the medicine out, don't struggle with him, but instead disguise the medicine in one ounce of juice, given by bottle or cup. Pills can be ground up and mixed with applesauce. Never let the giving of medication become a power struggle with your youngster. Remember, the child does not have a choice in this matter. The medication is prescribed for his own well-being, and he should cooperate in taking it. If he is old enough to express frank distaste for the drug, ask his help in selecting a food to disguise it in. Chocolate syrup, peanut butter, jelly, honey, and ice cream can all be used for this purpose. Because many medications, especially elixirs and syrups, have a very high sugar content, you might have your child rinse his mouth after taking his dose of medication.

CREATURE COMFORTS

You will want to make your child as comfortable as possible during an illness. Your presence alone will help to comfort and assure him, so if you work outside the home, you will probably want to take a few days off if possible. Sending a sick child to school, a babysitter, or day care to expose other children is unfair to your child and thoughtless of others. Although I have taken my own sick child to work with me, I now consider it inappropriate. Besides, I think it is a sad message to a child that the needs of others outweigh his own needs during illness. Your child will likely be most comfortable at home in his own bed and receiving your undivided attention.

You should evaluate your child fully every few hours. Take his temperature. Check to be sure he is urinating.

Find out if he has any complaints, discomforts, or new symptoms. See if he seems to be responding appropriately or is willing to smile or play.

Be sure to tend to your child's physical needs and keep him comfortable. If your baby has diarrhea, change and clean him promptly after each stool to prevent diaper rash. If he already has a raw bottom, gently rinse him in a basin of lukewarm water after bowel movements and apply Desitin to protect his skin from the next stool. If he vomits, clean him, change his clothes or sheets, and let him rinse his mouth. Give him a container to keep nearby for the next episode. If he has a cold and is too young to blow his nose, use your bulb syringe to clear his nostrils whenever he seems congested and especially before feeding him so he can breathe comfortably.

Remember that your sick child may be whiny and emotionally needy. Try to recall how miserable and cranky you can get when you don't feel well. This is the time to pamper him, hold him, and, yes, "baby" him if necessary, instead of telling him to "be a big boy." Minor discomforts might be relieved with home remedies such as a heating pad or ice pack. Distraction works wonders, so a new toy may be in order. Reading stories, playing a quiet game, or watching TV will help keep his mind off his illness. In general, just do all those obvious little things that appear to relieve his symptoms and reassure him with your presence and love. I will always remember my own parents' doting attention and obvious concern when I had the measles at age four and spent many miserable days in bed clinging to a comforting small rubber doll they had bought me.

12 Illnesses and Disorders

THE FOLLOWING MATERIAL provides an easily accessible reference to specific childhood illnesses and disorders. Most of the conditions discussed require treatment by your baby's pediatrician or another healthcare provider. The purpose of this material is to increase your familiarity with each condition, *not* to replace your physician's advice and care. By increasing your understanding of specific conditions affecting your child, I hope you will be better prepared to ask questions, understand and comply with treatment, recognize possible complications, and prevent recurrences. Included are a few illnesses and disorders that are not very common, but about which little information is available to parents from other sources.

Allergy

Definition: An allergy is the body's reaction to a foreign substance, such as a food or medicine, an inhaled particle like pollen or dust, or a skin contact with a substance, like soap or wool.

Cause: The actual chain of events in the body that triggers an allergic reaction is caused by the union of protein substances known as antibodies with particles from foreign substances, leading to the release of a chemical called histamine.

Symptoms: The symptoms of an allergy vary according to the offending substance. Allergies to inhalants cause symptoms of hay fever, including wheezing, runny nose, and watery, itchy eyes. Skin contacts are more likely to cause localized skin irritation, whereas an ingested or injected substance may cause widespread symptoms, including hives, or itchy wheals, congestion and wheezing, or diarrhea and vomiting. An allergy will produce symptoms following exposure to the offending substance.

Treatment: If you suspect an acute allergic reaction (see page 405) or chronic allergic symptoms in your child, you should discuss these with her pediatrician and have her examined. The most important treatment of an allergy is to avoid exposure to the substance the body is reacting to. For some substances, such as foods and drugs, this is relatively easy to do. For other allergens, like pollens, it is not always possible to avoid them entirely. The kind of drug most commonly used to combat allergy symptoms is an antihistamine, such as Benadryl, which works to block the body's release of histamine and the allergic response that follows. Antihistamines are particularly helpful with hives and hay fever.

Complications: The most feared complication of an allergy is anaphylaxis. This is a rare, life-threatening reaction in which shock and airway obstruction occur, and it requires emergency medical treatment with adrenaline, oxygen, and intravenous fluids. (See page 406 under "Emergencies!")

Prevention: Allergies can't really be prevented, since it is not clear why some people develop allergies to particular substances while others don't. Some food allergies may be prevented by delaying the introduction of solid foods in the diet, and avoiding known allergenic foods for the first year, such as citrus fruits, egg whites, corn, berries, peanut butter, and fish.

Inhalant allergies are less likely to occur if one avoids recurrent exposure to the same pollens. I didn't develop hay fever until we settled permanently in Colorado. As a youngster, I had moved every two or three years, and I think that's why no one in my family ever had hay fever.

If your child has a known inhalant allergy, symptoms can be minimized by staying indoors with the windows closed during heavy pollen periods, dusting her room daily with a damp cloth, and giving her a daily bath or shower. If your child has allergic symptoms of unclear origin, avoid contact with all animals, dust collectors, and dust producers, such as venetian blinds, cotton quilts, toys stuffed with plant or animal products, flannel bedding and pajamas, and chenille bedspreads, drapes, and rugs.

A child with a known drug allergy should wear a Med-Alert necklace or bracelet with this information, in case of an emergency when the drug might be given without a full history being available. If your child has ever had a severe allergic reaction, for example to a bee sting, she should receive desensitization by a pediatric allergist and you should own a bee-sting kit (Ana-Kit) to combat a severe reaction until medical care can be obtained.

Additional Information: If you have a family history of milk allergy, it would be wise to breast-feed your children as long as possible. If you switch to formula feeding, you might consider using soy formula or one of the hypoallergenic preparations. If you suspect a food allergy, try removing that food from the diet (check food labels to be sure it is not an ingredient in a packaged food) and wait a week to see if symptoms resolve. You can then challenge your child again with the food

and look for the reappearance of symptoms to confirm your suspicions. I am now convinced that a variety of vague complaints among young children, ranging from leg pain, headaches, chronic cough or abdominal pain, fatigue, and irritability are due to unsuspected allergies. It may take a lot of patience and detective work to finally figure this out, so discuss your suspicions with your child's pediatrician or an allergist.

ANEMIA

Definition: Anemia is a term describing a low red blood cell count.

Cause: Iron is needed in the formation of hemoglobin in red blood cells. The most common cause of childhood anemia is inadequate intake of iron in the diet. Anemia can also be caused by loss of blood, from severe bleeding, for example. Conditions such as sickle-cell disease, in which the red blood cells are abnormal and don't survive very long in the circulation, also lead to anemia. Premature infants are prone to anemia, since they didn't get their full share of iron stores at birth. Finally, anemia can be due to leukemia or other major medical problems.

Symptoms: With mild anemia, there may be no noticeable symptoms, but the condition can be diagnosed by a routine blood test. With moderate or severe anemia, the child usually looks pale and tires easily with feedings or play. The infant may be weak, chronically irritable, and delayed in her development. Her appetite is usually decreased, although she often drinks large quantities of milk and may be overweight. She may have an unexplained craving, known as pica, to eat clay, dirt, ice, or starch. Anemia due to iron deficiency is most commonly discovered in infants six months to two years of age.

Treatment: If you suspect your child may be anemic, have her seen by her health-care provider, so that a hematocrit can be performed. The treatment of anemia will vary, depending on its cause. If anemia is due to iron deficiency or loss of blood (which contains iron), iron-rich foods, such as meats, fish, poultry, eggs, green vegetables, beans, iron-fortified cereals and formula, should be increased in the diet. Limit the intake of whole milk to three glasses a day, since milk contains little iron.

Also, fresh cow's milk can cause microscopic blood loss into the intestinal tract in young children.

Iron supplement should be prescribed and given several times a day for a couple of months, until the body's stores of iron are replenished. Since iron can upset the stomach, it is best to give it with meals. Iron supplement can stain the teeth, but the discoloration will brush off. To avoid tooth stains, you can mix the medication with whatever your child is drinking. Iron medication also turns the stools greenish-black, but this causes no problem. After a week or more on iron, a follow-up blood test should be done to see if anemia is improving. Later follow-up is also necessary to be sure the blood count is back to normal.

Rarely, a blood transfusion is required to rapidly correct severe anemia. Obviously children with chronic anemias, such as sickle-cell disease, will need long-term follow-up by a specialist.

Complications: Mild anemia has no complications, but *severe* or chronic anemia can cause an increased susceptibility to infections, a strain on the heart and even heart failure, developmental delay due to weakness, impaired learning, and bowel problems.

Prevention: Nutritional anemia due to iron deficiency can be prevented by providing iron-rich foods in the diet as soon as a newborn outgrows her iron stores, at around four to six months of age. Breast-fed infants and those fed iron-fortified formula are much less likely to become anemic than those fed whole cow's milk before a year of age. Routine screening for anemia is performed at nine and/or eighteen months of age, and again at four to five years.

Additional Information: Please remember that iron medication is very dangerous! Don't just leave it around where your child or her sibling can get at the bottle. Ingestions of iron medication can be fatal.

APPENDICITIS

Definition: Appendicitis is the most common gastrointestinal problem requiring surgery in childhood. It is an inflammation in a little wormlike portion of the large bowel known as the appendix.

Cause: The cause of appendicitis is unknown, although one theory is that the appendix gets blocked and an infection starts up behind the obstruction.

Symptoms: The classic symptoms of appendicitis are persistent pain in the right lower part of the abdomen and tenderness when the abdomen is touched. Fever, nausea, vomiting, and constipation are often present. The pain is worst just below and to the right of the belly button, or umbilicus. It can be so severe that the person is doubled up and refuses to move or walk.

Unfortunately, in children under five years, appendicitis is very difficult to diagnose. The younger the child, the more likely the appendix will have ruptured before appendicitis is finally suspected. Part of the problem is that with very young children who cannot explain their symptoms and are unable to cooperate with a physical examination, it can be difficult even to tell where they are hurting. This is where your observations as a parent can prove extremely helpful. You can hold and comfort your child and touch her in various places to try to determine if abdominal tenderness is present. With appendicitis, the white blood cell count is usually high, and X rays can help suggest the diagnosis.

Even though appendicitis is uncommon under five years of age, it is often misdiagnosed with unfortunate consequences. Any ill-appearing youngster with a stomachache present for two hours or more should be evaluated by a physician.

Treatment: Appendicitis must be treated by an operation to remove the inflamed appendix, preferably before it has ruptured. In order not to miss cases of appendicitis, it is clear that appendectomies will be performed more often than appendicitis is actually present. This is not overoperating; it is good medical practice. The consequences of missing appendicitis make a few unnecessary operations worth doing.

Complications: The main complication of appendicitis is perforation of the appendix with spilling of·pus into the abdominal cavity. This causes a severe inflammation of the abdominal cavity called peritonitis. Peritonitis can spread to life-threatening infection in the blood.

Prevention: There is no known way to prevent appendicitis. Complications can be prevented, however, by suspecting the condition and confirming the diagnosis early, before rupture.

ASTHMA

Definition: Asthma is a respiratory condition in which the large airways to the lungs, or bronchi, become temporarily narrowed due to contractions of the muscle around the respiratory passages. The narrowing causes respiratory distress, with particular difficulty breathing out, or exhaling.

Cause: The cause of asthma is not entirely known, but certain factors can trigger an asthma attack, including a respiratory infection or allergy to some type of inhalant, such as animal danders, house dust, pollens, molds, et cetera. A trigger is an invisible substance that gets into the lungs and causes spasm, or narrowing, of the airways. Other common triggers are tobacco smoke, rapid changes in temperature or barometric pressure, city air pollutants, paint fumes, and exercise.

Symptoms: The classic symptom of asthma is a whistling noise, known as a wheeze, made during breathing out, or exhaling. Wheezing may be mild and heard only with a stethoscope, or can be loud enough to be heard directly. A frequent, loose cough is common and may be the only sign. Noisy, rattly breathing may be present, due to mucus production. During an asthma attack, the child usually will have signs of difficulty breathing, including tugging in between her ribs, at the lower rib margins, or at the spot where the neck joins the breastbone.

Treatment: There is medication to relieve bronchial spasm. The common ingredient in most of these products is theophylline, a drug that relaxes the muscles in the bronchial tubes and relieves the narrowing. Usually theophylline is taken during an acute attack and for the following week or so. If you have theophylline medication at home, it is a good idea to begin giving it when your child starts wheezing, gets a bad cold, or has frequent cough. Children with severe asthma may need to take medication every day between attacks as well. Another prescribed medicine, which can be inhaled directly into the bronchial tubes, also helps relieve narrowing. You should encourage your child to drink lots of clear liquids during an asthma attack, as the extra fluid will help loosen the mucus and bring some relief. Do not give your child antihistamine/decongestant combinations, since these will dry out mucus and make it harder to cough up.

Danger signs that suggest your child needs immediate treatment include: a blue color to the lips or nailbeds, restlessness and inability to sleep, diminished fluid intake and decreased urination, or progressive difficulty breathing. Also, the onset of vomiting should be reported to your pediatrician, as it may be an indication that your child is getting too much theophylline.

During an attack, it may be necessary to take the child to your pediatrician. An injection of adrenaline may be required. Other things that can be done at the office or emergency room to help in a severe asthma attack include giving the child oxygen and starting intravenous fluids. If the wheezing clears, the child can be discharged home on theophylline, or another medication, given by mouth. If the child's respiratory distress cannot be sufciently relieved with these measures, temporary admission to the hospital may be necessary.

Complications: Because asthma increases the amount

of mucus in the bronchial tubes, it can make a child more susceptible to pneumonia or lead to temporary blockage of a part of one lung. Severe and repeated asthma attacks can cause permanent damage to bronchial tubes and chronic respiratory problems. Prompt treatment of attacks is always important, since severe asthma can be life-threatening.

Prevention: Asthma can be prevented by trying to avoid contact with known triggers. It might be necessary for a parent to stop smoking or to give away an offending household pet. Starting medication early when symptoms first appear can often prevent a full-blown attack. Keep your child's asthma medication handy; take it on trips and always get a refill if it starts to run out. During pollen season, give your child a daily bath and shampoo, avoid drives in the country, and stay indoors on windy days.

Contagion: Asthma is not contagious. Sometimes a respiratory infection will trigger an asthma attack, and in that case, the infection is contagious, but not asthma itself.

Additional Information:
Asthma is more common in older children and adults, but is sometimes diagnosed in youngsters under two years of age. It frequently runs in families.

BREATH-HOLDING SPELLS

Definition: Breath-holding spells are harmless but frightening episodes in which a youngster holds her breath after becoming upset and may turn blue and pass out.

Cause: Children breath-hold after becoming angry, frustrated, or frightened. Some use the spells for getting attention.

Symptoms: After intense crying, the child holds her breath and may turn blue or become pale from not breathing. The temporary lack of oxygen may even cause her to pass out, and occasionally the child will stiffen or have a brief convulsion while passed out. Obviously such spells are very frightening to parents who may then try to prevent their child from ever crying for fear of having it happen again.

Treatment: No treatment is necessary for breath-holding spells, except to protect your child from injuring her head if she passes out. Breath-holders almost always outgro. the episodes by four to six years of age. It is best not to respond with great alarm each time your child has a spell, as all the attention may just encourage her to breathhold more often.

Complications: The main complication of breath-holding is the risk of head injury if your child should pass out and fall down. Although her turning blue can be quite frightening, remember that she will automatically begin to breathe again as soon as she passes out, so she can't permanently harm herself. It is impossible to hold your breath until you die.

Prevention: Most children do not breath-hold. If yours does, there is really no way to prevent spells. Trying to keep your child from ever crying, getting angry or upset, is unrealistic. Ignoring spells (as best you can) will do more to prevent them than letting her see how panicked you are each time she holds her breath.

Additional Information: Breathholding spells begin after six months of age and seldom last beyond four years of age. Occasionally they are confused with epilepsy or convulsions. If a convulsion does occur with breath-holding, it always happens AF-TER the child has turned blue and passed out, never before. This type of convulsion is NOT true epilepsy. Any time a child has a convulsion, however, her doctor should be notified promptly.

BRONCHIOLITIS

Definition: Bronchiolitis is the inflammation and narrowing of the small airways, or bronchioles, of the lungs, and occurs most commonly in youngsters under two years of age.

Cause: Bronchiolitis is caused by one of several respiratory viruses. The illness may begin as a simple cold.

Symptoms: The symptoms of bronchiolitis are very similar to asthma, with signs of respiratory distress. The most typical symptom is a wheezing, or whistling, noise made when the infant breathes out. She may be tugging in, or retracting, between her ribs, at the lower rib margins, or where the neck joins the breastbone. The breastbone itself may sink in with each breath. The child usually breathes faster than normal. The difficulty in breathing often is accompanied by poor feeding, since the infant fatigues easily.

Treatment: All children with symptoms of bronchiolitis should be examined by

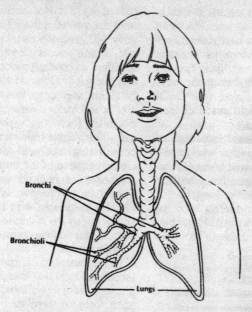

Bronchi

Bronchioli

Lungs

a physician. Mild cases of bronchiolitis can be treated at home by "supportive care," that is, just making the infant as comfortable as possible. Feeding lots of clear fluids will help, because the body loses water during rapid breathing. A cool mist vaporizer might help get moisture to the affected airways deep in the lung and will help clear congestion in your child's nose. Close observation is important to determine when the baby may need to be reexamined by a physician. Severe cases and those in young infants require hospitalization, so that oxygen and close monitoring can be provided.

Complications: Bronchiolitis can be complicated by lack of oxygen or pneumonia. Infants with bronchiolitis can stop breathing, and very rarely the condition is life-threatening.

Prevention: There is no way to prevent bronchiolitis, but complications can be avoided by your careful observations of your child and prompt medical attention for any signs of respiratory distress.

Contagion: Bronchiolitis is not contagious from one person to another, but the virus that causes it can be spread to another individual who might have different respiratory symptoms. The same virus is more likely to cause bronchiolitis in another child of similar age, whereas an adult would probably only get a cold.

Additional Information: Many children who experience repeated bouts of bronchiolitis in infancy will develop asthma later in life. Premature infants who had respiratory distress after birth are more prone to bronchiolitis.

BRONCHITIS

Definition: Bronchitis is an infection in the large airways, or bronchial tubes, leading to the lungs. The infection is lower in the respiratory tract than a simple cold, but it is not as deep as bronchiolitis or pneumonia.

Cause: Bronchitis is usually caused by a virus, and is thus self-limiting.

Symptoms: The main symptom of bronchitis is a loose cough that brings up mucus. The cough is usually worse in the mornings. Breathing should not appear rapid or labored, and the child should not appear very ill.

Treatment: Because bronchitis is almost always caused by a virus, antibiotics are not effective. The body will gradually mend itself, within a week or two, as long as complications don't develop. Drinking lots of fluids will help loosen mucus and make it easier to cough up. Running a vaporizer will make the child more comfortable and will decrease irritation of the bronchial tubes. Any child with a cough present for over one week or associated with fever or signs of respiratory distress should be examined by a physician.

Complications: Usually bronchitis runs an uncomplicated course, although pneumonia can develop. Severe or recurrent infections can cause permanent damage to bronchial tubes, leading to repeated attacks of bronchitis.

Prevention: Bronchitis occurs more commonly in children who are exposed to cigarette smoke. Parents who do smoke should not smoke in a room where children are present. Coughing up the mucus is important in the treatment of bronchitis, so it is unwise to give cough syrups to suppress coughing.

Contagion: Bronchitis is not transmitted from one person to another. The same germs that give one individual a cold may cause bronchitis in another and perhaps pneumonia in someone else.

Additional Information: Children with underlying respiratory problems, such as cystic fibrosis or asthma, are more prone to bronchitis. Bronchitis occurs in adults and older children, but is seldom diagnosed in infants.

CELLULITIS

Definition: Cellulitis is a serious skin infection in which organisms invade the deeper tissues of the skin.

Cause: Cellulitis is caused by a bacterial infection, usually a staph or strep germ, or an organism known as Hemophilus. It often begins as an insect bite or little scrape that becomes infected.

Symptoms: A child with cellulitis may look very ill and should be seen by a physician promptly. She may act listless, have a high fever, or have enlarged lymph nodes draining the area of infection. The area of cellulitis appears swollen, warm, red, and is very painful to touch. Although cellulitis can occur anywhere on the skin, two common and very dangerous types of cellulitis are: periorbital cellulitis, in which the eyelids are red and swollen and the white of the eye is red; and buccal cellulitis,

in which the cheek is swollen, red, and warm.

Treatment: Cellulitis must be treated with antibiotics. Some mild cases can be treated orally and followed closely on an outpatient basis. If the child has a fever, or the area of cellulitis is large, or periorbital or buccal cellulitis are present, hospitalization is necessary. These serious infections are treated with intravenous antibiotics. It is important to obtain cultures to find out the specific germ causing the infection in order to prescribe the correct antibiotic.

Complications: Cellulitis can spread rapidly to surrounding tissues and to the bloodstream, causing life-threatening illness. Periorbital cellulitis can cause permanent *eye* damage if not treated early. Both periorbital and buccal cellulitis can spread to the brain and cause meningitis.

Prevention: Cellulitis often starts from a little break in the skin that your child touches or scratches with dirty hands. Keep her nails clipped and wash all cuts, scrapes, and insect bites. If you think an area is beginning to look red, is developing pus, or seems to be tender, bring it to medical attention early, so that cellulitis doesn't develop.

CHICKENPOX (VARICELLA)

Definition: Chickenpox is a common childhood disease that lasts about a week; symptoms include an itchy rash and fever.

Cause: Chickenpox is caused by a virus in the family of herpes viruses.

Symptoms: There are usually no symptoms until the first appearance of the rash. The rash begins as reddened bumps, much like mosquito bites. Within a day or so, the bumps become tiny blisters that break open and develop scabs within a few days. The rash erupts in crops over the first several days of the illness, so there will be little bumps in all stages from first erupting to completely scabbed. The rash is usually very itchy. It begins on the trunk, then spreads to the arms, legs, and face. It can occur anywhere, including the mouth, eyelids, and vagina. Fever is usually present, especially during the early days of the illness.

Treatment: Because penicillin and other antibiotics do not work against viruses, they are not effective in treating chickenpox. Usually no specific treatment is given except to keep the child comfortable while the disease runs its course. Frequent baths will help relieve the itching. An antihistamine, such as Benadryl, may be given every six hours to combat itching and is especially helpful at nighttime. The dose is one teaspoon for each twenty-five pounds of body weight (up to one hundred pounds). Calamine lotion can be applied to the rash to also help control itching. Caladryl lotion contains Benadryl, and while it may provide more relief, it is also more likely that your child could develop a sensitivity to it. Have young babies wear cotton socks over their hands to prevent scratching. Older children should wear pants and long-sleeve shirts.

You can give acetaminophen to your child to help relieve the fever and make her more comfortable. DON'T give aspirin during chickenpox, however, as Reye's syndrome has occurred in children following aspirin treatment for chickenpox. (See page 376.)

Complications: The most common complication of chickenpox is infection of the rash, due to scratching with dirty fingernails. To prevent infection of the pox, bathe your child frequently, keep her fingernails trimmed, and give Benadryl if needed to minimize the itching.

Chickenpox can be very dangerous to persons with impaired immunity, such as someone with cancer, a newborn baby, or a person taking anticancer drugs or high doses of steroids. Such individuals may have difficulty fighting off the virus and can develop overwhelming illness. An infant of a mother who developed chickenpox during the last few weeks before delivery would be at risk of getting chickenpox during the first week of life and becoming seriously ill. When someone is exposed to or gets chickenpox who may not be able to fight it off, they are given a special kind of gamma globulin that is high in antibodies against the chickenpox virus. This preparation is expensive and precious, so it is prescribed only for persons at high risk.

Rare complications include chickenpox pneumonia, encephalitis, impaired blood clotting, and others. Be sure to notify your pediatrician whenever you think that your child's course of chickenpox is not typical.

Prevention: Almost everyone gets chickenpox before adulthood, and it is really preferable to do so, since adults often have more serious cases than youngsters. A vaccine with weakened chickenpox virus has recently been developed in Japan and is currently undergoing testing in the U.S. I expect that routine vaccination against chickenpox will become a reality within the next few years.

Contagion: Chickenpox is highly contagious. After close exposure to someone with chickenpox, there is an 85-percent chance that your child will get it. It is rapidly spread by respiratory droplets. The incubation period is from eleven to twentyone days, but children most commonly come down with chickenpox around fourteen to fifteen days after exposure. The biggest nuisance is that children are very contagious the day *before* they break out with the rash. The most conscientious parent may have sent their child to preschool the day before the rash appeared, without being aware she was sick. An entire class of children may be exposed before anyone realized it.

Additional Information: I commonly get asked by parents when their exposed child might come down with chickenpox. Let's say you want to figure when your daughter, Lisa, might develop chickenpox after being exposed daily to her brother, Jason, who broke out June 8. Jason was contagious a day before (June 7) the rash broke out and until all the lesions are scabbed over, which takes about a week. Lisa could come down with chickenpox as early as eleven days from June 7, or June 18. But she also might not get the illness until as late as twenty-one days from June 15, the last probable time that Jason was contagious. If she hadn't gotten sick by July 6 (June 15 plus twenty-one days), then she did not catch chickenpox from Jason. You should think twice about exposing her to other children who might be at risk for chickenpox during the period from June 18 to July 6. For example, that interval would NOT be a good time to have her admitted to the hospital for routine repair of a hernia. Since she could come down with chickenpox during that time, she might expose a very sick hospitalized child to the illness.

COLD (UPPER-RESPIRATORY INFECTION)

Definition: A cold is an upper-respiratory infection in the nasal passages and throat, and is the most common illness among both adults and children.

Cause: Colds are caused by one of many viruses and are thus self-limiting illnesses.

Symptoms: Colds often begin with a general feeling of achiness and fatigue. The nose may first be stuffy and then begin to run and drip profusely with a clear watery discharge. Later, the nasal secretions may become thicker. There may be sneezing, a slight sore throat, mild cough, or low-grade fever. Nasal congestion may cause the young infant to have difficulty nursing, since she may have to pause periodically to breathe through her mouth. She may be slightly fussy, but should not appear seriously ill. Symptoms may last one to two weeks.

Treatment: There is no specific medicine known to shorten the course of a cold by killing the virus that causes the infection. Antibiotics are not effective against viruses, so the body must fight the infection on its own.

Drinking lots of clear fluids will help. Infants should be offered more clear liquids and less milk, since milk tends to produce mucus. Young infants can be given Pedialyte or Lytren, while older infants can be given juices. Breast-fed infants can keep nursing, of course.

Over-the-counter medications are available to make cold sufferers more comfortable and help them get sufficient rest to allow their body defenses to overcome the infection. If the nose is very runny, an antihistamine-decongestant, such as Triaminic, Sudafed-Plus, Actifed, or others, may be given to help dry the secretions and allow the child to breathe more comfortably. If your child is under six years of age, verify the dose with her physician.

For the younger child, saltwater nosedrops can be made (1/2 teaspoon table salt in one eight-ounce glass of water) and instilled into the nostrils to loosen mucus and make it easier to suction out with a bulb syringe. Lay the child on her back on your lap and use a clean eyedropper to place a few drops of the saltwater solution into her nostrils. She will hate it and protest vigorously. After a minute, use a bulb syringe to suction out the secretions. Do this before feedings so she will be more comfortable while nursing. Make a fresh solution daily. Commercial saline nasal sprays (Ocean or Ayr) can be used as nosedrops, and are better tolerated than homemade saline solutions.

Cough expectorants can be given to older children to diminish the frequency of cough. Remember, you don't want to really suppress a cough, since it is the body's means of clearing secretions from the respiratory tract.

Complications: Although most colds are self-limiting, a variety of complications can occur. The most common complication of a cold in young children is an ear infection, often suggested by the onset of fever and irritability. Other complications include sinus infection, bronchitis, and pneumonia. Whenever new symptoms or sudden worsening occur during a cold, you should consider the possibility of a complication and contact your baby's doctor.

Prevention: There is no effective way of preventing colds entirely, and most of us are destined to have several colds each year. Good handwashing, using disposable tissues and discarding them after blowing the nose, and avoiding taking your child to large day-care settings will all help control the spread of colds.

Contagion: The viruses that cause colds are spread from one person to another by sharing common utensils, on the hands, or through the air by coughing or sneezing.

Additional Information: Since so many viruses cause the same "common cold" symptoms, it is not possible to develop immunity to colds. Most people have three to six colds each year, no matter how careful they are.

Our mothers and grandmothers probably cautioned us against getting cold and wet in order to prevent "catching cold." While the role of cold exposure in causing colds has never been proven, it is probable that one's resistance to infection can be lowered by various stresses, including environmental elements like cold exposure. Allowing the nasal passages to get cold and wet (by vigorously shoveling snow, for example) does make the nasal lining less resistant to invasion by viruses. So, our grandmothers may have been right after all!

CONSTIPATION

Definition: Constipation is a change in one's regular pattern of bowel movements toward infrequent stools of a firmer consistency and passed with difficulty.

Cause: Constipation can be caused by a change in diet, too little water intake, change in exercise level, certain metabolic conditions, as a side effect of specific medications, or by intestinal problems that affect how food moves through the bowel.

Symptoms: The main symptom is a change in stooling pattern. Stools become harder, and may be firm little balls, passed with difficulty. Usually the child will grunt and strain and appear uncomfortable when having a bowel movement, and several days may elapse between bowel movements. Sometimes, the passage of a large, hard bowel movement will tear the anus, causing a painful fissure that leaves a small streak of bright red blood on the stool, diaper, or toilet tissue. Consult your baby's doctor if a fissure doesn't heal in three days, the bleeding increases, or you ever see blood in the stool and aren't sure if a fissure is present.

Often, constipation is overdiagnosed and the term may be used incorrectly. If your child grunts when having a bowel movement, but passes a normal, soft stool, that is not constipation. If she passes a normal movement once every several days, this may just be her regular pattern. However, if her bowel movements usually occurred every day and were passed without discomfort, but now she hasn't stooled in three days and strains uncomfortably when she tries to have a bowel movement, she is probably constipated.

If your child is under one month of age, has been constipated from birth or experiences chronic problems with constipation, you should consult your pediatrician. She may have an abnormality in the bowel that interferes with the normal passage of stool. It will be important to diagnose and correct the problem in order to prevent her from suffering a lifetime of bowel difficulties that disrupt a normal life-style.

Treatment: There are two approaches to constipation, one from above and one from below. "Above" refers to dietary changes and use of oral agents that act in the intestines to relieve constipation. This method may take several days to work and is most effective in pre-

venting constipation from recurring.

The "below" approach refers to the use of an infant glycerin suppository or an enema to produce a stool promptly and bring relief. This approach, however, should never be used long-term or in a preventive fashion. It is reserved for cases of *severe* constipation. Most children grow up without ever needing an enema.

Specific treatment of constipation in a bottle-fed baby is the addition of 1 tablespoon of Karo syrup to each bottle. Karo can also be added to supplemental water bottles. Karo acts in the gut to draw water into the bowel and keep stools looser. If the baby is on solid foods, you can alter the diet to increase the amount of strained apricots, prunes, pears, peaches, and beans. Provided your baby is over a month of age, you can try an over-the-counter natural laxative called Maltsupex. It comes in both powdered and liquid forms. Start with a teaspoon in a bottle of formula or water twice a day. You can increase to a teaspoon in every bottle if necessary, or decrease to the lowest maintenance dose that seems to work for your baby.

In breast-fed infants, constipation is quite rare. A breast-fed infant under a month of age who stools only every few days should be examined and weighed since inadequate milk intake is a likely cause of her infrequent stooling. After the first several months, an exclusively breast-fed infant will commonly stool only once every several days without any problem. This is a normal pattern. A constipated older breast-fed baby on solid foods can be given the nonconstipating solids outlined above.

For a child older than a year of age, increase the amount of raw fruits and vegetables in her diet, such as raisins, pears, prunes, apricots, peaches, beans, lettuce, and cabbage. Be sure she is old enough to eat these items safely, however. They will work even more effectively if you leave the peelings on. Prune juice can be mixed 1:1 with 7-Up to make a tasty laxative. You can also make a bowl of bran cereal with milk. Let it sit out until the cereal softens to an easy-to-feed slush form.

If your child hasn't stooled in several days and clearly has the urge to have a bowel movement, you can use a piece of an infant glycerin suppository inserted into the rectum to provide relief. With an infant, some parents find that simply taking a rectal temperature will produce a stool. Another way to stimulate the rectum is by gently inserting the tip of your little finger (wrapped in lubricated plastic wrap).

I consider giving an enema to be drastic treatment for constipation. Enemas have been overused in the past, and there are many risks associated with them. I have never given an enema to one of my own children and have prescribed them in practice only rarely. Please contact your pediatrician before ever giving your child an enema.

Your pediatrician may prescribe a laxative for constipation, but since these will interfere with the natural urge to pass a stool, it is best to avoid them and try to solve the problem with dietary changes whenever possible. Stool softeners may also be prescribed temporarily for constipation, especially when the problem is associated with an anal fissure making stooling uncomfortable, or when a behavior problem is contributing to constipation.

Danger signs associated with constipation include: fever, a bloated abdomen, vomiting, or severe abdominal pain. Have your child examined if any of these are present.

Complications: The main complication of constipation is the development of dependency on laxatives, suppositories, or enemas in order to have a bowel movement. Many children who overuse these treatments will gradually lose the natural urge to push out a stool and become increasingly dependent on treatment. This is particularly unfortunate, since such drastic treatment of constipation is seldom really necessary.

Prevention: There are two main dietary approaches to the long-term prevention of constipation. One can avoid "constipating solids" and increase the amount of "nonconstipating solids" in the diet. Common constipating solids in youngsters include milk and milk products, especially cheese. Pasta, white rice, applesauce, bananas, and cooked carrots also tend to be constipating. Many children will become constipated as they switch from breast milk or formula to cow's milk. It is best to make the switch gradually over several weeks in order to prevent constipation.

We can all benefit from eating more raw fruits and vegetables, and natural unprocessed cereals and grains, such as whole wheat and brown rice. Drinking plenty of water and juices will also help keep stools softer.

Additionl Information: Each person's bowel propels food along at a different rate. Some people are naturally prone to constipation, and others tend to have loose, almost diarrhealike, stools. Such patterns often run in families. Many new parents place excessive emphasis on their baby's stooling pattern, and such undue focus may make toilet training more difficult or contribute to certain lifelong bowel habits. I'm almost relieved when I ask the parent of an older child when the youngster last stooled and they reply, "I really don't know."

CROSSED EYES (STRABISMUS)

Definition: Strabismus, or crossed eyes, refers to one or both eyes that turn in or out instead of focusing on the same object. The result is that the child sees double. Approximately 5 percent of children have crossed eyes.

Cause: There are many causes of crossed eyes, including abnormalities of the muscles that move the eyes, the nerves that control the muscles, or the eyes themselves.

Symptoms: Crossed eyes are most often noticed either shortly after birth or around age two to three years. One or both eyes may turn inward or outward or be deviated upward or downward. They may be fixed in position, or noted to be in the abnormal position only briefly. If you notice one or both eyes to be deviated, notify your baby's physician promptly. You observe her many hours each day, while an office visit may last only a few minutes. If the doctor doesn't notice the problem, insist that you have seen it. It is better to have your child

evaluated by an ophthalmologist if you suspect an abnormality than to postpone diagnosis. Crossed eyes DO NOT go away on their own!

Treatment: Crossed eyes need to be treated by an ophthalmologist. If one eye is involved, sometimes the good eye will be patched for a while, to encourage the child to use the weaker eye. If both eyes are affected, the patches can be alternated each week. Eventually, surgery may be needed to align the eyes correctly. Early surgery (six to twenty-four months) is preferable.

Complications: The most feared complication of crossed eyes is amblyopia, the suppression of vision in the bad

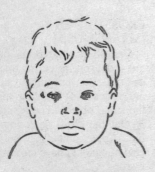

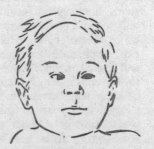

PSEUDOSTRABISMUS; NORMAL EYES

CROSSED EYE: BABY'S RIGHT EYE IS DEVIATED INWARD

eye. Amblyopia happens like this: A crossed eye makes a child see double; seeing double is frustrating, so the child begins to block out the image from the crossed eye and uses the good eye instead. Chronic disuse of the crossed eye during the early years of life can result in permanent impairment of vision. It is important to treat crossed eyes right away in order to preserve good vision for the rest of your child's life.

Prevention: Crossed eyes can't be prevented, but amblyopia can. Don't let it happen to your child. Have any suspicions about your child's eyes checked out with an ophthalmologist.

Additional Information: Many infants have "pseudo-strabismus," or normal eyes that look like they are turned inward. The reason for this appearance is that the bridge of the nose may be somewhat flat and there may be skin creases near the corners of the eyes, making it difficult to see the whites of the eyes in the inner corners. This gives the illusion of the eyes being turned in, when in fact they are normal. Your doctor can reassure you if you have any doubts about your baby's eyes.

CROUP

Definition: Croup is a viral infection of the upper airway that causes inflammation in the area around and below the vocal cords. This inflammation causes difficulty inhaling air into the lungs, or inspiring.

Cause: Croup is caused by one of several viruses. These organisms tend to occur during the winter months, so there appears to be a "croup season."

Symptoms: The main symptom of croup is a hoarse, or barky, cough, often called a "croupy cough." It can actually sound like the bark of a seal. With severe croup, the child will have difficulty breathing in and may make a sound with each inhaled breath. This sound is known as stridor, and it may be associated with rapid breathing or signs of labored breathing, such as tugging in at the spot where the neck joins the breastbone. A low-grade or moderate fever may be present, along with other signs of a cold.

Although symptoms most commonly develop over a period of several days, they can occur suddenly. Symptoms tend to get worse at night, so if your child is croupy during the day, you should check her carefully before putting her to bed at night. Look in on her during the night, too. Danger signs include:

√ the presence of stridor, even when the child is resting
√ a pale or blue skin color
√ a very anxious child (this can mean lack of oxygen)
√ drooling or inability to swallow her own saliva
√ any sign of severe difficulty breathing

Whenever any of these danger signs occur, take your child to the nearest emergency room immediately.

Treatment: Mild croup can be treated at home by methods that get moisture into the inflamed upper airway. A cold-mist vaporizer will help. The child can be brought into the bathroom and held on your lap while the room is steamed up by running the hot shower. Even being taken into the outside air seems to bring temporary relief to a croupy child, perhaps because the air outside is more humid than the heated air inside most homes during winter. Drinking lots of clear fluids also helps to bring moisture to the airway. Since most

cough preparations tend to dry out airway secretions, they should NOT be given to children with croup.

Complications: Though it is rare, croup can cause *severe* complications, including fatal respiratory arrest. Breathing may need to be assisted by machinery or an emergency tracheostomy. Complications can usually be avoided by seeking medical attention early and observing your child closely, especially at night.

Prevention: There is no sure way to prevent croup, but you are wise to protect your child from other children with colds involving hoarseness.

Contagion: The viruses causing croup can be readily spread from one person to another. The infection may have varying effects on different individuals. Children under three years, whose airways are the narrowest, tend to be most prone to croup. An adult with the same virus may have only a hoarse voice, or laryngitis, while an infant develops full-blown croup.

Additional Information: Unfortunately, once an infant has had croup, she is prone to a recurrence, either in the same season, or the following year. Croup is less common in humid climates and occurs more frequently in dry environments.

DIABETES

Definition: Diabetes (diabetes mellitus) is a condition in which the pancreas produces insufficient insulin for the breakdown of sugar in the body. This results in high levels of blood sugar and many other chemical abnormalities.

Cause: Diabetes is believed to be inherited to some degree, with certain viral infections possibly making individuals more prone to developing it. Although the inheritance pattern is by no means clear-cut, diabetes does tend to run in certain families. Although obese adults are more likely to develop diabetes, it is not true that eating too much sugar causes the conditon.

Symptoms: The classic symptoms of diabetes are weight loss, fatigue, excessive drinking of fluids, and frequent urination, which may include bedwetting. Tests of the urine will reveal large amounts of sugar, and the blood sugar is high as well. Diabetes may be discovered in its early stages by a routine urine test, or rarely it may be overlooked until the child goes into an unexplained coma due to very high blood sugar.

Treatment: The most important treatment of diabetes is the daily replacement of insulin in the body to break down sugar. Insulin will not work when taken orally, so it must be given by injection. The dose is very carefully calculated and adjusted whenever the child is sick or changes her activity level. The child's urine is tested daily at home for excess sugar, and it is now possible to test the blood sugar level at home with a machine that determines the blood glucose level within minutes.

Diet is also important in the management of diabetes. A normal diet is recommended, with the child eating at regular times each day, and having midmorning, afternoon, and evening snacks and an extra snack before vigorous exercise. Foods high in sugar should be limited, but this does not mean that a diabetic child can never eat sweets or dessert. Occasionally diabetes will get out of control because of illness or other stress, and hospitalization may be required so that intravenous fluids and insulin can be administered and careful monitoring provided.

Complications: Several complications can occur with diabetes. One is an insulin reaction, in which the giving of insulin makes the blood sugar level fall too low, known as hypoglycemia (see page 426). This can be very dangerous, as the brain needs sugar for energy, and convulsions can occur with hypoglycemia. Hypoglycemia is suspected whenever a diabetic becomes faint, feels hungry, starts to sweat, looks pale, or becomes irritable or drowsy. The child should be given a lump of sugar, orange juice, or candy right away. Some parents keep a strong glucose solution, known as Instant Glucose, on hand to rub on the inside of the lips if the child can't drink.

The second main complication is due to excessively high blood sugar, and is known as ketoacidosis. The child usually has abdominal pain, vomiting, an acetone smell to the breath, and excessive urination leading to dehydration. Intravenous fluids and insulin will be required, and prompt medical attention is necessary.

Complications of diabetes involving several organs can occur later in life. However, good diabetic control will help minimize complications.

Prevention: Since the cause of diabetes is not clearly understood, it is impossible to prevent. When a family history of diabetes in a close relative is present, periodic urine screening can be done on children to detect the disease early. The avoidance of obesity by developing wise eating habits in childhood may heip prevent the disease later.

Additional Information: Childhood, or juvenile, diabetes is uncommon, and the condition is extremely rare under the age of five years. Around the age of ten years, diabetic children can learn to give their own insulin shots and assume increasing control of their disease. They can participate in all activites, including vigorous exercise, which is actually beneficial, provided hypoglycemia is avoided. It is advisable to have a diabetic child followed regularly at a children's diabetes center, in addition to her own pediatrician.

DIAPER RASH

Definition: Diaper rash is a skin irritation in the area covered by the diaper.

Cause: Recent research has clarified the exact cause

of diaper rash. Diaper wetness is the first step in weakening healthy skin. Wet skin is more susceptible to damage by various irritating agents. Digestive proteins found in stools can also attack the skin and make it more susceptible to other rash-causing irritants. When urine and stool are in contact with each other, the digestive proteins in stool cause greater damage to the skin. Chafing of damaged skin can then lead to a rash. Or weakened skin can be invaded by stool organisms, such as yeast, causing longer lasting cases of diaper rash. Rarely, a rash in the diaper area is associated with a serious infection or problem elsewhere in the body.

Symptoms: Diaper rash begins with a reddish coloration of skin in the diaper area. Yeast infection (see page 392) tends to look very bright red with little bumps on it. Infection with bacteria may look like little pimples. A particularly worrisome infection causes blisters in the diaper area. Be sure to notify your pediatrician if you ever see intact or broken blisters anywhere on your baby's skin. Diaper rash associated with diarrhea often leaves the area around the anus red and raw. The baby usually is fussy and uncomfortable and may cry after wetting or soiling or when you wipe her bottom during diaper changes.

Treatment: Whatever the cause of diaper rash, it helps to leave the baby's bottom uncovered each day for as long as possible. You can lay her on a clean diaper and let her bottom air dry after each change. A boy baby may spray the walls; you can place him on his tummy to prevent this.

If you use cloth diapers, avoid rubber pants until the rash is healed. Change your baby as soon as you realize she is wet or has had a bowel movement.

Since your baby may be uncomfortable, gently wipe her during diaper changes with something soft. I always cringe when a parent grabs a rough paper towel in the examining room to clean her baby's red, raw bottom. One comfortable method is to fill a wash basin with lukewarm water and gently immerse the baby's bottom in it.

For ordinary rashes, I recommend Desitin ointment. Be sure to apply it after first cleaning the bottom and letting it air dry. You should get up at night to change your baby every four hours or so when diaper rash is present to keep it from getting worse by contact with a wet diaper all night.

Diaper rash that lasts for more than three or four days and is not getting better is almost always infected with yeast. It should be seen by your pediatrician, so specific treatment can be started. Diaper rash associated with white material in the baby's mouth or that starts while she is taking antibiotics is also probably due to yeast.

Complications: Complications of diaper rash are rare, but include skin infection that can spread elsewhere. The most common complication is prolonged, unnecessary discomfort for your child.

Prevention: When diaper rash first begins, you can usually prevent it from getting worse by good air drying, applying Desitin, and changing your baby more frequently. New disposable diapers made with materials that lock wetness inside the diaper itself and away from the skin have been shown to be effective in preventing diaper rash.

Additional Information: No child grows up without experiencing diaper rash. If she gets a rash now and then, it doesn't mean you are an inattentive parent. On the other hand, if your child is in day care and frequently has diaper rash, you might wonder how often she is getting changed. Some children's skin is more sensitive than others'.

DIARRHEA

Definition: Diarrhea is an increase in the number and water content of bowel movements, often due to an infection in the gastrointestinal tract. It is one of the most common illnesses of infancy.

Cause: Diarrhea is usually caused by an infectious organism. Viruses cause a large proportion of diarrhea cases, most of which are self-limiting. Bacteria, parasites, and other germs can also cause diarrhea. In infants, an infection elsewhere in the body often causes an increased number of bowel movements. For example, an ear infection or bladder infection is often accompanied by diarrhea. Diarrhea can also be due to intestinal allergies, malabsorption, immune deficiencies, and other disorders, but these are far less common than infectious diarrhea.

Symptoms: The main symptom of diarrhea is an

increased number of bowel movements. The movements are looser than usual and may contain a large amount of water, which is seen as a wet ring on the diaper surrounding the solid substance of the stool. Diarrheal stools are often green or yellow, and in severe cases, mucus or blood may be present. Diarrhea is often associated with vomiting and/or fever.

The number of bowel movements alone may not be a good indicator of diarrhea, since a normal formula-fed young infant may have only one or two stools a day, while a normal breast-fed newborn may have six or eight. When the number of bowel movements increases over the baby's usual pattern, or the bowel movements become very loose and watery, diarrhea is present.

Treatment: The usual treatment of diarrhea is to rest the gastrointestinal tract by taking the infant off formula and solids for twenty-four to forty-eight hours. During this time, the baby should be fed generous amounts of clear liquids. Infants under six months of age are usually placed on a balanced solution of sugar and electrolytes, which is clear like water. Brand names

for these solutions include Pedialyte and Lytren. By feeding your baby one of these products, you can be assured that she is getting the proper balance of minerals she needs to replace losses in the stool, as well as sugar for energy. Although she will lose weight for a day or two by not drinking milk, she will probably resolve her diarrhea sooner and be back on her regular diet faster, with less overall weight loss than if the diarrhea continued for many days.

Older babies can be offered a variety of clear liquids (but don't begin new juices at this time), including natural juices, broth, Jell-O water (made with twice the water the recipe calls for), and soda pop that has gone flat. While some of these solutions don't sound particularly nutritious, remember we are simply trying to provide a balance of easily absorbed electrolytes, water, and sugar while the bowel rests for a day or so.

Since the drinking of either hot or cold liquids tends to cause the gut to contract and a bowel movement to occur, it is best to offer the liquids at room temperature. If there is no vomiting associated with diarrhea, you can offer as much to drink as the baby wants. If she is also vomiting (see pages 303 and 390), feed her small amounts frequently. It is always best to feed the baby a variety of clear liquids unless she is receiving one of the balanced electrolyte solutions mentioned above. It is not a good idea, for example, to drink apple juice exclusively for two days.

Breast-fed infants generally should continue to nurse throughout their bout of diarrhea. For one reason, breast-fed infants may be unfamiliar with bottles and resist trying a new diet and new method of eating when they don't feel well. In fact, nursing may be an important source of comfort to them during an illness. Breast milk is often well tolerated during diarrhea. Finally, to interrupt breast feeding may cause the mother's milk supply to diminish and make the resumption of breast feeding difficult after diarrhea resolves. However, in some instances of severe diarrhea, infants will have difficulty digesting breast milk. Thus it may be necessary to temporarily interrupt breast feeding for a few days.

If the diarrhea has slowed down after twenty-four to forty-eight hours on clear liquids, the baby can gradually return to her regular diet. This can be done by introducing the "ABC," or "BRAT," diet in children who are already on solids. These letters stand for Applesauce, Bananas, Carrots, and Bananas, Rice cereal, Applesauce, and Toast. Such foods are also known as "constipating solids." If the baby has been formula-fed, it is a good idea to return to formula gradually by first feeding a soy formula for several days to a week. Soy milk is prepared with a sugar that is easier to digest than the sugar in regular formula and breast milk. In some instances, it takes a few days for the gastrointestinal tract to recover from diarrhea and to be able to fully digest regular formula.

Complications: The main complication of diarrhea is dehydration (see page 391). Dehydration is most likely to occur when diarrhea has been present for several days or is associated with vomiting or fever. Occasionally, however, an infant may have sudden onset of diarrhea with several massive bowel movements causing dehydration within the span of only a few hours. The first sign of dehydration is decreased urination, followed by mild lethargy, sticky saliva or a dry mouth, and lack of tears. Late signs are sunken-appearing eyes, a sunken soft spot (fontanel) in young infants, and severe listlessness and lethargy. Dehydration requires prompt medical attention and intravenous therapy may be necessary.

Protracted diarrhea may result in a prolonged period of recovery until the child can tolerate a full diet again. Diaper rash often complicates diarrhea.

Prevention: Diarrhea is almost inevitable during the first year of life, since it can be caused by so many viruses and bacteria and is so contagious. Helpful precautions include:

- √ Always wash your hands thoroughly after changing diapers or using the bathroom, especially when any family member has diarrhea.
- √ Take care not to feed your baby any food that is not fresh. Discard all baby food jars with broken seals and all unused cans of formula that have been open for forty-eight hours.
- √ Always store opened cans of formula or bottles of milk in the refrig-

erator. Take extra precautions during warm weather.

- √ Never feed a raw egg to a baby. (Frankly, no one should eat raw eggs; they can carry dangerous diarrhea-causing germs. I recall an entire family who became violently ill after eating homemade ice cream made with raw eggs from their backyard chickens.)

Contagion: Infectious diarrhea is highly contagious. The incubation period is usually several days. It is very important for people whose job involves preparing or serving food not to work if they have diarrhea. With a few types of diarrhea, people can continue to pass the germ in their bowel movements long after their diarrhea resolves.

Additional Information: While most cases of diarrhea can be managed at home with diet changes, it is important to have your child examined by a physician if:

- √ there is no improvement after twenty-four hours on a clear liquid diet
- √ there are other symptoms, such as diarrhea

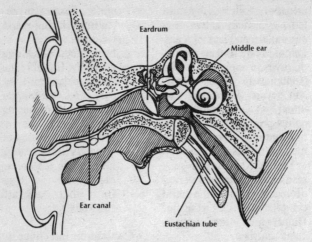

INNER EAR

and fever or diarrhea and earache, et cetera
- ✓ there are signs of dehydration
- ✓ there is blood in the diarrhea

EAR INFECTION (OTITIS MEDIA)

Definition: An ear infection refers to an infection in the middle ear, behind the eardrum. Ear infections are among the most common illnesses in young children, and scarcely a child reaches school age without at least one bout of otitis.

Cause: An ear infection occurs when germs get trapped in the middle ear, which is normally drained by the eustachian tube into the back of the throat. During a cold, the opening of the eustachian tube can become blocked, trapping germs from the nose and throat area in the middle ear where they start an infection.

Symptoms: An ear infection usually occurs in a child who already has a cold. Often the child over two can indicate to you verbally that her ear hurts. The child between one and two may pull on her ear or act uncomfortable. Infants under a year of age often have difficulty localizing ear pain and will simply be cranky and irritable. Ear pain is usually worse at night because the infected fluid in the middle ear presses against the eardrum when the baby lies flat. Sucking and swallowing may also be uncomfortable, causing the baby to feed poorly. A fever is common, but infection can occur without fever. In young children, diarrhea and/or vomiting may also be present.

If pus is draining from the ear, it almost always means that the eardrum has ruptured due to a severe infection, with pus under pressure. Although the child will usually feel better after the eardrum has ruptured, it is very important to have her examined and treated properly. Some parents mistake the pus for "wet ear wax."

If your child complains of an earache, pulls on her ears and acts uncomfortable, runs a fever with a cold for more than two days, or has any drainage from her ears, she should be examined by a health professional.

Treatment: To prevent a recurrence, ear infections must be treated with a full ten-day course of antibiotics, even if your child seems perfectly well a few days later. Many of the germs that cause ear infections are resistant to penicillin, so that a penicillin shot alone is usually not adequate treatment.

All ear infections require a followup examination to be sure the infection has been adequately treated. There is no other way to be certain without examining the child approximately three weeks after the infection was diagnosed. Occasionally the infection does not respond to treatment and a second course of therapy with another drug is required. Or, the infection may clear up, but leave residual fluid behind the eardrum, making additional follow-up necessary.

Complications: The most common complication of an ear infection is a temporary decrease in hearing, often at a time when the child is rapidly gaining language skills and needs to hear well. An important part of followup is to assure that hearing is normal. Undetected impaired hearing can lead to abnormal speech patterns in the early years of life.

Rarely, untreated ear infections can lead to serious complications, such as spinal meningitis or infection in the mastoid area.

Prevention: Several things predispose a child to ear infections. One of these is lying flat on her back while drinking a bottle. Milk can enter the eustachian tube and then become trapped in the middle ear if the eustachian tube gets blocked off. Germs multiply rapidly in milk, so that an infection can easily occur. If your child has had an ear infection, you should make an effort to hold her propped up in your arms for all bottle feedings.

In children with multiple ear infections (a common problem), several things might be prescribed to prevent further infections. One of these is prophylactic treatment with low-dose antibiotics, particularly during the winter months when colds and ear infections are most common. Another treatment is the placement of tiny plastic tubes (known as PE tubes) in the eardrum by an ENT (ear, nose, and throat) specialist. With the tubes in place, the middle ear drains well to the outside even if the eustachian tube becomes blocked from time to time. The tubes will remain in place from months to years and will eventually work their way out as the eardrum heals behind them. Hopefully, by then your child will have outgrown the tendency to have ear infections.

Contagion: Ear infections are not caught from person to person. They are due to germs that can cause upper-respiratory infections in gen-

eral. One child may have a cold, another might develop pink eye, another might get an ear infection, while still another harbors the same germ but has no apparent symptoms. Contrary to popular belief, ear infections are NOT caused by cold air blowing on a child's ears when she goes outdoors without a hat.

Additional Information: Allergies can also predispose a child to ear infections, since it is believed that the eustachian tube doesn't drain as well in children whose mucus membranes are swollen by allergies.

A child who develops an ear infection in the first six months of life is at risk of having repeated ear infections, known as chronic otitis media.

The only way to accurately diagnose an ear infection is to have the eardrums examined by your baby's health-care provider. Often the pediatrician's view of the eardrums is obscured by ear wax, which is commonly present in the outer canal. Individuals form ear wax at different rates, and there is nothing you can do about it. It is impossible for you to clean the wax out yourself at home, and attempts to do so with a Q-tip only drive the wax deeper into the canal, making your pediatrician's job even harder. Many an eardrum has been ruptured by a Q-tip—keep them away from the ears altogether!

If the pediatrician needs to clear wax from the ear canal, he will use a delicate spoonlike instrument. It is not uncommon for the canal to be scratched by the instrument and for a small amount of bleeding to occur. This can happen even in the best of hands and should not be cause for alarm, as the scratch will heal quickly. In order not to scratch the ear canal during the exam, the nurse or doctor may restrain your child firmly to avoid her moving during the cleaning procedure. This is simply for her own safety, although it looks like a lot of muscle is being used on one small baby. The ear exam itself is not painful, but most babies will protest vigorously since they don't like being held down. The ear exam is one of the most important parts of the physical examination.

It is now possible to purchase at a drugstore the instrument your physician uses to examine ears, known as an otoscope. It is doubtful that you can make any meaningful interpretation with an otoscope, however, without specific medical training in its use. Trauma to the child's ear canal could occur, and proper medical treatment might be delayed while well-meaning parents attempt to diagnose an ear infection at home. While parents are certainly capable of a wide variety of accurate observations about their child's condition, medical diagnostic instruments cannot be used safely or with any meaningful results by an untrained examiner.

Fortunately, as children grow older, they outgrow the tendency to get ear infections.

Inflammation of the skin lining the ear canals is known as *otitis externa,* or swimmer's ear. It causes pain and itching in the ear and severe discomfort if the outer ear is moved. The condition is uncommon in young children and is treated with prescription eardrops.

ECZEMA (ATOPIC DERMATITIS)

Definition: Eczema is a chronic itchy skin rash that can begin in infancy and last through adolescence.

Cause: Children who develop eczema have very dry skin. Dry skin often itches, especially when it is in contact with rough materials or detergents, and the chronic scratching leads to redness and irritation. It has been suggested that eczema is an allergic disorder, but this has not been confirmed, although many patients with eczema also have asthma or hay fever. In some infants certain foods seem to aggravate eczema, and in older children other substances, such as animal dander, sometimes make eczema worse.

Symptoms: The typical skin rash of eczema differs in location according to age of the child, but it is always very itchy. Infantile eczema occurs from about two months to two years of age. It first affects the cheeks and forehead, then spreads to the arms and legs and body. There are oval patches of redness and scaling, which can get infected and become weepy. During childhood, eczema tends to be present in the creases of the knees and elbows, the neck, the wrists, and hands and feet.

Treatment: Eczema should be treated by a health professional and requires ongoing medical care. During flare-ups, cortisone cream should be prescribed and used on affected areas of the skin. Infection, if present,

needs to be treated with antibiotics.

Ongoing treatment for eczema involves adding water to the skin so it won't be so dry and itchy. The child should be given two "dripdry" baths each day for less than five minutes each and without using soap. Cetaphil lotion is a good soap substitute. While the skin is still wet, a lubricating oil or ointment should be applied to the whole body. Good choices include Alpha-Keri bath oil or Keri lotion, Nutraderm or Lubriderm lotion, or Eucerin cream. A bedroom humidifier may help by adding more moisture to the air.

Another way to add moisture to the skin and cut down on itching during flare-ups is to use wet-to-dry dressings. This can be done by getting two pairs of long johns or cotton pajamas. The first pair is wet with warm water and then wrung until no more drops come out. These are put on the child and covered with a dry pair of long johns or pajamas to slow down evaporation. Your child will probably tolerate this quite well because she will finally feel comfortable. You can change the wet clothing every three to four hours.

Avoid irritating skin agents, such as soaps, harsh shampoos, and rough or woolen clothes. Sweat will also irritate the skin. Keep your child's fingernails trimmed to cut down on scratching.

Complications: The main complication of eczema is infection with staph or strep germs due to frequent scratching. Chickenpox can be more severe in children with eczema.

Prevention: It is not possible to prevent eczema, but some studies show it is less common among breast-fed infants. Flare-ups can be minimized by daily baths, application of a lubricating oil, and avoiding the irritating substances mentioned and any foods or agents that have been observed to make eczema worse.

Additional Information: Most children with infantile eczema will outgrow it around age two, but about 30 percent will go on to have childhood eczema.

EPIGLOTTITIS

Definition: Epiglottitis is a serious life-threatening respiratory disease that causes sudden obstruction of the upper airway.

Cause: It is caused by bacteria, almost always the Hemophilus germ.

Symptoms: Epiglottitis is most common between the ages of three and seven years. The child becomes ill suddenly, over a period of several hours. A high fever is usually present, and the child has trouble breathing and looks very sick. She usually complains of difficulty swallowing and has such a severe sore throat that she cannot swallow her own saliva. Some children actually hold a container in front of them to collect drooling saliva. The child's voice may be muffled, and she may make a croupy noise when she inhales. The symptoms are caused by tremendous swelling of the epiglottis, a structure in the airway above the windpipe. The epiglottis can get so large that no air enters the windpipe.

Treatment: Epiglottitis is an emergency! The child could stop breathing at any minute. If you suspect it, get to an emergency room as fast as possible without endangering yourselves in traffic. Allow your child to be in whatever position is most comfortable for her. DON'T force her to lie down, as this may obstruct her airway. Try to keep her calm.

Epiglottitis must be treated in an intensive care unit. A

specialist will pass a tube into the child's windpipe, past the swollen epiglottis, so she can breathe safely. Antibiotics will be given by IV to combat the infection. Children are usually much improved within a few days.

Complications: The most feared complication of epiglottitis is complete airway obstruction and respiratory arrest.

Prevention: Since epiglottitis is usually caused by the Hemophilus bacteria, some cases will no doubt be prevented by the new Hemophilus vaccine.

Contagion: Hemophilus organisms are contagious, but children don't catch the same disease from each other. One child with Hemophilus may have an ear infection, another epiglottitis, another cellulitis, and still another meningitis, while others harbor the germ without being sick at all.

EPILEPSY (CONVULSIONS OR SEIZURES)

Definition: Epilepsy (sometimes called convulsions or seizures) is a sudden, temporary disturbance of brain function that causes involuntary movements, and/or other body reactions, sometimes accompanied by loss of consciousness.

Cause: Epilepsy can have many causes, such as lack of oxygen to the baby during labor or delivery, infections of the central nervous system, chemical disturbances in the blood, birth defects or brain injuries, and inherited conditions. Often the cause of epilepsy cannot be determined.

Symptoms: There are many forms of epilepsy, with each category having a characteristic type of seizure. Generalized seizures cause the child to have jerking movements of all extremities, to pass out, roll her eyes, and often to lose urine or stool and be very sleepy for a time afterward. Other types of seizures include brief lapses of consciousness and vacant stares, movements of the tongue, face, or mouth with throaty sounds, and a sort of jackknife jerking of the body. Newborn seizures may be hard to notice and might consist only of eye-rolling, blinking, mouthing, or chewing motions. Depending on how severe the case of epilepsy is and what it is due to, the child may have a seizure only once every few months or years, or have many each day.

Treatment: Children with epilepsy need to take medication every day to prevent seizures. Many types of seizure medication are available, with different ones working better for different types of epilepsy.

There are many causes of epilepsy, and it is important to determine and treat the cause whenever possible. If a one-month-old's seizures are thought to be due to lack of oxygen at birth, then the cause cannot be treated now. On the other hand, if a three-year-old develops seizures due to meningitis, obviously the meningitis must be treated promptly.

Complications: The greatest risk of epilepsy is a very prolonged seizure that cannot be stopped. Another complication occurs if parents abruptly discontinue their child's seizure medication; this can cause seizures to increase suddenly. In some instances, the problem causing epilepsy also causes mental retardation, but many children with epilepsy have perfectly normal intelligence. It all depends on what is causing the epilepsy. Other complications include the risk of having a seizure in a dangerous place, such as while swimming, on a slide or swing, et cetera.

Prevention: Some causes of epilepsy can be prevented, such as head injuries. Certain factors can provoke seizures in an epileptic child, like hyperventilating, getting too tired, and suffering from emotional tension. Avoiding such stresses can help prevent some seizures. The best prevention of seizures once epilepsy is diagnosed is to give the prescribed medication as directed and to maintain close follow-up with a pediatric neurologist.

Contagon: Epilepsy is NOT contagious.

Additional Information: In about one third of cases of epilepsy, there is another family member, either distant or close, who also has epilepsy. Brainwave tests will show seizure activity. When a child has been seizure-free for several years and has a normal brainwave test, it may be possible to gradually discontinue medication, but only under the close supervision of a physician.

FAILURE TO THRIVE

Definition: Failure to thrive is a general term used for infants who fail to gain adequate weight for various reasons. An infant is said to be "failing to thrive" if her height and weight consistently plot below the third percentile or if she has experienced a noticeable decline from her previously established growth pattern.

Cause: There are many causes of failure to thrive, but the most common is simply inadequate intake of calories. This can be due to an inexperienced parent with a baby who is difficult to feed, an error in formula preparation, inadequate breastfeeding technique, or insufficient breast milk supply. Or, a baby may consume adequate nutrition but lose many calories because of chronic vomiting and/or diarrhea. Other times, a baby may have an underlying medical condition that keeps her from being able to consume or metabolize her food adequately.

Symptoms: Infants with failure to thrive are thin, with little fat in the usual places; their buttocks are wasted instead of plump. When plotted on a growth curve, their weight percentile is much lower than their height percentile. They often are delayed in their motor development because they are too weak to hold their head up, roll over, sit, etc. They may be chronically irritable due to hunger, but eventually they may give up demanding and become somewhat unresponsive and

listless. Chronic malnutrition eventually lowers their resistance and makes them prone to infection.

Treatment: The first approach to the treatment of failure to thrive is to assure adequate caloric intake. If the infant is bottle-fed, generous volumes of formula are offered frequently, and the formula is nutritionally enriched if necessary. For breast-fed infants with failure to thrive, liberal quantities of supplemental formula are offered in addition to nursing to nutritionally restore the infant while attempts are made to increase the mother's milk supply. Infants may be admitted to the hospital for a brief period in order to accurately monitor their caloric intake. Appropriate laboratory tests are performed to rule out the presence of any underlying condition requiring treatment. Parental support and counseling for feeding difficulties is provided.

Complications: Chronic malnutrition can predispose an infant to infectious diseases. Severe malnutrition early in life can permanently affect growth and brain function. Infants with underlying medical conditions causing failure to thrive can have complications associated with the medical problem. Prolonged failure to thrive due to underfeeding can cause emotional damage in the infant.

Prevention: The best way to prevent failure to thrive is to have your infant followed carefully after birth to document that she is gaining weight adequately. Early follow-up is especially important for breast-fed infants since it is difficult to determine just how much milk the baby is taking when you can't see it in a bottle. Getting the help and support you need with a new baby will also help prevent difficulties associated with feeding her.

Additional Information: Sometimes failure to thrive results from parental neglect, but other times infant failure to thrive occurs despite the best efforts of well motivated, conscientious parents. The important thing is to detect the problem as soon as possible and work with your baby's doctor to remedy it promptly, without experiencing unnecessary guilt.

GASTROESOPHAGEAL REFLUX (EXCESSIVE REGURGITATION)

Definition: Gastroesophageal reflux is the name for frequent regurgitation of stomach contents into the esophagus in young infants.

Cause: It is caused by a lax muscle between the stomach and esophagus, so that stomach contents can easily roll back into the esophagus, especially if the baby is placed horizontally.

Symptoms: The main symptom is frequent spitting up or vomiting of significant volumes of milk. In severe cases, failure to thrive may occur, as well as chronic irritation of the esophagus by stomach acids. Occasionally a baby with reflux will choke on milk or inhale it into her lungs, causing chronic pneumonia, frequent cough, and wheezing. X-ray studies and/or esophageal pH monitoring can be performed to confirm the diagnosis.

Treatment: Mild cases can be treated by keeping the baby in a semiupright position after feedings, so that gravity helps keep the feeding down. Many parents do this by propping the baby in her infant seat after eating. Laying her on her abdomen with the head of the crib elevated actually works better. If the baby is formula fed, the milk can be thickened by adding rice cereal to the bottle. Frequent small feedings are also recommended. In most instances, gastroesophageal reflux is a mild, transient condition that disappears by six months of age and is compatible with perfectly good health.

In rare severe cases, the infant may need to be maintained on her abdomen at a 30-degree angle for twenty-four hours a day, positioned on a special board. Occasionally medication is prescribed, and often a specialist in gastrointestinal disorders will be consulted. Rarely surgery is performed to prevent further vomiting.

Complications: Severe gastroesophageal reflux can lead to impaired growth, recurrent pneumonia, and damage to the esophagus.

Prevention: Gastroesophageal reflux can't be prevented, but early detection and medical management should prevent most complications.

GLOMERULONEPHRITIS

Definition: Glomerulonephritis is a kidney disorder that affects the part of the kidney that filters the blood. It is rare under three years of age.

Cause: Glomerulonephritis often occurs about ten days after the onset of a strep infection, either strep throat or impetigo.

Symptoms: The first symptom is often tea- or Coke-colored urine, due to the presence of blood. Abnormally colored urine should always be reported to your child's pediatrician. The production of urine may be decreased, and the child may retain water, suddenly weigh more, and be puffy. High blood pressure is common, as well as headache, fatigue, vomiting, and abdominal pain. When medical care is sought and a urine sample is examined, characteristic findings are present.

Treatment: The strep infection should be treated with antibiotics if it is still present. If the child's blood pressure is elevated, it should be treated with antihypertensive medication. Otherwise, no specific treatment may be needed other than bedrest while the child is followed carefully. She usually gets better within two to three weeks and recovers completely.

Complications: High blood pressure may be severe and difficult to control. A few children go on to have longterm kidney problems.

Prevention: Glomerulonephritis can be prevented by prompt and complete treatment of strep infections, including strep throat and impetigo.

Contagion: Glomerulonephritis itself is not contagious. The preceding strep infection is.

HEPATITIS

Definition: Hepatitis is an infectious disease causing inflammation of the liver.

Cause: Several specific viruses can cause hepatitis, and others are suspected.

Symptoms: The typical symptoms of hepatitis are fever, loss of appetite, vomiting, headache, and abdominal pain. The urine becomes dark, the stools turn clay-colored, and jaundice develops. Children often have few symptoms. Blood tests help confirm the diagnosis by showing liver abnormalities. Blood tests can also help distinguish the specific type of hepatitis.

Treatment: There is no specific treatment for hepatitis. Bedrest is recommended while jaundice is present. Although the child may have poor appetite, a wholesome diet should be encouraged. Severe cases require hospitalization.

Complications: Almost all children recover without problems. A few suffer severe hepatitis with liver failure, chronic disease, or relapse in illness.

Prevention: Infectious hepatitis, also known as hepatitis A, can be prevented in 80 percent to 90 percent of people if they receive a gamma globulin shot within one to two weeks of known exposure. All close contacts of a child with infectious hepatitis should therefore receive gamma globulin. Gamma globulin does NOT prevent serum hepatitis, also known as hepatitis B. A newly developed hepatitis B immune globulin does appear to help prevent serum hepatitis in exposed individuals.

Recently, a vaccine against hepatitis B virus has become available. It is recommended in a 3-dose regimen for individuals in families in which someone has hepatitis B or is a chronic carrier of the infectious particles in the blood. It is also given to newborns delivered to such mothers.

Contagion: Hepatitis is very contagious. The virus is shed in bowel movements, urine, blood, and saliva. Careful hand washing is important after using the bathroom.

Additional Information: Hepatitis A, infectious hepatitis, is usually milder, has an incubation period of fourteen to fifty days, and occasionally occurs in preschool

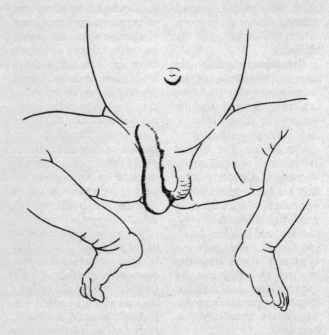

HERNIA

outbreaks through contaminated feces. Hepatitis B, serum hepatitis, has a slower incubation period of twenty-one to one hundred thirty-five days and is often passed by a blood transfusion or contaminated hypodermic needle.

HERNIA (INGUINAL HERNIA)

Definition: A hernia consists of abdominal contents or fluid that are forced through an abnormal opening in the abdominal cavity near the groin. Hernias are more common in boys than in girls.

Cause: During fetal life, a boy's testicles develop in the abdomen and migrate into the scrotum. Both boys and girls have a small abdominal opening near the groin that normally closes off during fetal life. If it doesn't close off completely, abdominal contents can protrude through the opening, making a bulge at the groin, where the thigh joins the abdomen.

Symptoms: Usually, the only symptom is a painless swelling in the groin that may extend down into the scrotum. It is more noticeable when the baby is crying or straining, and at other times may not be apparent. The hernia lump may contain a loop of bowel or abdominal fluid. Once you see a hernia, make an appointment with your pediatrician promptly.

Quite commonly, at the time of the office visit, the hernia bulge is not evident. It is important for you to carefully describe your observations. An accurate description of the hernia may be sufficient to prompt surgical correction.

If a hernia gets caught in the abnormal opening, or "strangulated," the baby may cry in pain and vomit. The hernia may look discolored and be very tender. In this case, the child should be examined by a physician immediately, as emergency surgery will be required.

Treatment: Although umbilical hernias go away, inguinal hernias do NOT. Surgery must be performed promptly to correct the problem and eliminate any risk of hernia strangulation. Even if a hernia is present on only one side, surgery is usually done on both sides. Often an opening is found on the presumed normal side and corrected at the time the hernia is repaired, saving the child another operation later.

Complications: The main complication of a hernia is the risk of strangulation of a piece of bowel caught in the groin opening. Prompt repair of hernias shortly after they are diagnosed should prevent this.

Prevention: The abnormal hernia opening is present at birth. It can't be prevented.

Additional Information: Inguinal hernias are even more common in premature infants. Five percent of all prematures have a hernia.

HERPES (ORAL)

Definition: Herpes infection in the mouth commonly occurs in children under five years of age upon their first exposure to the herpes virus. An infant infected at birth by a mother with active genital herpes can develop widespread illness.

Cause: Herpes infections are caused by the herpes

simplex virus. Two types have been identified. Type 1 is the usual cause of oral and skin herpes infections. Type 2 is responsible for genital disease and herpes infections of infants at the time of birth.

Symptoms: Most children will be exposed to the oral herpes virus before school age. Many of them will have infections so mild that they go unnoticed. Others, however, will become quite ill with fever, irritability, pain in the mouth and throat, fatigue and lethargy, and enlarged lymph nodes. Numerous yellowish ulcers will be present inside the mouth on the gums and tongue, inside the cheeks, on the tonsils and throat. The lips may be crusted, the breath is often foul, and the gums are very swollen. The disease lasts seven to fourteen days.

There is a chance that an infant born to a mother with genital herpes (type 2 herpes) will be infected at birth or become ill within the first week of life. The newborn may have tiny blisters on the skin, fever, jaundice, difficulty breathing, lethargy, vomiting, poor feeding, convulsions, or abnormal bleeding. The disease can be life-threatening.

Very rarely, a newborn exposed to type 1 herpes will become as seriously ill as the baby who gets type 2 herpes at birth. For this reason, it is always a good idea to protect your newborn from friends and relatives with cold sores.

Herpes virus can also infect the eyes, causing damage to the cornea and permanent impairment of vision. Herpes can enter the eye, either at the time of birth if the mother has genital herpes, or later if the child has oral herpes and rubs her eyes. Fortunately, this type of herpes infection is rare.

Children can get type 1 herpes infections in the genital area, usually by having their fingers in their mouth and then touching their genitals. The possibility of sexual abuse must always be considered in a child with genital herpes, however.

Treatment: Antibiotics are not effective against viruses, but new antiviral drugs are available and being used with some success against serious herpes infections in newborns and for herpes infections of the eye. Because of the seriousness of these infections, affected children should be under the care of a specialist.

For the most common type of herpes infection, oral type

l infection in a preschooler, treatment is aimed at helping the child feel more comfortable. The severe mouth pain leads to decreased fluid intake and can result in dehydration. Your pediatrician can prescribe a solution to rinse the mouth with several times a day. This will provide temporary relief and you can try to encourage the child to drink while she is feeling better. Most children prefer to drink cool liquids. You can offer Popsicles if you take care not to let them rub against her sensitive cheek skin (they can cause thermal skin injury). Acetaminophen can be given to combat the fever and relieve discomfort.

Complications: The most common complication of first-time oral herpes infection is the tendency to have recurrent cold sores. It is believed that the virus remains hidden in the body after the first infection and can be reactivated to cause fever blisters or cold sores during times of stress. Among the many stresses that can bring on a cold sore include sunshine, trauma, fever, menstrual periods, and severe illness. It is not clear why some people are plagued by these recurrent infections while others are not.

In children with eczema, a herpes infection can spread to the inflamed areas of skin and cause serious illness. In very sick children, or those with weakened immunity, many serious complications of herpes infections can occur.

Prevention: Type 1 herpes virus occurs so commonly that it is impossible to grow up without ever being exposed to it. You should avoid kissing, drinking from the same glass, sharing lip balm, et cetera, with anyone who has a fever blister, cold sore, or other suspicious sore around the mouth.

Type 2 herpes infections of newborns are prevented by inducing labor during a herpes quiescent period near term. A Caesarean section should be performed on mothers with active genital herpes sores. Such a mother can hold and feed her baby after delivery, provided she carefully washes her hands and lays a clean gown over her lap. She should also be careful not to let any clothing that has touched her genital area come into contact with the newborn. If a mother develops a cold sore shortly after delivery, she should not kiss her baby and should carefully wash her hands whenever she touches her mouth. Some mothers wear a face mask as a reminder not to touch their mouth when handling their baby.

Contagion: Herpes virus is highly contagious. It is said that one wipe of a cold sore could infect a whole room full of people. A person is contagious even before the cold sore fully erupts, so it is hard to avoid exposure to herpes virus altogether. The two dangerous herpes infections are type 2 herpes acquired at birth, and sometimes type 1 herpes acquired in the first few weeks of life.

Additional Information: We are presently experiencing "herpes phobia" in this country. Remember that type 2, or genital herpes, is dangerous to newborns but can be prevented by performing a Caesarean section if active lesions are present when labor starts or by inducing labor during a herpes-free interval. On the other hand, ultimate exposure to type 1 herpes is almost universal. There is no stigma associated with type 1 infection, and it is a shame the word "herpes" has created an alarmist attitude without reference to the type of infection.

HIGH BLOOD PRESSURE (HYPERTENSION)

Definition: High blood pressure *can* occur in children. Normal values for blood pressure differ according to the age and sex of the child, and blood pressure is considered high when it is greater than the 95th percentile for children that age.

Cause: There are many causes of high blood pressure, including kidney problems, heart problems, rare tumors, and others. Obviously, discovering the cause is very important, since the cause may require special treatment. The most common type of high blood pressure in children is called "essential hypertension," which means that the cause is unknown.

Symptoms: Only recently have pediatricians begun to take a child's blood pressure during routine check-ups. Often high blood pressure is found by such routine screening, with no symptoms being present. Symptoms of severe high blood pressure include frequent headaches or bloody noses, convulsions, and change in vision.

Treatment: Medication can bring high blood pressure down to normal. It may be necessary to use more than one medicine. If an underlying heart or kidney problem is present, it is important to treat that as well. Parents can acquire blood pressure equipment and learn to take their child's blood pressure at home. In older children, essential hypertension can often be improved by weight loss (if the child is obese), reducing dietary salt intake, and following an exercise program.

Complications: Complications of untreated severe high blood pressure include stroke, damaged vision, strain on the heart, and others. Another complication is the failure to discover the underlying cause of high blood pressure which may need prompt treatment.

Prevention: High blood pressure tends to run in families. If anyone in your family is prone to high blood pressure, you can start now to keep your child from being overweight, cutting down on salt for the whole family, and encouraging your child to exercise regularly and not to smoke. Complications of hypertension can be avoided by having your child's blood pressure checked regularly.

IMPETIGO

Definition: Impetigo, frequently mispronounced "infantago," is a skin infection that is particularly common in young children and often found on the face.

Cause: Impetigo usually is caused by the strep organism that causes strep throat. In fact, a child with strep throat may simultaneously have impetigo. The germs get under the child's fingernails, for example, after he picks his nose. Then, wherever he scratches a mosquito bite or touches an area where the skin is broken, he can introduce the germ and spread impetigo. Staph germs can also cause impetigo.

Symptoms: Impetigo usually starts as a small red pimple that develops a watery head and quickly ruptures to leave a weepy raw area that spreads. A scab soon forms, giving the sore a "honey-crusted" appearance. Impetigo commonly occurs near the corner of the mouth or the nostril, although it can be seen anywhere on the body. It is also frequently found in the diaper area. Parents often attribute early impetigo to another cause (irritation from her bottle, a scrape, or scratch). In fact, impetigo often starts as a simple scratch that becomes infected. After it goes several days without healing and with apparent spreading, parents should suspect an infection and seek medical help.

Treatment: Impetigo should be treated with local washing and the application of antibiotic ointment, such as Spectrocin, Bacitracin, or Polysporin. Oral antibiotics or a penicillin shot are also necessary. The nails should be kept short and clean so the germs are not spread by scratching. A daily bath helps prevent spread, hastens healing by soaking the scabs off, and makes the sores less irritating.

Complications: Some cases of untreated impetigo due to strep infection can lead to kidney disease. (See page 383). Rarely, severe infection of the skin or spread to other organs can occur from untreated impetigo.

Prevention: It's not possible to prevent impetigo, but you can decrease its likelihood by keeping cuts and scrapes clean and avoiding contact with other children with known strep infections or skin infections. A child in day care, or who has lots of siblings, or who lives in crowded conditions, will be more likely to get impetigo.

Contagion: Impetigo is highly contagious, and spreading within a family or day-care setting is common. Within forty-eight hours of starting treatment, the child should not be contagious and can return to preschool or day care.

Additional Information: Although poor hygiene can increase a child's chances of getting impetigo, most young children will have impetigo at least once (unless you manage to keep them in isolation). Impetigo doesn't mean your child is "dirty" or unhygienic—it is a common condition, especially where strep is prevalent. It is difficult to escape infection once exposed. When my children were small, they attended a large day-care center. It seemed that one of them always had a sore throat, one an earache, and another one impetigo. Strep "ping-ponged" around the day-care center and within our own family. By the time we treated one child, she had already passed it on to a sibling. Not until we changed babysitting arrangements did the incidence of strep in our family decline significantly. Yet we still experience a couple of bouts of strep each year, including someone who gets impetigo now and then.

INTUSSUSCEPTION

Definition: Intussusception is a rare condition causing intestinal obstruction in the first two years of life. It is due to the bowel inverting into itself, like a telescope.

Cause: The cause of intussusception can seldom be determined, though in some instances, an abnormality in the intestinal tract can be found.

Symptoms: The symptoms include sudden onset of intermittent waves of abdominal pain, vomiting, and bloody bowel movements, often resembling currant jelly. At first the child may look normal between the waves of pain, but soon the baby will become weaker and lethargic and will look seriously ill. The infant should be brought for medical care promptly as soon as symptoms appear. The telescoped segment of bowel can often be felt by the pediatrician when the abdomen is palpated. A barium enema X ray examination will confirm the diagnosis.

Treatment: Reduction (correction) of intussusception is an emergency procedure that needs to be carried out immediately after the diagnosis is made. Sometimes the barium enema will actually reduce the intussusception, as the barium pushes the bowel back into its normal position. When this fails, emergency surgery is necessary to correct the problem. Intravenous fluids will often be needed.

Complications: If treatment is delayed until the child is very ill, death can occur.

Prevention: There is no way to prevent intussusception. Complications can be prevented by seeking prompt medical care for a child with sudden onset of intermittent abdominal pain, vomiting, and bloody stools.

KAWASAKI'S DISEASE

Definition: Kawasaki's disease is a serious, newly described disease of early childhood.

Cause: The cause has not yet been determined; research is underway.

Symptoms: Specific criteria exist to diagnose Kawasaki's disease, including:

1. fever for over five days that does not respond to antibiotics
2. pink eye, or red, inflamed whites of the eyes
3. cracking of the lips and inflammation in the mouth
4. enlarged lymph nodes

5. a rash on the body and arms and legs, with reddened palms and soles

6. puffiness due to retained fluid.

Sometimes the joints are swollen and painful.

Treatment: No specific treatment is yet known, although aspirin therapy diminishes complications. New research has found intravenous gamma globulin to be helpful. Treatment mainly consists of relieving symptoms and monitoring the child carefully, often in the hospital.

Complications: Kawasaki's disease can be complicated by severe cardiac problems, especially in young infants. During and after the illness, children should be carefully screened for these heart problems.

Prevention: Since the cause is not known, there is yet no way to prevent Kawasaki's disease. Early diagnosis and close monitoring should prevent heart complications from going unrecognized.

Contagion: It does not appear that Kawasaki's disease is contagious.

LICE INFESTATION

Definition: Infestation with lice can occur in the scalp and on the body, and in the pubic area of adults (where it is known as "crabs").

Cause: Lice are tiny gray bugs, about 1/16″ long that cause sores in the scalp and on the body. Lice infestation is highly contagious, even among hygienic people.

Symptoms: Head lice cause itching and sores in the scalp, especially at the back of the head, just above the hairline. Their white eggs, known as nits, can be tightly attached to the hairs, and are visible. (They can look like small "beads" strung onto the hair.) Body lice cause little bumps that are intensely itchy, especially at night. The louse is not usually seen on the body but can sometimes be found in the seams of underwear. Babies can get pubic lice at the time of birth if the mother is infested.

Treatment: Lice infestations can be readily treated. Most physicians use a prescription product, Kwell. Hair lice and nits can be treated by shampooing with Kwell. Then comb the hair with a fine-tooth comb to remove the nits. You may have to pick them out by hand as well. You can repeat the shampoo in a week to be absolutely sure you have cured the infestation.

For body lice, you can use Kwell cream or lotion as prescribed by your physician. After treatment, wet-mop or vacuum your child's room, and wash the bed linen in hot water. Wash combs and brushes in Kwell. Hats should be washed or set aside for two weeks, since nits hatch in about one week.

Complications: The main complication of lice infestation is the anxiety it causes parents when they learn that their child was exposed to someone with it. You don't need to take drastic measures like shaving the head. It's easy to cure.

Prevention: Lice infestation can be prevented by avoiding contact with anyone known to have the infestation. Make it a practice never to share hats, scarves, combs, brushes or barrettes.

Contagion: Lice are very contagious. You should check the scalp and skin of other family members and close contacts. If they have nits, sores, or an itchy rash, they should be treated, too. After one treatment with Kwell, your child is no longer contagious, provided her clothes and linens were deloused as well. Lice can't exist off the human body for more than seventy-two hours.

LEUKEMIA

Definition: Leukemia is a form of cancer affecting the white blood cells.

Cause: The cause of leukemia is unknown.

Symptoms: Common symptoms include unexplained fevers, chronic fatigue, enlarged lymph nodes, pallor, and easy bruising or bleeding. Have your child examined if any of these symptoms are present. The abnormal white blood cells can crowd out other types of blood components, including red blood cells and platelets. For this reason, children with leukemia are usually anemic, too.

Treatment: Present available treatment with chemotherapy has greatly improved the chances of survival. With modern chemotherapy, the majority of children are free of disease five years later. Of course, a child with leukemia would need to be managed by a specialist, probably at a major medical center.

Complications: Complications of leukemia include anemia, bleeding disorders, frequent infections, and invasion of organs by leukemic cells.

Prevention: Since the cause of leukemia is not known, we cannot yet prevent it.

LYMPH-NODE INFECTION (LYMPHADENITIS)

Definition: Lymphadenitis is an infection of a lymph node and occurs most often in preschool-aged children.

Cause: A lymph-node infection usually results when an infection in the ear, nose, or throat spreads to a nearby lymph node, usually one in the neck. Bacteria, such as staph or strep, are the most common germs causing lymph-node infections, although other germs sometimes are involved.

Symptoms: The child usually has a fever and sudden appearance of a large, very tender lymph node that should prompt you to seek medical attention. The infected node is usually located below the angle of the jaw, making the neck and face appear swollen. Sometimes the skin over the lymph node will be red.

Treatment: A lymph-node infection needs to be treated with prescribed antibiotics for ten days. Sometimes pus forms in the lymph node, and it may need to be lanced and drained. If the lymph node is not better after one

to two days on antibiotics or the child appears very ill, she may have to be admitted to the hospital, so antibiotics can be administered intravenously.

Complications: A rare complication of an untreated lymph-node infection is spread of the infection to the bloodstream or extension of the infection into the vital structures of the neck.

Prevention: Lymph-node infections can be prevented by prompt treatment of the original nearby infection, such as an ear infection, an abscessed tooth, strep throat, et cetera.

Contagion: The original infection, such as strep throat, may be contagious, but a lymph-node infection is not contagious from one person to another.

Additional Information: A lymph-node infection in the neck is sometimes confused with mumps, mononucleosis, and other conditions.

MENINGITIS

Definition: Meningitis, or spinal meningitis, is an infection of the lining of the brain, known as the meninges. It is more common in infants than in adults. Unless treated promptly, meningitis can lead to death or permanent disability.

Cause: Meningitis can be caused by both viruses and bacteria. Viral meningitis is usually miid and self-limiting, although it can be serious in young infants. Bacterial meningitis may be rapidly fatal unless promptly treated with antibiotics and other measures. In children from six months to six years, the most common bacterial cause of meningitis is the Hemophilus germ. This bacterium also commonly causes ear infections, deep skin infections (cellulitis), bone infections, and other serious infections in young children.

Symptoms: Meningitis often follows an upper-respiratory infection, such as an ear infection. There is usually a high fever, though a low-grade fever can occur. Because meningitis causes pressure in the brain, the child has a headache and may be very irritable or very lethargic, not wanting to move. Vomiting commonly occurs, and the child feeds poorly. The inflammation around the brain causes a stiff neck and there is pain when the spine is stretched. The child prefers a position in which the head is bent backward and the back is arched. If the baby has a soft spot, or fontanel, it may be bulging or raised up

above the skull. In general, the longer meningitis progresses without hospital treatment, the sicker the child will appear, and the worse the outcome will be. If you ever suspect your child has symptoms of meningitis or other serious illness, contact your physician at any hour of the night or day.

Sometimes meningitis occurs with an ear infection. Early meningitis may go undetected by a health professional who simply treats the ear infection with oral antibiotics. This is not adequate treatment for meningitis, so the child will not improve, but will soon begin to get worse. Always call your pediatrician or return to the office when an illness under treatment is not responding promptly.

Treatment: A child with meningitis must be admitted to the hospital and treated with intravenous antibiotics for at least ten days. Intensive care may be necessary for the first several days of illness.

Complications: A serious complication of meningitis is delayed diagnosis and progression of disease. Death can occur. The most common complication is hearing loss, so hearing should be followed carefully in any child who has had meningitis. Mental retardation, cerebral palsy, or water-on-the-brain (hydrocephalus) may occur in severe cases or when treatment has been delayed.

Prevention: The recent availability of the Hemophilus influenza type B vaccine, known as Hib vaccine, will undoubtedly prevent many cases of meningitis. (See page 161.) The vaccine should be given to children eighteen months of age who are in daycare settings, and to all two-year-olds. Children between two and five years who have not received the vaccine can also be immunized. Since the vaccine doesn't work in children under eighteen months of age, young infants unfortunately remain unprotected from Hemophilus infections.

Contagion: The Hemophilus bacterium is contagious, but meningitis is seldom spread from child to child. One child may have an ear infection with Hemophilus, while another has meningitis, and still another carries the germ in her nose without becoming ill.

MONONUCLEOSIS
Definition: Mononucleosis is a self-limiting infectious disease common in childhood and adolescence, usually associated with a sore throat.

Cause: Mononucleosis is caused by the Ebstein-Barr virus (EBV).

Symptoms: Common symptoms of mononucleosis in older children and adults include a sore throat, fever, headache, general fatigue and muscle aches, swollen lymph glands, and abdominal pain. Occasionally a rash may be present, and the eyelids may be very puffy. Additional aids in the diagnosis include a blood test for mono, the presence of characteristic kinds of white blood cells on a blood smear, and an enlarged spleen that the physician can detect on physical examination. Mono is most common in adolescents, but it can occur at all ages although the symptoms are less typical in younger children. Youngsters under two usually have no symptoms.

Treatment: There is no specific treatment for mono, except for general measures to make the child feel better. Bedrest, lots of fluids, and acetaminophen will usually do the trick. The child may be ill for several weeks, but complete recovery almost always occurs.

Complications: A rare but dangerous complication of mono is rupture of the enlarged spleen by a blow to the abdomen. This could lead to severe internal bleeding and possible shock.

Prevention: Almost everyone gets mono by the time they reach adulthood, but some cases are so mild they go undiagnosed. Although mono is known as the "kissing disease," there are many other ways to transmit it from child to child, for example by saliva left on toys or drinking from the same glass. Obviously, it would be wise to avoid intimate contact with a person known to have mono.

Contagion: The virus causing mono is found in the saliva of infected persons and is excreted for many months after they have recovered. The incubation period for mono after being exposed is thirty to fifty days in young adults, and may be shorter in children.

Additional Information: Mono is often mistaken for strep throat, and may not be suspected until after the strep culture is negative and the child has not improved on penicillin therapy.

NEPHROTIC SYNDROME
Definition: Nephrotic syndrome is a kidney disease that usually begins between two and seven years of age and causes leaking of protein into the urine.

Cause: The cause of childhood nephrotic syndrome remains unknown, although the condition often follows a respiratory infection.

Symptoms: The child first may be noted to have puffy eyelids and to be urinating less frequently, prompting you to seek medical attention. Within a few weeks, she may develop generalized puffiness and excessive weight gain due to water retention. She may be tired and lethargic and have abdominal pain or poor appetite. Rarely, high blood pressure and difficulty with breathing occur. A urine test will show excess protein in the urine. Blood tests help confirm the diagnosis by revealing certain specific abnormalities.

Treatment: Children with nephrotic syndrome require close medical supervision by a physician, and often a kidney specialist. They usually respond very well to treatment with steroids, and many remain permanently well. Sometimes, however, the condition relapses and proves to be a chronic problem.

Complications: Children

with nephrotic syndrome are more prone to infections and the formation of blood clots. The main complication is the risk of relapses and chronic disease.

Prevention: Since the cause is unknown, there is no known way to prevent nephrotic syndrome.

Contagion: Nephrotic syndrome is not contagious.

NURSEMAID'S ELBOW

Definition: Nursemaid's elbow is the name for dislocation at the elbow of one of the bones in the forearm.

Cause: Nursemaid's elbow is caused by sudden, longitudinal traction of the arm, such as lifting a young child up by the hand or dragging a reluctant child by the arm. The sudden traction pulls the radius bone out of place and tears one of the ligaments attached to it.

Symptoms: The child suddenly refuses to move her arm and holds it slightly bent at the elbow and turned inward. The area over her elbow is tender to the touch, and she cries in pain if her arm is bent. An X ray will not show the abnormality.

Treatment: The pediatrician can reposition the displaced bone easily by rotating the child's arm outward and slowly straightening it.

A click may be felt as the bone pops back into position. The child usually starts using her arm again within twenty minutes. You should not try to manipulate the arm yourself, as without training, you could injure the child further. Occasionally, a parent will have inadvertently repositioned the bone while handling the child on the way to the office. I have also seen the problem be corrected in X ray, while the arm was being positioned for the film.

Complications: Complications of nursemaid's elbow are rare. Delayed diagnosis can occur if a parent fails to notice the injury in a preverbal child. Without proper education of the parents and caretakers, the condition may occur multiple times in the same child.

Prevention: Nursemaid's elbow can be prevented by parents not picking up their child by the hand or jerking on her arm.

PINKEYE (CONJUNCTIVITIS)

Definition: Pinkeye is an infection of the lining, or conjunctiva, of the eye. The conjunctiva covers the inside of the eyelid and the eyeball. The infection causes the white part of the eye to look pink or red, thus the name "pinkeye."

Cause: Pinkeye is usually caused by one of many viruses or bacteria and is often associated with a cold, ear infection, or other upper-respiratory infection. Pinkeye is common during the first month of life and can be caused by germs that enter the eye during the birth process. Later in life, other causes of eye contamination may occur, such as swimming in dirty water, or simply rubbing the eyes with dirty hands.

Symptoms: The white part of the eye usually looks red and irritated, and the lids may be slightly puffy. Mucuslike drainage accumulates and may dry on the eyelashes, causing the eyelids to be stuck together upon awakening. The eye discharge often reappears throughout the day, and can be either watery or thick greenish-yellow. Either one or both eyes may be involved. Older children may complain of mild stinging of the eyes, and young children may try to rub their eyes. Cold symptoms are often present, including a low-grade fever. Severe redness, swelling of the eyelids, or a high fever in the child are danger signs suggesting a more serious eye infection requiring prompt medical care, such as periorbital cellulitis (see page 325).

Treatment: Mild pinkeye with scant watery drainage and only slight redness can be managed at home by gently cleansing the discharge with a sterile cotton ball moistened with warm water. The drainage is an excellent growth medium for the infecting germs, so it is important to wipe it away. Wash your hands before and after you touch your child's eyelids and discourage her from rubbing her eyes. Throw the cotton ball away after each wipe and never use the same cotton ball on the other eye.

Pinkeye with profuse drainage, thick green or yellow discharge, or moderate redness is probably caused by bacteria and should be treated by your child's doctor with ophthalmic (or eye) antibiotic ointment or drops. Be sure NEVER to put any medication into the eyes unless it is specifically labeled as an eye preparation. Don't touch the tip of the bottle or tube to the eye, so it will remain uncontaminated. You will probably need someone to help you instill eye drops or ointment. Try to do this when the baby is quiet, perhaps sleeping. Someone can hold the lids open while you drop in the medication.

Complications: Complications of pinkeye are rare, but occasionally the infection spreads to deeper and surrounding eye structures. Any time an eye infection gets worse or has not responded to several days of medication, you should have the child reevaluated. High fever, eye pain, light sensitivity, or swollen, red eyelids are also worrisome signs that call for evaluation by your child's doctor.

Prevention: State laws require the instillation of eye medication at birth to prevent many cases of neonatal conjunctivitis. Teaching your child not to rub her eyes will help prevent pinkeye. Careful hand washing after eye care will also help prevent its spread.

Contagion: Some cases of pinkeye occur in epidemic-like form, so you should keep your child home from the day-care setting or preschool if she and several members of the family have pinkeye, since it is likely to be highly contagious. Pinkeye is easily spread from one eye to the other by eye rubbing and is often caused in the first place when nose and mouth germs on the hands

get rubbed into the eyes.

Additional Information: Pinkeye can also be due to noninfectious causes. For example, allergies can cause red eyes, as can opening the eyes in chlorinated swimming pools, or getting an irritating substance splashed into or rubbed into the eyes. It may be difficult to always determine the cause of pinkeye, but infection is more likely when other cold symptoms are present.

Eye ointment is more difficult to instill, but it lasts longer and thus requires fewer daily doses. It may blur the vision for a while after being instilled, so older children may complain about it. Eye drops are easier to get into a child's eye, but they are rapidly washed out by tears and will thus need to be given more often. You should never reuse leftover eye medication without a doctor's permission.

Excessive tearing in a young infant without other signs of pinkeye is probably due to blockage of the tear duct. Because the tears don't drain normally, these babies are prone to developing pinkeye. The blocked tear duct usually opens on its own by six months of age, but occasionally it needs to be probed by a pediatric ophthalmologist.

PINWORMS

Definition: Pinworms are little white worms about half an inch long that infect the large intestine of children and adults all over the world.

Cause: Symptoms are caused when the female worm crawls out the anus, especially at night, and lays her eggs in the skin folds of the anus. When the child scratches the anus, the eggs get under her fingernails. She can then continue to infect herself or pass the eggs on to other family members.

Symptoms: The main symptom of pinworm infection is itching of the anus. In little girls, the worms can crawl into the vagina and cause itching of the vagina and labia as well.

Treatment: Several drugs are effective in treating pinworms. Most of these are given as a one-time-only dose, calculated by weight of the patient. It is preferable to treat all family members who have symptoms once pinworms have been confirmed in one member, since close contacts can easily keep reinfecting one another. It is probably unnecessary to treat family members who have no symptoms.

For three days after treatment, be sure your child wears clean underwear to bed each night and keep her fingernails trimmed so she cannot scratch as much. Give her a shower each morning and carefully rinse the anal area where new eggs have been laid. The bedclothes and underclothes should be gently gathered up (shaking will spread the eggs) and washed daily. Machine washing kills eggs. Vacuum or wet-mop your child's room to prevent scattered eggs from infecting someone.

Complications: Pinworms have been blamed for all kinds of symptoms from insomnia to appendicitis, but there is little proof that they cause more than anal itching. In severe cases, ulcers in the bowel and anus can occur. The main complication is reinfection of a child and her family by failing to eradicate all the eggs during treatment.

Prevention: There is really no sure way to prevent pinworms. They occur worldwide and all of us probably have had them at some point in our lives without even knowing it. Wearing clean underwear to bed, keeping nails clipped, teaching our children to wash their hands after using the bathroom and before eating will help minimize pinworm infections.

Contagion: Pinworms are very contagious by passing eggs from the fingers of an infected individual to another. It takes about three to four weeks for the eggs to mature into adult worms who cause symptoms by laying more eggs. Eggs remain infectious for up to two weeks.

Additional Information: Pinworm infection is diagnosed by seeing the eggs under the microscope. Parents are usually given several small rectangular glass slides and asked to awaken their child early (before eggs are rubbed off or washed off) and place a piece of transparent cellophane tape over her anus. The eggs will stick to the tape. The tape is then placed over the glass slide and brought to the pediatrician's office, where it is examined under the microscope for the presence of eggs.

Be sure to check the details of the pinworm medicine your child and other family members are given. Some of these are not safe during pregnancy and should not be taken by a woman in her childbearing years. Others cause temporary red staining of stools which can permanently stain clothes.

Sometimes a second dose is given two weeks later in case reinfection occurred. Many parents suffer from pinworm phobia and undertake elaborate housecleaning efforts to eradicate invisible pinworm eggs. Don't let this happen to you. Twenty percent of all children have pinworms at any one time, and most of them are never bothered by it.

PNEUMONIA

Definition: Pneumonia is an infection of the lower respiratory tract, within the lung itself.

Cause: There are many different causes of pneumonia. Pneumonia caused by a virus is often mild and self-limiting, sometimes labeled as "walking pneumonia." Pneumonia caused by bacteria can be serious, even life-threatening. If food or a toxic substance, such as gasoline, is inhaled into the lungs, aspiration pneumonia, also known as chemical pneumonia, can occur from irritation to the lungs.

Symptoms: Common symptoms of pneumonia include fever, persistent cough, rapid breathing or difficulty breathing, poor feeding, poor color, and listlessness. Undress your child and watch her as she breathes. If her breathing is associated with sinking in of the breastbone or tugging in between the ribs, or at the lower rib margins, pneumonia should be considered. A grunting noise heard each time the child breathes out can also be a sign of pneumonia. Have your child examined promptly if any of these symptoms are present.

Treatment: Mild viral pneumonias do not require antibiotic therapy. The child should get well within two weeks, but during the first few days, appropriate fever control, lots of clear liquids, and rest will be necessary.

Pneumonia caused by bacteria must always be treated with antibiotics, and close medical follow-up is necessary to be sure the illness responds to treatment. Occasionally, hospitalization is necessary for bacterial pneumonia or severe viral pneumonia to provide oxygen or intravenous fluids.

In all cases of pneumonia, it is important not to try to suppress the cough, since coughing up the mucus within the lungs helps speed recovery. The cough is also an important sign by which to monitor the child.

Complications: If pneumonia is treated promptly and adequately, the child should recover quickly. Severe pneumonia or recurrent pneumonia may damage the airways and lead to more chronic lung infections. Rarely, with severe or untreated pneumonia may be fatal.

Prevention: There is no specific way to prevent pneumonia, but careful observations of young children with upper-respiratory infections will alert parents to the early signs of complications of simple colds. Giving the complete course of antibiotic therapy for early pneumonia will usually prevent complications. Keeping furniture polish, gasoline, and other substances which can be drunk and inhaled into the lungs out of the reach of children will help prevent aspiration pneumonia.

Contagion: Pneumonia is not spread directly from one person to another. The same germ that causes a cold or sore throat in one individual may lead to pneumonia in another. Many of the germs causing pneumonia are found in the nose and throat of healthy people.

Additional Information: Pneumonia is usually more serious in young infants than in older children or adults. Frequent coughing in a young infant should always be investigated by a health professional. The diagnosis of pneumonia is confirmed by taking a chest X ray.

In some children, an underlying condition may exist to make them more susceptible to pneumonia. For example, children with cystic fibrosis are particularly prone to pneumonia because they produce thick mucus in their lungs, which encourages the growth of germs.

PYLORIC STENOSIS

Definition: Pyloric stenosis is a condition in which the stomach is partially blocked from emptying into the small intestine, causing progressive vomiting. It occurs most commonly around six weeks of age and in males.

Cause: The cause of pyloric stenosis is not known. The muscle located where the stomach empties into the small bowel enlarges, becomes hard, and blocks the emptying of food contents into the bowel. A familial tendency toward developing pyloric stenosis seems to exist.

Symptoms: Infants appear entirely normal and feed well for the first few weeks. Between three and six weeks of age, they begin vomiting after eating. At first, stomach flu may be suspected and a clear liquid diet recommended. Soon it becomes evident that the child is vomiting everything. She tends to be constipated since so little food is getting into the bowel. If the vomiting is allowed to persist for long, she will become dehydrated, with the first sign being decreased urination. When seen by a physician, the diagnosis can be confirmed by X ray tests or ultrasound of the abdomen. The doctor may be able to feel the olive-sized, hardened muscle when the infant's abdomen is examined.

Treatment: The treatment of pyloric stenosis is a relatively minor operation in which the enlarged muscle is cut and widened. Often the baby can go home in a day or two.

Complications: The main complication is delayed diagnosis by failing to suspect pyloric stenosis. Persistent vomiting could lead to chemical disturbances in the blood, malnutrition, and severe dehydration.

Prevention: There is no known way to prevent pyloric stenosis.

REYE'S SYNDROME

Definition: Reye's syndrome is a rapidly progressive condition causing coma that has been recognized only recently and is being reported more often.

Cause: The exact cause of Reye's syndrome remains unknown, but the disorder does seem to follow chickenpox, influenzalike illnesses, and infections with other viruses, especially when a child has been treated with aspirin during the illness.

Symptoms: The child usually is first sick with an upper-respiratory infection. Soon afterward, she begins to have progressive vomiting, irrational behavior, deep breathing, gradual unresponsiveness, and finally coma. Convulsions may occur.

Treatment: Reye's syndrome can be life-threatening, and requires intensive therapy in the hospital. Many organs experience disturbed function with this disorder, including the brain, liver, kidneys, and lungs. With intensive care, however, the majority of children survive and ultimately do well.

Complications: Complications can occur in any of the organs affected by the condition. Permanent brain damage sometimes occurs, especially in children under two years of age.

Prevention: Because of the association between Reye's syndrome and aspirin use, parents are advised not to give aspirin to their children during chickenpox and influenza. I recommend not using aspirin in young children altogether until more information is available.

Contagion: Reye's syndrome is not contagious. The preceding viral illness that occurs in some children is contagious, however.

RINGWORM

Definition: Ringworm is a scaly, red infection of the body or scalp.

Cause: Ringworm is not a worm. It is caused by a group of fungi that live in humans, dogs, and cats. The same family of fungi also cause athlete's foot and "jock itch" in older individuals.

Symptoms: Ringworm in youngsters is most commonly found on the scalp or body. In the scalp, ringworm looks like circular, hairless, slightly reddened areas covered with grayish scales and broken stumps of hair. It can be very itchy. Ringworm on the body causes enlarging ring-shaped pink patches, with scaly red borders, usually on the face, arms, legs, or body. It may be mildly itchy. As the borders spread, the central part clears up.

Your child's physician can confirm ringworm by shining a special light on your child or by gently scraping the affected area and examining the scales under the microscope.

Treatment: For body ringworm, your physician will probably prescribe Tinactin cream to be applied two to three times a day until the ringworm patch has been gone for one week. If the ringworm appears to be spreading despite treatment or isn't cured within six weeks, you should return to your physician.

Ringworm of the scalp must be treated for up to six weeks by oral medication prescribed by your child's physician. In addition, applying Tinactin cream to scalp ringworm twice a day for a week helps prevent further spreading of the infection.

Complications: In severe cases of scalp ringworm, swollen areas with pus can develop and leave permanent scars and areas of baldness.

Prevention: Ringworm can be prevented by not exchanging hats and headgear with others and avoiding mangy animals. If one family member or pet has ringworm, thorough treatment and follow-up will help assure others don't get it.

Contagion: Ringworm is contagious, and can be caught from infected people or pets, or even from hairs left on furniture. After only forty-eight hours of treatment, however, ringworm is no longer contagious and you needn't worry about it spreading to others.

ROSEOLA

Definition: Roseola is a common childhood illness with fever, followed by a rash, occurring most commonly between six months and three years of age.

Cause: The cause of roseola has not been determined although it is probably a virus.

Symptoms: The child has sudden onset of a high fever, sometimes as high as 104° F. The fever lasts for about three days, but other symptoms are absent and the child appears relatively well. After about three days, the fever suddenly drops to normal or below normal and a faint, pink, pinpoint rash appears. It is mainly on the trunk and is usually gone within twenty-four hours.

Treatment: No specific treatment is necessary for roseola. By the time the rash appears, the child is essentially well. During the period of fever, you can't yet know the child has roseola. The fever should be treated with lots of clear liquids and acetaminophen.

Complications: During a high fever of roseola, convulsions can occur and raise concern about possible meningitis. The biggest complication of roseola is not knowing what is causing the fever until the rash breaks out. During the three days of fever, you and your doctor may worry that your child has something more serious. Actual complications are exceedingly rare.

Prevention: It is not a good idea to expose your child to another child with fever and rash. However, no matter how careful you are, your child will probably get roseola sometime before the age of three years.

Contagion: Roseola is contagious and has an incubation period of ten to fourteen days. Your child is probably not contagious after the rash is gone. You can get roseola only once.

SCABIES

Definition: Scabies is an itchy skin infection that is occurring in epidemic form in the United States.

Cause: It is caused by an insect mite that burrows under the skin and lays her eggs.

Symptoms: Scabies classically causes little bumps with raised lines where the mites burrow under the skin. The sores are found mostly on the wrists, ankles, between the fingers, in the armpits, behind the knees, in the crease of the elbows, and in the groin area. They are very itchy, especially at night and when it is warm. The sores and surrounding areas may be scabbed over due to scratching.

In infants, scabies may look different. Burrows may be absent, and the itchy bumps may be present on the face, scalp, palms, and soles, which are uncommon sites in older children and adults.

Treatment: Before treating, scabies should be confirmed by a physician by gently scraping the top of one of the sores and looking at it under the microscope. Scabies is treated by prescribing Kwell cream or lotion or an alternative medication. Even after successful treatment, itching may continue for about a week. Cool baths and calamine lotion will help the itching.

To prevent reinfection machine wash bed linen and pajamas. Anything that can't be washed, e.g., sleeping bags or blankets, can be put aside for four days, since the mite cannot live away from the human body for that long.

Complications: The main complication with scabies is impetigo, or infected sores, due to the child's intense scratching. If any of the sores look weepy or have pus, they are probably infected and antibiotics will be needed.

Prevention: It may not be possible to prevent scabies, since it is so common. If one family member gets it, you can prevent it from spreading to others by the treatment measures mentioned.

Contagion: Scabies is very contagious. Since it takes thirty days to develop scabies after contact with it, the whole family should be treated if one member has it. Close contacts, such as friends who spent the night, should also be treated. Your child is no longer contagious after one treatment with Kwell.

SINUSITIS

Definition: Sinusitis is an inflammation of the membranes lining the sinuses, or chambers extending from the nose that help warm and humidify air.

Cause: The sinuses are commonly inflamed with upper-respiratory infections and allergies. Sinusitis occurs when bacteria enter the sinuses and start an infection, usually when the sinus passages get blocked during a cold.

Symptoms: The symptoms may vary according to which sinus is infected. The sinuses are not all formed at birth, so obviously infants can't get infections in all the sinuses, as an adult can. There may be pain overlying the infected sinus, for example, above the eyebrows, over the cheekbones, or behind the eyes, or the child may simply have a bad headache. Nasal congestion, a thick discharge from the nose, and a postnasal drip are usually present. Bad breath is a common symptom. Swelling around the eye, especially the upper eyelid, is seen with sinusitis in infants, and fever is usually present. The diagnosis is confirmed by X ray of the sinuses, but the condition often goes undiagnosed in early childhood because it is seldom considered.

Treatment: Sinusitis is treated with oral antibiotics for ten to fourteen days. An antihistamine-decongestant will usually help the sinuses drain. Mild decongestant nosedrops, such as ⅛ percent Neo-Synephrine can also be used if the nasal passages are congested. Acetaminophen can be given to relieve discomfort.

Complications: Complications are rare but can be serious. Sinusitis can spread to the bones around the sinuses and cause cellulitis (see page 325) or even meningitis (see page 366).

Prevention: Older children should be discouraged from jumping into a swimming pool feet first, as water can get into the sinuses.

Contagion: Sinusitis is not contagious, but the upper-respiratory infection that may be associated with it is contagious.

SORE THROAT

Definition: A sore throat is one of the most common infections of childhood.

Cause: More than 90 percent of sore throats in children are caused by an upper respiratory virus. Strep throat and mononucleosis can also cause sore throat.

Symptoms: The child usually has other symptoms of an upper-respiratory infection, including runny nose and mild cough. The throat is mildly or moderately sore. It is often worse at night because the child has been mouth breathing due to nasal congestion. Fever may be present, and the lymph glands in the neck are often enlarged. The tonsils normally appear large in children under six years of age, even in the absence of a sore throat. After six or eight years, the tonsils begin to shrink.

Treatment: Unless strep throat (see page 382) or mono (see page 368) is suspected, no specific treatment is necessary. Older children can gargle with warm saltwater. Acetaminophen may be given for fever or discomfort. If the child is old enough, sucking on butterscotch-flavored hard candy may bring relief. Although many parents request a penicillin shot or oral antibiotics for every sore throat, antibiotics should NOT be given unless the infection is shown to be due to strep throat.

Complications: Complications of ordinary sore throats are extremely rare.

Prevention: It is virtually impossible to avoid getting several upper-respiratory infections each year and occasional sore throats. Avoiding contact with persons with known upper-respiratory infections will help.

Contagion: Viruses causing sore throats and upper-respiratory infections are contagious.

Additional Information: In the recent past, it was believed that repeated sore throats or tonsillitis could be prevented by removing the tonsils. Back then tonsillectomy was performed so commonly, it was almost an American ritual. In fact, very few children really can benefit from a tonsillectomy, and the operation carries a significant risk. Tonsillectomy will NOT help: "large tonsils," frequent colds and sore throats, recurrent strep throats, frequent ear infections, chronic tonsillitis, or bad breath. Yet the majority of tonsillectomies are performed by parental pressure for these poor reasons. Almost always, the risk of surgically removing the tonsils is greater than leaving them in. A competent ear, nose, and throat specialist can counsel you thoroughly on the valid indications for tonsillectomy.

STREP THROAT

Definition: Strep throat is a sore throat caused by a specific bacterium.

Cause: A throat culture will confirm the presence of the causative streptococcal bacteria. In addition to sore throats, strep can also cause ear infections, skin infections, or infections in other sites.

Symptoms: The classic symptoms of strep throat are usually seen in children four years and older. They include a mild to severe sore throat, with white patches on the tonsils, which may be enlarged. Tiny red dots may be present at the back of the roof of the mouth, and foul breath may be noted. The lymph nodes in the neck are often enlarged and tender. The child usually has a fever and headache, and may also have a stomachache and vomiting. Runny nose and other symptoms of a common cold are usually absent. Impetigo, or skin infections, around the nose and mouth are commonly associated with strep throat.

Certain strains of the strep germ cause a skin rash with strep throat. The rash is rough and sandpapery, with tiny red bumps and areas that look blushed. It is worse in skin folds, and there may be a pale area around the mouth. The rash can last a week or more and be very itchy. Later, the skin peels. Strep throat with the rash is known as scarlet fever.

Strep throat is uncommon in infants. When it does occur, their symptoms are mainly those of a cold, not a sore throat.

Treatment: If strep throat is confirmed by throat culture, your child should be treated, either with a penicillin shot, or with a ten-day course of oral penicillin or another antibiotic. Never allow her to receive penicillin (especially a shot) unless you are absolutely sure she is not allergic to penicillin, however! If she is allergic, another antibiotic can be given by mouth instead.

Your child should begin to feel better within two days after antibiotics have been started. You can help keep her comfortable by giving acetaminophen every four to six hours and offering cool or warm liquids to drink. Keeping the nose clear so mouth breathing won't be necessary also helps diminish sore throat symptoms.

Complications: Although strep infections will resolve on their own if untreated, complications can occur. The most feared complication of strep throat is rheumatic fever, which can permanently damage the heart. Rheumatic fever is much less common today than in previous decades, but it still occurs. Prompt treatment of strep infections will prevent rheumatic fever. Other complications of untreated infections include impetigo and kidney damage.

Prevention: There is no sure way to keep your child from ever getting strep throat, since she will be in close contact with other children in preschool, school, and many other settings. Avoiding day-care centers with large numbers of children will help decrease her exposure to strep. Encouraging all parents of sick children to keep them home during illnesses would keep all of our children healthier.

Any child who has had rheumatic fever MUST be protected from future strep infections and from reactivation of rheumatic fever by taking penicillin or another antibiotic prophylactically for the rest of her life.

Contagion: Strep throat is highly contagious, so your child should be kept away from other children for at least twenty-four hours after antibiotics have been started. It is considerate to tell other parents whose children have already been exposed to your child that she has confirmed strep throat. Then they can get their children cultured too if they become ill. If one family member has strep throat, other family members with symptoms should be cultured, too. The incubation period for strep is about three days.

Additional Information: A throat culture is taken by rubbing the tonsils and throat with a special cotton-tipped swab that is then wiped on a culture plate. Unfortunately, it takes one to two days to get the result of a throat culture, so treatment may be deferred for a few days. Other times, your doctor may start treatment temporarily, on the presumption that strep is present, while waiting for the cultural tests. A rapid test for strep has been recently developed, but it is still less reliable than a throat culture.

Some parents—especially those with difficulty giving all the antibiotic doses for a full ten-day course—prefer a penicillin shot if their child has strep so that they can be confident the illness is treated as soon as they leave the doctor's office. Others prefer oral medication, but it is important that all the prescribed antibiotic be given. Severe penicillin reactions, although uncommon, are more likely to occur with a shot than with oral medication.

SUDDEN INFANT DEATH SYNDROME (SIDS)

Definition: SIDS is the sudden and unexpected death of an infant or young child for no apparent reason.

Cause: Numerous causes of SIDS have been suggested, but so far *none* has been proved; no association has been documented between SIDS and DPT vaccine. The cause remains unknown, although extensive research continues to look for a common thread among these babies.

Prevention: No one knows how to prevent SIDS. Respiratory monitors are commonly recommended now for infants with a previous blue spell, premature infants who have stopped breathing in the past, or infants who have had a sibling with SIDS. These at-risk infants are hooked up to a monitor during the first year of life whenever they sleep. If they were to stop breathing, the monitor alarm would sound to alert the parents to stimulate the baby to breathe again. Obviously, having a baby on a monitor is disruptive to routine family life, but for some families, the worry about possible SIDS proves to be even more disruptive.

Additional information: SIDS has been known for centuries but is receiving more attention recently as other causes of infant death become preventable. One in five hundred babies dies each year of SIDS. The peak incidence is between two and four months of age, and 91 percent of deaths occur within the first six months of life. SIDS is more common during an upper-respiratory infection, in the winter months, in low-birth-weight infants, and in siblings of a previous child who died of SIDS.

SIDS is certainly an unpleasant topic, but not one of us parents can say we have never thought about it. Every time one of my children slept through the night for the first time, I bolted awake in the morning, fearing the worst. I know you will do the same. We needn't be phobic about SIDS, but we should keep a close watch on our babies, especially during respiratory illnesses. A child with SIDS risk factors can be monitored during the first year.

UMBILICAL-CORD INFECTION (OMPHALITIS)

Definition: Omphalitis is an infection of the base of the umbilical cord during the first few weeks of life, before it has completely healed. The infection can spread to the surrounding skin or down into the blood vessels of the cord and from there to the bloodstream and other organs.

Cause: Infections of the umbilical cord can be caused by a variety of bacteria.

Symptoms: Symptoms of an infected umbilical cord include a foul-smelling cord that oozes yellowish puslike material. The surrounding skin on the abdomen may be red and tender. Other symptoms that may be noticed are nonspecific and are the same symptoms a newborn shows whenever she is ill. These include poor feeding, irritability or lethargy, vomiting, elevated or low temperature, jaundice, or any significant change in usual behavior. Seek medical care immediately if any of these symptoms are present in your newborn.

Treatment: An umbilical-cord infection is a serious matter, requiring prompt treatment with antibiotics. Often hospitalization will be necessary so that antibiotics can be administered intravenously. Part of treatment also includes frequent cleaning of the cord base with alcohol.

Complications: Because the three major blood vessels in the cord lead directly into the bloodstream, a cord infection can be complicated by serious spread of the infection.

Prevention: Careful cleaning of the umbilical cord stump will help prevent infection. Gently lift the cord stump and squeeze alcohol from a generously soaked cotton ball down into the base of the cord. Clean away any drainage that is present, since bacteria grow readily on dried discharge. Try to keep the cord exposed to the air so it will dry up and fall off sooner. Keep the diaper folded down away from the cord.

Contagion: Cord infections are not contagious, although some of the germs that cause an infection, such as staph or strep, can be caught from another family member with a skin infection or sore throat.

Additional Information: Fortunately serious umbilical-cord infections are not common these days. Standard hospital policy requires treatment of a baby's cord at birth with an agent that inhibits the growth of germs.

UMBILICAL HERNIA

Definition: An umbilical hernia is a soft swelling covered by skin that protrudes from the umbilical area when a baby cries, coughs, or strains. It is especially common in black babies and premature infants.

Cause: An umbilical hernia is due to imperfect closure of the umbilical opening under the skin, where the umbilical vessels once entered the body. The swelling consists of portions of the small intestine and abdominal contents that protrude through the opening whenever the infant strains.

Symptoms: An infant has no symptoms with an umbilical hernia. The only finding is the periodic bulge that is visible at the umbilicus. The opening through which the abdominal contents protrude can be a fraction of an inch in diameter to an inch or more. When the baby is calm, you can reduce the hernia by gently pushing the bulge back through the opening at the base of the navel, and feel the umbilical ring with your fingertip.

Treatment: Treatment of an umbilical hernia is seldom necessary. The opening under the skin gradually closes off on its own, usually by a year of age. Large hernia openings may take several years to close. Binding the belly button does not speed the process, as was once believed. You don't need to worry about the hernia protruding when the baby cries; this can't hurt her.

Complications: The main complication of an umbilical hernia is parental anxiety over its cosmetic effect. Medical complications are extremely uncommon. Very rarely, a piece of bowel can get caught in a small hernia opening. The infant would appear to be in pain, the overlying umbilical skin would probably become discolored and the hernia would not be reducible.

Prevention: There is no known way to prevent an umbilical hernia.

UNDESCENDED TESTICLE

Definition: An undescended testicle is one that is not in the scrotal sac at birth. One or both testicles may be involved.

Cause: The cause of undescended testicles is unknown. The problem arises in fetal life when the testicles normally migrate from the abdomen into the scrotal sac. Three percent of fullterm males and 30 percent of premature males have undescended testicles at birth.

Symptoms: The child has no symptoms, but on physical examination, the involved testicle is not felt in the scrotum. Sometimes this is a false alarm, and the testicle

has simply pulled up into the body because the child is cold. Placing him in a tub of warm water may allow the testicle to drop back down. A true undescended testicle is never felt in the scrotum.

Treatment: Treatment may not be necessary. Over half of undescended testicles will descend by two months of age, and 80 percent by one year.

A child with an undescended testicle that has not spontaneously dropped into the scrotum by one year of age should be seen by a urologist. Operating to bring the testicle down is now recommended as early as two years of age.

Complications: An undescended testicle that is not brought down into the scrotum early in life has an increased risk of developing cancer and is less likely to produce sperm normally.

Prevention: An undescended testicle is present at birth; there is no known way to prevent it.

URINARY-TRACT INFECTION

Definition: A urinary-tract infection (UTI) is an infection in the bladder and/or kidneys. UTIs are the second most common infections in children, after upper-respiratory infections.

Cause: A UTI is caused when germs get into the urine. Normally, urine is sterile, but since the urinary opening is so close to the anus, especially in girls, it is possible for stool germs to enter the urinary opening and then ascend up the urethra into the bladder, or up the ureters into the kidneys. Children who take bubble baths may be more prone to UTIs, because the chemicals irritate the urinary opening and allow dirty bath water to enter the bladder. Children who wait long periods between urinating, instead of emptying their bladder frequently, are also prone to UTIs.

Symptoms: In older children and adults, the symptoms of a UTI include painful urination, the urge to urinate frequently even though only a small amount of urine may be passed, fever, and tenderness over the lower abdomen. Young infants may have vague symptoms like diarrhea, vomiting, poor feeding, fever, and irritability. Foul-smelling urine, at any age, suggests a UTI. In children who are growing poorly without an obvious cause, a chronic urinary-tract

infection may prove to be to blame.

If the infection spreads to the kidneys, the child is usually much sicker. The temperature is usually higher and back pain may be present in the area where the lowest ribs meet the spine on either side.

Treatment: A child with symptoms of a urinary-tract infection should be seen promptly by a physician to have a urine specimen obtained for culture. Antibiotics are necessary to treat the infection. Treatment should continue for ten to fourteen days, and close follow-up with repeat urine cultures should be performed. Drinking large volumes of fluid will help flush out the infection and can be a helpful part of treatment. In the case of infection in the kidneys, the child will probably have to be hospitalized and treated with intravenous antibiotics for several days.

Following treatment, the child's doctor may order X ray studies of the urinary system to be sure no abnormalities exist that would make the child prone to more UTIs.

Complications: Any untreated bladder infection can spread to the kidneys, causing a much more serious infection. Chronic UTIs that go unrecognized and untreated can cause permanent kidney damage. In young infants, an untreated infection can spread to the bloodstream and become life-threatening. In preschoolers, undetected UTIs can cause daytime and nighttime wetting that is mistakenly assumed to be emotionally based.

Prevention: UTIs can be prevented by encouraging your child to urinate regularly and discontinuing bubble baths. Teach your daughter to wipe from front to back after bowel movements, so she won't wipe fecal material into her urinary opening. When an abnormality exists in the urinary tract making a child prone to infection, surgery can usually be performed to correct the problem.

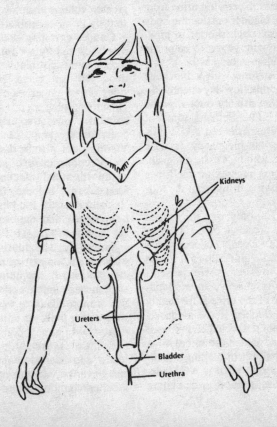

Contagion: UTIs are not contagious. They arise within a person from their own natural germs due to individual susceptibility.

Additional Information: During early infancy, boys have more UTIs than girls because more boys are born with a blockage in the urinary tract that can lead to infection. After infancy, far more girls experience UTIs than boys, mainly because the tube carrying urine from the bladder outside the body is so much shorter in girls, allowing germs to enter the bladder more easily.

Anyone with a blockage to urine flow anywhere within the urinary tract is prone to UTIs. Perhaps some of you experienced a UTI during your pregnancy, because the weight of the pregnant uterus presses on the tubes carrying urine from the kidneys.

The only way to confirm the presence of a UTI is to take a cleanly collected urine sample and culture it to see if any germs are present. Unfortunately, an examination of the urine is frequently overlooked if the diagnosis is not suspected. Looking at urine under the microscope is helpful in making the diagnosis, but it is NOT adequate alone. A urine culture must be taken to confirm the presence of a UTI. Parents of a child with chronic urinary tract infection can be taught how to check the urine at home for signs of infection.

VOMITING (See page 303)

Definition: Vomiting is the process of bringing up stomach contents. It is both more forceful and involves greater volume than simple spitting up or regurgitating.

Cause: Vomiting is commonly caused by a viral infection in the gastrointestinal tract, but can occur as a symptom of numerous other infections, such as urinary-tract infections, strep throat, pneumonia, and others. Vomiting can also be due to noninfectious causes, such as an intestinal blockage, food allergy, a loose muscle between the food pipe (esophagus) and the stomach, and many others.

Symptoms: The child with stomach flu, or gastroenteritis, typically has symptoms of diarrhea and vomiting. She is more likely to vomit after eating milk or solids, especially in large amounts. The child is usually nauseated and has poor appetite. Fever may be present. When vomiting is associated with dehydration, follows a head injury, is associated with lethargy or diminished responsiveness, occurs with abdominal pain or a distended abdomen, or when blood is present in the vomited material, your child should be examined by a physician promptly.

Treatment: Vomiting is usually lessened by feeding the child very small amounts of clear liquids at frequent intervals. You may need to start with as little as a teaspoon and increase from there. Young infants should be given Pedialyte or Lytren, which are balanced sugar and electrolyte solutions specially prepared for young infants. Older babies and children can be given clear juices, flat pop, Jell-O water (made with twice the amount the recipe calls for), broth, et cetera. Soda pop often works best. The purpose is simply to keep down enough fluids to prevent dehydration, provide sugar for energy, and replace electrolytes lost from vomiting. Don't give milk or any solids while the child still has vomiting. With this regimen, vomiting seldom lasts longer than twenty-four hours.

You can purchase an over-the-counter medication known as Emetrol that helps settle the stomach. The dose for children is one teaspoon; wait twenty minutes and offer sips of fluids. You can repeat the dose of Emetrol if necessary.

In general, pediatricians don't like to use prescription medications for vomiting, as they can have side effects in children and really don't work as effectively as the dietary management outlined.

Observing for signs of dehydration is an important part of the treatment of vomiting. Be sure your child is urinating at least once every six hours.

Complications: The most common complication of vomiting is dehydration. (See page 307.) A practical complication is the mess of vomit on clothes and beds. I always taught my kids as soon as they could walk to try to make it to the toilet when they felt like they were going to vomit. Keep a bucket or other collection container around when your child is ill with vomiting.

Prevention: Vomiting can be minimized during an illness by avoiding milk, ice cream, and heavy meals whenever your child has a fever.

Contagion: Vomiting due to a gastrointestinal infection is contagious. Many other causes of vomiting are not.

YEAST INFECTIONS (MONILIA AND THRUSH)

Definition: Yeast are germs that live naturally in our mouths, gastrointestinal tracts, and vaginas in balance with other organisms. When the growth of yeast gets out of balance in proportion to other germs, a yeast infection occurs.

Cause: A yeast infection is more likely to occur after a course of antibiotic treatment that kills bacteria and allows the yeast to overgrow and flourish. Because yeast are so prevalent, nearly every infant develops a yeast infection, either in the mouth or diaper area, at least once during infancy.

Symptoms: Yeast grows best where moisture is present, so the most common sites affected by yeast are the mouth, the diaper area, and skin creases, such as the neck and armpit. Symptoms vary with the site of infection. Yeast in the mouth, known as thrush, causes white patches on the inside of the cheeks and lips, the tongue, and the roof of the mouth. Although milk can appear white on the tongue, yeast won't wipe off as eas-

ily as milk, and yeast also tends to cover the other mouth surfaces described. The baby may be fussy during feedings or have no symptoms at all.

If yeast is present in the mouth, it is likely to be in the rest of the gastrointestinal tract as well. Thus yeast can be excreted with each bowel movement and infect the skin in the diaper area, causing a troublesome rash known as monilia. This rash looks very red with little red bumps, especially at the edge of the rash. Despite your best efforts with over-the-counter ointments and frequent diaper changes, the rash may not improve. Yeast in the groin, neck, and armpit creases often looks like a red, weepy area.

Treatment: Yeast in the mouth is treated by a prescribed medication given by dropper into the mouth, usually four times a day. It may also be necessary to boil your baby's pacifier or bottle nipples daily for the next several days, since yeast is often harbored on the nipples and can be reintroduced. It is important for breast-feeding mothers to air dry their own nipples after nursing an infant with thrush, so their nipples don't become infected by yeast.

Yeast skin infections can be treated by a prescription cream. Frequent drying of the affected area is also important. This may mean you will have to change your baby's diapers more often than usual for a few days, even including temporarily getting up at night to change your sleeping baby's diaper. I have seen many instances where diaper area yeast failed to respond to prescribed medication until the nighttime changes were instituted.

When yeast occurs in an older baby already on solids, you may want to give natural yogurt to the baby daily, especially if she is receiving antibiotics for any reason. The yogurt will reintroduce the natural gut organisms necessary to keep yeast in check.

Complications: Untreated yeast infections may persist and make your baby uncomfortable. Skin rashes can become infected with other germs as well. Serious complications are rare, however.

Prevention: It is almost impossible to prevent yeast infections entirely, since the germs are so common. However, changing your baby's diaper whenever you notice it is wet, air drying her bottom during changes and whenever any skin irritation is apparent, will help minimize chances of infection. Feeding yogurt during treatment with antibiotics will also help prevent yeast infections.

Contagion: Yeast is present in everyone's body and can be readily passed from one person to another. When infection occurs, however, it is usually from the overgrowth of one's own yeast, rather than something that is "caught." Infants first get introduced to yeast by passing through the birth canal, since the vaginas of most pregnant women contain yeast organisms.

Additional Information: Once your child is toilet trained and her skin is no longer in frequent contact with moisture, yeast infections become uncommon. Although vaginal yeast infections are common in women, because of the different pH in the vaginas of little girls, vaginal yeast infections are rare before puberty.

If you would like to read more about these and other childhood medical conditions, I recommed *Your Child's Health* by Barton Schmitt, M.D. (Bantam).

13 Emergencies!

EMERGENCY! The very word quickens your pulse and hastens your breathing. Fortunately, the chances of a medical emergency ever arising can be minimized by routine attention to safety precautions, diligent supervision of our young children, and early medical care for serious illnesses. But only in fairy tales can a parent raise a child who never needs stitches, breaks a bone, chokes momentarily, develops trouble breathing, or has an allergic reaction. It is almost inevitable that your child will someday require your quick and appropriate response in a crisis. Preparing today for such a potential emergency may help you keep a cool head, take effective emergency action, and calm your child instead of panicking unnecessarily.

So STOP! READ THIS SECTION TODAY! Learn the emergency techniques described, implement the safeguards outlined, and review the conditions that follow. Then you will know how to use the information promptly and efficiently should you ever really need it.

First, let me emphasize that, although we cannot prevent every potential crisis in a lifetime, it is certainly true that an ounce of prevention is worth a pound of cure. In fact, the majority of tragic childhood accidents can be averted altogether by these preventive measures.

SAFETY MANDATES FOR PARENTS

1. ALWAYS secure your baby in an approved infant restraint, and your older child with a seat belt, when traveling in an automobile. Begin using your own seat belt if you don't already do so. Enforce this habit when your child travels with others, and NEVER make an exception. A child held on your lap is never safe in a moving automobile. He will become a projectile, crashing against the dashboard, during the smallest fender bender. Your loving arms are powerless to restrain him during an accident and your own weight will crush him. Remember, automobile accidents are the leading single cause of childhood deaths and permanent disability!

2. Remove all poisonous substances from the reach of your child before he can even crawl, and continue to do this until well beyond school age. If your child visits Grandma or anyone else regularly, be sure they take the same precautions. Despite your own diligence at home, your toddler could ingest Grandma's heart medicine while she is babysitting at her house. Keep the number for the regional poison control center near the phone, and always have a bottle of syrup of ipecac in the house in order to induce vomiting if a poisonous substance has been ingested (and *only* if so directed by poison control or your health-care provider. They will advise you how much to give.).

3. Set the thermostat on your hot-water heater at 124° F. This single maneuver would prevent more than half of all burn accidents to infants and children. Test the temperature of your own hot water by letting it run a few minutes from the tap that is closest to your water heater. Then use a meat, candy, or water thermometer to measure the temperature. If it is above 124° F, turn the thermostat on your hot-water heater down to a lower setting and wait a day for the water to reach the new temperature before testing it again.

4. NEVER keep a loaded firearm in your home if children will ever be present. Many tragedies are caused by the accidental discharging of loaded guns by small children. If you own a gun, unload it and store the ammunition separately from the gun.

5. Install a smoke detector on every level of your home. Small children are powerless to protect themselves in case of a fire, and they can be overcome by smoke inhalation within a few minutes.

6. NEVER leave your young child home alone, not even for a few minutes. It is appalling how often parents will "take a chance" by leaving the baby in his crib or their preschooler playing alone while they run an errand, drive the babysitter home, take their partner to work, or whatever. Almost all of us have done it, yet it is absolutely foolish and totally irresponsible. Don't ever take this chance with your baby or youngster.

7. NEVER leave your child with a babysitter under twelve years of age or in an environment where there are too many children and too few caretakers. Review with babysitters how to respond appropriately in an emergency.

8. Get rid of dangerous pets before bringing a baby into your home. I recall with horror an infant whose ears were viciously chewed off by a wild ferret kept as a pet. Infants have been crushed by pet boa constrictors, mauled by dogs, or clawed by cats. If you have a dangerous or exotic pet, or an aggressive young male dog or one that is skittish around children, find a new home for the animal to avoid placing your child at risk.

9. Institute age-appropriate safety precautions in your home, including covering electrical outlets, keeping electrical cords from the reach of toddlers, buying safe toys, barricading stairways from crawling infants and toddlers, keeping matches away from *all* children, turning pot handles against the wall, and using the back burners on the stove.

10. NEVER leave an infant or small child alone for even an instant in a tub or near a pond, ditch, or pool of water. Never take a child onto a boat or flotation device without having him wear a life vest.

11. NEVER bicycle with a child unless you are a proficient cycler yourself. Always have the child wear a helmet and secure him appropriately in a passenger seat. If the child is old enough to ride alone and you are riding with him, keep your bike behind his.

12. DO NOT allow youngsters under the age of four years to eat nuts, popcorn, hard candy, pitted fruits, raw carrots, celery, or other food items they might choke on, and don't permit children to eat small foods while traveling in the car.

13. NEVER allow your toddler or preschooler to play in the street or driveway.

Although half of all children will be injured each year severely enough to require medical attention or to require restriction of their activities, it is probable that by adhering to these outlined safety mandates, your own child will be among those who escape injury. Meanwhile, the following guidelines will help you respond to emergencies that do arise.

EMERGENCY READINESS GUIDELINES

1. Keep your physician's phone number handy and know how to call other emergency resources, such as the fire department, police, ambulance, poison control, paramedics, and the nearest emergency room that cares for children. As soon as your child is able, teach him to dial "0" and to ask for help should an emergency arise. If he can say the name of his street and knows not to hang up the phone, the call can be traced and help can be sent even if something has happened to you.

I recently saw a fifteen-year-old girl who called her mother at work when the house was on fire instead of calling the fire department. Fortunately, her mother was able to mobilize help in time to rescue the girl, but I couldn't help wondering what would have happened if her mother had been out of the office. We need to prepare ourselves to react in an emergency as well as review age-appropriate responses with our children from time to time.

2. Learn to perform cardiopulmonary resuscitation (CPR). Take a CPR class so that you can respond calmly and effectively in a life-threatening emergency involving a victim of any age. Take a first-aid course, too. Your preparation may allow you to make the life-saving difference to someone someday, either a member of your own family or a complete stranger.

3. Keep the following items stocked in your medicine cabinet for use in minor emergencies.

√ syrup of ipecac to induce vomiting in the case of poisonous ingestions. NEVER administer ipecac, however, without directions from a poison control center

√ or your physician, since there are a few ingested
   substances that should NOT be vomited, such as lye
√ hydrogen peroxide (3 percent) to cleanse cuts and
   other wounds (although soap and water are quite
   adequate)
√ topical antibiotic ointment, such as Bacitracin, for
   covering minor wounds
√ Benadryl elixir or 25 mg capsules (prescription no
   longer necessary), to be administered in case of an
   allergic reaction while you seek medical care. The
   dose is 1 teaspoon of elixir per 25 pounds or one 25
   mg capsule for a 50-pound child
√ Band-Aids, gauze pads, and adhesive tape to cover
   wounds and keep them clean
√ material to be used as a tourniquet in the event of a
   severe reaction to multiple bee stings, a poisonous
   spider or snake bite. String, rubber tubing, or a strip of
   cloth can be used. Tying the tourniquet around a bitten
   extremity between the bite and the body will minimize
   the amount of toxin absorbed into the body while
   medical help can be sought. The tourniquet should be
   tight enough to make the veins stand out but not tight
   enough to cut off the pulse. Release the tourniquet for
   a few seconds every fifteen minutes
√ an Ace bandage to be used to support a joint that has
   been sprained or a muscle that has been strained. In the
   case of a possible broken bone, a magazine can be wrapped
   around the extremity and held in place by the Ace bandage until you reach medical care
√ tweezers to remove splinters or stingers

In an emergency, there is no time to learn how to
perform CPR, the Heimlich Maneuver, back blow, chest
thrust, or stop heavy bleeding. Take the time today to
learn these procedures so that you can respond efficiently
if you ever need to carry them out.

Pressure Points

Even severe bleeding will usually stop when firm, direct
pressure is applied over the wound. In the rare event that

hemorrhage cannot be controlled by direct pressure, it can be helpful to know the location of the major arteries of the body. Pressure over the artery between the wound and the body will help stop the hermorrhaging. Pulsations in the major arteries in the extremities can be felt as follows: the brachial arteries in the elbow crease, the radial arteries in the wrist crease, and the femoral arteries in the groin. Try to find these pulses on your own body.

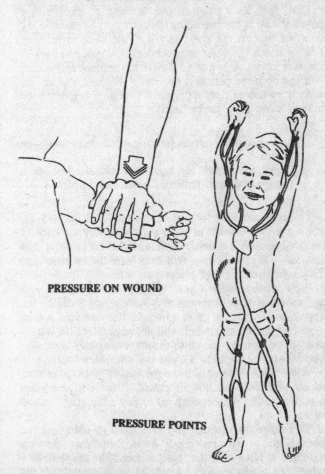

PRESSURE ON WOUND

PRESSURE POINTS

CPR

In the event a child's breathing or heartbeat, or both, ever stops (for example, with severe trauma or electrocution), both functions need to be restored immediately until professional help arrives. Each minute lost in returning his pulse and maintaining his body's oxygenation will diminish his chances for survival and full recovery.

First, feel for a pulse in one or more of the pressure points shown in the preceding illustration. You can also lay your ear against the chest to tell if the heart is beating. Briefly watch the chest for breathing motions and look at the skin color. A mirror held next to the nose and mouth will fog up if the person is breathing. Without a heart rate and/or respiratory rate, a person will rapidly begin to look blue or ashen gray. Immediately:

√ Call or send someone for help—but don't leave the victim.

√ Check the mouth for vomited material, gum, or a foreign body and remove it with your fingers.

To begin breathing for a child, lay him on a flat surface. Place a folded blanket or other padding under the back of his head to raise it about an inch, and pull the jaw and chin forward. This positioning will help open the air passages. Tiny infants can be laid across your arm.

With a baby under a year of age, cover both his nose and mouth with your mouth and blow gentle puffs of air, approximately twenty times a minute. Remove your mouth after each breath and the air will automatically flow out. If you are performing mouth-to-mouth respirations correctly, you should see the baby's chest rise with each breath.

With older children, cover the mouth with your own mouth and pinch the nostrils closed. Breathe fifteen times a minute, using only enough air to move the chest up and down.

To restore circulation, you will have to compress the breastbone, or sternum, firmly against the heart. Be sure the child is lying on a flat, hard surface, like the floor or a table, not a bed or sofa. Apply pressure directly in the

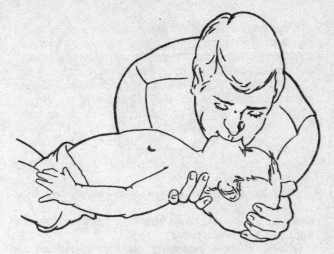

MOUTH-TO-MOUTH RESUSCITATION

midline over the breastbone, or else your compressions will be ineffective and you will break ribs.

For an infant under a year, use the index and middle fingers of your dominant hand to push down on the midportion of the breastbone between 100 and 120 times a minute. The sternum should depress about ½" to 1½" each time you compress the chest.

In a child over one year, you can press with all four fingers together, or use the base of one hand to apply more pressure. The older the child, the firmer pressure will be needed and the fewer compressions per minute. A child over one year would require 80 to 100 beats per minute and the breastbone should depress about 1" to 1½". If your chest compressions are effective, you or a companion should be able to feel a pulse with each heartbeat at one of the pressure points described.

If help is available, one of you should breathe for the child while the other compresses the chest. Give one breath after each five chest compressions. If you are alone, you will have to both breathe for the child and provide cardiac

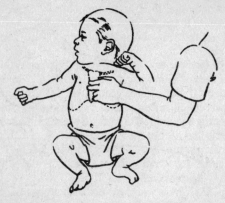

METHOD OF CHEST COMPRESSION FOR AN INFANT

massage. To do this, pause after each ten chest compressions and give two breaths.

Obviously, these maneuvers are very specialized and require instruction and practice if they are to be performed effectively. If you ever need to use CPR, it will probably involve only a few quick breaths to restore breathing if your baby turns blue. Although it is unlikely that you will ever need to perform sustained CPR, in order to do so successfully, you should take a formal course through the Red Cross, local fire station, or other community organizations. In these courses, you receive written instructions as well as practice with both adult and infant models, so you can be sure of the right amount of pressure to use to compress the heart and how hard to blow to inflate the lungs. Without such expertise, CPR can lead to broken ribs or be ineffective. NEVER try to learn CPR on a real person who doesn't need it, as you can cause serious internal injuries.

Heimlich Maneuver or Abdominal Thrust

The Heimlich Maneuver has been credited with saving many lives from sudden obstruction of the windpipe, or trachea, by inhaled food particles. It is now taught to restaurant workers and medical personnel. The idea behind the maneuver is that there is always some extra air in the air sacs of the lungs. If a piece of food has blocked the trachea, forcing this remaining air out of the lungs can blow the object out.

Heimlich Maneuver: The Heimlich Maneuver should be performed *only* if a choking victim's airway is completely obstructed or if he is unconscious. If he can breathe at all, his own cough reflex should be allowed to cough out the obstructing material. To perform the Heimlich Maneuver, encircle the victim with your arms from behind and lock your hands into a fist, with the thumb side against the victim's abdomen. Your arms should be just below the lower ribs but above the waist. While leaning the victim forward, give a firm upward squeeze, known as an abdominal thrust, with your fists against the victim's abdomen. You can repeat the maneuver four to five times. The food particle will be forcefully expelled from the trachea as air is pushed out of the lungs. To perform the maneuver on a small child, place him on his back and kneel next to him. Place the heel of one hand on the child's abdomen in the midline between the belly button and the rib cage. Give a series of 6 to 10 rapid inward and upward thrusts until the foreign body is expelled. The Heimlich maneuver is not presently approved for use in children under one year of age. Back blows and chest compressions (see pages 402, 404) are recommended instead for young infants.

Back Blows: If the Heimlich Maneuver fails to expel the obstructing material, other measures for relieving airway obstruction should be attempted immediately. With the heel of your hand, deliver four sharp blows rapidly and forcefully between the shoulder blades. An infant should be draped over your arm head down, and a larger child can be draped over your lap. These back blows may dislodge the foreign body, and a repeated Heimlich Maneuver may then force it out.

Chest Thrusts: If back blows are unsuccessful, four chest thrusts should also be tried. These can be performed, just as is done in external cardiac massage, with the child lying on his back, preferably with his head lower than his body. Or, you can place your arms under his armpits to encircle his chest. Grab one fist with the other hand and

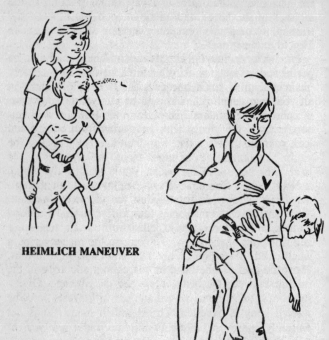

HEIMLICH MANEUVER

BACK BLOWS

place the thumb side on the middle of the breastbone. Press inward with quick backward thrusts.

Remember, a combination of methods may be necessary to dislodge a foreign body in the airway. Don't give up; keep trying all three methods.

Now that you have rehearsed these procedures mentally or on a mannequin (never on a person who doesn't need it), incorporated routine safety precautions into your daily life, and reviewed the guidelines for handling emergencies, you are prepared to respond efficiently and calmly in an emergency. The following outline of various medical crises provides specific plans of action and caution against commonly performed practices that are harmful. Remember, in any emergency: Calmly reassure your child; remain with him throughout all evaluations and procedures if possible; stroke, sing to, or otherwise comfort him; and explain everything that might seem foreign to him. Regardless of your own level of anxiety, always try to convey to him a calm and confident manner. Your presence will help assure your child that what is being done to him by others has your approval.

ANAPHYLAXIS (SEVERE ALLERGIC REACTION INCLUDING BEE STINGS)

What: A severe allergic reaction (anaphylaxis) can immediately follow exposure to certain medicines, bee stings, insect bites, and, rarely, foods or other substances. An itchy, weltlike rash may erupt, and in severe cases, the child's air passages may swell shut. Often, the child has had a previous serious reaction to the same substance.

Danger Signs and Dangers: Difficulty breathing manifested by wheezing or a harsh noise, pale and anxious appearance, chest pain, nausea, vomiting, stomach cramps or diarrhea are all worrisome signs indicating the need for immediate medical attention. Shock and complete respiratory arrest can occur without prompt medical intervention.

1. DO get the child to a hospital or emergency room immediately. Call an ambulance if necessary.

2. DO give the child an antihistamine, such as Benadryl. Give a teaspoon of Benadryl for every twenty-five pounds of weight (up to one hundred pounds).

3. If the reaction is from one or more bee stings and the stinger(s) is still present, DO remove it by scraping it off with your fingernail or using tweezers. Apply an ice cube to the sting.

4. If a severe reaction results from an insect bite or one or more bee sting(s) on an extremity, DO tie a tourniquet around the bitten arm or leg between the bite and the body, in order to decrease the absorption of poison into the body. The tourniquet should be tight enough to make the veins stand out, but not so tight as to turn the extremity white or cut off the pulse. Release the tourniquet for a few seconds every fifteen minutes.

5. If you own a bee-sting kit because of a previous severe reaction, DO give a premeasured injection of epinephrine if you are sure the dose is correct for your child.

6. DO raise the child's legs if he looks very pale.

1. DON'T delay getting the child to a hospital if he appears to be suffering a severe reaction. In the case of a severe reaction, injectable drugs will be needed, as well as oxygen and other forms of treatment you don't have at home. Severe allergic reactions can be life-threatening.

2. If the reaction is due to a bee sting, DON'T squeeze the stinger when removing it.

Prevention: Never allow your child to be given an antibiotic or other medicine, especially in injectable form, to which he has reacted in the past. Don't give him foods to which he is known to be allergic. Keep an antihistamine on hand in your home, especially if your child has had a previous allergic reaction. Ask your child's physician to prescribe

an emergency kit (Ana-Kit) to use in case of bee stings if your child has had a severe reaction to a bee sting in the past. A child who has had a previous anaphylactic reaction to a bee sting should be referred to an allergist for hyposensitization treatments to prevent a future reaction.

BLOODY NOSE (EPISTAXIS)

What: Nosebleeds are common in young children and are usually due to dryness of the nasal passage, combined with picking the nose, which all children do from time to time. A nosebleed can also be caused by an upper-respiratory infection, trauma to the nose, high blood pressure, or a bleeding disorder. Most often the bleeding comes from the front part of the nose and will stop promptly with continuous pressure to the tip of the nose.

Danger Signs and Dangers: Young children often swallow the blood from a bloody nose. This can be very irritating to the stomach and cause vomiting and/or diarrhea. Also it can mask the amount of blood lost, since you can't see how much blood was swallowed.

1. DO pinch the nostrils closed and hold steady pressure for at least ten minutes. Ask your child to breathe through his mouth.

2. DO have the child lean forward so the blood will not run down his throat. Give him something to spit blood into.

3. DO try to estimate the amount of blood lost and seek medical attention if your child is lightheaded when he stands up or has fainted (these symptoms suggest excessive blood loss), the bloody nose has lasted longer than thirty minutes, or hasn't stopped with two trials of direct pressure for ten minutes each.

4. DO report repeated bloody noses or a bloody nose that occurs in a child with unexplained bruises to your child's physician. A medical problem could be present.

1. DON'T lean the child backward, or he will be forced to swallow blood.

2. DON'T peek every few minutes to see how the nosebleed is doing. Each time you release pressure to peek, the clot can wash off and bleeding will start again.

3. DON'T apply a cold cloth to your child's forehead or back of his neck; it doesn't hurt, but it doesn't help either.

Prevention: Try to discourage your child from picking his nose. You can apply a thin layer of petroleum jelly to the inside of the nostrils along the center wall, using the tip of your little finger or a Q-tip. You'll probably only need to do this every few days to keep the nasal passage moist and decrease irritation. Running a humidifier in your child's room might also help prevent dryness of the nasal lining.

BROKEN BONES

What: Young children are less likely to break bones than older people, since their bones are less calcified. The first bone to calcify is the clavicle, or collarbone, which is commonly broken by a fall onto the shoulder. A fall onto the wrist can break the bones in the forearm. The bones in the lower leg are much more easily fractured than the long bone in the thigh.

Danger Signs and Dangers: Severe tenderness at one spot over a bone, pain upon movement of the area, or swelling over a bone after an injury each suggest a fracture. Fractures in young children should also be suspected if a child begins to limp, won't use one extremity, or an infant cries inconsolably. Compound fractures, or those that break the skin, are at great risk of infection. Fractures through the part of an arm or leg bone known as the growth plate may affect ultimate bone length. Multiple fractures, or unexplained fractures, should always raise the suspicion of child abuse.

1. DO immobilize an extremity that is obviously or possibly broken while you seek medical attention. For an arm or shoulder, you can use a triangular piece of cloth to fashion a sling. For a leg injury, wrap the extremity in a magazine surrounded loosely by an Ace bandage and carry the child to prevent putting weight on the injured part.

2. DO bring your child to medical attention for any injury following which he won't use the extremity.

3. DO bring your child to medical attention for any poorly explained injury that occurred with another caretaker.

4. DO apply a sterile dressing to an open fracture, splint it, and take special care not to move the limb while you seek medical attention.

1. DON'T move the affected extremity unnecessarily; further damage can occur.

2. DON'T move a child with a neck or back injury until an ambulance arrives.

Prevention: Most preschool injuries severe enough to cause fractures occur from car accidents or child abuse. You can prevent the former by regularly using car restraints. You can prevent the latter by careful screening of all caretakers with whom you leave your child and by seeking help yourself if you ever feel you are losing control with your child.

BRUISES

What: A bruise is usually the result of trauma that breaks blood vessels under the skin and causes bleeding into the skin. The bleeding turns the tissues blue-black or purplish at first, and as the blood is gradually absorbed by the body, the discoloration changes to blue-green, yellow-green, and yellowish. It may take a week or more for a bruise to fade completely.

Danger Signs and Dangers: A bruise that is growing in size is worrisome, as it suggests that the bleeding is ongoing. A bruise over certain places may be alarming, such as: abdominal bruising (an organ may have been ruptured); bruising around the eyes or behind the ears after head trauma (suggests skull fracture); bruises that cannot be explained by the nature of the injury (suggests child abuse); bruises that occurred without trauma (suggests a bleeding problem). In the case of severe trauma, massive bruising may be associated with severe blood loss, which may lead to shock.

1. DO apply a cold compress or ice bag to the bruised area for twenty to thirty minutes to help stop bleeding.

1. DON'T apply a warm compress until twenty-four hours after the injury. Heat may cause additional bleeding to occur.

Prevention: All children will receive minor bruises as they learn to walk and experience occasional falls. Major bruises can be prevented by following routine safety precautions and using automotive restraints. "Easy bruising" may suggest a disorder in the normal blood-clotting mecha-

nisms, and so should be reported to your physician.

BURNS

What: A burn is a thermal injury to the skin that can be caused by hot liquids (e.g., water, coffee), hot objects (e.g., radiators, cigarettes), flames, electricity, or lightning (see page 417). Burns are classified by severity as first degree (redness of skin only); second degree (blistering); and third degree (full-thickness of skin involved). Third-degree burns will always scar and often require skin grafts. A first- or second-degree burn can rapidly progress to third degree by infection. The skin of infants and children is far more sensitive to heat than that of adults, so babies can be severely burned faster than adults and at lower temperatures.

Danger Signs and Dangers: The seriousness of a burn depends on three things: the degree of burn (first, second, or third); the extent of the burned area (the percent of body surface area affected); and the location of the burn (face, hands, and genital areas are the most worrisome). ALL second- and third-degree burns in infants and children should be seen by a physician. Hospitalization is often required for severe burns to provide local therapy to prevent infection and to provide intravenous fluids, since large volumes of fluid are lost into burned areas and shock can occur.

1. DO immediately run cold water over the burned area. This will help minimize the degree of burn injury and will feel soothing to your child.

2. DO cover the burned area with antibiotic ointment and a clean bandage. If the burned area is too large to cover with bandages, apply a clean cloth. First- and second-degree burns are very painful when exposed to air. (Third-degree burns are often painless initially because of nerve damage.)

3. DO bring a child who has sustained any third-degree burn or a second-degree burn larger than a quarter to the physician or emergency room.

4. DO bring for medical care a child who has been burned on the hands, face, or genitals, regardless of the size or degree of burn.

5. DO seek prompt medical attention for any burn that appears infected several days later (weeping pus, growing area of redness a-round burn, fever in the child).

6. DO bring your burned child for a DPT injection if he did not complete his primary series, or for a tetanus booster if he has not had one within five years. Burns are prime sites for introduction of tetanus infection.

1. DON'T apply butter or oil to a burn. Butter contains salt, which will make the burn hurt more, and applying such foodstuffs may also introduce infection.

2. DON'T break burn blisters. They will rupture on their own, but while they are present they provide protection from infection. Breaking them may introduce infection. When they do break on their own, carefully remove the loose skin.

3. DON'T try to treat significant burns at home. If a burn becomes infected, it can rapidly extend to a higher degree, with serious complications.

Prevention: Most burns can be prevented by instituting routine age-appropriate safety measures, installing smoke detectors in the home, discarding old and unsafe electrical appliances and hot-water vaporizers, and replacing frayed electrical cords. Turning the thermostat on your hot-water heater down to 124° F will prevent more than half of childhood burns. Burn complications, including infection, fluid loss, and permanent disability can be minimized by prompt medical attention for all significant burns.

CHOKING

What: Choking can occur with milk, mucus, small objects, or solid food particles. The main windpipe (trachea) may be obstructed, or the material may be sucked into the bronchial tubes of the lungs. The degree of distress depends on the location of the obstruction.

Danger Signs and Dangers: The child may appear to make gasping movements but be unable to move air into the lungs or make any sounds. He may turn blue, cough, and gag. After initial choking, he may appear to have recovered. If he makes a wheezy noise with breathing afterward or continues to have coughing spells, this suggests that the foreign body is still lodged in the bronchial tubes. Failure to remove such particles can lead to pneumonia, collapsed lung, and other complications.

1. DO tilt the child forward and slap him on the back between the shoulder blades if he is choking on an object and not moving any air into his lungs.

2. DO look into the child's mouth with a flashlight to see if there is an object you can remove with your fingers.

3. DO perform a Heimlich Maneuver (abdominal thrusts) and chest thrusts if an object seems to be lodged in the main windpipe and is obstructing breathing (see page 402). Repeat back blows, too.

4. DO seek medical care after a choking spell if the child continues to cough or make a wheezy noise with breathing.

1. DON'T stick your finger down the child's throat unless there is a long object you could pull out, such as a balloon. If the object is round and smooth, like a marble, it is more likely you will push it down farther and completely obstruct the child's breathing. Perform abdominal thrusts or back blows and chests thrusts instead.

2. DON'T slap or pound on the child's back if he is breathing adequately between coughing. Let him catch his breath on his own.

3. DON'T assume that all is well just because the immediate choking spell is over. If the child coughs or wheezes, especially after choking on peanuts or popcorn, it is probable that particles are still in his lungs and prompt medical care should be sought.

Prevention: Most choking episodes can be prevented by not allowing children under four years of age to eat peanuts, popcorn, raw carrots, and other food items on which they might choke. Age-appropriate toys should be selected so that infants do not have access to small objects. Marbles, jacks, and other small toys should NEVER be allowed in the mouth. A newborn should be put down to sleep on his abdomen, and an infant should not be made to drink from a propped bottle.

CONVULSION

What: A convulsion, or seizure, is a sudden jerking movement of the body in response to an area of irritation in the brain. A brief, isolated seizure can occur, or rarely, seizures continue several hours without stopping and can be life-threatening. Both the convulsion itself, as well as the underlying cause, warrant treatment and investigation. Children who have seizure disorders will need to take long-term medication to prevent further seizures (see page 350).

Danger signs and Dangers: Any seizure is worrisome, unless it occurs with expected frequency in a child with a known seizure disorder. A first-time seizure is cause for concern, and the child should be seen promptly to determine the cause. Any seizure with fever should prompt a medical evaluation of the child to be sure he doesn't have meningitis. A seizure following head trauma suggests serious head injury.

1. DO take the child to your physician or emergency room promptly if it is a first-time seizure. If he has had previous seizures, call to report this one if it is in any way out of the ordinary.

2. DO gently restrain the child during the seizure to be sure he doesn't hurt himself.

3. DO observe to be sure the seizure is not affecting the child's breathing and he is not turning blue.

4. DO roll him to the side in case any vomiting occurs, and try to keep his mouth clear of any vomited material.

1. DON'T try to put something hard into the child's mouth to keep him from biting his tongue. It is more likely that the hard object will cause bleeding and potential choking. As long as he is not blue, he is breathing adequately and is not choking on his tongue.

2. DON'T try to give him any medicines, such as acetaminophen, while he is having a convulsion, as he is likely to choke on it.

3. DON'T dismiss a convulsion as a minor occurrence.

Prevention: Many convulsions can't be prevented. If your child has a known seizure disorder, giving him his prescribed medication regularly will help prevent convulsions.

CUTS

What: A cut can be superficial or deep, minor or involve vital structures, relatively clean or heavily contaminated, smooth or jagged.

Danger Signs and Dangers: A cut is worrisome if it bleeds heavily, seems to have resulted in impaired function of the part, or is very dirty. Puncture wounds are more likely to become infected. Signs of infection include redness around the wound, pus visible within the wound or coming from it, increasing tenderness of the wound, the onset of a fever, red streaking of the skin around the wound, or swelling. Cuts that sever an artery and produce pulsatile, brisk bleeding could cause life-threatening hemorrhage.

1. DO stop bleeding by pressing with a clean bandage or cloth over the bleeding part. For severe wounds causing hemorrhaging, direct pressure over the artery supplying the injured area may be necessary. (See pages 398 and 423-24.)

2. DO cleanse the wound with soap and water, followed by hydrogen peroxide (3 percent) if available.

3. DO take your child for a tetanus booster if he has been cut with an unclean object or received a puncture wound, and he never completed the primary series of DPT injections or has not had a tetanus booster within the past five years.

4. DO take your child to your physician or emergency room for sutures if: bleeding continues after five minutes of direct pressure; the wound is more than 1/8″ deep; the cut is jagged or wide or appears that it will heal with an unattractive scar; the injury involves the face or hand; the wound is filled with asphalt, pencil lead, or other debris that will leave a permanent tattoo and needs to be cleaned out.

5. DO have stitches removed at the scheduled time. Different parts of the body heal at different rates. Wounds may reopen if stitches are taken out too soon, but excessive scarring will occur if they are left in too long.

6. DO bring your child in if a wound appears to be infected several days later.

1. DON'T squeeze a wound to make it bleed more for cleansing purposes. Wash it well with soap and water instead.

2. DON'T use alcohol to cleanse a wound. Alcohol will burn and is a poor disinfectant.

3. DON'T insist on a tetanus booster for every wound. Most of us received far more tetanus shots as youngsters than were ever warranted, sometimes causing adverse reactions. We routinely need tetanus boosters only every ten years; for dirty wounds or puncture wounds, every five years.

Prevention: Your child will have many cuts and mi-

nor wounds. Most serious injuries can be prevented by instituting safety precautions at home and the use of car restraints when traveling. Infections can be prevented by thorough immediate cleansing of wounds, covering them with antibiotic ointment, and keeping a clean dressing on them.

DENTAL INJURY

What: Trauma to the teeth usually results from falling. Teeth can be knocked out, chipped, or permanently discolored. All chips that extend beyond the most superficial enamel layer of the tooth will require dental attention.

Danger Signs and Dangers: Any discoloration of teeth, dislodged teeth, loose teeth, cracked teeth, chips larger than about one-fifth of the tooth, or injured teeth that are cold-sensitive should be seen promptly by a dentist. Possible dangers are bleeding from the tooth or surrounding gums; immediate loss of teeth; later onset of severe pain in the damaged tooth; later onset of serious infection within the tooth, which can lead to permanent damage to the tooth nerve; unrecognized damage to the forming permanent tooth and later cosmetic problems. In the case of small babies, a loose tooth that falls out can cause choking.

1. DO call a perodontist or a dentist with much experience in children's dentistry promptly and arrange to have the damaged tooth examined if any of the danger signs are present.

2. DO pick up teeth that are knocked out and gently rinse them off without handling the root. Reinsert them in the gums if they are *permanent* teeth and get to a dentist promptly, within an hour.

3. DO keep your child on a soft diet for three days if any teeth are loose.

4. DO contact a dentist if dental pain begins a week or two after dental trauma.

1. DON'T assume that trauma is insignificant simply because the child has no immediate pain. A traumatized tooth may be numb for a week or more before severe pain ensues. Meanwhile, an abscess may have formed at the root.

Prevention: In older children, maloccluded or crooked teeth are prone to injury, so getting braces for a child who needs them will not only correct his bite, but will also help protect his teeth. Generally, protecting children from falls by safety-proofing the home will help prevent dental injuries, as will being safely restrained while traveling in the car. Don't let small children run with lollipops, toys—anything!—in their mouths.

DOG (AND OTHER ANIMAL) BITES

What: Dog and cat bites are common among toddlers and young children, since their unpredictable movements often frighten animals. The majority of bites are inflicted by large males of aggressive breeds. Risks of dog and cat bites include infection, permanent scarring, and the remote but very real chance of introducing rabies. Death can occur rapidly if the animal attacks the child's throat.

Danger Signs and Dangers: In general, the risk of dog and cat bites becoming infected is so great that stitching them closed is seldom attempted. Unsutured wounds can leave unattractive scars, however. Stitches are sometimes used with bites of the face, after extensive cleansing of the wound. Prophylactic antibiotics and close follow-up are necessary. Fever, swelling, redness, or tenderness of the wound are signs of infection.

1. DO try to stop the attack by pulling the animal's jaws apart. Pouring cold water on the dog or cat may also make him loose his grip. Be prepared to kill the animal if he is attacking the child's throat.

2. DO capture and detain the dog or cat and determine the status of its health and rabies immunizations.

3. DO wash the wound immediately with soap and water for five to ten minutes.

4. DO bring any child with a dog or cat bite that breaks the skin, especially on the hands or face, into the office, clinic, or emergency room so that careful cleansing can be performed and antibiotics can be prescribed if indicated.

5. DO bring in any child with a dog or cat bite whose primary series of DPT shots is incomplete, or who has not had a booster in the past five years, so that a tetanus booster can be given.

6. DO consider at risk for rabies a child who was bitten in an unprovoked attack by a skunk, raccoon, fox, bat, or unknown or ill-appearing dog or cat.

7. DO report the attack to authorities so that the dog or cat will be known to be dangerous. Occasionally, animals with repeated attacks will be disposed of, and rightly so.

1. DON'T pull the child from the jaws of a dog, as further injury may occur; pry the jaws apart.

2. DON'T lose track of a dog or cat that has bitten your child. The animal should be observed for ten days afterward to be sure it doesn't show signs of rabies.

3. DON'T keep a dog or cat that has bitten children. Get rid of it promptly before a tragedy occurs. Such a pet is a time bomb.

Prevention: The chances of your child receiving a dog or cat bite can be minimized by teaching your child not to pet strange dogs or cats and not to make rapid movements around animals or approach them while they are eating. Also remind your child that no matter how friendly the animal seems toward anyone else, he is still a stranger to the animal. Complications of bites can be prevented by careful cleansing of the wound and prompt medical attention, both immediately and if signs of infection appear later. Children should be taught never to approach *any* wild animal, not even a cute little squirrel, and especially not one that is sick or injured or in the presence of its babies.

DROWNING

What: Drowning is the third most common cause of accidental death of children in the United States. Toddlers are especially at risk. They can panic and drown in even a few inches of water. During drowning, the airway goes into spasm and the body's supply of oxygen is cut off.

Danger Signs and Dangers: Within seconds of being under water, the body begins to be deprived of oxygen. By two to four minutes, the circulation is impaired, and within six minutes of submersion, irreversible brain damage may begin. By the time you pull a drowned child from water, both his heart and respiration may have stopped.

1. DO begin mouth-to-mouth resuscitation IMMEDIATELY after quickly clearing any material from the mouth. Every minute counts! You may have to do mouth-to-mouth while treading water yourself.

2. *DO* begin external cardiac massage if you cannot detect a pulse or heartbeat.

3. DO send someone to call an ambulance and administer oxygen as soon as it is available.

4. DO turn the child's head to the side if he begins to vomit. Drowning victims usually swallow lots of water and vomit easily.

1. DON'T stop CPR until the child reaches a medical facility. In coldwater drowning, children have miraculously survived long periods of submersion and have eventually recovered.

2. DON'T waste precious time trying to drain water out of the lungs. Just start mouth-to-mouth resuscitation.

3. DON'T bend or twist the neck if there is a chance of neck injury, for example, if the victim has suffered a diving accident.

Prevention: Constant vigilance will prevent most childhood drownings. Never turn your back on your child in the tub, near a pool, at the beach, or anywhere near water. Teach your child to swim at an early age. See that all members of a boating party wear life jackets.

ELECTRICAL SHOCK (AND LIGHTNING INJURY)

What: Injury by electrical shock or lightning is very

similar. Both can damage the heart and nervous system and cause local burns from intense heat. The degree of injury depends on the duration of contact with the electrical source, the type of current (AC is more dangerous), and the path it takes in the body. It can range from a minor burn to full cardiac and respiratory arrest. A common electrical injury in children is a mouth burn from biting an electrical cord.

Danger Signs and Dangers: An electrical injury leaves entry and exit burns where the current enters and leaves the body. There is usually a period of impaired neurologic function, such as headache, tingling, paralysis, or inability to speak. Heart damage often occurs, including a heart attack, irregular heartbeat, or complete cardiac arrest. The eardrums can be ruptured, causing hearing loss or ringing in the ears.

Children with lip and mouth burns should be hospitalized for several days since hemorrhage can occur when the damaged skin sloughs later. Unfortunately, scarring at the corner of the mouth always occurs, but it can be repaired by plastic surgery later.

1. DO interrupt the power source or knock the wire away from the skin with a wooden pole or other non-conducting material.

2. DO begin mouth-to-mouth resuscitation and/or external cardiac massage immediately as indicated.

3. DO look for entry and exit burns. The former resembles a sharply defined, painless, gray area with a charred center, while the latter is less distinct and may be larger.

4. DO bring for medical care every child with an electrical burn or who has been struck by lightning. The degree of burn can look deceptively minor, while the extent of tissue destruction may be apparent only later. An EKG (electrocardiogram) may be needed to be sure the heart wasn't damaged.

1. DON'T be misled into thinking that the burn is minor; it may take days or weeks to tell the full extent.

Prevention: Cover all exposed electrical outlets with safety plugs. Don't let small children play unsupervised with electrical toys. Teach children not to fly kites in the vicinity of high wires or during stormy weather. Instruct children to come indoors whenever they see lightning in the area and to fall quickly to the ground if their hair ever stands on end during an electrical storm.

EYE INJURY

What: Eye, or ocular, injuries include black eyes or injuries to the tissues around the eye and injuries to the eye itself by blunt trauma, cigarette burns, splintering objects, et cetera. Superficial injuries and foreign bodies are common on the white portion of the eye, or sclera, and the colored part of the eye, or cornea.

Danger Signs and Dangers: The biggest worry about eye injuries is that vision will be permanently affected. A foreign body, scratch, or chemical spilled onto the cornea may affect vision, whereas mild injuries to the white portion of the eye will not, even though such injuries might make the white portion bright red. A painful eye, tearing eye, or any eye experiencing significant trauma should be seen promptly, as well as any eye in which impaired vision is suspected.

1. DO rinse the eye generously with lukewarm tap water whenever a chemical has been spilled into the eye. Wrap the child in a towel and pour tap water from a cup into his eye continuously for ten to fifteen minutes. Refill the cup as often as necessary. You don't need to keep his eye pried open the whole time, but keep pouring. If you choose to hold his head under the tap, use a low-pressure stream. Keep his head turned sideways.

2. DO cover an injured eye with the lid shut with gauze, and tape lightly until you can get to a physician.

1. DON'T let the child rub his eye, as this may cause more damage.

2. DON'T attempt to remove foreign bodies lodged in the eye. Further trauma may be inflicted.

Prevention: Eye injuries can be prevented by not allowing infants to play with toys with sharp points, not smoking in the presence of small children, and not allowing children to play with kittens or other pets near their faces.

FAINTING

What: Fainting is falling down and being unconscious for a brief period. It is uncommon in young children, but occurs more often in adolescents. It can occur from overheating, standing too long, getting too excited, hyperventilating, or having a breath-holding spell (see page 321).

Danger Signs and Dangers: Fainting is usually a benign condition, unless the child injures himself falling. The greater danger is that a serious condition is mistaken for mere fainting. For example, could the child have suffered a head injury and passed out because of that? Did the child actually have a seizure, shaking and jerking while unconscious? Does he have a medical problem, such as hypoglycemia or a heart defect, causing him to pass out?

1. DO keep your child lying down with his feet elevated for at least ten minutes after fainting.

2. DO talk to your child about what may have upset him and give him something to drink.

3. DO seek medical care if your child is not back to normal within an hour or if he ever faints again.

1. DON'T use smelling salts to arouse your child. They are very irritating, and he will arouse on his own.

Prevention: Teach your child not to lock his knees when standing for a long period. This prevents recirculation of the blood. He should periodically flex his knees and tighten and relax his leg muscles.

FROSTBITE

What: Frostbite is thermal damage, usually to the extremities, that occurs in children exposed to extreme cold. The severity of frostbite depends on the intensity of cold (wind-chill factor), how long the child was exposed, and how rapidly he was rewarmed. Children are very vulnerable to frostbite because their skin is more sensitive than adults.

Danger Signs and Dangers: Frostbite is common on the tip of the nose, the fingers, and the toes. Mild frostbite causes redness of the skin, but no permanent damage. Moderate frostbite causes cold, white areas, blisters, and even blackening of skin. Severe frostbite leads to gangrene and actual loss of the affected parts. Even mild and moderate frostbite can cause numbness, long-term cold sensitivity, and pain.

1. DO remove any wet clothing in contact with the skin and loosen any tight clothes.

2. DO cover the frostbit-

ten areas with dry, bulky garments.

3. DO protect the area from trauma.

4. DO move the child to a warm environment and rewarm the frostbitten area by dipping it in warm water (about 102°F or 39°C) for twenty minutes.

5. DO give the child a dose of acetaminophen, since rewarming may cause the frostbitten areas to hurt.

6. DO seek medical attention promptly.

7. DO keep the child at bedrest, with the frostbitten part elevated.

1. DON'T rewarm before transporting the child if there is any chance of refreezing on the way. This causes more damage.

2. DON'T vigorously rub the frostbitten area; such trauma can cause further damage.

3. DON'T rewarm with an oven, fire, or dry heat, since unequal exposure may result in tissue burns.

Prevention: Be aware just how easily a youngster can get frostbite. Don't let your child out in the cold unless he is dressed appropriately, including waterproof gloves and boots. Remove wet garments promptly. Think twice about driving in a snow-storm, since your car could break down with your family inside. If you must drive, be sure everyone is dressed appropriately and you keep blankets in your car trunk during the winter.

HEAD INJURY

What: A head injury results any time your child strikes his head, causing significant trauma. It may be an open or closed trauma, depending on whether an open wound exists. Serious head injuries can lead to coma and death.

Danger Signs and Dangers: The child should be examined promptly if: (1) the fall was from a significant height (two feet or greater) or onto concrete; (2) the child displayed significant symptoms afterward, such as being unconscious for a period after the fall, having visual disturbances, a dilated pupil, convulsion, nausea, vomiting, dizziness, headache, trouble speaking or walking, acting lethargic or disoriented; or (3) there is a swelling on the head, active bleeding, black-and-blue marks behind the ears or around the eyes, clear liquid coming out of the nose, or blood from the ear.

1. DO call 911 or 0 to

NORMAL dilated pupils, equal in size

NORMAL pupils equally constricted after exposure to light

**ABNORMAL left pupil remaining dilated
while right pupil has constricted to light**

request paramedics immediately if your child is unconscious or not responding normally.

2. DO call and discuss the fall with your physician or personnel at the emergency room if you have any questions, even if the trauma seems minor.

3. DO observe the child closely for the next forty-eight hours, including awakening him from sleep every four hours, to check for responsiveness, and speech ability, reaction of pupils to a flashlight (the pupils should be the same size and both should get smaller when the light is shined on them). In the case of an infant, see if he awakens and seems to recognize you, will nurse or take a bottle, and responds appropriately. For an older child, see if he recognizes you and his surroundings, can answer simple questions, and acts like himself. Observation is easier if your child sleeps in your room for two days after the injury.

1. DON'T try to keep the baby awake. Accidental falls often occur around bedtime when a child is tired and cranky and careless. You can't "prevent a coma" by trying to keep a child awake. If the child does fall asleep, awaken and check him regularly as described above.

2. DON'T give the child anything to eat or drink for at least an hour. Children are prone to vomit following head injuries and could choke on the vomited material. You can offer clear liquids for the next few hours.

Prevention: Head trauma commonly occurs when infants fall off changing tables, down unprotected stairways, from high chairs and strollers. Safety-proofing the home to prevent falls and using safety restraints in the car will help prevent most childhood head injuries.

HEMORRHAGE

What: Hemorrhage is severe, profuse bleeding. If not controlled, hemorrhage could lead to shock and ultimately death. Stories exist of individuals with relatively minor gunshot wounds, for example, who bled to death because no one was present to stop hemorrhaging. Although hemorrhage usually results from major trauma, it can occur with a minor injury in a child whose blood doesn't clot normally.

Danger Signs and Dangers: Hemorrhage can be from a vein or an artery. If the blood pumps or spurts from the wound, it is probably arterial bleeding which results in more rapid blood loss. The child may look pale and the hands and feet may feel cold if a significant amount of blood has been lost.

1. DO call an ambulance or rush the child to the nearest hospital if you believe life-threatening blood loss has occurred.

2. DO have the child lie down, with the feet elevated about ten to twelve inches.

3. DO place a clean cloth or bandage on the wound and then apply strong, direct pressure over the wound, using the palm of your hand.

Do this promptly, as arterial hemorrhaging can quickly lead to shock.

4. If direct pressure has failed to control bleeding, then also apply firm pressure over the artery between the wound and the heart until help arrives (see page 399).

5. DO apply an arterial tourniquet ONLY under the following rare circumstances: the bleeding is definitely arterial; it is coming from an amputated or mangled extremity and can't be controlled by direct pressure; the child is very far from emergency care. You apply the tourniquet as follows: Use a thin strip of cloth, such as a necktie, scarf, or folded handkerchief. Tie it around the arm or leg above the wound; then insert a short stick and tie the tourniquet again. Twist the stick until the tourniquet is tight enough that bleeding stops. Tie the stick in place and don't release it until you reach the hospital.

1. DON'T ever tie an arterial tourniquet unless the above conditions exist.

Prevention: Most bleeding will stop with continuous, firm pressure. Bad injuries leading to hemorrhage can usually be prevented by close supervision of young children and regular use of car seats and seatbelts.

HUMAN BITES

What: Human bites occur commonly in toddlers who may bite one another as part of normal exploration with their mouths. The human mouth contains over forty different germs, making human bites even more likely to get infected than dog or cat bites.

Danger Signs and Dangers: Teeth marks may be noticeable, with surrounding bruising. If the skin is broken, medical attention will be necessary. Bites of the hands are particularly prone to infection.

1. DO vigorously wash the bite with soap and water for ten to fifteen minutes.

2. DO seek medical care for any human bite that breaks the skin.

3. DO observe the child carefully for signs of infection, such as fever, or pus, redness, or tenderness of the wound, and report these to a physician

4. DO bring the child's tetanus immunization status up-to-date, if it is not already current.

1. DON'T ever have stitches placed in a human

bite. The risk of infection is too great.

Prevention: If your child has ever bitten, curb this habit promptly (see page 280). If he is in day care with another biter, get assurance from the babysitter that she will not leave the biter alone with other children. Teach your child to withdraw from another youngster who looks as if she intends to bite. Don't ever bite your child in an attempt to teach him not to bite others. The message is confusing and you risk breaking his skin.

HYPOTHERMIA

What: Hypothermia occurs when a person's temperature is below 95°F., or 35° C. In children, it is usually caused by prolonged exposure to the cold, such as being stranded in a car during a snowstorm. Hypothermia can also occur after near-drowning in cold water. Newborns are at particular risk of developing hypothermia.

Danger Signs and Dangers: Hypothermia causes loss of appetite, lethargy, and cold, swollen, hardened skin. There is progressive loss of mental function, with the child eventually becoming unconscious. Heart irregularities can occur; death from severe hypothermia is usually due to cardiac arrest.

1. DO provide CPR as indicated.
2. DO move the child to a warm environment.
3. DO use warm blankets and warm water bottles to raise the child's body temperature.
4. DO seek medical attention to assure no underlying problem exists, to check for frostbite, and so on.

1. DON'T use HOT water bottles to warm a small child, as you can burn the skin.

Prevention: Hypothermia can be prevented by avoiding traveling during a snowstorm, not letting youngsters walk home from school in a snowstorm or play outdoors when the wind-chill factor is below freezing. Schools are often canceled on extremely cold days because children have become hypothermic waiting for a late school bus. I even hesitate to discharge a newborn from the hospital on a very snowy day for fear the parents' car will break down.

INSULIN REACTION (HYPOGLYCEMIA)

What: Although diabetes is not common in early childhood, it occasionally does occur among preschoolers. Diabetics can experience wide swings in blood sugar and are at risk of hypoglycemia (low blood sugar), particularly if they skip meals after taking their insulin or exercise vigorously without snacking. All diabetic children and their parents should be taught the signs of low blood sugar and how to respond. Hypoglycemia due to many other causes can also occur in infants.

Danger Signs and Dangers: Signs of hypoglycemia include sweating, irritability, nervousness, pale and cool skin, hunger, lethargy, and lightheadedness. These may be hard to detect in a baby or very young child, so you should be highly observant if your child is diabetic. The brain requires sugar for energy, so in severe cases, seizures, coma, and permanent brain damage can occur.

1. DO immediately give a high-carbohydrate liquid to drink (e.g., orange juice). If the child is unresponsive, apply Instant Glucose (most families with a diabetic member have a tube of this solution in their home) inside his lips.

2. DO seek medical help immediately, unless he responds right away.

3. Do call your doctor to discuss insulin dosages for the remainder of the day.

Prevention: Insulin reactions can be prevented by paying careful attention to insulin dosages and closely monitoring your diabetic child's blood sugar, urine sugar, and ketones. Permanent damage can be prevented by maintaining a high level of suspicion for insulin reactions and providing a source of carbohydrate promptly.

POISONING

What: Anything potentially toxic that has been eaten, inhaled, or spilled onto the skin constitutes a poisoning. Pills, household products, gasoline, plants, gasses, or spoiled foods can be poisonous to your child.

Danger Signs and Dangers: The risks depend upon the specific actions of the toxic substance ingested. The reactions may be delayed several hours, so that you may falsely think nothing is wrong. Common effects after the ingestion of drugs include lethargy, depressed respirations, high or low blood pressure, coma, heartbeat irregularities, and many others. ANY changes noted in your child after he ingests a poison are very worrisome.

1. DO remove the child from the substance and rinse it off if spilled on the skin.

2. DO call your local or regional poison control center to receive up-to-date advice about the toxic risk and treatment of the ingested material. Report exactly what was ingested, how much is missing, the time of the event, how the child acts, and so on.

3. DO be prepared to give your child syrup of ipecac but only *if* poison control tells you to do so. Ipecac will cause the child to vomit up the poisonous material. Since some things should not be vomited (because they will cause damage to the food pipe or cause choking), be sure that you have called poison control *before* giving ipecac. The usual dose for children over a year in age is 1 tablespoon.

4. If ipecac was recommended and has been given, DO follow it with large amounts of liquids. Vomiting occurs faster on a full

stomach, so encourage the child to drink.

5. DO go to your physician's office, hospital clinic, or emergency room promptly if advised to do so by your poison control center. Any delay in seeking medical care can be dangerous.

1. DON'T give syrup of ipecac if the child has passed out. He will choke if he vomits without being fully awake.

2. DON'T forget to bring the various containers of possibly ingested substances with you. This is the best way the doctors can tell what your child might have taken and how to treat him.

3. DON'T believe the child about how much of the substance he has taken. If two or more children are involved in the ingestion, DON'T believe any of them about who took what. It must be assumed that each one could have taken the full amount.

4. DON'T delay in calling Poison Control. Many very dangerous substances don't show their side effects right away, so the child may look just fine initially.

5. DON'T call your doctor first. Poison Control is faster and more up-to-date. They will call your doctor

for you, or you can call your physician later. If you do not have access to a regional poison control center, then do call your physician or emergency room.

6. DON'T follow the antidote cited on the label of the ingested product until you call Poison Control. Many of these instructions are wrong.

Prevention: Don't ever leave medicines or other toxic substances where children can reach them, including vitamins with iron. (Iron is very toxic.) Be sure to keep syrup of ipecac on hand from the time your baby first learns to crawl. Never refer to medicine as "candy" or talk about it tasting good.

SNAKEBITE

What: Almost all poisonous snakebites in the United States are caused by pit vipers (rattlesnakes, water moccasins, and copperheads). The outcome depends on the size of the child, where he was bitten, how much venom was injected, and how quickly he is treated. Sometimes venom is not injected by a bite. If no reaction has occurred within thirty minutes, this was probably the case.

Danger Signs and Dangers: A poisonous snakebite causes a severe reaction at the site of the bite, with pain, swelling, and discoloration. You can see a double puncture mark with surrounding bruising. Bites by pit vipers cause bleeding disorders, and the child can vomit blood, cough up blood, or have blood in his stools. Nausea, vomiting, sweating, and chills also typically occur, and children may have convulsions. Although death is rare, when it does occur, it is usually due to respiratory distress and shock. Death usually takes at least six to eight hours, so there should be adequate time to seek medical help.

1. DO wash the wound well, and keep the child quiet and inactive to slow the absorption of venom. Carry him to minimize his activity.

2. DO apply a tourniquet between the bite and the body, if the bite is on an extremity. The tourniquet should be at least two inches above the bite and tight enough to make the veins stand out, but not tight enough to cut off circulation. Release the tourniquet for a few seconds every fifteen minutes.

3. DO seek medical care promptly.

4. DO keep the bite lower than the rest of the body.

1. DON'T pack the extremity in ice, as the child could suffer frostbite in addition to the damage from the snakebite.

2. DON'T try to make a cross-cut in the wound and suck out the venom. This really doesn't work very well, and there is great risk of inadvertently cutting through tendons, nerves, and blood vessels. If you are far from medical care and are sure the bite was poisonous, then it may be worth trying to remove some venom. Use a clean (flamed) knife or razor blade and make a single cut about ½" long and ⅛" deep in the longitudinal direction over each fang mark. Try to squeeze the venom out for a minute or two; then use your mouth or a suction cup from a snake bite kit to try to suck it out for about ten minutes. Do not swallow the venom. Wash the wound thoroughly afterward. Suction does not help after thirty to sixty minutes have elapsed.

Prevention: Children in snake-infested areas should wear boots and long trousers, should not walk barefoot, and should not be permitted to explore under ledges or holes.

SPIDER BITES

What: The two main poisonous spiders in North America are the black widow and the brown recluse. The female black widow can be identified by a red hourglass-shaped mark on the underbelly. It is found in almost all areas of the United States. The brown recluse is ½" to 1" long, has violin like markings on the back, and is found most often in the central and midwestern states.

Danger Signs and Dangers: A black widow spider bite causes a sharp fleeting pain, with a severe reaction beginning within half an hour to a few hours. Two fang marks should be evident, and a severe local reaction may be noted around the bite. Marked muscle rigidity can occur, including severe abdominal cramps, nausea, and vomiting. Small children can have convulsions. Hospital admission may be required, and deaths have occurred in small children who were bitten by one or more spiders

The brown recluse bite causes a severe reaction around the bite that is extremely painful and can go on to necrosis of surrounding skin. A black scab forms within a week and lasts two to five weeks. Although death is rare, the child can develop symptoms within twenty-four to forty-eight hours after the bite, including headache, fever, vomiting, joint pains, weakness, rash, seizures, and blueness.

1. DO kill and capture the spider and bring it with you to the clinic or emergency room so that it can be accurately identified.

2. DO examine the child for evidence of the bite (two fang marks with black widow).

3. DO bring the child promptly to medical care if a black widow or brown recluse spider bite is suspected. Intravenous therapy and hospitalization may be necessary.

4. If the bite is on an arm or leg, DO tie a tourniquet around the limb between the bite and the body, so that the amount of poison absorbed into the body will be slowed. Release the tourniquet for a few seconds every fifteen minutes. The veins should stand out, but you should still be able to feel a pulse.

1. DON'T pack the bit-

ten arm or leg in ice, as this may cause frostbite in addition to the injury from the spider bite.

2. DON'T tie the tourniquet so tightly that the circulation is cut off.

Prevention: Spider bites can be prevented by knowing what type of spiders are prevalent in your geographic area. Don't let your child play in places likely to harbor spiders, such as garages, dark closets, around old shoes, rubber tires, et cetera. Suspecting a spider bite, and looking for bite marks, in a child too young to report the incident, will make treatment more rapid.

SPINAL-CORD INJURY (NECK OR BACK)

What: Automobile accidents are the leading cause of spinal injuries in children. Fortunately, many are incomplete injuries, so that partial or full recovery often occurs. It is very important *not* to move a child with a possible spinal injury until expert help arrives, as certain movements can cause further spinal-cord damage.

Danger Signs and Dangers: A spinal injury should be suspected in any child with serious trauma, such as a major automobile accident; a child with severe head, face, or back injury; a child who complains of neck or back pain following trauma; a child who is unconscious after an accident; a child who has weakness, tingling, numbness, or paralysis of his arms or legs after an injury. It is possible to still have fractured vertebrae even though the child is walking around okay, a sudden movement could lead to paralysis if the injury isn't detected and properly treated.

1. DO immobilize the child immediately and wait for an ambulance to arrive with a neck collar and spine board. If the child MUST be moved (if, for example, there's immediate danger of fire), use several people to support every part of the body. The body should be kept in a straight line and not allowed to bend. If the child is in water, help him float flat on his back until a spine board can be brought or several people can move him by supporting the head and back as a unit.

2. DO place sandbags or books on either side of the head so it cannot be turned until expert help arrives.

3. DO check to be sure the child can breathe. High neck injuries can impair breathing. If mouth-to-mouth resuscitation is necessary, try to move the head as little as possible, while still providing effective respiration.

4. DO cover the child with a warm blanket and try to keep him calm, so he won't try to move.

1. DON'T assume that no serious injury has occurred just because the child walked away from the accident. Get X rays for any significant neck or back injury.

2. DON'T bend, twist, or turn the neck or back in anyone who could have a spinal injury. Well-meaning bystanders have caused permanent paralysis by moving accident victims.

Prevention: The regular use of automotive restraints would prevent many spinal injuries. Children should be taught never to dive into shallow water. Trampolines should NEVER be used for recreation, but rather used in supervised athletics only.

SPRAINS AND STRAINS

What: A sprain is a tear of a ligament conecting two bones around a joint. A strain is a tear in a muscle or a tissue connecting muscle to bone. Neither is very common in small children, although they do occur commonly in athletic adolescents.

Danger Signs and Dangers: Mild or moderate swelling can be present, with localized tenderness, a surrounding bruise and pain when the child tries to put weight on the extremity. The pain may start immediately or be delayed a few hours. Consider the possibility of a broken bone, since sprains and strains are uncommon in young children.

1. DO apply a cold compress or ice bag for the first hour.
2. DO elevate the extremity to decrease swelling.
3. DO apply an Ace bandage to help protect the sprained area. Be sure it is not too tight.
4. DO bring the child for an X ray if he is not better in a few days. A fracture could be present.

1. DON'T apply heat for at least a day or two, as it will increase any bleeding and make swelling worse.

Prevention: Sprains are more common among children who play competitive sports, especially when running on a wet field or when already exhausted.

SWALLOWED OBJECT
What: Small children tend to put everything in their mouths, and often swallow nonedible objects, such as coins, safety pins, buttons, fruit pits, et cetera. Most such objects will pass without difficulty in the bowel movement a few days later. Problems arise when objects block either the windpipe, food pipe (esophagus), or intestines. Occasionally an unrecognized object in the esophagus or bowel can cause chronic irritation and a partial blockage.

Danger Signs and Dangers: Immediate choking, coughing, or noisy breathing suggests that the object is partially blocking the windpipe (trachea). This requires emergency medical care. Refusal to eat solid foods and complaints when swallowing suggest that the object has partially blocked the esophagus. Later on, vomiting, a distended abdomen, and decreased stooling suggest that the object has partially blocked the intestines.

1. DO bring in a child for emergency treatment who chokes on an object and has noisy or labored breathing afterward.
2. DO look in the child's mouth with a flashlight to see if an object is visible

and can be removed with the fingers.

3. DO perform chest thrusts, abdominal thrusts, and back blows on a child who is unable to breathe after choking on an object.

4. DO search for the swallowed object in the child's bowel movements for the next few days even if the child appears well after swallowing an object.

5. DO bring a child for an X ray to detect a swallowed object if he has any difficulty eating afterward, either immediately or even weeks later.

1. DON'T push your finger down the child's throat if he is gagging on an object; you might block off his airway completely.

2. DON'T assume a swallowed object has passed normally through the gut without finding proof of it! Until seeing it in the stool, you should assume it is still lodged somewhere.

Prevention: Virtually all children will swallow a foreign object sometime. You can minimize this by giving small children only age-appropriate toys and foods and supervising them when eating any potentially troublesome foods, such as fruits with pits.

14 Contemporary Concerns

TODAY we parent with the advantage of safety, medical, and psychological information never before available. Yet we also confront harder, more complex issues than parents faced in the past. Some of the information contained in this chapter may strike you as intrusive because it deals with topics most of us would rather not contemplate. But in spite of our reluctance to dwell on some difficult issues, we are fortunate that others have given much study and thought to these topics. Our children will benefit by our increased awareness of social safety, family values, and certain aspects of breast feeding. Keeping an open mind as you explore these and other controversial issues will allow you to make the best possible decisions for your child and your family.

PREVENTING KIDNAPPING

The subject of childhood kidnapping is so terrifying that you may view it as an unkind intrusion in a baby care book. Even if kidnapping weren't covered here, it probably has occurred to you. Many parents confide that they fear kidnapping, because it must be obvious to child snatchers that their child is the most beautiful and desirable youngster in the world.

But your fear is useless to your child unless it motivates you to protect her. Although no one can absolutely guarantee your child's safety, you can take many steps yourself and teach your child safety rules that will dramatically improve her odds of ever being abducted, without instilling excessive fear.

What You Can Do

Communicate your child's worth. Let her know how much she means to you. You want her to keep herself safe because she knows she is important to you and loved, and the idea of separation would be as unbearable to her as it is to you.

Reinforce for your child that she is NEVER to take any chances. Her safety has to be an imperative. Keep good communications open and comfortable, so your child will share any frightening or even suspicious incidents with you.

NEVER leave your child alone in the car, even if the doors are locked, even if it's just for a minute. Don't leave your child, EVEN FOR A MOMENT, unattended in a stroller or shopping cart while you look for something. And, please don't ask a stranger to keep an eye on your baby in a store for "just a second." That's all it takes. This same principle applies to leaving your child in a restaurant or other public place while you pay the bill or make a quick phone call.

If you are leaving your child in a nursery at church or for a meeting or class, make sure that children are signed in and out in some organized and safe manner. Do not leave your child in the care of someone you have just met or don't know at all. Meet new babysitters in advance and get references.

It is very dangerous to let your child feel it is permissible to wander off from you in public. Make it a firm rule from the beginning that if she is out of her stroller, she is to stay at your side.

Don't allow your child to go into a public restroom alone. If your child is over five and with the opposite-sex parent, choose between taking her in anyway, sending her in with a same-gender friend if you're with one, or waiting just outside the door and investigating if the child doesn't appear in a reasonable amount of time.

If you will be dropping your child off at a birthday party

or at a friend's house for the day, find out if the parents plan to take the child out anywhere. You will want to know where your child will be and to pass on some of your safety standards to the person supervising your child.

Of course, never leave your child home alone.

If you are in a public place and your child is suddenly missing, even for a short time, do call for help immediately. If stores and shopping malls had an automatic policy of closing all exits as soon as a lost child is reported, many abductions might be thwarted.

What You Can Teach Your Child

Talk to your child about strangers. Tell her that strangers are people she doesn't know. Most strangers are good people, just like her friends, but a few strangers are bad people. STRESS that we can't tell the difference between good and bad strangers just by looking. A "bad guy" may even look like a "nice lady." Tell your child that when she is with you she can talk to strangers you talk to, but when she is alone she can NEVER talk to anyone she doesn't know.

Teach your child that if a stranger tries to come close to her or asks her to come closer, she must ALWAYS run and scream for help. Make sure that this idea is so ingrained that she would never stop and evaluate the situation, but would always run and scream for help.

Teach your child that if she thinks a stranger wants her to go with him (or her) she should forget her manners, stop listening to that person, forget any toys she may leave behind, and not worry about causing a scene. She should run, scream, yell, and if necessary, fight, bite, kick—do anything to attract attention and escape.

Your child should know that it is okay to say no to adults! Some children have been abducted without a struggle because they felt they couldn't argue with an adult.

Teach your child through role playing that she must resist every temptation in order to keep herself safe. Go over as many sample situations as you can think of, making your scenarios as irresistible as possible.

For example, say to your child, "If a strange woman,

who was very nice and pretty, told you she had some kittens in her car and asked you if you wanted to hold one, what would you do?" Or, "If a man told you that he had a little girl just your age and he would like to take you both to Disneyland, would you go with him?" Or, "If a man came to your preschool and said that I had been in a car accident and was in the hospital, and that I sent him to bring you to me, would you go with him?"

While role playing sample threatening situations, remind your child that you would NEVER send a stranger to pick her up. List examples of who might pick her up in case of emergency, perhaps her grandparents or friends she knows well, but never someone she doesn't already know. Some parents teach their child a "code word" that anyone picking the child up must give. This is confusing, because after all, you just promised that you would NEVER send a stranger to pick her up. Why would her grandmother need a code word? Forget the code word idea and assure your child that there is NO circumstance under which she is permitted to go with a stranger.

Many children imagine that if a stranger tried to abduct them, they would fight off the stranger (a little superhero syndrome). Convince them that this is absolutely not an option. To be safe, they must run and scream for help; there simply are no alternatives.

Teach your child that if someone were to try to carry her off, she should scream specific information, like "This is not my dad (or mom). Help! He's trying to kidnap me." It has also been suggested that you teach your child to address such cries of help to a specific person like "You in the gray coat I need help; he's trying to kidnap me." It may be harder for a person who has been singled out to ignore cries for help.

By the time your child is three, she should know her name, her parents' names, her address, her phone number, and how to dial the operator. As soon as your child is old enough, teach her how to use a pay phone, so she could call home if necessary.

Teach your child who to approach for help if she needed it, like people in uniforms or people who clearly work in the place where she is. Help her learn to identify these people.

Help increase your child's awareness of her surroundings, to recognize people who seem suspicious, and to describe places and people's appearance, should it ever be necessary.

Teach your child that if she is wearing something with her name on it, people may use her name when talking to her. Unless you teach her otherwise, she may assume that they know her or are her friend.

Teach your child never to go into the home of someone she doesn't know, even if she is with another child who seems to know that person.

Never let your child play alone or unsupervised. Children are far more likely to be snatched when playing alone. Children are safe when with a responsible adult and are even relatively safe when playing with other children.

Your child should know that only adults should answer the door, even if you are nearby.

We would all like to think that something as horrible as kidnapping could not happen to our child. But our unwillingness to face the reality of kidnapping puts our children at greater risk. You need not and should not scare your child, but you should teach her how to keep herself safe. By behaving more cautiously, you will not take risks with your child.

AVOIDING SEXUAL ABUSE

Again we find ourselves faced with a subject so distasteful we would rather ignore it than face it. But the incidence of sexual assault forces us to acknowledge this reality and learn how to protect our children from it.

Sexual abuse ranges from mutual viewing of genitals, handling of genitals, or oral contact, to attempted or actual penetration. Children who are victimized in this way always carry the scars. Their world will never feel as safe and secure again.

The frightening facts are:

√ Among the pupils in an average classroom, there are two or three victims of sexual assault.

√ One out of four girls has been molested in some way before the age of eighteen.

√ More children between the ages of eight and twelve are abused than those in their teens.

√ Ten percent of sexual abuse victims are under the age of five.

√ Ten percent of victims of sexual abuse are boys.

√ Eighty-five percent of child sexual assaults occur by family members or friends.

√ Incest occurs in 10 percent of all families.

√ Most children don't tell.

These statistics lead us to wonder what kind of a person would assault a child sexually and what type of child is most often a victim? There are no definite answers to either question. Absolute predictability about sexual assault and those who perform it would make prevention very easy. Unfortunately it's not so simple, but there are some generalizations that often apply.

Contrary to popular belief, sexual assault of a child is not usually a sudden violent attack. Typically the child is assaulted by someone with whom she has a trusting relationship. It is most often a gradual process. Sexual abuse may start with wrestling or tickling sessions that come to include some "accidental" touching of genitals.

Sadly, the person who sexually abuses a child is often somone she knows well and trusts: a friend, her mother's boyfriend, her stepfather, a babysitter, an uncle, a cousin, or even her own father. Only rarely is the perpetrator of sexual abuse a woman. In general, sexual abusers come from rigid and authoritarian backgrounds and have been sexually abused themselves in childhood. They may indulge in heavy alcohol use, batter their wives, and physically abuse children as well.

Behaviors to suspect include a disrespect for a child's feelings or requests, like someone who tickles a child too much, or someone who imposes more hugging or kissing than the child clearly wants. Also beware of adults who have a sexual or flirtatious manner toward a child or who refer to the child in a way they would another adult they are attracted to—calling a little girl "a real knockout," for example.

Anyone who entices children into his home or his company, no matter how nice he seems, should be viewed suspiciously. A person who has trouble interacting socially with adults and prefers to relate to children may use his age and power over a child for an abusive purpose. And, of course, anyone who is known to have committed a previous sexual offense should NEVER be trusted with your child.

Any time your child says she feels uncomfortable with someone, her feelings should be heeded. Your child may be perceiving subtle inappropriate behavior. Although any child can be a victim of sexual abuse, a child is more easily victimized if she is so obedient and respectful of adults that she can't say no.

What You Can Do

Always respect your child's right to say no to *anyone* if what they ask doesn't feel right. Never urge a reluctant child to kiss or hug someone. This only teaches her that she must submit to the physical demands adults make of her and contributes to "abuse victim training." If any kind of physical affection or attention is unwelcome to your child, this MUST be respected.

Not only should you never force your child to give or accept unwanted affection, you should stand up for and protect your child's right of refusal. Perhaps at goodbye time, when your child has refused to give a kiss, you can take your child by the hand and say, "Okay, let's go home now." This clearly shows that you support your child's decision to kiss or not, and that you approve of her behavior.

You can set family boundaries on what you feel is acceptable in the areas of touch, affection, privacy, and nudity. This helps your child recognize inappropriate behavior. Let your child know that she has rights, including rights to privacy with her body and rights not to be touched when she doesn't want to be.

Make your child feel important. Children with low self-esteem are more vulnerable to abuse. Also, help your child develop a good body image. Point out positive aspects of her body, like strength or coordination. Don't let her develop the feeling that parts of her body are bad, naughty, shameful, or dirty. If she feels this way, she will be unlikely to tell you anything concerning these areas.

Use common sense. How many times have we read in the newspaper that a child was repeatedly abused while in the care of the mother's boyfriend. Watch for situations that could be inappropriate, that make the child fearful or unhappy, and that give you even the slightest feeling of suspicion.

Evaluate babysitters carefully. Talk to other parents who have used them. Question your children after using a new babysitter. Follow up on anything that doesn't sound quite right.

Observe your child for the development of new symptoms and behaviors commonly recognized to be associated with sexual abuse. These include nightmares, bed-wetting, public masturbation, fear of men, fear of going to the babysitter, discomfort with urination, and abdominal pain. Many children display one or more of these signs, but if several are present together or new ones appear, consider the possibility of sexual abuse.

Of course, any physical signs suggestive of sexual abuse, in a girl or boy, should prompt you to obtain a medical evaluation of your child. Such signs would include genital bruises or cuts, an enlarged vaginal opening, rectal fissures, or vaginal or penile discharge. But remember, the absence of physical findings never rules out the possibility of sexual abuse if the child tells you that abuse has occurred.

NEVER assume your child is not telling the truth about sexual abuse, no matter how much you want to deny it. Young children simply don't lie about such issues.

What You Can Teach Your Child

Caren Adams and Jennifer Pay, authors of *No More Secrets*, offer parents a great deal of important information in their book. The following points should be emphasized.

Let your child know that she does not need to decide why the other person is doing what he is doing. If the child is uncomfortable, she can just say no.

Teach your child the concept of "private parts." Tell

your child these are the parts of her body that a bathing suit covers, and no one has the right to touch these parts. When teaching your children about sexual abuse, start out by talking to them in terms of unwanted touching. Then you can progress to the possibility of someone touching their genitals.

As an educational technique, I now ask parents' permission in their child's presence before examining a youngster's genital area. This is very helpful in teaching that genitals are private and NO ONE—not even a doctor—should feel free to touch them. I reinforce to the child during the exam that others should not be allowed to touch her genitals.

Help your child become comfortable with vocabulary words for genitals, breasts, and nipples. Children who are afraid to use words like "penis" or "vagina," might be too embarrassed to tell you if someone touched them there.

Discuss who might do something like this. Mention that it could be someone who seems nice, even someone they know and not always a stranger. Also point out to your child that the abuser does not always use force. Gifts, bribes, and promises are common. They can take the form of favors or money in exchange for certain behaviors, then bribing or threatening the child not to tell.

Teach your child not to keep secrets from you, especially those made with an adult. Tell her it is always okay to share secrets with parents and this type of secret MUST be shared. Explain the difference between secrets and surprises, like birthday presents or an unexpected trip to the zoo.

Many public education programs now regularly convey to youngsters the importance of saying no to adults who try to initiate sexual behavior. An unfortunate backlash we are seeing among young victims of sexual abuse is tremendous guilt after being unable to say no. Although you will teach your child that she has the right to say no, in reality adults can be very convincing and intimidating, and children are really very trusting and vulnerable. It is not always within your child's ability to say no to an adult, especially a trusted person. If your child is ever sexually abused in any way, do all you can to reassure her that she bears no guilt, regardless of how she handled the situation.

Tell her you know that she is small and that the adult was bigger and more powerful and should have known better. Make it clear to your child that in a case of sexual abuse, the adult is ALWAYS at fault.

Unfortunately, the problem of sexual abuse has always been with us. Has it only reached greater proportions in our society recently? Or has society refused to tolerate it any longer? The damage it does to our trusting and vulnerable children is too great! We must protect them by educating ourselves and our children, by using good judgment, and insisting on stronger prosecution for perpetrators. As parents, you must instill in your child the importance of following the above precautions. Urge schools to offer preventive education, such as the excellent and effective program developed by Lutheran Social Services of Washington called *My Very Own Book About Me*. Such efforts demonstrate that society and its institutions do care about the protection of our children.

If you have reason to suspect that a child is being sexually abused, state law requires that you report it. This is not an option! You must report sexual abuse if you suspect it, although you can report anonymously if you request.

AVOIDING GETTING LOST

It is a rare parent who cannot relate a terrifying incident of temporarily "losing" their child. Regardless of the duration of the "loss," those moments are surely among the worst in our lives.

One mother recounted to a group of other parents the horror of losing her five-year-old son at an amusement park. Because she had taught him to stay where he was if he ever got lost, she found him without assistance. The tone of her voice and her expression reflected her anguish as she recalled this incident. One of the parents asked how long the child was lost. The mother replied seriously, "Oh, it must have been at least three minutes." Perhaps a childless couple might have laughed, but the other parents just shook their heads sympathetically. The point of this story is that losing a child, whether the experience lasts for only three minutes or for hours, is terribly frightening and painful.

Teach your child to never wander away from you. Don't allow your child out of her stroller or backpack until she knows that she must stay with you. If in doubt, hold hands at all times. Although the sight of a toddler on a leash may be offensive to some, this is a practical way to assure that your youngster doesn't wander off in a crowd. I suspect many parents who use them have already endured at least one harrowing experience.

If you will be in a crowd or in an open space like a park, dress your child in a bright color, like red. She will be much easier to spot. Also, at the beginning of the

outing, point out to your child what you are wearing so you will be easier for her to keep an eye on.

If you will be on a hike, or in the mountains, at the beach, camping, or doing a similar outdoor activity, let your child wear a whistle around her neck. Instruct her to blow it loudly if she becomes lost (but not otherwise) and to keep blowing it periodically until she is found.

Teach your child her neighborhood limits, like "You can ride your tricycle from our house to the corner and back, but not farther." You may have to reinforce these boundaries daily.

What Your Child Should Know

Every child should know her name, address, phone number, parents' names, and their work numbers as soon as she is able. Younger children can probably learn their own name and the name of their street. Add information as capabilities grow.

If your child becomes lost, she should stay where she is and wait for you to return. Explain that you will go back to find her. If she has waited for you for what seems like a very long time, and you still haven't found her, she should seek help from someone who works on the premises or someone in a uniform.

Assure your child that you will not be angry at her for being lost. Many children have hid while they were lost because they were so frightened of their parents' anger. Encourage your child to make herself more visible when lost. Promise your child that you would never give up looking for her. This will give her hope and courage and will keep her out in the open trying to be found.

What to Do If Your Child Is Lost

If your child is lost and you can't find her quickly, DO react immediately. Ask for help, especially in a store or shopping mall. It is possible that your child is not lost but has been kidnapped. If you announce your need for help, insist that the management lock all exits until your child is found. If your child is lost outdoors, waiting to ask for help could waste precious minutes of daylight that may mean her spending the night outside.

Be able to furnish a good description of your child and a current photo. Make a mental note each day of what your child is wearing.

Regardless of the amount of caution you exercise with your child's safety, no one can promise that she will never become lost. Each one of us has had a moment of carelessness in which we turned our backs or "took a chance" that put our child in jeopardy. If it happens to you, don't let feelings of guilt overwhelm you to the extent that they interfere with your good judgment. Keep in mind that you need to stay calm and make good decisions, not punish yourself.

Try not to be obsessive about these fears. If you have implemented as many precautions as possible and have taught and rehearsed with your child actions for getting found, you have protected her as well as you can.

PHYSICAL ABUSE

Physical abuse of children is a crime that horrifies parents, and yet it is almost always parents who commit the abuse. In our best moments, beating our children is beyond our comprehension, but in reality no parent loves their child every minute of every day. Every parent has the potential to reach a point of great enough stress and low enough impulse control to hurt their child. Acknowledging that even you, as a good and loving parent, could possibly lose control and abuse your child is the first step toward prevention.

Professionals who work with abused children and their parents have developed some guidelines to help parents prevent child abuse. The last thing you want to do is hurt your child.

Abuse is more likely to occur when parents have unrealistic expectations for the child's age. A large number of abused children are beaten, for example, over toilet training and night-wetting issues. In these cases the children were simply not capable of greater urinary control, but an uninformed or immature parent perceived the child as uncooperative and rebellious.

All parents occasionally need a cooling-off period. If you feel yourself becoming very angry and in danger of hurting your child, separate yourself from your child. Go outside or into another room. Do not feel you must conclude the issue over which you and your child are entangled. Leave and don't come back to your child until you have cooled off.

The stress that leads to child abuse is often mistakenly thought to be the result of one major incident, like losing a job. In fact, a series of small but stressful events are more likely to produce an explosion of uncontrolled anger. On days filled with aggravation (the washer breaks, the toilet overflows, the dog wets on the carpet, and your child misses the bus), force yourself to take a break. In times of stress we are least likely to do something for ourselves, but we most need to. Don't let yourself become completely depleted and more prone to loss of control.

Holidays, especially Christmas, are known times of great stress when the incidence of child abuse increases. Parents are frazzled, children are overly excited and often impatient. Instead of releasing your pent-up tension on your children, think of ways to make the holiday period easier. For example, as Christmas approaches and my children are out of school, their anticipation becomes unbearable. To ease matters, each day I let each child open one small present sent from out of town.

Another time when both parents and children are typically overstressed is when one child in the family is very ill. The parents are tired, worried, and overextended, and the other children are jealous of all the attention directed toward the sick one. Remember that this is a high-risk time and take the necessary precautions to get through it successfully.

If you can avoid ever spanking, you run far less risk of losing control and hurting your child physically. Parents who do occasionally spank should always observe these rules:

—Use only your open hand
—Spank only through clothes

—Hit only the buttocks or thigh
—Hit one time only

One parent is often present while the other is abusing their child. If you see your partner getting out of control, it is your obligation to interfere and stop the abuse. If you stand by and watch, you are just as guilty.

If you feel you are close to losing control at times and need help, turn to someone who is sensitive and supportive, such as a close friend or relative, one you're sure you can count on to give appropriate and constructive help. Most counties have a hot line you can call to talk to someone if you are having a hard time. Look in the White Pages under Child Abuse. Use these resources to help you cope. Parents Anonymous is an organization for parents who are working on turning around abusive behavior.

If you're asking for help to prevent yourself from abusing your child, don't hesitate to share your feelings with a health professional, fearing you'll be punished. If you have not yet hurt your child, you will receive only help.

If you are a person who has been violent in the past, was abused as a child, or frequently uses alcohol or drugs (which lower impulse control), you are at high risk for committing child abuse. Recognize your status if this description fits you, and love your child enough to get preventive help from the beginning. If your partner is a high-risk parent, urge him to get help and be on guard for times when you might need to intervene.

Realize that when extremely exhausted, none of us is rational and we are certainly at our worst for dealing with the sometimes irrational demands of a child. Try to avoid becoming very exhausted, but if you do, arrange an alternative caregiver for your child. Accept the fact that your perspective is altered, and make an effort to stay calm with your child.

Parenting is difficult, and sometimes abusive behavior comes from the frustration of not having effective skills to use with our children. Parenting classes such as PET (Parent Effectiveness Training) are available in most communities. The better your parenting skills, the less likely you will find yourself out of control with your child.

Children are not always abused by their own parents.

The abuser is sometimes a stepparent; someone the parent is dating; or a babysitter caring for the child.

If your child returns from someone else's care with any kind of injury, ask for a full explanation. If the story sounds unlikely, investigate. Be your child's advocate.

If you have abused your child, you may feel so remorseful that you're sure it won't happen again. Don't trust your feelings. If you have hurt your child in the past, you will probably do it again, unless you seek some help.

In the past children were most often hurt as a result of deliberate corporal punishment meted out by parents who thought they were doing the right thing. There are still cases like that today, but now abuse more commonly stems from an explosive incident. Parents no longer have the help extended families once offered and face many economic and life-style stresses.

If you understand that child abuse is an everyday risk and that you must work on preventing it, you are far less likely to commit it. If you have abused your child, get help; don't wait for it to happen again. Loving our children is more than feeding, clothing, and protecting them from outside dangers; we must also protect them from the possibility of hurting them ourselves.

TRANSMITTING SEXUAL VALUES

Transmitting sexual values may not sound like a "contemporary concern." After all, sex has been with us since the beginning of the human race. What is new for parents today is the base of knowledge we now have about human sexuality, thanks to researchers like Kinsey, Masters and Johnson, and Calderone.

In the past, parents rarely transmitted sexual values consciously. Inadvertently, of course, sexual values were transmitted, but were often negative and guilt-laden. Parents tended to react to any hint of sexuality with embarrassment, superstition, or ignorance. Now, with all we know about healthy and positive sexuality, there is no excuse for failing our children in this important area.

The first step will be to examine your own sexual values. Most of us have inherited some ambivalence about our sexuality. Let's recognize these unhealthy attitudes and decide not to burden our children with them. Do you believe:

- ✓ that men are more sexual than women?
- ✓ that men experience sex actively while women experience it passively?
- ✓ that masturbation is bad or harmful?
- ✓ that "good girls" are asexual but "normal, healthy boys" should be in constant pursuit of their next "sexual conquest"?
- ✓ that men NEED to release their sexual energy and women are obligated to fulfill that need?

This is only a sampling of attitudes that could interfere with fostering healthy sexuality for your daughters and sons.

Sexual values are transmitted by example through your relationships with friends, spouses, or lovers; your feelings and reactions to your body and your children's bodies; your vocabulary; and the knowledge you share or withhold as you teach your children about sexuality.

Body Image

Children cannot feel comfortable with their sexuality if they don't feel comfortable with their bodies. Although children start out with good feelings about their bodies, they often pick up negative attitudes as they grow older.

Your first opportunity to communicate feelings about your child's body will be in the way you hold your infant. Are you comfortable holding your baby close? Do you enjoy that closeness and the skin-to-skin contact? Or do you feel a need to limit intimacy with your baby and hold her less often or at some distance, avoiding skin-to-skin touching?

Your own comfort with physical contact with your baby will begin to teach her about her body. Many parents experience sensual pleasure from holding, stroking, and kissing that sweet, smooth baby skin. Naturally these babies, in turn, learn the healthy pleasure received through the sense of touch.

When changing the baby's diapers, parents also influence the baby's body image. Do you make faces and communicate disgust as you change an unpleasant diaper? Your baby must interpret this disgust to be a reaction to her body. It's a good idea to be pleasant or at least neutral while changing even the messiest diaper. Your baby cannot distinguish your reaction to the odor or bowel movement from revulsion about her body.

Another opportunity to communicate positive or negative feelings about your child's body is your reaction to normal genital play, which is inevitable throughout infancy and childhood. We know that sexual feelings are present from birth. Newborn boys have erections and newborn girls experience vaginal lubrication. If you seem upset by genital handling, and push your child's hands away, express that this behavior is undesirable, or refer to it as "dirty" or "naughty," your child may begin to absorb negative feelings about her genitals. Such a message is confusing, since the baby or child clearly enjoys genital fondling and has every reason to think that this touching is good. In fact, pleasure is good. We need to acknowledge that it is both natural and good when children pleasure themselves this way.

As our babies become toddlers and preschoolers, self-exploration will expand into body exploration with other children of the same and opposite sex. Again, this is normal, universal, and healthy as long as the children are all about the same age and mutually agreeable to the exploration. You can ignore (and thus allow) such exploration unless you are completely unable to accept it. In that case, please react in a neutral, rather than negative, way. Practice responses such as, "It seems a little cold in here; wouldn't you like to put your clothes on?" Or "Would you kids like to play a game?"

If you are comfortable with your child's natural curiosity and no harm is being done (e.g., putting objects into orifices), you can pretend not to notice sexual exploration. Sex educators and researchers Dr. Mary Calderone and Dr. James Ramey state in their book, *Talking with Your Child about Sex,* "Sex play between children of the same and opposite sexes goes on right through childhood without observable harm except when adults make an uproar about it.''

Language

In addition to reacting to genital touching and exploration, another way parents indirectly impart sexual values is through their vocabulary. One of the first verbal lessons we offer our children is naming parts of the body. (''What's this?'' ''Nose!'') If parents freely and enthusiastically name all parts of the body, but name genitals only when asked, they have probably confused the child already.

Once parents do provide labels for the genitals, some interesting discrepancies arise. Most families are quite comfortable with the term ''penis.'' But if women of our generation are asked what name was taught to them by their parents for their genitals, many answer ''none,'' and others reply, ''down there.'' The message girls received was very negating and devaluing. Boys had a penis, but girls' sex organs weren't even worth naming or acknowledging. Some families still explain gender differences by saying, ''Boys have penises and girls don't.'' Again, what boys have is noteworthy, special, and identified. Either girls don't have anything, or it's nothing worth mentioning.

Besides being incorrect and insulting, withholding comfortable vocabulary for genitals also creates an aura of secrecy. If genitals are something ''we just don't talk about,'' how good can they be?

Many modern families have tried to improve on traditional gender identification by saying, ''Boys have penises and girls have vaginas.'' But, this still isn't quite right. Since reproduction is seldom the issue toddlers are interested in, it seems odd to highlight the vagina. It is also confusing. We are usually referring to how children urinate when we discuss their genitals, and girls certainly don't urinate with their vaginas! Because both boys and girls do pleasure themselves, it might make sense to equate the penis and clitoris. A more informative response would be: ''Boys have a penis. Girls have a vulva and inside it are three special parts: the urethra, where urine comes out;

the clitoris, that's the part that feels good when you touch it; and the vagina, which mommies use when they give birth to a baby. For boys, the penis does all of these things. It's where urine comes out; it's what feels good; and it's what daddies use when they do their part in making a baby.''

OFFERING INFORMATION AND ANSWERING QUESTIONS

Most parents recognize the importance of passing on sexual knowledge to their children and may resist sharing this responsibility with the public schools. However, only twelve out of one hundred parents have ever discussed sexual intercourse with their children and only four out of one hundred have talked about contraception.

Many of us find it awkward to discuss sex with our children, since so few of our parents ever discussed sex with us. Even if you find it difficult, embarrassing, and uncomfortable, you owe it to your children to educate and equip them to function sexually as adults.

The easiest way to discuss sexuality is to begin early. Answer your toddler's questions about anatomy and excretion freely and matter-of-factly. This will communicate your willingness and availability to answer any kind of question. You should also offer age-appropriate relevant information. For example, if your daughter says, "Did my penis fall off?" instead of answering, "No, you never had one," you might state, "No, girls are born with a vulva with a clitoris, a vagina, and a urethra," et cetera. Or if your child asks, "Do storks really bring babies to people?" instead of answering, "No," you can reply, "No, mommies and daddies make babies." This response may trigger additional questions. As you review the same information over and over throughout her childhood, she'll absorb what she can from each conversation and your explanations will become more elaborate.

Clear Messages

One of the biggest mistakes parents make in communicating sexual values is sending between-the-lines messages in their answers. For example, when a child asks how babies are made, a parent says, "When a mommy and daddy want to make a baby, the daddy puts his penis into the mommy's vagina." Sound familiar? There are two problems with this classic response. First, you have clearly communicated male activity and female passivity; the man does and the woman is done to. Since we all know that this doesn't reflect reality, how about saying, "The daddy's penis and the mommy's vagina fit together." Doesn't that sound more mutual?

Another common mistake is implying to children that the sole (or at least major) purpose of sex is reproduction. Now, as adults we know that simply isn't true. We make one, two, or maybe three babies in a lifetime, but we have frequent sex because we enjoy it. It's important for children to realize that adult sex is not just for reproduction but is also a means of expressing love, being close, and sharing pleasure. You could say to your child, "Sometimes moms and dads make love to create a baby and other times they make love just to have a close, fun, loving time together."

Naturally you'll gear both your answers and your volunteered information to your child's age, but don't abdicate your responsibility to educate your child. At every age, children are ready for some level of sexual knowledge. Your main messages should be: Your body is wonderful; it is good and natural to feel pleasure; and sex is a positive part of everyone's life when it is loving and mutual. Beyond that, you can add your own personal values.

Try to be as relaxed as possible in your discussions, so your child will really feel free to ask you what's on her mind. Children will ask the easiest person to talk to. Let it be you.

I regularly provide puberty education to fifth-grade girls at our neighborhood school. I try to emphasize that the class discussion is really just a springboard for many more such discussions with the girls' parents. It always saddens me when several girls announce that they could never talk to their own mothers about these issues. Such an atmosphere didn't arise overnight, but it must have evolved from years of muted responses to honest inquiries. The only way to ensure that your children will turn to you later for advice on intimate matters is to begin early in life to respect their inquisitiveness, respond with candor, and maintain open communication.

TELEVISION

Television is a perplexing issue for parents and requires their daily attention. On the one hand, we are sure that if our children haven't had their quota of *Sesame Street* before kindergarten, they will surely be placed in a remedial group. On the other hand, we hear authorities everywhere chastise parents for using the TV as a babysitter and allowing children to watch all the "wrong" shows.

Whether the influence of TV is predominantly positive or negative, TV is indeed a major influence in most children's lives. Children begin watching TV at the average age of 2.8 months, and by the time they are between three and five years of age, most are watching fifty-four hours a week! Thus, TV may be the greatest influence in a child's life outside her family. Even the amount of time spent in school does not compare to that spent in front of a TV. Some parents actually spend less time interacting with their child than the child spends watching TV. This phenomenon is having the greatest impact on the present generation of children, so we really don't yet know the full effect of TV on our children.

Positive Features of TV

TV is a powerful and effective educational tool. Both children and adults learn a great deal from TV. For example, many children have learned to read effortlessly by routinely watching *The Electric Company*.

TV can be a broadening influence in a child's life. Through TV children become aware of environments, people, and life-styles different from their own. This contrib-

utes to a more openminded and accepting attitude toward
other cultures. In addition, TV can enrich a child, exposing her to events she may never have seen otherwise, such
as elections, space launches, the Olympic games, or ballet
and theatrical productions that might be unavailable in
your town.

Watching a special TV program can offer an experience
of family togetherness that might not have occurred otherwise. Watching TV with your child offers an opportunity
to teach consumerism, especially during commercials. Ask
your children questions such as these:

√ How many times do you think they had to film this
  toy car commercial to get the car to jump so far?
√ Do you think cleaning with brand X would really
  make anyone enjoy housework as much as that woman
  seems to? Do you know that she is an actress who is
  paid to look happy while she pretends to clean?
√ Do you think people will really like us more if we
  use a certain brand of soap or mouthwash?

Negative Features of TV

Watching TV is the most passive thing a person can do.
By watching TV many hours each day, children may learn
to be passive listeners and to expect to be continually
entertained. Watching TV takes the place of personal interactions with parents, siblings, or friends; it also takes the
place of physical exercise.

Skillfully packaged children's shows that change scenes
frequently may contribute to shortening children's attention spans and cause later difficulty with schoolwork. Dr.
Werner Halpern, a psychiatrist at a mental health center in
Rochester, New York, claims that some children's programs, with their pulsating, constant visual and auditory
stimulation, may be overwhelming to a young child's
nervous system and contribute to emotional instability.

All parents are at least somewhat concerned about the
amount and nature of violence on TV. The Surgeon General's Committee on Television and Social Behavior has
claimed a causal link between violence watched on televi-

sion and some forms of aggression and violent behavior. Children who are very aggressive, frustrated, and poorly adjusted already may be especially vulnerable.

How much violence do children really see on TV? Whether they watch only "children's and family shows," or whether, like five million other children under twelve, they are still watching TV at the adult hours of 10:30 to 11:00 P.M., the answer is: PLENTY! Three out of ten programs contain violence, and cartoons contain one aggressive act per minute. (In all fairness, the older cartoons we watched, like *Tom and Jerry,* are far more violent than the new ones.) As a matter of fact, an hour of children's programming has more violence than an hour of adult programming. By the time most American children have reached the age of eighteen, they have seen 18,000 murders and countless scenes of other violent crime.

In her excellent book *Growing Up Free,* Letty Cottin Pogrebin cites research that says,

> Children who watch hours of TV suffer an increase in nightmares, fears, and appetite disturbances. They develop greatly distorted ideas about death and suffering. Their behavior is altered in small and large ways. They become insensitive to the sight of someone being hurt. They use violent scenarios as a guide for their own actions when playing with others. They are capable of reproducing hostile acts exactly as they saw them on TV eight months earlier. When given the opportunity to either help or hurt a child in need, kids were more likely to HURT after seeing a fighting scene than after seeing an exciting sports event. And an appalling number of juvenile crimes—torture, kidnappings, rapes, and murders—have been traced to events portrayed on television dramas.
>
> Most sobering of all, I think, is this fact that affects all children, not just the criminal few: Kids who watch four or more hours of TV a day tend to overestimate the number of violent crimes that happen in real life and exaggerate the danger of their own victimization. Children needn't mimic violence to be damaged by it; they are wounded spiritually by the FEAR of violence and the suspicion that they are unsafe in our world.

Another harm TV inflicts on our children is subtle brain-washing about damaging and limiting sex roles. TV teaches children a distorted lesson about men and women. A perceptive five-year-old girl asked her mother why almost all the characters on Saturday morning cartoons are boys and when girls are on "all they ever do is get saved?" She added emphatically, "I'm tired of it!"

It has been found that heavy TV viewers between the ages of three and twelve have more stereotypical views of occupational sex roles. Following exposure to programs showing somewhat counterstereotypical women (a school principal, a police officer, a park ranger, and a TV producer), both boys and girls were more likely to say that these were jobs to which girls could also aspire.

We know that children believe what they see on TV. Do we want our boys to think they need to be tough and macho like Mr. T., and our girls to think that they need to be dependent on a man's approval like the women they see on programs, cartoons, and commercials?

When you monitor TV programs for moral values, language, sex, and violence, please add stereotyped sex roles to your list. It may be the most far-reaching and long-lasting damage TV does.

How Much TV Is Okay?

The amount of TV you allow your children to watch will reflect your personal values. But you might be interested to know that by the time the average American child enters kindergarten, she has spent more time in front of a TV than a college grad with a B.A. has spent in the university classroom! And by the time that same child has graduated from high school, she will have spent almost twice as much time in front of a TV as in front of a teacher.

Many families would like to cut down their TV consumption (after all, it really may be bad for their health). Here are some suggestions for limiting your family's TV viewing time:

√ Move the TV to a less accessible, less comfortable room. Make it a little harder to automatically turn it on by unplugging it each time you turn it off.

√ Put books you and family members are currently reading on top of the TV. Seeing the books might make you decide to read instead of watching TV.

√ Turn the TV off *immediately* after each show you watch, before the music and previews of the next program lure you into another hour.

√ Set limits and require choices in your family TV viewing. For example, you might let each child choose five shows a week. You will find it is interesting to hear your child weigh one show's merits against another in deciding on the best show for her.

√ Select specific programs to watch, instead of just turning on the TV set to see what's there.

√ Avoid using the TV as a regular babysitter. If the only reason the kids are in front of the TV is because you need some time, try putting them in front of puzzles, clay, building blocks, or a game instead.

√ Go on a TV diet by systematically cutting back on the number of shows you watch. Maybe cut out one show a week (or a month) until you are more satisfied with your TV viewing level.

√ Watch TV with your children as often as possible, so you can monitor and discuss the material you're viewing. Also, since you can't afford to waste time in front of the TV, they're apt to spend less time there.

Guidelines for the TV You Do Watch

√ Choose quality shows with good writing and acting, and without sex-role stereotypes and violence. You need to exercise censorship, even for very young children. They absorb more than we often realize.

√ Teach your child consumerism. Point out how a commercial or TV show is trying to influence us, how they are doing it, and how that idea jives with reality.

√ Become active consumers. Write stations, shows, and advertisers and tell them when something has offended you and when you like what you see. As soon as your children are old enough, let them write, too.

√ When watching a toy commercial, ask your child what the children in the ad are doing. Are they playing with the toy or watching it? Which is more fun?

√ After your child has seen an irresistible toy advertised on TV, take her to a store and show it to her. Doesn't it look smaller, more breakable, less imaginative, and less fun in real life?

√ When you hear your children refer to a toy as a "boy's toy" or a "girl's toy," ask why. If the answer is, "Because I saw it on TV and only boys/girls were playing with it," ask if they can think of any other reasons.

√ To demonstrate to your child the values conveyed by a TV show, especially cartoons, ask them to count the acts of kindness shown during one program.

√ After any show, ask your children which characters would they like to be regardless of sex. Notice how rarely the women's roles are the appealing ones. Point this out and talk about it.

√ Raise your children's consciousness and standards about the quality of TV shows. Tell them which programs you like, which you dislike, and why.

√ As you watch TV with your young child, talk to her about the program's story line and ideas to make sure she understands what she sees.

Many authorities who have researched TV's effects on children believe you simply should not own a TV. This may be somewhat unrealistic and might make your child feel "deprived" in relation to her peers, besides causing you to miss worthwhile programs. In addition, by refusing to own a TV, you abdicate your voice in TV programming. Rather than turning our backs on TV and its harmful elements, we can be effective consumers by selective watching and by voicing our opinions through letters and purchasing power. We can object to what we don't like and reinforce what we do.

THE FAMILY BED

The "family bed" refers to the practice of family members sleeping together in the same bed. In most families, this usually means the baby or toddler sleeping in bed with her parents. Although this is an ancient practice, its benefits are being rediscovered and its use reinstituted in some modern families, making the acceptability of the family bed a contemporary concern.

There seem to be four kinds of parents. There are those who strongly believe in the family bed as a philosophy. A large number of parents occasionally bring their babies in bed with them because the babies are happier and the parents sleep better. They may bring a frightened toddler into their bed during a storm or after a nightmare but don't make a regular practice of letting their child sleep with them. Other parents have never had their babies in bed with them because the thought has never occurred to them or they find the idea somewhat uncomfortable. Then there are the parents who are adamantly against the idea of having a baby or child in their bed and, furthermore, think it is a perverted practice.

Those parents and authorities who object to the family bed cite the harm they think it causes. And those parents and authorities who favor the family bed cite the benefits they think it offers. Perhaps some perspective can be brought to this issue.

Objections	How Much Truth Is In It?
Your child will become a sexual pervert.	None.
Sexual contact may be occurring between the parents and children.	This is most unlikely. The family bed is offered by loving, nurturing parents, not parents who would victimize a child. The sick parent who would do that would do it no matter where the child slept.

Objections	How Much Truth Is In It?
Parents will not sleep as well.	If the child is a very restless sleeper and the parents are light sleepers, this may be true. In most cases, everyone seems to sleep fine. Parents may sleep better feeling sure that their baby is okay.
The parents will never have a chance to make love.	Parents are more imaginative than that! They either move the child temporarily, or go to another location themselves. Actually most parents go to bed without "company," make love, and then a few hours later are joined by the baby.
Parents may roll over and suffocate or crush the baby.	There is really NO truth to this. Parents, even very heavy sleepers, instinctively know the baby is there and never roll over on her. In addition, no baby would passively lie still if something were obstructing her breathing; she would squirm and fight in a very noticeable way.
The child will be sleeping with her parents for the rest of her life.	I know of no reported cases of this. Children grow toward independent sleeping and outgrow the need to come into their parents' bed.

Objections	How Much Truth Is In It?
If a child is still sleeping with her parents at a very late age, this may be abnormal.	There could be some truth to this. If the child does not seem to eventually outgrow coming into her parents' bed, perhaps she is not being appropriately guided toward independent sleeping.
Keeping the baby in bed at night encourages more night nursing.	It might, but there is nothing unhealthy about a baby receiving extra closeness and nourishment. Most mothers adjust to night nursing with minimal disruption of their sleep.

Benefits	How Much Truth Is In It?
The child will feel safe and emotionally secure sleeping with her parents.	This is likely to be true.
Some parents sleep better with the baby in bed.	This is true, partially because the mother needn't get up for night feedings and partly because the parents aren't worrying about the baby and listening for every little sound.
Babies benefit from this opportunity to spend extra time with their employed parent or parents.	Parental contact at night can help substitute for missed daytime interaction.
A working mother's milk supply can be maintained more easily if her baby nurses freely at night.	Night nursings can be important to an employed mother's milk supply, and keeping the baby in bed is one way to ensure that adequate nursing will take place.

If Your Child Likes the Family Bed, But You Don't

✓ Bring your baby into bed when she wakes up to nurse, but instead of falling right back to sleep, attempt to move your sleeping baby back to her crib after the feeding.

✓ Start offering the night nursings from a rocking chair instead of your bed, and try returning the baby to her crib.

✓ Place a single or double mattress on your baby's bedroom floor and nurse her there at night. When she falls asleep, you can quietly slip back into your own room.

✓ You can put a mattress on your bedroom floor next to your bed so your child can sleep nearby without being in your bed. Then use the same technique as in the previous tip.

The Usual Course of the Family Bed

If, for reasons of increased sleep or increased closeness, you find yourself bringing your baby into bed, the following guidelines will help you derive its benefits while still encouraging the ultimate goal of growth toward independent sleeping.

✓ After the baby initially nurses to sleep, lay her in her crib. When you go to bed, you will have some time alone together before the baby awakens for her first night feeding. At that point one parent can bring her into your bed to be nursed, allowing everyone to fall back to sleep quickly.

✓ If the baby is still waking during the night by the time she can walk, you can arrange her bed so she can get out of it without help, perhaps using a mattress on the floor, or a very low bed. When she feels the need for closeness, she can simply walk into your bedroom and climb into bed herself. Often neither parent is awakened.

✓ As the child grows older, she will feel more and more secure sleeping by herself. She will come into her parents' bed less often, until eventually she won't come at all.

Although the family bed has benefits, any child could grow up securely without it. The cautions are based mostly on myth, not on real safety or psychological factors. The family bed is a personal decision, not anyone else's concern, and is a healthy and restful way to sleep while parenting young children.

BREAST FEEDING ISSUES

With the rising incidence of breast feeding, some old practices have appeared anew. Old practices in a new world will give rise to questions, concerns, and even judgments. And that's just what has happened with some time-honored aspects of the nursing relationship.

Nursing in Public

Even advice columnists have been consulted about the propriety of breast-feeding a baby in public. By public, I mean in a restaurant, on an airplane, in a park, or at any other location outside your home.

Why has the question of nursing in public arisen? Because some people claim to find this practice "offensive." One might wonder what could possibly be offensive about a mother feeding her baby? Those offended claim she is exposing a sexual part of her body.

It is a sad commentary on our society that breast feeding is rarely publicly visible and the sexual exploitation of women's bodies is so prevalent that breasts have lost their maternal associations and only the sexual ones remain. No one would deny that breasts play a role in our sexual experience. The primary biologic purpose of the breasts, however, is to lactate and provide nourishment for our offspring.

Breast feeding is how human mothers naturally feed

their babies. It is not offensive, nor inappropriate in any situation. It is nature's plan. If observers are so unfamiliar with natural human feeding that they find themselves reacting with embarrassment, that's their problem, not the mother's or the baby's.

In consideration of both our right to breast-feed and the sensitivities of a portion of the public, however, a compromise can be reached. Nursing can be accomplished in a discreet way. If the mother pulls her blouse up from the bottom (rather than unbuttoning from the top), the top of her breast is covered by her blouse and the bottom by the baby. Nursing can be accomplished with virtually none of the breast exposed. If anyone objects to discreet nursing, they are objecting to the very fact that a baby is being nursed, and *that's* offensive.

Objectors often claim that mothers could nurse in the privacy of a restroom. But the sad state of many public

restrooms renders them unfit even for their intended use, much less for feeding a baby. Objectors and breast-feeding mothers alike would appreciate better facilities for nursing babies. If restrooms had couches or chairs, most mothers would be delighted to have a comfortable, clean, private place to nurse. Currently mothers who are relegated to the restroom for nursing may find themselves feeding their babies in a stall. Would you want to eat your meal in a bathroom stall?

Breast-feeding mothers find themselves facing a real societal dilemma. On the one hand, society endorses and encourages breast feeding for providing optimal infant nutrition, but at the same time qualifies its acceptance with "not in front of me." It is time for our society to stop talking from both sides of its mouth. For now, though, when the rights of those who find nursing embarrassing and those who depend on nursing for their nourishment are weighed, there can be no question that the babies are the ones who must win, even "in public."

Tandem Nursing

Tandem nursing is the practice of simultaneously nursing two children who aren't twins. If this idea is unfamiliar to you, you may wonder how a mother might find herself in this situation.

If a nursing mother becomes pregnant, her nursling may or may not wean voluntarily. Many babies will wean by the time their mother is a few months pregnant. Her milk supply usually diminishes within two to three months, becomes more colostrumlike, and tastes different. Some mothers will wean their baby during a pregnancy because they do not want to nurse two babies. But other mothers believe that their baby's nursing needs remain and will allow the baby to continue breast feeding.

Some worry that the practice of nursing through a pregnancy could be harmful to the fetus or mother, but there is no need for concern on this count. Since actual milk production declines in the early months of pregnancy, there is little additional caloric drain on the pregnant mother by continued lactation. Of course the older baby cannot depend on breast milk alone for all of her nutritional needs and must be supplemented with formula or milk and solids, depending on her age.

The biggest problem the pregnant mother faces is discomfort. Since nipple and breast tenderness usually accompany pregnancy, nursing can become uncomfortable. Each mother needs to decide for herself if the advantages of continuing to nurse her baby outweigh the discomfort of nipple soreness.

Other areas of concern arise once the mother is nursing both babies. First, will the newborn receive enough of the milk? The extra stimulation to the breast will cause more milk to be produced, as it would be with twins. Enough milk can be produced for both the older and the newborn baby, but the mother does need to exert some control over the nursing patterns to ensure that the newborn receives first priority, since breast milk is her only food source. The older baby can be offered a partically empty breast and make up for the extra calories with solid food and other drinks in her diet.

Some people also express concern about whether the older baby will ever wean. In fact, tandem nursing may lead to longer nursing in the older baby. But certainly, an older tandem nurser can wean either voluntarily or with some gentle guidance from her parents.

Some mothers who tandem nurse claim that the practice leads to closer feelings and less rivalry between the siblings. There is no scientific evidence to prove this, but the practice may have that effect in some families.

In modern American society, tandem nursing is still unusual. With the increased incidence of breast feeding and the tendency toward longer nursing, however, more parents are considering tandem nursing. This is a personal decision. While tandem nursing can be physically draining to the mother, many mothers feel that weaning the first baby before she is ready would be even more of a strain. Decisions concerning tandem nursing are neither right nor wrong; it's a matter of personal choice.

Late Nursing

Several decades ago any breast-feeding mother was an exception. Nursing for three months was certainly long enough and six months almost unheard of. Now the American Academy of Pediatrics has recommended that all infants be breast-fed exclusively for the first four to six months of life and continuing throughout the first year.

The expression "late nursing" certainly has a different meaning in every time and culture. In underdeveloped settings and less industrial societies, nursing until three years is often the norm. But, in our present culture, nursing past the age of two years is considered unusual.

Why, you might wonder, is late nursing even presented as an issue for discussion? Mothers of late nursers know the answer. For some reason, many people unconnected to the nursing relationship have strong negative views about late nursing and often express these to both the mother and the nursing toddler. Even some pediatricians discourage late nursing, based only on their personal reactions, rather than any medical basis.

Objections you may hear will include:

- ✓ She'll be a momma's girl; he'll be a momma's boy.
- ✓ Late nursing is a sexual, and therefore perverted, activity.
- ✓ It will cause homosexuality.
- ✓ She will go to kindergarten, high school, or college still nursing.

Of course these are all myths; none is a real concern. In fact, to the contrary, late nursing has some benefits. It provides emotional security, nutrition, and immunologic protection.

If you choose to nurse a toddler, develop a word for nursing that is not obvious to other people. Explain to her that nursing is something "special" that we try to do at home, not in public. And when challenged by outside people, as you will be, you can always truthfully answer "we're weaning" (it is a slow process).

Once again, late nursing, which often goes hand in hand with baby-led weaning, is a personal parenting decision. Read your own child's needs; follow your own parenting instincts; and turn a deaf ear to all that well-meant but inappropriate advice.

15 Nonsexist Child Rearing

I SAW A POSTER RECENTLY that read, "We haven't come a long way, and I'm not your baby." It first struck me as an angry, radical feminist slogan, but it started me thinking. We see more women than ever in professions like law, medicine, and engineering, and women are taken more seriously as athletes, too. Women are in politics and in space; women are in the fire station and in the board room. Men are teachers and nurses and full-time homemakers. But in 1986 the number of women in traditionally male occupations is too few, and women are still earning considerably less than men. That isn't such a long way, baby.

Sexism is stereotyping, bias, or prejudice about a person based on gender, just as racism is prejudice based on race. Interestingly, even though racism is socially unacceptable, sexism carries less social stigma. The populace just assumes that innate differences exist between boys and girls, women and men.

The scientific community has studied the topic of sex differences in many ways. And for almost every "conclusive" study, there is another that "proves" something different. Inherent problems in the studies make this topic a very difficult one. You can't raise children in a vacuum in order to ascertain which traits are due to environmental influence, and the very scientists making observations are themselves influenced by societal sexual bias. The language of studies is often misleading, too. For instance, "Males are more aggressive than females" does not mean that *all* males are more aggressive than *all* females, or that

470

any male will be more aggressive when compared to any female. It means that more males than females exhibit aggressive behavior . . . in this study.

In fact, for all traits, the range of difference is greater within either sex than it is between the sexes. All we really know for certain about the differences between males and females is just what we learned in eighth-grade health class. Girls mature about eighteen months faster than boys. Boys end up with greater bone size and muscle mass. Girls and boys also have different genitalia. But society continues its quest to discover just how else men and women may differ.

We don't hear that men and women have differing muscle strength, we hear that men are stronger. Whatever the trait, it is not judged neutrally or simply differentiated; the quest is not really to find out how men and women are different, it is to find out which sex is "better" in which areas. And that is where sexism becomes limiting. If boys are "supposed" to be stronger, and Timmy is not very strong, he is seen as less male. If girls are "supposed" to be weaker, and Tammy is very strong, she is seen as less female. Why are each of these children devalued for not performing to stereotype, instead of being valued for their true talents?

Sex-role stereotypes, although not accurate measures of skill, interest, or potential, become behavior predictions, and thus behavior restrictions. Although you may not think your four-year-old leads a very restricted life, children see sex-role restrictions in every social setting. They select sex-role "appropriate" birthday gifts for friends, they shun opposite-sex stereotypical play, and they have clear images of sex-role-linked occupations.

Even if we claim to value our female and male children equally, the children themselves know the truth. In our patriarchal society, being male is superior, and any male-emulating behavior in girls is condoned, but female-emulating behavior in boys is scorned. A four-year-old may not understand it in those words, but she already knows that it's okay to be a tomboy, while for a boy to be labeled a sissy is deadly. It is okay for a girl to wear jeans, but a boy could never wear a dress. A girl who beats a boy in a race may not get dates, but she will be spared the ridicule directed at a boy who cooks the best soufflé in class. Is it just as good to be a girl as it is to be a boy?

By far the most conclusive evidence of the fact that children recognize society's gender-based expectations comes from children themselves. When asked what they want to be when they grow up, most girls say a mommy or a teacher, and then have trouble thinking of other possibilities. Most boys fail to mention being a daddy, but have myriad other ideas in mind—cowboy, fireman, football player, president, or doctor.

When asked what they would be if they were boys, the girls' options open up immensely and they report they'd be a baseball player, a bus driver, an astronaut, a fireman, or a scientist. Boys, on the other hand, become quite thoughtful and often frustrated when trying to decide what to be if they were a girl, and usually say "just a mother." The most telling of all, though, is the little boy who replied, "If I was a girl, I guess I'd grow up to be nothing."

So how do we do it? How do we raise children without sexist restraints? In our society, which is highly socialized to expect sex-role behaviors, nonsexist attitudes are exceptions to the rules that our child absorbs in every sphere of life. Nonsexism is not easily taught and will be slow to sink in. Such insignificant gestures as giving a truck to a girl or a doll to a boy, or having Dad cook when Mom is sick, contribute little to a child's education in nonsexism. Indeed, even children from very nonsexist homes may be well rooted in sex-role behavior. Our societal messages are simply so strong that only consistent, conscious efforts can alter its impact on our children.

The ongoing commitment to imparting the new value system required for raising nonsexist children is difficult to maintain without a firm belief that nonsexist child rearing is really beneficial to children, parents, and society. Many well-intentioned parents, are so firmly socialized into sexism that they harbor doubts and misconceptions about nonsexist child rearing.

Misconception # 1: Nonsexist child rearing will produce unisex children.

Nonsexist child rearing does NOT mean raising a generation of sexless children. It is not the insistence that all girls and all boys both play soccer and study ballet. Rather, it allows broader choices for both sexes. Nonsexist child rearing acknowledges that all children are not the same, but recognizes that the differences result from their varied skills, interests, and talents, rather than the genetic allocation of genitals.

Sexism discourages variety by imposing arbitrary limitations, like assigning pink infant clothing to girls and presuming athletic interest in all males. Nonsexist child rearing allows for infinite variety. By removing limits based solely on the accident of gender, the world is opened up to our children.

Jordan's gender should not predict athletic interest or academic skill, and we should not press either upon Jordan. Rather let Jordan pursue what is really best for healthy development and enjoyment. While experience may tell us that most boys do like to play with cars, let us not assume that all do, or that not one girl does. Sexism generates pressure to behave according to gender role. Remove the *role* expectations and you leave more doors open to all children.

Misconception #2: Children need to identify with the same-sex parent for proper development.

The assumption that the parent role model must be of the classic gender role type is fallacy. Children do learn about being a girl or being a boy from seeing their parents operate in the world and identifying with that image. Unfortunately, what most children perceive is a clear reflection of a patriarchal society in which men are valued and women are mothers. Examine how such messages are conveyed in daily life.

"Don't get crumbs in Daddy's chair, Robin." (Does Mommy even have her own chair?)

"Ask your Dad for money to go to the movie." "Ask your Mom if we can have some cookies." (Dad controls important things like money, and Mom handles the more mundane things like food.)

"Don't track through your Mother's clean kitchen." (Everybody has a bedroom, the living room belongs to all, but a kitchen is Mom's.)

"Shhhh! Dad's taking a nap!" (He must be hardworking

and important, if he is tired and cannot be disturbed.)

Children routinely see men as policemen and newscasters, construction workers and priests, doctors and bus drivers. They see women as waitresses and cashiers and mothers. Rare is the child who does not formulate from these observations that men do important and interesting things and that women generally take care of others and do less exciting things.

How utterly refreshing and healthy it would be if children developed gender identity by modeling a confident, competent, caring adult of their same sex, but not necessarily performing according to sex-role expectations.

Sexism also hinders healthy gender identity in another way. Imagine the anxiety experienced by a young boy admonished not to "cry like a girl." As he tries hard to be like a boy "should" be, he has to wonder if he is a boy at all, since he really wanted to cry and "boys don't cry."

Misconception #3: *If we raise our sons to be soft and our daughters to be strong, they will never fit in with their peers.*

The purpose of nonsexist child raising is not to weed out all traits associated with the child's gender and to insert the traits of the opposite gender. That notion is just as limiting as the status quo.

Nonsexist child rearing seeks to allow our soft children to be soft, and our strong children to be strong, regardless of gender. Since this ideal will take generations to come about, the problem of peer acceptance is minimized. If all children with traits or talents of the opposite sex-role stereotype were allowed to express those attributes freely, there would be enough nonconformists within each group that "fitting in" wouldn't be a problem.

Misconception #4: *When offered trucks and dolls, little boys always choose trucks anyway. This nonsexist stuff just doesn't seem to work.*

When a two-year-old boy prefers a truck to a doll, it is not because it is natural for him to like trucks or because nonsexist child rearing does not work. It is because sex-role expectations and stereotypes are omnipresent, flavoring every sight, sound, and touch he has known in his short years.

Misconception #5: Nonsexism has already been achieved.

Look first at the social role model and you see that most male-dominated areas, like law, engineering, medicine, or sports, are valued in the most direct way, monetarily. Most traditionally female roles, like parenting, cleaning, caring, and teaching are not. Society does not value stereotypically male and female skills, talents, and traits equally.

What's wrong with finding value in those traits and actions stereotyped to gender? Girls feel good when praised for appearance and boys feel good when praised for achievement. True, but what about the pressure such behavior places on them? Girls spend countless hours and dollars trying to be pretty, even at the expense of their health. Although they are often spared some of the anxiety of achievement pressure that boys bear, they often simply turn off athletic or academic talent or achievement in the hope of being more appealing to boys.

Where girls are expected to be pretty simply because they are female, boys are expected to do well in sports and math because of the mere random assignment of chromosomes and genitals. When you think of the number of competitors versus the number of winners in team and individual sports, simple math reveals that most boy competitors will not be winners or superstars.

Although boys do worry about their appearance during adolescence, current fashion is less crucial, and makeup is not a time, financial, or health concern. A few extra pounds will be far less noticed and less likely to trigger anorexia or bulimia, and pimples, the curse of teenage years, will not stop the roar of the fans for the touchdown. These would destroy the self-esteem of any girl if she is dependent solely on her appearance for approval.

The first step to communicating nonsexist child rearing is to become aware of the sexism all around us. Begin to attune to the subtle sexism in your life. When can you substitute the opposite sex without a jar to your ear? When can you predict big/active for maleness and small/passive for femaleness in cartoons, greeting cards, furniture, personality expectations? At first it may not be easy to notice sexism, but soon you'll recognize it more and more. Before long you'll see that sexism and its limiting effects are rampant in our culture.

As you begin to think in this way, let a mental click register each time you perceive sexism.

"Jeff, will you watch Sarah for me for a few hours while I go to the hardware store?"

versus

"Jessica, I'm going to the hardware store. I'll see you in a couple of hours." *Click.*

Bill, a single parent, is sainted by the women he dates for being able to do so well with his children—he even takes them to their afternoon piano lessons!

but

Jeannette, a single parent, is credited with being strong, spunky, and/or gutsy for supporting herself and shoveling her own snow. *Click.*

Susan, age five, comes home from her medical checkup with Dr. Jane Norton and proclaims, "When I grow up, I'm going to be a nurse, just like Dr. Norton!" *Click.*

"Jane, I did the dishes for you." "Thanks, Joe." *Click.*

Watch some prime-time TV or some Saturday morning cartoons. First, count the number of men/boys, then the number of women/girls. Then do a little analysis of who is active (doing, chasing, thinking, saving, winning, fighting) and who is passive (cute, helpless, chased, saved). Then, brace yourself; try some commercials. Who sells what to whom? How? Why? *Click.*

Yet most of us overlook even the most blatant clicks. An educational spot about the American Constitution shown between cartoons uses mostly male cartoon characters to represent early Americans. A group of men shout, in a cartoon dialogue bubble, "Life," then "Liberty," and as the rest of the phrase is sung a man is seen chasing a woman across the front of the screen. Just who is pursuing and who is happy?

By applying some basic ground rules for parenthood, infancy, and childhood, and making the eradication of sexism a family quest, you can minimize limitations on your children's development.

Opponents of nonsexism first point to language as evidence of how hard and futile it is to change. Using "he or she" or "s/he" is too awkward, they claim. And we all know that "man" refers to the entire human race, so why all the fuss? The objectors don't even hear what is offensive in the term "lady doctor."

All sexism in language devalues females in one fundamental way: Male is presumed to be normal, the majority, the standard, and female is different, less common, other-than-the-standard. Have a nonbeliever try this test: Substitute female for male and apply equal adjectives in everyday conversation. "My friend, a male attorney, told me . . ." "As woman evolved, she began to hunt for food." "If an engineer recommends soil samples, she may suspect the following possibilities." "Peace on earth, good will toward women."

The addition of an adjective that identifies sex—such as male nurse or lady doctor—degrades either person. By noting that the job performed is other than the gender-role stereotype, the language points out that the man is lowering himself or that the woman has been elevated above her proper place.

The other substantial hindrance to achieving nonsexist goals is inherent in the function of language. If we are sexist, our language evolves with sexism built in; if we learn and use language that is sexist, the sexism in each of us is reinforced. Begin to repair your language in each of these areas so that your children will have at least some exposure to vocabulary free of the baggage of expectation and stereotype based on gender.

Nouns: If someone told you that a boy at the doctor's office gave you some pills, you would probably envision a young male drug dealer. If the girl at the doctor's office gave you pills, the vision is of the adult female who works for the doctor. Adult males are referred to by the term "men," but females are too often called "girls" or "ladies," when "women" would be the term of choice. The parallel term "gentlemen" is almost never used. (Notice public bathroom door signs: many read "Men" and "Ladies.")

Noun repair: Females are girls until age eighteen; after that they are women. Male adults are men and female adults are women.

Pronouns: Everything in the world from people to animals to inanimate objects are presumed to be male. Exception: Most temperamental things, like storms and boats, have long been assigned female pronouns. At least this has begun to change.

Pronoun repair: Animals and things won't be offended to be called "it," and personal pronouns can be for people only. The use of the phrase "she or he," although cumbersome at first, does work, and has the added benefit of

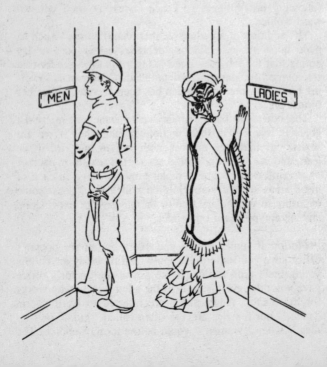

being noticeable in use. Each time we hear it, we are reminded that children, doctors, parents, writers, students, poets, marathoners, scientists, gigglers, bricklayers, lovers, and babies can be female or male.

Adjectives: As applied to people, they are used very differently for men and women. He's a dashing playboy; she's a loose woman. She's an aggressive businesswoman; he's an assertive businessman. Even babies get different words for the same traits. She's petite; he's very small for his age. He's a go-getter; she's very active. She's cute or pretty; he is handsome.

Adjective repair: Any time you use an adjective, choose one to describe the person or event, void of sex-role expectations. The standard test of opposite gender will guide you. He's a playboy, she's loose; they are both sexually promiscuous. They are adept at business, and they are nurturing parents.

Sentence structure: Girls are usually described physically or referred to in the passive mode: She is a cutie, she's a charming hostess; she's a lovely wife. Boys are more likely to be discussed in active sentence structures: he dresses sharp, he cooks up a storm, and he outsmarts everyone in his class. This is no surprise, since active boys and passive girls are the very basis of the gender-role expectations placed on children. Language simply reflects our expectations that boys do great things and girls are great looking.

General language repair: Notice and avoid language that employs or perpetuates any assumption about a person based on gender. For trash collectors' dignity, we changed to "sanitation engineer"; for minorities we changed language in accord with their preferred description. In the same vein, we must continue to mold our language for the female population.

PARENTING

Your life-style models for your children the value system by which you live. By eradicating traditional roles in your home and establishing parity parenting, you will erode some of the sexism that society instills in your child. Toss out the old patriarchal notion that the value of the work performed is measured by the income earned. If one partner earns more, this does not buy immunity to an equal share in maintaining the home.

Eliminate the words "for you" from your household vocabulary. No longer can you think in terms of changing the oil "for you" or doing dishes "for you."

Tasks may be assigned by almost any method *other* than sex-role expectation. Consider preference (one hates cleaning toilets; one hates vacuuming stairs), priority (the barefoot partner loves clean floors; the slipper-wearing one could not care less), and practicality (it's hard to make the bed with your partner still in it). Talent, skill, and knowledge rarely apply to any menial task of household maintenance. Even tasks never before performed like mending clothes or changing oil can be taught and traded. Learn new skills from your partner and feel free to exhibit and enjoy your newfound competence.

Parity parenting means that each parent is interchangeable with the other for the varied family responsibilities. One parent does not defer punishment, as in "wait until your father gets home." One parent does not always buy the new shoes or accompany the child to the doctor. One parent does not always take the family out to dinner or buy the new car.

Either parent disciplines or pampers. Either parent takes children to the dentist or the circus. Either parent plays ball or kisses away a scrape.

INFANCY

Why do we dress our baby girls in ruffles and pink, and our boys in practical blue? Because babies are so much alike, we want people to know she is a girl or he is a boy. Why do we want people to know that? Because people have no idea how to react to a person (even a one-week-old) of unknown gender.

A baby's bedroom is one area that reflects some sense of creativity, only because most are decorated before the sex of the child is known. Pastel green and yellow are genderless, as are animal motifs or graphic murals. Apply the same thinking to other areas of your baby's life.

As babies grow, their choice of toys is molded around parental expectation instead of such practical issues as expense or developmental readiness. Even infant boys are offered baby-version planes, trains, or trucks, and girls are given lambs and dolls. Toddler boys push lawn mowers and toddler girls push doll strollers. A healthy mix of "boy" toys, "girl" toys, and neutral toys will minimize the influence of this set of limits and expectations.

Our expectations of behavior for even young children are very strong, and are almost entirely based upon the sex role society expects the child to grow into. We expect girl babies to sit sweetly in our lap and we reinforce that behavior. We expect boy babies to crawl fast and far to explore and get into things, and we seldom reprimand that kind of behavior. We expect messiness in boy children and timidity in girls. We expect boys to be loud, boisterous, and active in every way, and girls to be sweet-tempered, calm, and cute. Our expectations play a vital, if not the most significant, part in the development of the child. We expect sweet, so when she is sweet, we are pleased. She senses our pleasure, and displays more sweetness to please us again. Et cetera. "Aha!" we think. "We are right. She is very sweet."

Healthy expectations will be those based on things other than gender. She may be athletic if both parents are athletic. He may be calm if raised in a calm atmosphere. This is a tough area to repair, so begin to be conscious of what you truly see in your child and what is really only a mirror of gender-based expectation.

CHILDHOOD

Expectation for behavior or traits based solely upon sex will only handicap any child. Boys miss out by not knowing "girl things," like how good it feels or how much confidence and self-esteem come from being clean and looking attractive. Girls miss out by not knowing "boy things," like the thrill of that strong *whack* of ball against bat. Girls suffer by constantly wondering if they are as pretty as another girl. Boys suffer by constantly trying to do everything as well as some other boy.

Sexist expectations never enhance; they always detract from real potential. They impose unnecessary limitations on our children. From sports, play, and friends to cooking, crying, and caring, don't impose limits on your child because of gender.

Sports is one area where girls have been truly starved for too long, and boys have been overfed for too long. Girls used to know sports as something boys did, and are only now beginning to view sports as an area where they can participate or compete. Boys know sports, at younger

and younger ages, as something else they need to excel at. Encourage sport as play. Soccer, dodge ball, cartwheels, and running don't have to be competitive; they are supposed to be fun. If you add to the girls' agenda and subtract from the boys', eventually the role of sports in your family will be in appropriate balance. They are a fun way to exercise, interact, learn, and grow.

When we have gender-based roles or expectations for children, we limit and damage the very people we want to nurture. If she *should* be feminine, and feminine is passive and attractive, then she'll probably always strive to be more of what that is, and continually feel inadequate—not feminine enough. If he *should* be masculine, and masculine is strong and achieving, then he'll probably always strive to be more of what that is, and continually feel inadequate—not masculine enough. But if your children's self-worth does not hinge on expected appearance or achievement, if they feel lovable and loved just for who they are, they will be more able to achieve their full potential in every area. And that is what nonsexist child rearing is all about. For more on this subject, I recommend Letty Cottin Pogrebin's *Growing Up Free*.

16 WORKING STRATEGIES FOR WORKING PARENTS

STUDIES SHOW that working parents tend to feel inadequate about their parenting. What working parents may not realize is that *all* parents—regardless of how many hours they are at home or away from home, how many hours they are with their child or separated from them—feel they are not parenting well enough. It is the nature of parenthood that our best never feels quite good enough.

Contrary to our fears, more than forty well-researched studies have failed to demonstrate any ill effects on children of working parents. A California psychologist traced four hundred schoolchildren and found that their emotional adjustment was not related to whether their mothers worked outside the home, but rather to how their mothers felt about their work and their lives. Researchers have concluded that the more satisfied a woman is with her life, the more effective she will be as a parent, and the better adjusted her children will be. So, parents with a need and/or desire to work must consider the emotional costs to themselves and their children of staying at home and being frustrated compared to going to work and feeling guilty about not being "Supermom" or "Superdad."

Who are working parents? They could be a two-career family or a single father or single mother employed outside the home. A growing number of families now fit one of these descriptions. Seventeen million women with children are working outside the home, including more than 40 percent of all mothers of preschool children. The rising divorce rate means that many children are living with a single working parent. These parents have additional challenges, among them finding quality day care for their children, managing guilt, having too much to do in too little time, sharing responsibility equitably for care of the children and house, and having no time for themselves.

Whether you work part-time or full-time, great care must be given to selecting the best possible day care for your child.

Your decision about day care will depend on your resources, job location, your child's nature, and your personal needs. Consider all day-care options with these criteria in mind. Day-care options include having a family member or a caregiver in your home, a day-care home (licensed or unlicensed), or a day-care center. Most day-care providers are very special people. They generally work for a low salary in the face of high expectations and do it because they enjoy working with children.

The person you select to care for your child must have special qualities. Why else would you have entrusted your child to her care? You should offer her at least the same consideration you would give to any employee.

After a year, offer her a raise even if she does not request one. When in doubt, be generous. If you pick up your child a few minutes late or ask for some special arrangement or consideration, give your caregiver a small bonus. The investment in good feelings will more than pay for itself.

If your child is sick or you go on a vacation, do you expect your caregiver to go without pay? Her income depends on payment for caring for a certain number of children. She cannot simply bring in another child to watch while yours is sick. Why should her income suffer? A place in her home is still reserved for your child even when she is sick or you are on vacation, and your caregiver should be compensated for that.

Whatever your child-care arrangements, try to be as prompt and reliable as possible with both dropping off and picking up. Express your appreciation for the care your child receives and the peace of mind this allows you.

Each day-care option and each type of day-care provider has pros and cons and unique considerations. If you manage to find day care near your place of employment, you may be able to nurse your infant or eat lunch with your preschooler during the workday. Many parents appreciate the opportunity for additional contact with their child, while others find separating again to be difficult. Here are suggestions for selecting a day-care provider in your home, a day-care home, a day-care center, or using a relative for regular day care.

CAREGIVER IN YOUR HOME

This option appeals most to parents of infants. The one-to-one care is important during infancy. A baby probably feels more secure and settled in her own home and has less need for the social stimulation provided by other children in a day-care center. Parents also find day care in their home convenient because they do not need to pack diapers, bottles, food, blankets, and changes of clothing each morning.

Some parents prefer a caregiver who does not have housekeeping duties as well. This assures the baby will receive the caregiver's full attention, something you cannot assume with any other day-care arrangement.

Of course, there are some drawbacks. First, day care pays poorly, making it hard to find someone capable who is willing to work outside their own home for so little. This fact accounts for the high turnover rate, which can be a problem for you and your baby. In spite of the low wages caregivers receive, care in your home is still the most expensive option to you. Only parents with a fairly high income can consider spending so much on day care.

One more consideration is that if things aren't going well and your child is nonverbal it may take you a long time to figure it out. In a group situation, chances are that you would hear something from the other parents if a blatantly bad situation existed.

If you desire a day-care provider to come to your home, start by asking friends and others who might be good sources (other day-care providers, college employment offices, church, or synagogue), put an ad in the paper or contact a home services agency. Include essential information or requirements in the ad to eliminate unlikely applicants. A sample ad might read as follows: "Mature woman to care for infant in our home. Approximately thirty hours a week. Southeast part of town. Must have own transportation. Long-term commitment. Nonsmoker. References.'' These exact specifics may not be essential to you, but you need to include as much important information in your ad as possible.

The next step is to screen out applicants whose needs and yours don't match up well enough to warrant an interview. In the course of a telephone conversation, you may discover, for example, that one woman will take the job only if she can bring her own child along. This may or may not be acceptable to you. You may discover that the wage you are offering is too low for some, and so on. Those who seem like possible candidates should be scheduled for an interview. Ask them to bring along the names of their references.

Before you even begin your interview, watch for certain signs. How does the applicant react to your request for references? If she has worked in this capacity before and cannot provide you with references, be very suspicious. Inquire about her health. You certainly don't want someone in your home who might give your baby an illness. It will also be important to you that she is healthy so she won't be missing work and will be energetic enough to care for your baby.

Think twice about those who also offer to do housekeeping in order to earn a higher wage. You are still getting one person for the same number of hours. What you may really be paying for is someone to spend less time with your baby. Is that what you want? If you do expect housekeeping duties to be performed, you might want to state that the housework is to be done when the baby is sleeping, or that you expect her to put the baby's needs first and housekeeping second.

Are neatness and cleanliness important to you? If so, notice the applicant's appearance. Do you feel that you can trust this person? She will have access to all your possessions (including, of course, your most precious one) each day.

At some time during the interview, hand the baby to the applicant. How does she respond? Is her manner gentle?

Do you like the way she handles your baby? How does the baby respond to her?

Older women often apply for caregivers' jobs. They have the advantages of maturity and experience, but sometimes they can be very opinionated about child rearing and less than openminded about your own methods. After all, they may have raised several children and feel their techniques worked for them. Try to gauge an older applicant's flexibility: Does she seem receptive to your ideas?

Very clearly outline the duties you expect her to perform. If you intend for her to do the baby's laundry, wash her bottles, and change her sheets, say so and make sure she agrees to it.

Ask questions that help you discover if your values are similar. Is she comfortable with your feeding and nutrition practices? Does she express value judgments about dual-career marriages with children? How does she feel about the importance of a regular schedule, fresh air, TV, and so on? Incompatible values are difficult to resolve.

Discuss discipline thoroughly. You need to know her views on discipline, and she needs to hear your views. Ask her what she would do if the baby made her angry. Be extremely explicit about the fact that you would never give *anyone* permission to hit your child *under any circumstances*. Outline what kinds of discipline would be acceptable to you.

Ask her what she would do if an emergency arose. She may not follow through precisely on her words, but you'll have an idea of what she considers appropriate action.

Ask her what she would do with the baby all day. You'll be surprised by the variety of answers you hear.

Base your final decision on the responses given to your questions, the recommendations provided by her references, the observations you make, and your gut-level reactions.

Once you've hired someone, it is very important that you sit down and go over guidelines for caring for your child. Put them in writing. View this as a long-term relationship. Invest time in the beginning to make sure that what you expect is clear. Eventually the small things may drive you crazy, so establish open communication from the beginning and don't let those little things pile up. State very clearly that you are the parents and that you will be making the decisions about your baby's care. Indicate that you are looking for a day-care provider, not a third parent.

Have a meeting before your new caregiver begins work and lay out your expectations. Listen carefully to her and respond. Make sure you understand each other. Try to spend a few hours with her and your child as training and orientation and to reassure your child during the transition to a substitute caregiver.

List an approximate schedule of your baby's meals and sleep times. If you are loose about scheduling, you could simply list food suggestions and predicted nap times like this:

—Breakfast: Amy usually has cereal or eggs with toast and juice.
—Offer Amy a mid-morning snack. She likes bananas, raisins, crackers, or rice cakes.
—Amy usually needs a morning nap around 10 or 11 A.M.
—Lunch: Give Amy yogurt, cheese, or peanut butter on bread, plus a piece of fruit and juice.
—Amy usually naps again around 2 or 3 P.M.
—Offer a snack when she wakes from her nap.

If there are specific foods you do not want your child to have or which she cannot tolerate, list them. If there are certain activities you want or don't want in your child's life, be specific. For example, you may state that you don't want the TV on, but you would like at least one book read to her each day and for her to have a walk when the weather permits.

If you want something done a particular way, show your caregiver. Demonstrate how *you* change her diaper, bathe or feed her, for example.

Do you want her to reinforce certain programs you may be doing with your child, such as a gymnastics program? Explain it to her and show her exactly what you want her to do.

Be specific about sleep. If you want your baby rocked to sleep, make sure that is understood. Also be specific about her crying. Is she to be picked up immediately?

You might suggest that your caregiver keep a notebook of your baby's day, recording such things as when she ate, slept, and had bowel movements. Any coughs, vomiting, unusual fussiness, and such could also be recorded. This is especially helpful if you are asked such questions by your pediatrician. You'll have the answers and won't have to consult your caregiver.

If you are concerned about the caregiver's attention being focused solely on your baby you may need to request that she not watch TV during work hours, or at least that TV viewing be limited.

Once your caretaker has been working for you for a short time, evaluate how things are going. In addition to your valuable gut-level feelings, look for the following:

√ How does your baby look when she sees her caregiver arrive?
√ How does the caregiver greet the baby in the morning?
√ When the caregiver holds her, talks to her, and plays with her, is the baby responsive? Do they seem to be on the same wavelength? Is she sensitive to the baby's reactions? Does the baby seem happy in her arms?
√ From your observations, does the caregiver display common sense?
√ If your child is verbal, listen to what she has to say about her time with her care provider. Do not discount what she says. Follow up on it.

If your caregiver is not what you had hoped for, change. You don't have a binding contract. It takes a great deal of work to start over with a new ad and interviews, but it is important. Do not stay with someone unless you are comfortable with her and confident in her care.

If you are happy with the quality of care your child is receiving, show your appreciation. You are lucky; treat her well and hope for a long-lasting relationship.

A DAY-CARE HOME

The advantages of a day-care home are a homelike atmosphere with siblinglike children for social stimulation.

A day-care home is usually less expensive than a caregiver in your home.

However, day-care homes vary greatly in the quality of care provided. The day-care mother may have little or no training for working with children. Sometimes the disposition of a saint may be enough qualification, but not always. You have no way of controlling how your child's day is spent. Does the day-care mother plan structured activities with the children? Does she play with them or does she put them in front of the TV or keep them in the backyard while she visits with her friends or does her housework? If you are patient and visit several day-care homes, chances are good that you can find warm, quality care for your child. But do look carefully.

A parent about to return to work may feel at a loss about finding good day care and not know where to begin the search. If you are lucky enough to know someone whose child is in an excellent day-care home, start there. A personal recommendation is your best bet. You can also find day-care homes through the newspaper, your church or synagogue, or calling the United Way for a listing of licensed day-care homes in your area.

Once you have a list of possibilities, call and find out if the home has an opening. If so, make an appointment to visit and interview the day-care mother. It is a good idea to make your appointment just before lunch or near the end of the day. This will allow you to see her at her worst and most harried. Compare how the various day-care providers you visit handle stress.

Consider whether the home is licensed or unlicensed. Licensing means something different in each state, but it usually refers to safety and health standards and maximum number of children. Find out what licensing means in your state and decide if it is a priority to you.

When you visit the day-care home, there are several aspects of the overall situation for you to evaluate. The first is the environment. Notice the children who are being cared for. Are they happy, calm, wild, unnaturally subdued? What kind of atmosphere is it? Are the children supervised and free to interact with the day-care mother, or are they delegated to the "play room" or the TV?

Ask to be shown around the house. Where do the children play, eat, sleep? Do you approve of these settings? What type of equipment does she have for the children? What would you need to provide? As you consider this aspect, you may be reminded that in any day-care home, there are trade-offs to be made, so evaluate your priorities.

Is the house safe? Are the stairs protected? Are cleaning supplies and other toxic substances up out of the reach of children? Is the yard fenced and in good repair? Look around carefully with an eye to safety. In addition to safety for its own sake, the home's safety level is a good indicator of how much energy and commitment this day-care mother brings to her job.

Does she have enough room for the number of children she cares for? Do they have adequate opportunities for play? Very crowded conditions will make a calm atmosphere harder to achieve. Is more than one environment available for play?

Next, focus your attention on the day-care mother herself. You need to be very careful not to overlook her obvious drawbacks because you are desperate and you want her to be wonderful. This has happened to me.

First, notice how she interacts with the other children. You can assume that she'll be nice to you and attentive toward your child for the purpose of this interview, but how is she with her routine charges?

Notice the chemistry between the day-care mother and your child. If you have an infant, hand her to the day-care mother. Do you like the way she handles your baby?

Since you scheduled your visit at a stressful time, like just before lunch, you may get a feel for this care provider's capacity. Is she already overloaded? Is she capable of handling one more child? Do you like the type of lunch she prepares and the way the children are fed? Are the children required to bring their own lunches? Will she heat up a hot meal if you send it?

In addition to your observations, you need to question the day-care mother directly about a number of issues. Some important topics are suggested here. Add whatever else is critical to you.

Discipline is a crucial issue. Observe carefully if any discipline occurs while you are visiting. Discuss your respective philosophies in detail. Find out just what her rules and limits are and what disciplinary actions she takes. Make it very clear what is acceptable to you. Emphasize that you will not give her permission to hit your child under any circumstances. Such permission could be very dangerous. You have no way of gauging her ability to control her impulses. You know nothing of her temper, but you can be assured that, like everyone, she allows herself to get farther out of control when no other adults are present.

If "firsts" (like the first step, the first sentence, and so on) are important to you, ask her not to mention them to you if they occur while you're at work. Surely the baby will repeat this "first" at home and you can experience the thrill of it.

If your child has any special dietary needs, like breast feeding, a vegetarian diet, or allergies to be monitored, be sure you have the day-care mother's wholehearted support. Her cooperation is vital.

Ask about her policy on sick children. I hope they are not allowed in the day-care home. This system offers your child the best protection. If sick children can come, how do you feel about the extra exposure to illnesses for your child? State that you would expect the care provider to warn you if a child in her care came down with a contagious illness.

If either of you have specific expectations or requirements, they should be spelled out very clearly in advance. An example of this might be hours. Will you pay her overtime if you are late? How much? How late or early will she watch children?

Ask about the number and ages of children present on a regular or part-time basis in case you are not seeing the entire care load during your visit. Find out if there are children near your child's age.

Ask her how long she has been doing day care. Ask about her background and why she likes her work.

Inquire about her policy on vacations, both hers and yours. You probably need to have a backup babysitter for her vacations or in case of her illness. Ask what her payment policy is for your vacations and sick days. Interestingly, women often have difficulty talking about money matters. Make sure both what she is charging and what you think you will be paying are clearly out in the open.

Call other parents who use this day-care mother and listen carefully to what they tell you. This is your best source of information for evaluating a caregiver.

Do not decide to leave your child in the care of anyone unless you are convinced that she has an understanding of the age characteristics of children.

Once you have selected your day-care home and your child is going there regularly, how do you evaluate the quality of care she is receiving? Drop by unannounced. Are things about the same as when you arrive at your scheduled time? Ask what your child ate for lunch. Is it satisfactory to you?

In the beginning of your relationship with a new caregiver, you might want to bring a certain number of diapers each day, rather than just leaving a box. That way you can tell how often your baby is changed. Also watch for diaper rash.

Does the caregiver talk to you negatively about the other children and parents? If so, you can probably assume that she also airs complaints about your child or you behind your back, rather than to you directly.

Does the day-care mother seem relieved when you pick your child up? Does she seem very upset if she has to care for her longer than usual?

Always observe the way your child and the day-care mother greet each other. Are they genuinely happy to see each other? Is there reluctance on either side?

Ask your caregiver how she handled a certain situation. Be specific and ask for details.

If your child tends to be fussy, cry, and have temper tantrums once she gets home, this is not necessarily a sign of trouble at the day-care home. Most children, and even infants, will hold in some of their negative feelings away from home. Once home, in the safest place, they can express their negative feelings from the day. Initially they may also be acting out some resentment about your leaving them. This is normal.

If your child is verbal, listen carefully to all she has to say about her experiences at day care. Do not discount what she says. If she volunteers little, question her. If your child is not verbal, you need to look for other clues. The most important is probably how the baby acts when she is dropped off at the day-care home and when you pick her up. How does she react when you hand her to the day-care mother? When you return? Keep in mind, however, that many children around the age of two will cry any time they are separated from their parents.

Signs of trouble at the day-care home can include:

√ your child's sudden reluctance to go
√ increased crying
√ sudden increase in temper tantrums
√ onset of bed-wetting or thumb-sucking
√ becoming less communicative or more irritable
√ signs of poor physical care, like diaper rash, for which the caregiver does not express concern
√ bruises or burns, especially if the explanation seems unlikely
√ the day-care mother making negative comments about your child
√ your child suddenly having sleep problems or night-mares
√ a sudden decrease in appetite

You may notice other signs that are troublesome to you. Perhaps any of these behaviors alone could simply be part of normal childhood difficulties, but if more than one appears, check it out. Many parents have left their children in unhealthy or even abusive day-care homes simply because they failed to read the signals and investigate.

Young children may experience some unhappiness as they adjust to a new day-care home, especially if you are leaving them for the first time. If you feel confident that the situation is a good one, give your child a month to adjust. If after a month your child is still unhappy, you should probably change day-care providers. Sometimes there may just be personality incompatibilities or such radical differences from your own home practices that your child is upset or confused. Be considerate of your daycare provider, but always be your child's advocate first.

Developing a good relationship with your day-care provider takes some work but is worthwhile. As soon as a concern arises, sit down and talk it over with her. Don't hold it in until it becomes much harder to discuss. Most issues can be discussed in an unemotional, matter-of-fact way when they arise, but feel so much bigger if you wait. You are paying for services, so don't be timid about expressing your expectations. Taking care of your child is your caregiver's job—she's not just doing you a favor.

Realize that you won't find perfection in any day-care mother. Think in terms of trade-offs. For each imperfection is there something that balances it? For example, does the fact that your day-care provider rocks your baby to sleep lovingly make up for the fact that her house is messy?

One complaint many mothers have about their caregiver is that she doesn't give them a summary of the day's events when the child is picked up. If you want to know what your child did during the day, ask! Ask about her behavior, how much she ate for lunch, when she napped, and anything else that's important to you. If you take a little initiative, the relationship may feel more satisfying to you.

Your relationship with your day-care provider is unique. Even though you may start out as employer and employee, you often end up as friends. When friendships develop, there is probably more personal investment in the well-being of your child, but it's harder to handle problems or make a demand. Hopefully your relationship will develop into one of mutual respect, and you may even find yourselves modeling mothering behavior from each other.

DAY-CARE CENTERS

A day-care center is selected by many parents, especially those with preschool-aged children. One reason preschoolers predominate at day-care centers is that few centers accept infants. Others require toddlers to be potty trained. Another factor is parental concern about how much attention an infant will receive in a day-care center.

There are many reasons why a day-care center appeals to parents. There is no concern over a day-care mother becoming ill, going on vacation, or quitting. Even if one of the day-care teachers is sick, the center remains open.

Day-care teachers may have training in child development and some may even have a degree in early childhood education. More educational stimulation is probably offered at a day-care center than in a day-care home.

On the other hand, a day-care center may not have as flexible a range of hours as a day-care home. In addition, children older or younger than the preschool years may not be able to attend. Another disadvantage to centers is the traditionally high turnover rate of caregivers.

If you are interested in a day-care center, visit several. A good idea is to make a form with your questions and fill out one for each center you visit. This way when you go home and want to remember and compare certain features, you'll have the information.

Sample questions that you might ask the center's director are:

- ✓ What are your hours?
- ✓ What would happen if I were late to pick up my child?
- ✓ What is your teacher to child ratio?
- ✓ What type of training do your teachers have?
- ✓ What is your staff turnover? What is the average length of time your teachers have been here?
- ✓ What about substitutes?
- ✓ How many different teachers will work with my child in one day?
- ✓ How do you help the child adjust to the center?
- ✓ Could I stay a while for the first few days if it seems necessary?
- ✓ What will you do if my child becomes sick?
- ✓ Where do the children eat, sleep, play?
- ✓ How do you handle discipline?
- ✓ What do I need to send with my child each day?
- ✓ If my child is unhappy, will you let me know?
- ✓ Who is in charge when you're not here?
- ✓ What type of reports do you give the parents?
- ✓ What type of food do you provide?
- ✓ What is the approximate schedule of activities during the day?
- ✓ Can I stay and observe?

If the answer to the last question is no, you should have no further interest in that day-care center. Any center that is proud of its program will be happy to let you and your child visit.

As you observe the center, focus first on the children. Look at their faces; are they happy? Do they seem comfortable and at ease? How do they interact with the day-care teachers? Warmly or hesitantly? Are the teachers affectionate or formal? Do you hear the sounds of happy children and encouraging teachers? Or do you hear conflicts, crying, reprimanding?

Is the center reasonably clean? Are there any obvious hygiene problems or bad odors?

Notice what type of equipment is available for play. Is it safe? Are the children having fun with it? Are there games, bikes, playground equipment, and educational materials?

Try to observe a meal. You might even ask to sample the food. Is the meal well-balanced and nutritious? Are the servings adequate, the mood cheerful and calm? Are children forced to eat things they don't like?

Just as with any other day-care option you will make trade-offs in a day-care center. Look over your forms, compare both the concrete answers and the feelings you had. Try to make your decision based on both factors.

Once your baby or child is attending the center of your choice, use the guidelines offered to evaluate the other day-care options. Monitor your child's and her teacher's reactions to each other. Listen carefully to your verbal child and watch your baby closely. Ask for progress reports from the teachers. For a very social child, a day-care center can be a happy solution to the day-care dilemma.

RELATIVES AS DAY-CARE PROVIDERS

Some parents leave their children in the care of their own parents or other relatives. The advantages of this type of child care include the possibility that it may be free and that the child is probably more genuinely loved by a grandparent or relative. The problems parents have encountered, however, sometimes offset the advantages. Your own mother, mother-in-law, or sister probably feels much freer to impose her own child-rearing philosophies on your child than would an outsider you employed. This can lead to conflicts that can be difficult to resolve. Think this option over first, decide how compatible your ideas are and leave your child with a relative only if you feel comfortable and confident about the situation.

Regardless of your day-care choice, it is difficult, at least at first, to leave your child in someone else's care. It may help you to remember that bringing up children in the past was often a job shared with grandparents, aunts, siblings, and hired help. The team approach to child rearing is not really so new, and as long as the "teammates" you choose are caring, it can work well.

In using full-time day care for twelve consecutive years, I guess we've tried all varieties. We've taken babies with diaper bags to other women's homes and had babysitters come to our home to care for children. During the internship year, we used a live-in sitter, since I stayed overnight at the hospital regularly. We've used preschools, day-care homes, and day-care centers. We've tried all-day care, after-school care, and even combinations of care for different children at the same time.

Although losing a babysitter or day-care arrangement was incredibly traumatic, in the long run things always seemed to work out for the best. In talking with other parents and reviewing my own experience, it appears that changing day-care arrangements every year is not uncommon. You may lose a good sitter, or often your living and work circumstances change, or you will recognize the changing needs of your child. The sitter who responds optimally to an infant, for example, may not be the best person for a busy, active toddler. A preschooler might prefer the opportunity to interact with other children to one-to-one care in the home. Provided the arrangements you make are based on the needs of your child, along with your life-style, resources, and preferences, and as long as you keep reevaluating the situation, you'll discover that many day care options are capable of working out fine.

DILEMMAS OF WORKING PARENTS

It would be unfair to suggest that families with one parent at home full time do not face dilemmas. They most certainly do. Raising children under any circumstances is difficult. Two-career families and working single parents, however, face an additional set of dilemmas. These parents typically report having lots of guilt feelings, a chronic lack of time, and problems with sharing parenting and household responsibilities.

Guilt

Although guilt is common among all parents, and especially among mothers, employed mothers seem to take the largest dose on themselves. Society has always expected a father to be a "working father," has extolled him for doing it, and condemned him for not doing it. So naturally he feels justified whenever something else doesn't get done because of his "work."

Women, on the other hand, are still expected to some extent to stay home and be wives and mothers. Even though it is certainly more and more acceptable for mothers to have careers, somehow failing to fill the "Aviance woman" 's, shoes is still not easy to justify.

Any number of items can provoke guilt in a working mother, such as the child's attachment toward the caregiver, not baking cookies, not doing projects with the school, not spending enough time with her child, not making a clever homemade Halloween costume, and any undesirable behavior in the child.

When a large guilt attack hits, parents often behave unwisely. In *The Working Parents Survival Guide*, author Sally Wendkos Olds lists six common mistakes made by guilty parents. They are:

1. Overprotecting the child
2. Giving unnecessary gifts
3. Giving in to demands
4. Feeling sorry for the child

5. Allowing the child to escape home responsibilities
6. Ignoring misbehavior

What should guilt-ridden parents do instead? They should simply do the best they can, acknowledge to themselves that this is their best and then—give themselves a break! Be just half as understanding of your own limitations as you are of others'. If you genuinely love your child and let her know it, your imperfections won't have lasting effects.

Most working mothers desperately want a wonderful, warm day-care provider for their child. Once they find one, the child attaches to this carefully selected woman, and then the mother feels jealous of their relationship and guilty that she's not doing all the mothering! It is a rare working mother who has not at some time worried, "Will my child know I am her real mother, not the caregiver?" The answer is yes, your child always knows who her real mother is, regardless of how attached she may be to the caregiver. Toddlers often call any nurturer they are attached to "Mommy." It's a compliment to the caregiver, not an affront to you. Nurturing fathers sometimes get called "Mommy," too.

Mother in the best way you can when you are with your child and try to bypass the jealousy. Feel grateful your child is receiving the nurturing you'd like her to have during the day.

Older children will often express jealousy of your co-workers, causing you to feel guilty. "You must love the people you work with more than me 'cause you're always with them and you leave me at the babysitter's." Could any parent fend off guilt in the face of that? Probably not. You need to reassure your child that you indeed love her more than your coworkers or your work. She may feel less jealous of your work world if you bring her to your place of work occasionally. She probably has fantasies about your office, the people in it, and the work you do. Let her see just where you are and what you do when you're not with her. This may reduce jealousy by making her feel less excluded from your work world, and it is always helpful for children to know what jobs their parents perform.

Not Enough Time

Combining a career and parenting leaves little time for anything else. As a matter of fact, there's not enough time in most days for both a career and parenting! How do working parents manage?

For one thing, parents with less time to spend with their kids work hard to make that time effective, satisfying, and worthwhile. Parents manage the time limitations differently and often creatively. Some parents change their hours while their child is an infant to allow for more time at home. Some husbands and wives change their work hours so they don't overlap as much, meaning less outside care for the baby. Others with part-time jobs concentrate their hours into fewer days, finding that whole days with the baby are more satisfying than several harried half days.

Some parents temporarily cut back on their work hours while their baby is young. This type of flexibility may not be possible for you. But one thing all working parents have found is the need to cut down on activities other than working and parenting. This is the time in your life for prioritizing. You simply cannot do it all. Some parts of your life will have to go. You need to decide what they will be.

Other solutions for making more time to parent include structuring family time on weekends. It works best if you make a concrete plan to go somewhere as a family. You'll have to resist the temptation to do all your washing, shopping, and cleaning on weekends. If you stay home, chances are that the parents will end up doing household tasks instead of focusing on the child. Many families find hiring household help well worth the expense because of the time and energy it frees.

Some parents make a policy of spending uninterrupted time with their child from the time they get home from work until the child's bedtime, delaying any work brought from the office or housework until the child is asleep. Not only is this good for the child, who really needs your focused attention, but it also will relieve your guilt. In reality, you can't accomplish much with your child up anyway. Devoting this short period of time to your child makes both of you feel good.

The dilemma of not enough time often leads to illness and fatigue. Chronic fatigue among dual-career couples can erode their relationship because one or both are "too tired" to have fun together. In addition, if you are trying to do too much, your body just may rebel. You can become run-down, and with your physical defenses low and your stress high, you are more prone to illness. To avoid this, in addition to limiting your activities, and learning to say no, also pay attention to your diet. Make extra efforts to eat healthfully and find a source of exercise you can fit into your hectic schedule. Rest when you know you are getting exhausted, and schedule an annual physical checkup. If you do become ill, take care of yourself appropriately and promptly.

In addition, as difficult as it may be, you must find some time for yourself, even if it's only a little. Whether you take a walk or take a bath, you'll still feel emotionally refueled.

Sharing Responsibilities

Sharing responsibilities, both parental and household, is the natural solution to lack of time and an essential part of a two-career family's life. If both parents are employed, they must support each other in order to make it work.

Although this concept is obvious, right, and just, it is rarely implemented. Many young families still hold on to role models from the past, where women took full responsibility for house and children. Now that women share in family wage earning, it is nothing less than absurd to expect them also to solely manage the home front. Men and women alike agree with this concept: It's the implementation that seems to be the problem. Couples who have struggled with this conflict report that sharing responsibilities calls for some structure, at least in the beginning when it's not second nature. Ideas that others have tried include:

✓ If one partner vacuums, the other one bathes the children. Alternate these jobs.
✓ Some families set certain times of the day when Mom's on call or Dad's on call for the kids.

√ One parent prepares supper and the other parent feeds the baby or toddler (or clears the table and does the dishes, or puts the food away).

√ Certain household tasks are scheduled for each evening and accomplished together, leaving the weekends for "family time."

√ No major housework is done during the working week and major family cleanup time is set for a fixed time on a weekend day.

Remember that if you've split your household tasks and a certain job is yours, whether it's laundry or the oil change, you have full responsibility for it. This includes noticing that it needs to be done, and doing it promptly, not after your partner has reminded you. On the other hand, you should not feel apologetic about asking your partner to do the tasks he or she has agreed to. You should expect them to come through on their agreement just as you do.

As a working parent, your most important goal is to provide the best possible parenting in less time than you'd like, but your next most important goal is to give yourself credit for the good job you're doing. Remember, you don't need to be a perfect parent, just "good enough." Instead of putting your energy into berating yourself for what you haven't done, put it into streamlining your housework, finding special moments with your partner, and spending focused time with your child. Your best gauge of your success as a parent is the well-being of your child.

17 ALL KINDS OF FAMILIES

NOT TOO LONG AGO, the typical American family consisted of a married set of parents with several children and some extended family members in the home. But who is the typical American family today? Is it a two-parent family with mother at home, with father at home, or with two-career parents? Is it the interracial family, the gay- or lesbian-parented family, or the childless family? Is it the stepfamily, the adoptive family, or the single-parent family?

Statistics demonstrate the recent rapid change in family constellations. Today, a mom, dad, and child occupy only 29 percent of all households, and family size is diminishing. For the first time in American history, the average household has fewer than three people in it. In fact, 55 percent of all households consist of only one or two persons. Married-couple households have increased only 12 percent in the last fourteen years, compared with an 82-percent increase in all other types of households. Demographers predict that by 1990 married couples will represent 57 percent of the population; in 1950, 80 percent of the adult population was married.

What do these statistics indicate? Some people would suggest that the "American family" is eroding, but I believe it is evolving. Just as societies of the world have grown more interrelated and interdependent through history, families are changing from tight-knit, clanlike kinships to diversified and cross-cultural units.

Gone are the exclusionist days when any nonstandard circumstance was considered taboo. The labels "illegitimate child" and "unwed mother" are losing their stigma, and the single-parent family is now common. It seems the derogatory term "broken home" is also losing its impact. A little boy came home from an afternoon at a friend's house and demanded that he and his mother inspect their house for damage. His friend's mother had referred to his "broken home."

Social rules are stretched as couples choose to marry or not; to bear children, adopt, or remain childless; to confine themselves to racial boundaries or not. Divorce, too, has lost its stigma. Remarriage is so commonplace that a blended family (one with children who are yours, mine, and ours) is a significant social phenomenon of the 1980s.

Then how do we define a family? Is it just any potpourri of people who happen to live under one roof? No. A family is a group of persons glued together by emotional commitment, persons bonded to one another through time by the investment they have in one another's wellbeing. They may be related by blood, by marriage, by legal adoption, or by personal commitment alone, but whatever the outward manifestation of their union, each member of a family is a valued, integral component. Although at first glance atypical families seem far from the norm, the stories these people tell reveal their likeness to any stereotypic normal, happy family.

John, a single father of two sons, aged six and seven, always wanted a family; kids are important to him. He feels that single parenting, although much more difficult than coparenting, makes him a better father. He concentrates more on parenting than he did when he was married, and he really tries to be nurturing. John's youngest son appreciates his dad's efforts, and with his limited vocabulary explains, "My dad is nicer than other dads."

Making time for himself is difficult because of his continuing concern about robbing from time that could be spent with his children. He does date, though, and finds women tend to lionize him (especially single mothers) for the quantity and quality of his parenting.

John feels that his family is very much like other families, except that he works harder at being a good parent, since he is the only one. In a matter-of-fact way, he states that what he thinks his children gain from their life-style is "a better father." Having always been heavily involved in parenting, he has trouble empathizing with men who find single fatherhood overwhelming after having been less involved when married. To those new single fathers who have been previously inactive in parenting, he recommends reading and/or support groups at first if they feel the need, but then says simply, "Don't sweat it—it's just like being a parent."

When Rich and Sue learned she was carrying twins, they were overcome with excitement, finding it hard to believe that their pregnancy was among the 1 in 80 singled out by this "specialness." When identical twin girls were born a month early, the smaller one had some medical problems not present in the larger, sturdier baby. "In a way, I'm glad that they were clearly distinguishable early on as two individuals, even if it was unfortunately by their medical condition," says Sue. "For me, it was the first stark reality that we had two distinctly unique children with different needs, not an identically matched pair of babies." The parents discarded their original twin names of Kara and Tara in favor of clearly separate identities, Stephanie and Melinda. "Soon after bringing them home," relates Rich, "we began to recognize personality differences, varying likes and dislikes, strengths and weaknesses. Learning to view our daughters as *two* babies instead of *one set* of twins was an important challenge to us as new parents."

Sue vividly recalls the physical exhaustion of the first few months. "The sheer effort of just feeding, changing, bathing, dressing and caring for two babies was often more than I could handle. It seemed like they never slept at the same time, and I grew more and more tired and discouraged. While other mothers would ogle my twins, I started envying women with one infant to whom they could give their undivided attention." Before long, with Rich's support and the help of Sue's mother who came to stay, the family settled into a routine, allowing Rich and Sue to enjoy more time with each baby.

Now at age six, the girls have a strong physical resemblance and many similar qualities. But Rich and Sue have continued to maintain each daughter's individuality. "They

have different haircuts and we avoid dressing them alike,"
explains Rich. "Although they do spend considerable time
together, they have separate rooms to allow them time
alone and a space of their own." Stephanie and Melinda
were in the same kindergarten class, but have different
first grade teachers this year. They both play soccer on the
same team, but Stephanie goes to gymnastics while Melinda takes dance lessons.

According to Rich and Sue, raising twins has been a
challenge and a treat. Most aspects are a double blessing,
but admittedly lots of things are double effort. "A recurring
problem," insists Sue, "is well-intentioned outsiders who
focus on the girls' sameness, while we constantly strive to
relate to them as distinct individuals."

Jan is from a white, rural environment, and Greg was
raised in an inner-city black neighborhood. Culture and
skin color placed them far apart, but love brought them
together. They now have the welcomed outcome of that
love, three beautiful children aged eight, three, and one.

This family chose to live in a successfully integrated
neighborhood, so their children feel at ease with their
black friends, their white friends, and their interracial
friends. They seek out other interracial families, in order
to feel supported, and because of the bond they feel with
them. The children in this family feel no different from the
rest of the world.

Although Greg and Jan did experience some prejudiced
reactions for dating and marrying outside their race, they
feel far more accepted in society now, and encounter few
uncomfortable situations. They feel no different from the
many other families who bridge various cultural gaps.

Their recommendations for a new interracial family are
few. "Remember that love is not prejudiced. To love
someone of another race and to bear children together is
very normal. Your comfort about your interracial family
will be evident to your children. How they feel about
themselves is a reflection of how their parents feel, so be
sure you are comfortable about your situation before you
have children. Then surround yourself with good support
and choose a neighborhood that is accepting of and includes other interracial families."

*   *   *

Although many families adopt because they can't conceive a biologic child, Connie and Guy elected to adopt as their first choice. Influenced early in life by books about adoptive families, by the World Population Control message of the 1960s, and by overseas military duty, this young (and fertile) couple decided to adopt interracial children. They are now the parents of Dominic, an eight-year-old Puerto Rican boy, and Jaimie, a one-year-old Korean girl.

Dominic has had the usual questions about being adopted, like "Why did my parents give me up?" His parents have always made adoption a regular part of conversation, and they inject as much positive input about his birth family as possible. Now, at eight, he has healthy self-esteem and full understanding about being adopted and racially different from his parents. He does, however, have difficulty dealing with new people or situations, "maybe from the trauma of early separation and loss," muses his mother, referring to his six months spent in foster care prior to being adopted.

But do these traits result from the adoption, or are they just a part of who Dominic is? That question is just one of many that Connie and Guy deal with as adoptive parents. From the beginning, knowing that their children's genetics are different, these parents have been ready to accept surprises and differences. That acceptance is the one trait that Connie feels is most crucial to successful adoptive parenting.

Jaimie and Dominic are lucky to have parents with the sensitivity, understanding, and love to have made adopting interracial children their choice. And Connie is proud that her children will grow up with a comfortable view of an interracial world, one step closer to worldwide understanding and peace.

My own family of five children is far from today's norm, and poses its own sets of concerns. The world presumes that nobody *wants* more than two children, so with each subsequent pregnancy the rude comments increase. "Oh, you must be Catholic," or the so-called joke, "Can't you figure out how to stop this? I thought you were a doctor,'' were two of many I endured. I remember being excited anew with each conception and noticing other people's lack of enthusiasm with my serial pregnancies.

As my family grew, it became easy to think only in groups; boys and girls, big and little kids, or all one family unit. One-to-one time with any child became hard for me because I never wanted anyone to feel left out. I learned, though, that if you start allocating solo time to your children, even if it's just to run an errand, a balance is quickly attained. Now I carry that principle one step further; when I travel, I try to take one child with me. Rather than bickering about fairness, they all eagerly await their turn for the combined treat of travel and solo time with Mom.

Another technique used in some large families is to proclaim one day a month for each person. On that day, the honored one sits at the head of the table, eats their favorite meal, chooses the television programming and in many ways is honored as a loved and special person in the family. Parents, too, get to be included in this esteem-building ritual.

In a large family, birth order establishes a family hierarchy that is hard to break. Older children become junior parents, and baby brother feels like baby brother for life. But children in large families learn parenting and responsibility. They have a choice of siblings when seeking a playmate, a confidant, or a role model. And most learn to state their needs clearly—they *have* to in order to survive the competition. Beware the occasional child who retreats instead of asking. In a busy family, it is easy to grease the wheel that squeaks the loudest and subtly neglect less demanding children.

Parenting a large family, like any other, presents many potential pitfalls and countless rewards. Let your children be individuals; praise each for their own talents and don't reprimand any one in front of the others. Use time, your grave enemy, as efficiently as possible. And enjoy the delightful breadth and diversity in your home.

When Ann and Mark first held their son, Brenden, in the birthing room at the hospital, they were awed by the preciousness of life and relieved that their child was healthy and whole. They didn't notice the worried look under their obstetrician's mask nor the astute observations the infant's nurse was recording. Within an hour their pediatrician arrived and after examining Brenden, she sat down with them and explained: "Your son has several physical features compatible with Down's Syndrome. We will be conducting a chromosome test to confirm the diagnosis, but I want you to know that the possibility exists. Brenden appears to be healthy in every other way and we will keep you informed of all we do to evaluate him more fully."

At first Ann and Mark couldn't believe that their new son could have a genetic problem. During the several days it took to confirm the diagnosis by chromosomal analysis, Ann and Mark remained numbed by the suggestion that their precious baby could be imperfect in any way. "Isn't Down's Syndrome something that only occurs in children of older women? I'm only twenty-seven," argued Ann. But the truth that their child was permanently different gradually settled upon Mark and Ann. When they returned to the pediatrician's office a few days later, they didn't need to see her somber face to know that Down's Syndrome had been confirmed. "That was the saddest day of my life," recalls Mark. "I felt so much sorrow for my boy and for Ann and myself. All I could think about were the future dreams that would never materialize. Ann and I just clung to one another."

The pediatrician empathized with their sense of loss, answered their many questions, and emphasized the positives: While many children with Down's Syndrome also have heart defects and other medical problems, Brenden had none of these associated problems. He would learn and develop, but at a slower rate than other children. He would give and receive love just as any child does. He would bring his parents many joys and insights. And he would need the routine baby care that any infant does, as well as specialized care to maximize his development.

"It was really hard at first," recollects Ann. "People didn't rejoice with us as they do when a healthy baby is born, and they didn't rush right over. In fact they avoided us. Eventually, Mark and I began to view Brenden more as an ordinary and wonderful baby than a Down's baby, and I wanted the outside world to welcome him as an individual, too. I guess it was my sister who was the turning point for us. She has four kids of her own, but she came out to stay with us and just started treating Brenden like any other baby. She noticed all his cute features and behaviors. She rocked him, talked to him, played with him, and burped him just like I had watched her do with her own. She was the first person to make me feel proud to be Brenden's mother.''

Now at age five, Brenden is enrolled in pre-school and has lots of neighborhood friends. He is slower than other children, of course, but his parents delight in each new milestone. He is thoughtful, loving, energetic and fun to be with. Mark and Ann have subsequently had a healthy daughter, Erin, now three. They have found that Brenden has brought them far more joy than pain and that coping with a chronically handicapped child has strengthened them spiritually. They sought marriage counseling shortly after Brenden's birth, but now feel their marriage is stronger than ever. In addition to the routine activities of other young parents, Mark and Ann have been very active in their local chapter of the Association for Retarded Citizens. ''Parenting a handicapped child makes you dig into your inner depths and find untapped strengths you never thought you had. I've never felt sorry for myself or Brenden,'' says Ann. ''He's taught me what unconditional love is all about.''

Shared parenting was their style when they were married, and shared custody was the logical arrangement after they divorced. Nancy's elementary-school-aged sons, Tad and Tucker, live one week with her and the next week with their father. No matter where they sleep, they have the same school, after-school activities, day care, and playmates.

A two-and-a-half-year veteran of this unusual custody agreement, Nancy finds that the practical aspects of her life-style fascinate friends and teachers. Clothing and paraphernalia are sent back and forth every week, and the boys have dressers at each home. They have few duplicate items, and the decision to purchase duplicates is usually based on size and portability as well as importance. Nancy found it worth the extra expense to purchase double sets of lunch boxes, soccer balls, and "moon boots," in order to avoid transporting them every week. Aside from always explaining their life to teachers, teammates, and friends, the boys' only practical dilemma is that no form ever has enough lines to list both parents' names, addresses, and phone numbers.

The children know that they live differently from most other kids, because they continually have to explain to other people how to phone them, where they live, and so on. But it is a fact of life. In preschool, Tad was faced with a potential problem. The class was given materials to make an ornament for home, but just enough for one ornament. He simply asked the teacher for more supplies. "I have to make two; I have two homes," he said as matter-of-factly as if he had been announcing that he had two arms. The boys often delight in the best parts of the two homes. At Dad's house they share a giant water bed, and at Mom's they have bunk beds. Dad has a big yard and a small park nearby, but Mom lives just three blocks from the best ice cream store in the city.

Tad and Tucker have learned about transition, but compared to horror stories of other divorces, their adjustment problems have been surprisingly minor. Actually, they had less to adjust to; there was no suddenly absent parent, and there were no tirades between the adults. Now that the routine is established, they continue to learn and grow from circumstances other children don't experience, like the responsibility for taking toys with them on Sunday, or doing without them for the week. (Clothes are the responsibility of the parents, but each child has to remember his toys.) The boys also gain better parents. Single parenting is hard work, but each parent gets one week off for each week on, so they are rested and eager to be parents when the children return.

Nancy has this to say to someone considering joint custody. "I would try to do this only if you have an incredibly good working relationship with the other parent. You will be on the phone a lot confirming details of time, place, and belongings. There is the potential for endless petty arguments; one didn't pack enough underwear; one arrives late; one sends dirty clothes back; and so on. Try harder than ever to coparent effectively. Discuss all decisions (take piano lessons? join a soccer team? how much allowance?) so that you can both live with the decision, and avoid competition between households. Most importantly, try hard to be considerate of the other parent; it will come back to you and your children tenfold.

"We are both careful to do more than our share each week. The receiving parent gets clean clothes and freshly bathed children, and we offer to babysit and chauffeur for each other when needed. Our dual commitment to shared parenting compels us to work hard, and keeps us from getting angry or feeling taken advantage of. I think that commitment to being good parents, married or not, is what makes our arrangement work."

Josh and Randy feel that their family is not very different from any other family. He is Christian, she is Jewish; they have four children; two are adopted and two are biological; of the four, two are biracial and two are Caucasian. Two of the children are learning-disabled and two are not; one is being raised as a Christian and three are being raised in Judaism.

They may be a lot like other families in many ways, but each of their differences, and differences in general, are a big topic of conversation in their home. The children—Megan, fifteen, Justin, thirteen, Mathew, ten, and Loren, eight—have an ongoing awareness and a broad appreciation of differences and limitations. The two children without learning disabilities see their siblings struggle with concepts and tasks that come easily to most. Living in a predominantly black neighborhood, Megan is proud to have a biracial brother.

Both Josh and Randy value differences, and make a point to highlight that in their home. They often host international guests to continue to demonstrate to their children the worldwide differences in culture. (Those visitors get a taste of many facets of America in just one home!) Josh has learned, though, that differences can be exciting and/or devastating. He found that his old notions about the whole family doing lots of things together just didn't pan out, because of the varying needs and tastes encompassed in one home.

As unusual as their family is, Josh and Randy do not

feel at all alienated or different, and they say of their family, "We have zero regrets. We think it is a totally enriching and good experience."

Every one of these kinds of families is a minority, yet every one feels like the All-American Family. Each of these families knows joy and sorrow, confidence and fear, and love and anger. The children in any of these families know that in their home they find comfort, love, and acceptance.

As your family grows, you'll notice the same development. You'll make decisions appropriate for you as your life evolves, whether or not you have the classic family of two children and two parents. You may easily find yourself in a nonstandard family, but whatever the constellation of your family, it will be normal for you, and accepted in our diverse society. The glue that bonds your family will be the same as that for any other family—love.

Index